Fall '87
Sydney W. Howard

# ADVANCES IN COGNITIVE SCIENCE 1

**ELLIS HORWOOD SERIES IN COGNITIVE SCIENCE**
*Series Editor:* MASOUD YAZDANI, Department of Computer Science,
University of Exeter

# ADVANCES IN COGNITIVE SCIENCE 1

*Editor:*

**N. E. SHARKEY,** B.A., Ph.D.
Lecturer in Artificial Intelligence and Cognitive Psychology
University of Essex

**ELLIS HORWOOD LIMITED**
Publishers · Chichester

Halsted Press: a division of
**JOHN WILEY & SONS**
New York · Chichester · Brisbane · Toronto

First published in 1986 by
**ELLIS HORWOOD LIMITED**
Market Cross House, Cooper Street, Chichester, West Sussex, PO19
1EB, England

*The publisher's colophon is reproduced from James Gillison's drawing of the ancient Market Cross, Chichester.*

**Distributors:**

*Australia and New Zealand:*
Jacaranda-Wiley Ltd., Jacaranda Press,
JOHN WILEY & SONS INC.
GPO Box 859, Brisbane, Queensland 4001, Australia

*Canada:*
JOHN WILEY & SONS CANADA LIMITED
22 Worcester Road, Rexdale, Ontario, Canada

*Europe and Africa:*
JOHN WILEY & SONS LIMITED
Baffins Lane, Chichester, West Sussex, England

*North and South America and the rest of the world:*
Halsted Press: a division of
JOHN WILEY & SONS
605 Third Avenue, New York, NY 10158, USA

© 1986 N. E. Sharkey/Ellis Horwood Limited

British Library in Cataloguing in Publication Data
Advances in cognitive science 1. —
(Ellis Horwood series in cognitive science)
1. Cognition
I. Sharkey, N. E.
153.4    BF311

ISBN 0–85312–921–5 (Ellis Horwood Limited)
ISBN 0–470–20346–3 (Halsted Press)

Phototypeset in Times by Ellis Horwood Limited
Printed in Great Britain by R. J. Acfords, Chichester

# Contents

*I dedicate this book to my daughter Amy*

# Preface

It is difficult to say when my interest in cognitive science started, but I was first introduced to the idea of linking psychology, linguistics, and artificial intelligence (AI) by Henry Shaffer in 1978 when I attended his undergraduate course on cognitive systems. Throughout my graduate work, I was encouraged by Don Mitchell to combine the experimental methodology of cognitive psychology with my theorizing about AI. I learned most about AI in my first post-doctoral year in the computer science department at Yale. Bob Abelson gave me that job and he taught me a lot of tricks that have stood me in good stead ever since. One of the most profound influences on my thought has been from my friend and mentor Gordon Bower with whom I also spent a post-doctoral year at Stanford. He set me straight about a lot of things and I hope will continue to do so.

This book, like my own career, has no single theme which connects all of the chapters except a commitment to the study of cognition. I have deliberately avoided collecting these chapters under traditional headings such as artificial intelligence, psychology, linguistics, or philosophy since most of the individual chapters have a foothold in at least two such disciplines. Similarly, I have not sectioned the book into areas like semantic memory, parsing, knowledge-based inference, thought, etc. Rather my intent was to present a selection from first-rate researchers whose work is not firmly constrained by the dogmas of their mother discipline. Each of the contributors in this volume (as well as those who nearly contributed) has influenced my research in cognitive science over the last five or six years as mentor, colleague, friend, neighbour, or some combination. I can find no better motivation for this collection. I offer it to you in the hope that you get some of the excitement out of this blend that I did.

I would like to thank the crowd at Essex for help with some of the reviewing: Gordon Brown, Amanda Sharkey, Richard Sutcliffe, and Peter Wright. I would also like to thank Aunt Thelma, Uncle Jack, Victoria, Joel, Henry, Pobble, Lucy, Micky, Ajit, Ravi, Mark, Andy, Christian, Chris, all the Johns, Hughie, Derek, Richard, Phil, Paul, Dawn, Masoud, Sarah, Ritu, Tenzing, Anthea, Monica, Peter, and last but not least Steve R., for their continued support. I would also like to thank Steve Evans and Jake McGoldrick for inspiring me to put this book together, but since they didn't I won't.

Noel E. Sharkey
Essex, 1986

# Contributors

Richard Alterman, Cognitive Science Division, University of California, Berkely, California, USA.

Debra Bekerian, MRC Applied Psychology Unit, 15 Chaucer Road, Cambridge, UK.

Gordon H. Bower, Department of Psychology, Stanford University, Stanford, California, USA.

Hubert Dreyfus, Department of Philosophy, University of California, Berkeley, California, USA.

Stuart Dreyfus, Department of Industrial Engineering and operations Research Department, University of California, Berkeley, California, USA.

Jerome A. Feldman, Department of Computer Science, University of Rochester, Rochester, New York, USA.

Marilyn Ford, Computing and Information Studies, School of Social and Industrial Administration, Griffith University, Queensland, Australia.

Carolyn C. Foss, Xerox Palo Alto Research Center, Palo Alto, California, USA.

Richard J. Gerrig, Department of Psychology, Yale University, New Haven Connecticut, USA.

Arthur C. Graesser, Department of Psychology, Memphis State University, Memphis, Tennessee, USA.

Debra L. Long, Department of Psychology, Memphis State University, Memphis, Tennessee, USA.

John D. Mayer, Department of Psychology, State University of New York Purchase, New York, USA.

Keith, K. Millis, Department of Psychology, Memphis State University, Memphis, Tennessee, USA.

D. C. Mitchell, Department of Psychology, University of Exeter, Exeter, Devon, UK.

John Morton, MRC Cognitive Development Unit, 17 Gordon Street, London, UK.

Christopher K. Riesbeck, Department of Computer Science, Yale University, New Haven, Connecticut, USA.

Lokendra Shastri, Department of Computer Science, University of Rochester, Rochester, New York, USA.

Paul Smolensky, Department of Computer Science, University of Colorado, Boulder, Colorado, USA.

D. Zagar, Department of Psychology, Dijon University, France.

# Introduction

## SO WHAT IS COGNITIVE SCIENCE?

Since I started putting this book together, I have asked quite a number of people what they thought cognitive science was. These were mainly people whose interests are, by self-report, within cognitive science. I also conducted an informal survey at the 1985 meeting of the Cognitive Science Society at Irvine (the 7th annual meeting). The answers were almost as many as the number of people I asked. They ranged from "... a new way to study the mind ..." to "... a good way to get research funding ...". Everyone seemed to have their own idea about what the new discipline should be. Judging by the replies, it would be easy to get the impression that cognitive science is a discipline in which researchers from cognitive psychology, semantics, linguistics, philosophy, pragmatics, and artificial intelligence get together to confuse each other about how to proceed. The only common features that emerged in answer to my question were that cognitive science is interdisciplinary, it uses the computational metaphor, and its subject matter is the study of cognition/mind/thought/intelligence.

Other writers have defined cognitive science as "... the domain of inquiry that seeks to understand intelligent systems and the nature of intelligence" (Simon, 1980), or as "the study of the principles by which intelligent entities interact with their environments" (Walker, 1978). Miller, Polson, and Kintsch (1986) propose that cognitive science may be viewed as "... the collection of several pairwise intersections among anthropology, computer science, linguistics, neuroscience, philosophy, and psychology" (e.g. neurolinguistics or cognitive anthropology). However, in his book *Computation and cognition,* Pylyshyn (1984) expresses his hope that cognitive science is not "... just an umbrella title for a number of different sciences ... attempting to understand the workings of the mind" nor "... a political union based on an interest in a broad set of questions". Instead, he wants to believe in the more exciting possibility "... that cognitive science is a genuine scientific domain like the domains of chemistry, biology, economics, or geology". Pylyshyn feels that "... there may well exist a natural domain corresponding roughly to what has been called 'cognition', which may well consist of a ... uniform set of principles". Time will tell (although waiting for Godot may be painful).

Whatever cognitive science is, it is certainly a field rich with debate about what it should be. As no doubt everyone is aware, we cannot simply throw away the protective armour of our own disciplines and rush naked to become born-again cognitive scientists. Yet we must be prepared to question our own formalisms and assumptions, to at least admit to the possibility that they may be ill founded. We must be prepared to beg, borrow, and steal the tools from the other disciplines. It seems that at this point in time, cognitive scientists have very little to gain from methodological squabbles (cf. Sharkey & Pfeifer, 1984; Sharkey & Brown, 1986). It is impossible to tell yet who has the right approach. All serious methodologies, whether they be neat or scruffy (Abelson, 1981), should be given serious consideration. For surely a major part of the cognitive scientist's work must be the exploration and examination of alternative methodologies.

Yet even at the Cognitive Science Society's annual conference we hear all the old grievances emerging. I suppose the best we can hope for is that our efforts inspire a new generation of researchers who will teach us what the discipline really is. It is really with the latter people in mind that I have put this book together.

## SO WHAT IS THIS BOOK ABOUT?

This book is a collection of chapters which, in my opinion, represent a cross-section of some of the most interesting advances in cognitive science. Having discussed some of the problems in finding agreement among the definitions of cognitive science, I would like to declare my own bias. For me, cognitive science is the study of the possible cognitive architectures (including representations and rules) and processes involved in understanding various parts of the world, including ourselves. Currently I think that the computational framework is important, in that it seems to be the rock on which the discipline was founded. However, this need not always be the case. Perhaps one day we will discover new technologies and new metaphors with which to explore the mind.

The chapters in this volume, and in subsequent volumes in the 'Advances' series, represent a selection of issues which I have wanted for some time to see aired in a single place. I have deliberately not compartmentalized the book in the hope that the reader will find some of the rich web of themes and controversies that run throughout. I shall outline some of these briefly before going on to describe the individual chapters.

Shastri and Feldman (Chapter 6) examine some of the constraints imposed on cognition by the neural architecture of the brain whereas Morton and Bekerian (Chapter 2) are concerned with the constraints imposed on human memory research by alternative cognitive architectures. A different type of constraint interests Mayer (Chapter 11). he investigates the constraints imposed on cognition by mood.

Several of the chapters examine the access and application of knowledge in understanding. Graesser *et al.* (Chapter 5) emphasize the use of many types of schematic knowledge in the process of comprehension. But Gerrig (Chapter 1) goes further in stressing that much of language comprehension hinges on aschematic knowledge such as that needed to understand the question "Shall we pizza tonight?" Foss and Bower (Chapter 4) on the other hand concentrate their investigation on the psychological processes necessary to retrieve our knowledge of intentionality in order to understand the actions of a character in a story. the knowledge retrieval process is at the centre of the chapter by Smolensky (Chapter 7). Alterman (Chapter 3) is also interested in knowledge application, but only with reference to the process of local text summarization. Much of the interest in knowledge structure, access, and retrieval in cognitive science results from an interest in the human inference process. This is seen clearly in the chapters by Graesser *et al.*, Alterman, and Shastri and Feldman.

Some of the chapters are more concerned with the so-called front end of language understanding: parsing. Ford (Chapter 9) presents an interdisciplinary account of the process of syntactic closure. In direct opposition, Riesbeck's direct memory access parser (Chapter 8) does not pass through a separate stage of syntactic analysis. But Riesbeck is also concerned with the process of memory retrieval as are Morton and Bekerian (Chapter 2), and Foss and Bower (Chapter 4). Mitchell and Zagar (Chapter 10) provide an empirical account of the parsing process and suggest (though not as strongly as Gerrig (Chapter 1)) that semantic and pragmatic factors should be taken into account.

Three of the models in this book have the mechanism of spreading activation as their central process: Riesbeck's (Chapter 8) marker passing system; Shastri and Feldman's (Chapter 6) continuous valued deterministic system; and Smolensky's (Chapter 7) non-deterministic binary system. The mechanism of spreading activation has received considerable attention in cognitive science recently, particularly in contrast to rule-governed or symbol-passing systems. In 'connection' systems like those of Smolensky, and Shastri and Feldman, the decisions that the system makes are not governed by a body of rules. Instead they 'emerge' as a response of the processes to the constraints imposed by the structure or architecture of the system. Dreyfus and Dreyfus (Chapter 12) argue strongly that truly skilled behaviour in particular cannot ever be produced by rule-governed systems but only by systems such as those used by connection machines.

## THE CHAPTERS IN BRIEF

### Richard J. Gerrig, 'Process models and pragmatics'

In the first chapter, Gerrig examines the traditional view of meaning as a division between pragmatics and semantics. In this view, the literal meaning of a sentence is first computed and only then is the sentence interpreted in relation to the current context. In the true spirit of cognitive science, Gerrig mixes objective psychological evidence with intuition and the close examination of examples. After examining various 'meaning recovery tasks' he argues that any process model of what we call language comprehension should contain sub-components that deal directly with context sensitivity. Gerrig reviews evidence against the literal meaning hypothesis and proposes that listeners and readers use shared knowledge automatically in the recovery of meaning. The strength of this chapter is not in the presentation of any new theory, but in drawing our attention to what current process models of language comprehension cannot, in principle, handle.

### John Morton and Debra Bekerian, 'Three ways of looking at memory'

Morton and Bekerian examine three different types of theory of human memory. In doing so they emphasize an important fact which is often overlooked: psychological theories are not falsifiable in *all* of their aspects. Although psychologists use objective experimental methods to test their theories, there are, nonetheless, always a number of kernel assumptions which remain untestable. The authors begin by stating the kernel assumptions of their own 'headed records' framework and then go on to compare these with the kernel assumptions of both associative network and schema frameworks. It is a very difficult task to pull out the kernel assumptions of such all-encompassing theories and some readers may find this to be a weakness of the chapter. In particular the associative network assumptions appear to be about one type of associative network (unlike those presented in Chapters 6 and 7 here). However, this does not detract from the force of the argument that there is a lot to be gained from a detailed comparison of assumptions rather than by making comparison only on the basis of experimental results.

### Richard Alterman, 'Summarization in the small'

In the next chapter Alterman presents a new AI model of human text summarization which has the unusual title 'Summarization in the small'. Alterman makes a useful distinction between text summarization in-the-large and in-the-small. The former deals with the text as a whole where issues such as salience, importance and interest value are the prime concern. The latter refers to local summarization techniques which do not require global text understanding. Rather they require an analysis of the underlyuing conceptual structure of pieces of text. The new AI model, SUM, piggy-backs on Alterman's earlier concept coherence analysis program NEXUS (Alterman, 1985). As such this chapter represents a logical development of Alterman's earlier work. He also provides us with a reivew of the AI summarization literature with respect to his two-part distinction.

### Carolyn C. Foss, and Gordon H. Bower, 'Understanding actions in relation to goals'

Chapter 4 is an excellent example of what psychology can offer artificial intelligence. Foss and Bower examine the psychological processes involved in drawing inferences about human intentionality. They are concerned with how readers utilize information about a character's goals in order to understand that character's actions. They begin by explaining how retrieval of knowledge of goal–action relationships can be thought of in the same way as retrieval of other information from memory. They then present three new experimental studies which take as their starting point a process model version of Wilensky's (1983) artificial intelligence system. The evidence Foss and Bower present suggests that goal relationships are understood by inferring subgoals which connect an action with a goal. They found that as the number of subgoals between a goal and an action increased so comprehension decreased. The authors conclude by discussing how their findings could be extended by further experimentation. This should provide the budding experimental cognitive scientist with exciting possibilities.

**Arthur C. Graesser, Keith K. Millis, and Debra L. Long, 'The construction of knowledge-based inferences during story comprehension'**
The next chapter (5) also examines how people make inferences to enable them to comprehend text. Graesser, Millis, and Long present important aspects of their new model of text comprehension. An important contribution which these authors make to cognitive science is in their use of converging methodologies. These consist of psychological experimentation, computational methods, and the systematic analysis of verbal protocols. After outlining some of the strengths and weaknesses of these methodologies, the authors explain how they have been used to determine which specific knowlege structures are constructed at multiple levels of discourse analysis. They conclude by pointing out the necessity of an interdisciplinary perspective in cognitive research and how it keeps psychological models from becoming set in particular inadequate paradigms.

**Lokendra Shastri and Jerome A. Feldman, 'Neural nets, routines and semantic networks'**
Shastri and Feldman present a connectionist model in which they introduce a set of formal mechanisms for the representation of conceptual information about 'natural kind' terms and script-like routines. In so doing they describe an evidential semantics which enables their system to make inferences from apparently inconsistent statements. Like other connectionist systems, the representational primitives are described as a network of nodes linked together by weights of varying strengths. The strength of connection between two nodes is a measure of their association and thus the knowledge of the system may be said to be stored in the connections (hence connectionism). Shastri and Feldman deliberately avoid the use of an interpreter on top of their network structure. Indeed, the only computational primitives in their model are the calculation and transmission of continuous activity states, in parallel, between the concept nodes. Underlying the model presented here is a deep concern for psychological 'reality'. In particular these authors take pains to build a system which obeys some of the same constraints of the neural architecture of the brain.

☆ **Paul Smolensky, 'Formal modelling of subsymbolic processes: an introduction to harmony theory'**

Smolensky presents his harmony theory here, which is a mathematical theory of information processing in the subsymbolic paradigm. He clearly demonstrates its power as a formal mechanism for the completion of partial descriptions of static states of an environment. Like the model presented in the previous chapter, Smolensky's may be called a connection system. He shares with Shastri and Feldman the fundamental notion that knowledge is stored in the connection between nodes and the access function is a mechanism driven by a process of spreading activation. However, unlike Shastri and Feldman, Smolensky utilizes a binary non-deterministic architecture (cf. Sharkey & Sharkey, 1986, for a comparison of the different types of connection systems). That is, the nodes in Smolensky's system do not have continuous values: they are either on or off. Furthermore, like the related Bolzmann machine, his model has a stochastic element which takes into account the global energy of the system in determining the probability that a given node will be on or off. It is interesting how Smolensky relates his model to the more standard notion of schemata. He ends his chapter with a concrete application of the system.

**Christopher K. Riesbeck, 'From conceptual analyzer to direct memory access parsing: an overview'**

In this chapter (8) Riesbeck introduces his new theory of direct memory access parsing. Unlike previous work at the AI laboratory at Yale, in which he has been closely involved, there is no separate lexicon in this system. Rather, language-specific information is stored directly in memory in the same way as other information. This means that the new parser emphasizes the process of memory search with highlighted importance given to linguistic cues. One of the nice features of the chapter is the way in which Riesbeck places his theory in its historical context. In particular, he points out the close relation with Quillian's (1969) teachable language comprehender, which employed a similar marker-passing architecture and intersection search.

**Marilyn Ford, 'A computational model of human parsing processes'**

In her chapter, Ford presents us with a competence-based computational theory of syntactic closure. In doing so she draws both upon the earlier work of Bresnan (1978) on which lexical funtional grammar was founded and Kaplan's general syntactic processor. Her aim, which is quite clearly a cognitive science aim, is to develop a psycholinguistic theory which is linguistically sound and computationally explicit. By psycholinguistic theory she means that it must be open to the normal objective test methodologies employed in psychology. Indeed, all through the chapter Ford presents evidence for her case from known psycholinguistic and linguistic data. Like any good scientist, Ford attempts here to capture generalities among phenomena which previously seemed unrelated. The importance of this paper is that by laying out her claims in such an explicit way, Ford leaves open a number of predictions which admit themselves to the possibility of falsification.

### D. C. Mitchell and D. Zagar 'Psycholinguistic work on parsing with lexical functional grammar'

Mitchell and Zagar present an experimental evaluation of the computational model of parsing put forward by Ford, Bresnan and Kaplan (1982) (this is the forerunner of the model presented by Ford in the previous chapter). The psycholinguistic evidence presented here suggests that several important features of human parsing are accurately reflected in this model. For example, the experiments lend support to Ford *et al.*'s fundamental assumption that human parsing proceeds by depth-first analysis. However, Mitchell and Zagar also point out a number of ways in which the model is underspecified or incomplete. In particular they suggest that a major shortcoming of the Ford *et al.* theory is its lack of precision concerning the mechanisms utilized in setting up syntactic preferences. Furthermore they argue that the semantic and pragmatic content of ambiguous phrases should be taken into account. Nonetheless, Mitchell and Zagar end on a positive note by commending the model and suggesting that it provides a useful basis for further psychological investigation.

### John D. Mayer, 'How mood influences cognition'

In the penultimate chapter, Mayer introduces us to the important role played by emotion in cognition. Emotion is one of those areas which congitive scientists have tended to push aside or disregard entirely. Indeed there is widespread belief that emotion is simply a global parameter which either acts to 'slow down' or 'speed up' cognitive processing. Mayer chooses one aspect of emotion, mood, and carefully reviews the detailed experimental evidence for and against its effect on cognition. He argues from the existing evidence that human probability estimation is strongly mood-linked. He concludes the chapter by attempting to answer the question "What is the purpose of the link between mood and probability estimation?" This question leads Mayer into a discussion of plan selection and long-term planning. All through this chapter the author points out how the various lines of evidence may be relevant to the construction of AI models.

### Hubert Dreyfus and Stuart Dreyfus, 'Why skills cannot be represented by rules'

The final chapter criticizes part of the field of artificial intelligence. Underlying the arguments put forward by the Professors Dreyfus is the notion that AI programs should have cognitive resemblance. As a critique of AI as an engineering exercise this may be misplaced, but not as a critique of AI within cognitive science. The authors particularly concentrate their attack on expert systems, a subfield of AI which is currently very popular among home computer enthusiasts. The authors point out some similarities between the current ideas of knowledge engineers and the 2000-year-old ideas of Plato and Socrates. In both cases the belief is that although experts can apply rules to give us examples, they find it difficult to articulate them. Dreyfus and Dreyfus argue that experts do not proceed by systematically applying a set of rules to a body of knowledge. That is what beginners do. Experts, they argue, have access to tens of thousands of typical situations, one or more of which may be rapidly and effortlessly applied to the current problem without the use of rules. They liken this to the computational models of the 'new connectionists' (cf. Shastri & Feldman; and Smolensky, this volume). One of the most interesting aspects of this chapter is the authors' careful reporting of some of the false rumours which have surrounded much of the expert systems literature.

Noel E. Sharkey
February 1986

## REFERENCES

Abelson, R. P. (1981). Constraint, construal, and cognitive science. *Proceedings of the Third Annual Conference of the Cognitive Science Society*, Berkeley, California.

Alterman, R. (1985). A dictionary based on concept coherence. *Artifical Intelligence*, **25**, 2, 153–186.

Bresnan, J. W. (1978). A realistic transformational grammar. In M. Halle, J. W. Bresnan & G. A. Miller (Eds.), *Linguistic theory and psychological reality*. Cambridge, MA: MIT Press.

Ford, M., Bresnan, J. W. & Kaplan, R. M. (1982). A competence based theory of syntactic closure. In J. W. Bresnan (Ed.), *The mental representation of grammatical relations*. Cambridge, MA: MIT Press.

Kaplan, R. M. (1975). On process models for sentence analysis. In D. A. Norman, D. E. Rumelhart & the LNR Research Group, *Explorations in cognition*. San Franscisco: Freeman.

Miller, J. R., Polson, P. G., & Kintsch, W. (1986). Problems of methodology in cognitive science. In W. Kintsch, J. R. Miller, & P. G. Polson (Eds.), *Methods and tactics in cognitive science*. Hillsdale, NJ: Erlbaum.

Pylyshyn, Z. (1984). *Computation and cognition: Toward a foundation for cognitive science*. London: MIT Press.

Quillan, M. R. (1969). *The teachable language comprehender*. BBN Scientific Report 10, Bolt, Beranek and Newman.

Sharkey, N. E. & Brown, G. D. A. (1986). Why artificial intelligence needs an empirical foundation. In M. Yazdani (Ed.), *Artificial intelligence: Principles and applications*. London: Chapman & Hall.

Sharkey, N. E. & Pfeifer, R. (1984) Uncomfortable bedfellows: artificial intelligence and cognitive psychology. In M. Yazdani and A. Narayanan (Eds.), *Artificial intelligence: Human effects*. Chichester: Ellis Horwood.

Sharkey, N. E. & Sharkey, A. J. C. (1986). KAN: A knowledge access network model. In R. Reilly (Ed.), *Communication failure in dialogue.* North-Holland: Elsevier.

Simon, H. A. (1980). Cognitive science: The newest science of the artificial. *Cognitive Science, 4,* 33–46.

Walker, E. (1978) (Ed.). *Cognitive science, 1978: Report of the State of theArt Committee to the advisors of the Alfred P. Sloan Foundation, October 1.*

Wilensky, R. (1983). *Planning and understanding: A computational approach to human reasoning.* Reading, MA: Addison-Wesley.

# 1

# Process Models and Pragmatics

Richard J. Gerrig

Speakers and listeners who share appropriate knowledge can find coherence in almost any sequence of utterances. Consider this interchange:

> Harvey: Shall I compare thee to an April day?
> Celia: The girl climbed over the dog.

These two uttances were generated by a pair of students who were asked simply to write down the first sentence that came to mind. The utterances weren't intended to inhabit the same interchange. It's hard to imagine how they could: without special information, comprehension is driven by knowledge held in common by the members of our culture, and there is no general shared structure — script, schema, frame — that binds these two statements. The interchange does make sense if we invent a private history of shared knowledge for Harvey and Celia. Suppose that it has become practice for this pair to comment on each other's emotional state by alluding to Shakespeare's Sonnet 18, which begins, "Shall I compare thee to a summer's day? Thou art more lovely and more temperate." By uttering, "Shall I compare thee to an April day," Harvey is noting — by a means transparent to Celia — that she seems unsettled, like a typical April day in New England. Celia's reply explains this emotional state: "The girl climbed over the dog." We can imagine that the consequences of this event (where *the girl* and *the dog* are mutually known to Harvey and Celia) will be evident to Harvey, and so make sense of Celia's state of mind.

If this example seems rather far-fetched, it is because we are only observers being introduced to a series of experiences that Harvey and Celia would actually have shared. If we were appropriately knowledgeable participants in this dialogue, we would find the interchange rather unremarkable. We would find ourselves accessing what seems from the outside to be rather esoteric shared knowledge and bringing it to bear in the course of language comprehension with little or no reflection. That is the proposition to which this chapter is devoted: listeners and readers use shared knowledge regularly and unreflectively in the recovery of meaning. In this chapter, I will outline this perspective on language comprehension and explore its consequences for process models of understanding.

## PRAGMATICS AND LANGUAGE COMPREHENSION

What do listeners do when they hear an utterance? Suppose that there is a set of *meaning recovery tasks*, the execution of which comprise different aspects of an answer to the question, "What did this speaker mean by performing this utterance in this circumstance?" Ideally, these tasks could be ordered with respect to some non-arbitrary criterion, perhaps by the frequency with which they must be carried out in everyday language use. At one extreme, we would find tasks that are required in all instances of understanding, say "Recover word meanings". At the other extreme, we would find low-frequency tasks, say "Count *b*'s in the utterances". Listeners perform at least some subset of these tasks every time they hear an utterance: faced by a language input, listeners regularly carry out some standard repertory of meaning recovery tasks. I take *comprehension* to designate the collection of moment-by-moment processes that listeners undertake obligatory to realize this subset of tasks.

Consider a formal device that is intended to mimic the process of language comprehension. The device takes as input an utterance and gives as output the meaning of that utterance. But — to mimic comprehension — what meaning ought that to be? Linguistic and philosophical theories of language suggest at least two alternatives, based on the traditional partition of meaning into *semantics* and *pragmatics* (Morris, 1946). *Semantics* is the study of the context-free, or literal, meaning of words and sentences. If our formal device incorporates semantics alone, we would expect its outputted meaning to be an interpretation of the utterance in some null or universal context. *Pragmatics* is the study of meaning when utterances are made by particular speakers on particular occasions for particular listeners — speakers' meanings (Grice, 1957, 1958). If our formal device incorporated pragmatics, we would expect the outputted meaning to be context-senstive. As an illustration of how different these outputs could be, consider Donna's utterance, "The dog is running through the field," another unconstrained elicitation. Our semantic device would express in "output language" the paraphrased content of the sentence, with more than one output for utterances with ambiguities. Our pragmatic device would give an interpretation appropriate to the context of utterance. Suppose Donna's utterance were a response to the question, "Is it safe to pull out of the driveway?" It would take on the meaning, "You needn't worry that the dog is under the car." Suppose Donna's utterances were in response to, "When will Lassie be home?" It would then take on the meaning, "Soon, she's getting close to home." What our pragmatic device offers as output is the total body of information Donna meant to communicate by using this utterance.

Why might we prefer the pragmatic to the semantic device? Simply, the output of the semantic device would be of little value in most communicative settings. We need to know which of an unlimited number of messages Donna intended by uttering, "The dog is running through the field." In only a handful of instances would she intend nothing more than the literal meaning. In practice, speakers rarely intend to communicate only the literal meaning of the sentence uttered. To determine all that speakers do intend, listeners must perform the sort of analyses incorporated in our pragmatic device. Namely, they must evaluate an utterance against context — speaker and situation (H. Clark & Carlson, 1981). Process models of moment-by-moment language comprehension should reflect that necessity: the process we choose to call language comprehension should include within its scope subcomponents that accomplish aspects of context sensitivity.

### The process of comprehension

Researchers in psycholinguistics have identified a number of component comprehension processes that act upon language inputs (see H. Clark & E. Clark, 1977, for a review). For example, they define *lexical access* to be the process that forges a connection between the words of an utterance and representations of their meaning in memory. They define parsing to be the process that reveals the syntactic structure of sentences. Theorists have generally agreed about what analyses are necessary. Controversy has centred around what knowledge is available to the comprehender as each process is executed. Consider the sentence, "The night sky was filled with stars." Suppose a comprehender has encountered all but the last word, namely, "The night sky was filled with ..." An *interactive* theory of language comprehension suggests that a comprehender could exploit the syntactic structure of the early parts of the sentence to speed recognition of the final word, "stars" (Marslen–Wilson & Tyler, 1980; Marslen-Wilson & Welch, 1978; Salasoo & Pisoni, 1985). An *autonomous*, or *modular*, theory of language processing claims that lexical access of "stars" would be unaffected by prior context, because grammatical and contextual information are unavailable to the process of access (Foder, 1983; Forster, 1976, 1979).

The importance of this difference in informational architecture lies in the consequences for the efficiency of language processing. Theorists in both the interactive and modular camps have claimed their conception of processing to be the more efficient. Fodor (1983) suggested, for example, that one virtue of the modular system he envisioned was that its operation would be quite fast. In his theory, functions like lexical access and parsing are mandatory and automatic; no time-consuming decisions are necessary to adapt processes to situations. In the context of an autonomy-inspired investigation of lexical access, Seidenberg *et al.* (1982) suggested that, "Automatic access of lexical information frees processing resources for other tasks ... [D]eciding which information to retain from a limited pool of alternatives may be simpler computationally than marshalling various types of knowledge to restrict lexical access" (p. 532). Interactive theorists, by contrast, have argued that the ready availability of many sorts of information at all times avoids more important processing costs. Marslen–Wilson and Tyler (1980) pointed out that comprehension in everyday conversation must occur very rapidly in time. The interactive processor is "designated for optimal efficiency and speed ... In every case of spoken word recognition, no more of the sensory input needs to be heard than is necessary to uniquely distinguish the correct word-candidate from among all the other words of the language ... that could occur in that particular context" (p. 61). What we can extract from these opposing views is not a resolution — the debate lingers — but an appreciation for the invocation of efficiency.

It is the quest for efficiency that leads me to champion a conception of language comprehension that includes within its scope aspects of traditional pragmatics. Just as there are processes like "lexical access" and "parsing" that are carried out obligatorily, whatever the proposed architecture, I believe that there are subcomponents of comprehension that yield context-sensitive, speaker's meanings with the same regularity. For utterances to have their intended communicative impact, comprehenders must recover these meanings. My belief is that the language-processing system is organized to reflect that reality.

Empirical evidence suggests that at least the most straightforward attempt to exclude speaker's meaning from comprehension is incorrect. Many accounts of language understanding have incorporated what Gibbs (1984) called the *literal meaning hypothesis*: "Sentences have well-defined literal meanings and [the] computation of the literal meaning is a necessary step on the path to understanding speaker's utterances" (p. 275). Searle (1975; see also Grice, 1975, 1978), for example, suggested that comprehenders first recover the literal meaning of an indirect request like, "Can you pass the salt?" When they examine the situation, and determine that the speaker must have meant more than the question of ability alone, they recover, at last, the intended meaning, "Pass the salt." This view presupposes two processing stages with very different characters. In the first stage, a comprehender recovers a literal meaning, presumably by deploying such processes as lexical access and parsing. In the second stage, the comprehender puzzles out the speaker's intended meaning. The processes that recover literal meanings and speaker's meanings are unintegrated.

Gibbs reviewed the evidence for and against this proposal and concluded that it has no psychological validity. Consider, for example, the prediction that comprehenders always recover the literal meaning of indirect requests. Gibbs (1979) tested this hypothesis by contrasting reading times for indirect requests (like, *Can you pass the salt?*), literal uses of the same utterances (where the utterance suggested a real question of ability), and direct requests (like, *Pass the salt*). Gibbs found the indirect requests took no longer to understand than did the other forms in appropriate contexts. If indirect requests require the same processing time as direct uses of the same utterances, it is impossible for theorists to maintain that comprehenders recover a literal meaning and then "puzzle out" the rest (see also Clark & Clark, 1979; Gibbs, 1983). Gibbs (1984) concluded from the overall evidence that comprehenders do not automatically recover literal meanings in the course of understanding.

This finding licenses speculation about what representation of meaning *is* automatically recovered through the activity of language comprehension. My unstartling proposal is that the comprehension process obligatorily recovers some aspects of speaker's meaning. Once we are committed to this proposal, two interrelated problems face us: (1) we must specify which aspects of speaker's meaning (which meaning recovery tasks) are subsumed by comprehension; (2) we must specify what processes, as subcomponents of overall comprehension, perform these recovery taks. In the next section, I will address these issues in the context of specific meaning recovery tasks.

## MEANING RECOVERY TASKS

The notion *meaning recovery* is necessarily vague — in principle, there are an unlimited number of tasks. Consider the task, "Count *b*'s in utterance." This procedure would be an important step in meaning recovery for a spy who knew that his context was communicating a meeting time by uttering a sentence with an appropriate number of *b*'s. the same message could be communicated through any pre-arranged system that involved counting surface features of the utterances. We would be quite surprised if any of the unlimited number of potential code systems were subsumed by ordinary comprehension. Instead, we would expect the listener-spy to comprehend the utterance, say "Buy me a blue bird-bath", in the usual moment-by-moment fashion, and then to count *b*'s deliberately. I will call whatever processes operate to recover additional meaning once comprehension is complete, *exploration*. In contrast to comprehension, we might not expect exporation to have any consistent character; the processes necessary to recover meanings beyond comprehension will depend on the situation. Before I turn to specific meaning recovery tasks, I will briefly illustrate a comprehension–exploration continuum.

Consider these utterances, all Dana's answers to Amy's question, "Would you like to go to the movies tonight?"

(1) Yes, I would like to go the the movies tonight.
(2) Yes, I would.
(3) I have to study for an exam.
(4) There's a full moon tonight.

Answer (1) comprises a straightforward answer to the question. The recovery of meaning in this instance is a clear case of what we would want to call language comprehension. Answer (4) seems to be an equally clear case of what we would intuitively want to call exploration. It is difficult to see how a report on the phase of the moon is relevant to going to the movies. Amy would be forced to do some conscious problem-solving: "Why would Dana think her utterance was relevant to my question?"

Intuitions about comprehension and exploration are fuzzier for answers (2) and (3). Answer (2) requires Amy to consult her memory for the question, to see what Dana has agreed to. The recovery of antecedent information — the interpretation of anaphors — is a process that we very well might want to consider part of regular comprehension (cf., Malt, 1985; Murphy, 1985). Finally, answer (3) is an example of a rather straightforward indirect speech act. Dana is replying to Amy's question with an utterance that suggests that an enabling condition for attending the movies, having sufficient free time, cannot be met (Searle, 1975). That makes Dana's utterance readily interpretable. But, does our process of comprehension compute Dana's indirect meaning, or must Amy explore the utterance's meaning?

This question becomes more compelling once we acknowledge that by endowing Amy with the correct shared knowledge we can accord to answer (4) the same status as answer (3). Suppose Amy and Dana mutually know that Dana is a graduate student in the astronomy department, and that her dissertion is a test of a theory of light refraction during full moons. With that shared knowledge, Amy will recover the same indirect meaning for "There's a full moon tonight" as for "I have to study for an exam." In both cases Dana has suggested — capitalizing upon either cultural norms or specific shared knowledge — simply, "I have to do something else." Do the same processes foster understanding in both cases? My speculation is that the processes are the same, and that they are subcomponents of the process of comprehension. I turn now to some specific domains of meaning recovery — contextual expressions, referring phrases, and ambiguous utterances — and identify some areas where this proposal can be tested.

### Contextual expressions

Consider this trio of sentences form Thomas McGuane's novel *The bush-whacked piano* (pp. 213–214):

> A good-natured, superior murmur passed over the potato salad ... The potato salad had begun to stir ... [T]he potato salad began to advance upon the podium.

Without the appropriate context, these sentences — given sufficient exploratory processing — evoke a horror movie scenario. *Potato salad* has somehow achieved animacy so it can murmur, stir, and advance. In the context McGuane established, however, *potato salad* has the straightforward (and relatively more mundane) interpretation of *people eating potato salad*. *Potato salad* is an example of a contextual expression (E. Clark & H. Clark, 1979): an expression with an unlimited number of possible meanings, one of which is selected in each context of use. In McGuane's sentences, *potato salad* could have designated any group if individuals who interact with potato salad: people who prepare it, people who paint pictures of it, people who bathe in it to keep their skin supple, and so on. The sentence, "A good-natured, superior murmur passed over the potato salad" would take on a new meaning in each case.

Although sometimes used by novelists for specifically aesthetic purposes, contextual expressions are pervasive in everyday language use (E. Clark & H. Clark, 1979; H. Clark, 1983). English incorporates several highly productive schemata for creating them. For example, with a small number of exceptions (see E. Clark & H. Clark, 1979) nouns can be transformed into verbs. Many such *denominal verbs* have become conventional in the language — *to shampoo, to litter, to telephone.* Innovative denominals can encode either mundane ("The chambermaid *pillowed* the bed") or unusual ("The bellhop *pillowed* his stomach to play Santa Claus") concepts. In each case, the meaning of the expression is determined from the context of use. Even young children, speakers of English, French, and German, seen to have internalized a rule that makes the noun-to-verb transformation permissible (E. Clark, 1982; see also, E. Clark, 1981; E. Clark & Hecht, 1982). Other types of innovations are *derived agentives* ("Jack is a *bookcaser*", where *bookcaser* could mean someone who builds bookcases, someone who lives in a bookcase, someone who juggles bookcases, and so on), *eponymous phrases* ("David *did a George Washington*", which could mean that David chopped down a cherry tree, or crossed a river standing up in a boat, or was first president of an organization, and so on; see H. Clark & Gerrig, 1983), and innovative compound nouns ("Stuart waved to the circus man", where *circus man* could mean the man Stuart met at the circus, or the man who works for the circus, or the man who studies the history of circuses, and so on; see Downing, 1977; Kay & Zimmer, 1976) — the list goes on.

Consider an utterance with a reasonably mundane contextual expression: Lee asks, "I'm tired of eating at the same old Chinese restaurant, do you want *to pizza* tonight?" How might her addressee, Robin, understand this utterance? *To pizza* could not be understood by means of a classical model of comprehension for at least two reasons. First, there is no ready-made representation of *to pizza* in memory, so the process of lexical access will come up empty (H. Clark & Gerrig, 1983). Second, and consequently, when a grammatical analysis is made of the utterance, the parser will have no ready-made information about the syntactic role of *to pizza* (H. Clark, 1983). This simple example of speaker's meaning puts us outside the operation of standard conceptions of comprehension. The framework I have established so far suggests two approaches to this dilemma: understanding can either be accommodated by a non-standard account of comprehension, or through exploration. Suppose meaning for contextual expressions were always recovered through exploration. To understand *to pizza* Robin would have to work hard to puzzle out what Lee had in mind; the representation of meaning passed on by comprehension, given the dearth of information about the meaning of *to pizza*, would be rather impoverished. The comprehension process would essentially be useless in the many instances of contextual expressions.

Suppose, instead, that understanding contextual expressions is a frequent enough meaning recovery task to be realized through comprehension. The challenge then is to specify how listeners could accomplish that in a moment-by-moment process. An initial suggestion might be to broaden the role played by knowledge structures that have already been implicated in comprehension — structures like schemata, scripts, and frames (cf. Minsky, 1975; Rumelhart, 1980; Rumelhart & Ortony, 1977; Schank, 1982; Schank & Abelson, 1977). For example, in the course of comprehension, we retrieve knowledge from memory about fish and post offices to select the correct senses of *scale* in "Lydia scraped the scales off the halibut" and "Lydia weighed the letters on the scale." Perhaps the same sort of knowledge can work a little harder to recover meanings for *to pizza*. For example, by mentioning "the same old Chinese restaurant" Lee prompts access of Robin's knowledge of restaurants, facilitating understanding of *to pizza*. If we amend the utterance to "I'm in the mood for cooking, do you want to pizza tonight?", Robin still has appropriate schematic information in memory. But what if Robin and Lee have been working on a jigsaw puzzle that pictures a pizza? Or they've been writing a cookbook on making pizzas? Or they've been making pizza-shaped refrigerator door magnets to sell at a local crafts fair? In each case, the meaning of the utterance "Would you like to pizza tonight?" would be apparent only to Robin and Lee by virtue of the knowledge they share.

This class of contextual expressions, I'll call then *aschematic*, suggests two processing possibilites. We could propose that aschematic expressions require exploration: if listeners can find no general knowledge to facilitate comprehension, they must puzzle out meanings. A more courageous theoretical move, however, would be to explicate the manner in which context operates during moment-by-moment comprehension, when context means more than structures stored in semantic memory. The greatest difficulty lies in having the necessary knowledge available at the correct instances. For example, let's return to "Do you want to pizza tonight?" when it has the meaning, "Do you want to work on the pizza jigsaw puzzle tonight?" If this expression is to be understood moment-by-moment, in the course of comprehension, then Robin must hear *to pizza* and have easy access to the appropriate shared information in memory. Note that easy access to just any information about pizza will not do. Robin might have another friend, Glen, with whom she habitually spray-paints pizza on brick buildings. When Glen asks her *to pizza* it means something completely different from when Lee makes the same request. So, Robin must have easy access to speaker-appropriate pizza information. A proposal that listeners recover meaning from contextual expressions as part of moment-by-moment comprehension presupposes a memory system that makes possible easy access of information indexed by topic and speaker.

Even if listeners accomplished the understanding of conventional words and schematic and aschematic contextual expresions through the same processes, comprehension need not be equally easy in each case. It might be easiest to access meaning directly from the lexicon, next hardest to access schematic information to create a meaning, and hardest of all to retrieve specific shared knowledge to create an aschematic meaning. Furthermore, there could be processes that are necessary to understanding either schematic or aschematic contextual expressions that are not necessary when lexical access is sufficient. What is important is that in each instance listeners carry out the recovery of meaning moment-by-moment: the representation of meaning output by language comprehension includes an interpretation of both conventional and contextual expressions.

As in other meaning recovery domains, there will be cases that require mixtures of comprehension and exploration. Consider an utterance like "I met a girl at the coffee house who did an Elizabeth Taylor while I was talking to her." When faced with this kind of sentence, readers are quite able to explain why it is that they can't fully understand it (H. Clark & Gerrig, 1983). They often give an explanation like, "I know who Elizabeth Taylor is, but I can't think why she'd fit into this sentence." An insight like this one might grow out of foiled comprehension followed by exploration. The reader finds information about Elizabeth Taylor in memory (through the normal action of comprehension), but is unable after exploring the phrase to determine one sufficiently salient and unique act of Taylor's to give the sentence meaning.

This section is replete with speculations, but these are made against the background of at least one solid fact: contextual expressions are ubiquitous in everyday language. They are a problem — a meaning recovery task — that a process theory of understanding must address. My approach here has been to suggest some of the theoretical challenges of having contextual expressions interpreted moment by moment in comprehension. As always, empirical research is needed to suppport a theoretical bias.

### Referring phrases

When a speaker, Judith, wants to select out some third individual in conversation with Janet, she has an unlimited number of alternative referring phrases. Suppose the third individual has the name James Andrews. If there is only one such individual who is salient in the common ground of Judith and Janet (H. Clark & Marshall, 1981), then a small number of conventional means will successfully refer to him: James Andrews, James, Jamie, Andrews. But Judith need not stop there. Suppose Andrews is a blond who grew up in Minnesota and attended Harvard, and that these facts are mutually known to Judith and Janet. Judith could call Andrews *our Minnesota friend*, *the blond beauty*, *Mr Harvard*, and so on. Judith can coin a referring phrase that employs any piece of knowledge that she shares with Janet that uniquely selects Andrews out from the group of individuals that they both know. In fact, the referring phrase can be based on information that is not even true of Andrews. For example, if he considers himself to be overweight despite his evident slenderness — and this is mutually known to Judith and Janet — Judith could refer to Andrews as *our fat friend*.

Objectively, if all Judith and Janet's mutual friends could be brought together, this phrase might better refer to some other individual. But, because of shared knowledge, Judith can use it to pick out Andrews.

This brief dissertation on references shares an important theme with the discussion of contextual expressions. We see again the importance of particularized, aschematic knowledge to understanding referring phrases. H. Clark and Marshall (1978, 1981) argued at length for the necessary inclusion of mutual knowledge in theories of references. They introduced the concept of a *reference diary* to designate knowledge structures in which people record their shared experiences with other individuals. This idea specifically incorporates the indexing to speaker and situation that was necessary for interpretations of contextual expressions. I am going to examine two sub-areas within the general realm of reference to illustrate further the role of mutual knowledge and to explore implications for process models.

### Definite pronouns

Consider the utterance, "She never eats white bread." We would expect, in conversation, that this utterance would only occur in a situation where it was evident who *she* was. Most theorists proposed that listeners understand definite references moment by moment in comprehension by seaching through a representation of discourse memory. Search is constrained by the structure of prior discourse and general world knowledge (cf. H. Clark & Sengul, 1979; Corbett & Chang, 1983; Ehrlich, 1980; Ehrlich & Rayner, 1983; Sandford & Garrod, 1981). For example, in a theory of text-processing, Sanford and Garrod (1981) presented experimental evidence to support the proposal that readers ordinarily restrict search for the referent of a definite pronoun to what they call *explicit focus*. Explicit focus is an easily accessible partition of memory containing representations of entities and events mentioned in the text. Pronoun resolution is efficient because readers need only search through this highly constrained region of memory to recover the meaning of a definite pronoun. But pronoun referents are not always in explicit focus (see Sidner, 1983) — or even implicitly present in the prior discourse. Consider an especially elegant exception from William Faulkner's *The sound and the fury*. Toward the end of the book, a librarian presents the aged Dilsey with a newspaper clipping. Faulkner describes the conversation between them in this way:

> 'It's Caddy!' the librarian said. 'It is! Dilsey! Dilsey'
> 'What did he say?' the old Negress said. And the librarian knew whom she meant by 'he', nor did the librarian marvel, not only that the old Negress would know that she (the librarian) would know whom she meant by the 'he', but that the old Negress would know at once that she had already shown the picture to Jason. (p. 418)

The referent of the initial *he* is not in explicit focus for the reader. Jason hasn't been mentioned for about a page, and a new episode has intervened. Furthermore, Jason certainly could not be in any sort of focus brought on by conversation between the librarian and Dilsey, because the librarian's utterance is the first that had passed between them in several years. Sanford and Garrod's model addresses itself only to what transpires between the reader and the text, and not with the conversationalists. Nonetheless, the characters and the readers must all resort to shared knowledge to interpret this *he*, although the knowledge was gained from different perspectives.

Any model of meaning recovery for definite pronouns that assumes that a referent can always be found in the near vicinity of a pronoun would fail on the Faulkner example. We can find many more examples of these *unheralded* definite pronouns in a junior high school scenario. Imagine a junior high host who us trying to get his friends to commit themselves to attending his party. Each time he asks the question, "Are you coming to my party?", a friend responds, "Not if *he* is going to be there" or "Not if *she* is going to be there." The young host must work his way through a maze of *he's* and *she's* to determine who will actually attend the party. He must have some processes that allow him to recover the right referent for each unheralded pronoun. Once again, we can speculate whether those processes are part of moment-by-moment comprehension, or whether some special exploration must take place.

Let's step back for a moment and examine the parallels between these unheralded pronouns and other types of referring phrases. Consider Heather's answers to Larry's question, *"Are you coming to the party tonight?"*

> Not if *he's* going to be there.
> Not if *that man* is going to be there.
> Not if *Mr Wonderful* is going to be there.
> Not if *that jerk with the Hawaiian shirt* is going to be there.

In each case, Larry must consult the common ground that he shares with Heather to determine who she is referring to (H. Clark & Marshall, 1981). There is consistency from the unheralded pronoun to the other cases in the processes we might suggest would facilitate meaning recovery. If referring phrases that require common ground checks are interpreted in moment-by-moment comprehension, we might expect the *he* to be understood through comprehension as well.

However, surface similarities are misleading: there might be an institutionalized distinction within language processing that makes the unheralded pronoun a case apart. Process theories of references concern themselves largely with specifying the partitions of memory that understanders must search to find referents. The more that search can be constrained, the easier referent recovery should be. If all pronouns were recovered through comprehension, we would expect the search instruction to be *look in (some analogue to) explicit focus and in common ground*. However, for most pronouns the search can be constrained only to explicit focus. Objectively, unheralded pronouns are infrequent. For most pronouns, the effort a comprehender would expend to search common ground would be wasted. Toward the goal of efficiency, we might conclude that the search of explicit focus is legislated within comprehension, and only a failure of this search, for something akin to an unheralded pronoun, requires exploration.

We can study unheralded pronouns to see if there really is a special process given over to the comprehension of pronouns. Note that the norm in understanding referring phrases is that some check of common ground must be made — even for mundane expresions like *Dick* and *Jane*, a comprehender must check memory to ensure that only one mutually known referent is likely in context (H. Clark & Marshall, 1981). If, for pronouns , no such check is routinely made, then completeness has been sacrificed for efficiency. If we take a common ground check to be a normal aspect of comprehension, then the constrained check for pronouns requires a special, restricting process.

We require here an ambiguity in what we might mean by *special process*. For pronoun understanding, we might suggest that both standard and unheralded pronouns are handled by special processes: the unheralded pronouns require special processing (in the sense of exploration) only beacuse there is a special process which institutionalizes efficient processing of standard pronouns. This ambiguity is seen in other domains of language use. For example, much research on metaphor understanding has focussed on whether special processes are needed to foster comprehension (cf. Gerrig & Healy, 1983; Gibbs, 1984; Gildea & Glucksberg, 1983; Rumelhart, 1979). Adapting the current framework, we might search for some global model of language comprehension that acccomodates literal and metaphorical utterances with equal ease. If our experiments then find any processing differences for three types of utterances, we would suggest that special subprocesses have been encapsulated within the global system to lead to greater efficiency for certain high-frequency meaning recovery tasks. This is an opposite approach to one like that embodied the *literal meaning hypothesis* (see earlier discussion). In that case, the literal meaning is given precedence, and any further processing that listeners undertake to recover speaker's meanings is special. Here, I take an inclusive model of comprehension to be the norm, so processes that have evolved to deal efficiently with high-frequency meaning recovery tasks, like pronoun resolution, are special processes.

### Referential and attributive descriptions

There are two possible interpretations for an utterance like, "*Someday, I'd like to meet the mayor of New York.*" The speaker, Colleen, could mean either that she'd like to meet a specific individual, say Ed Koch, or that she'd like to meet any individual who satisfies the description. The two interpretations of Colleen's utterance illustrate the distinction between *referential* and *attributive* descriptions (Donnellan, 1966, 1978). A referential use of a definite description picks out a particular referent; an attributive use characterizes any individual who fulfils the description. Colleen's utterance illustrates that the same phrase can function in both roles. Which role a particular phrase does fulfil will depend on the shared knowledge of speakers and listeners. Suppose Colleen, continuing her list, tells her friend Gregg, "I'd also like to meet the strongest man in the world." Colleen may have a particular person in mind, say Clinton Hogan. In that case, her phrase *the strongest man* would be referential for her. However, if Gregg doesn't know that Clinton Hogan is the world's strongest man, then the phrase will be only understood as attributive (Colleen wishes to meet the unknown individual who fulfils that description). But, suppose Gregg does know about Hogan, but believes that Colleen is unaware that he knows. He might then retrieve a referent from memory for *the strongest man*, but nonetheless infer that Colleen did not intend him to do so. Finally, if Colleen and Gregg mutually know that Hogan fits the description, Gregg might reasonably be expected to interpet *the strongest man* to mean *Clinton Hogan*.

What processes of meaning recovery underlie this tangle of knowledge states? At issue is under what circumstances Gregg, in interpreting *the strongest man*, would undertake a search of memory to find a specific referent. In some communicative settings, Colleen will expect Gregg to recover *Clinton Hogan*, in others she will not. Does Gregg's processing of the utterance mirror these expectations — are there any processing differences for attributive and referential descriptions? For a bare phrase like *the strongest man*, it's hard to imagine how the processor could be tipped off to (potential) attributiveness. Phrases do not come inscribed "This is referential" or "This is attributive." Gregg may have no choice but to initiate a search of memory. Listeners, in general, may have to undertake many useless searches of memory to discover that phrases are not being used referentially. But consider a variant on Colleen's first utterance: "I suppose I'll have to wait until Ed Koch is ousted from office, but someday I'd like to meet the mayor of New York." Would Gregg still have to undertake a memory search? We would like to know, essentially, how sophisticated a philosopher of language comprehension is: does comprehension know enough about definite descriptions to turn off a memory search in appropriate circumstances?

Let's return to the complications brought on by knowledge states. In one possible scenario, Gregg, unbeknownst to Colleen, has a referent for *the strongest man* in memory. In that case, Gregg might interpret Colleen's utterance to mean, *I'd like to meet Clinton Hogan*. But that's not what Colleen meant. If she discovered that Clinton Hogan is the strongest man in the world, she might no longer want to meet him: the concrete instantiation might not accord with the abstract desire. Does Gregg interpret the utterance to mean *Clinton Hogan* during comprehension, and then, through exploration, decide that Colleen didn't intend that specific interpretation? Or, because *Hogan* fails a common ground check (Gregg does not believe that *Hogan* is mutually known to Colleen) does comprehension produce a representation of the utterance that omits *Hogan*? We can add another level of complexity. Suppose Gregg knows that *Hogen* is the strongest man (he won the world championships), but also knows that he and Colleen witnessed a weight-lifting exhibition where another individual, *Robert Marvel*, billed himself as the world's strongest man. Gregg, in his search of memory, must disregard "true" information and find common-grounded information. Furthermore, many definite descriptions that appear to outsiders to be attributive will be referential to those with the appropriate knowledge. I know that a good friend will know what restaurant I have in mind, and that I am being ironic, when I report, "I just ate supper at the best restaurant in New Haven." A stranger would have no restaurant in mind (or perhaps the wrong one).

Which of these layers of complexity are accommodated by comprehension? Some illumination may come from an analysis of the memory representations listeners create when they hear the definite descriptions. Ortony and Anderson (1977), for example, demonstrated that there are differences in memory occasioned by the *directness* of the use of definite descriptions. They suggested that the use of a phrase like *the strongest man in the world* is *direct* when it picks out some special, relevant property, for example, *The strongest man in the world must be able to lift five hundred pounds*. It is used *indirectly* when the content of the description is irrelevant to the predicated concept, so that a proper name would be more typical, for example, *The strongest man in the world sings in a barbershop quartet*. In a test of recognition memory, Ortony and Anderson found a tendency for readers to recognize incorrectly versions of indirect sentences where proper names had been inserted, like "Clinton Hogan sings in a barbershop quartet." We can look for processing differences analogous to these memory differences. Study of the atributive/referential distinction may expose many aspects of the moment-by-moment recovery of meaning for referring phrases.

## Ambiguous utterances

Throughout this chapter, I have given examples of utterances that are ambiguous. Their interpretation is uncertain in the absence of appropriate shared knowledge. For example, a denominal verb like *to pizza* could be assigned an interpretation no more specific than *some action involving pizza*, in a null context. But suppose a stranger were to walk up to Debbie and ask. "Do you want to pizza tonight?" so that she could not come to a unique meaning. What would Debbie's processing look like? What representation of meaning would she arrive at through comprehension? Does Debbie assign a specific reading to the utterance, even when there is no disambiguating context? Consider this reconstructed radio sports broadcast with an ambigous utterance:

The Red Sox and Yankees played the third game of a four game series yesterday afternoon. The game was a disaster, 9 runs to 0. The Red Sox will have the opportunity to sweep the series this afternoon.

What did *The game was a disaster* mean? By the end of the news item, we know that the Yankees must have lost the game beacuse the Red Sox.have the opportunity to sweep the series. However, before that final utterance, *The game was a disaster* is ambiguous. Either the Red Sox or Yankees may have won. The correct interpretation depends on the sportscaster's loyalties. It is only from his point of view that a Yankee loss was a disaster. But when first interpreting it, what does an understander, Bart, do? One strategy would be for him to interpret the utterance in accord with his own team preference. That is what I did — as a sometime Red Sox fan, I took *The game was a disaster* to mean that the Red Sox had lost. When I heard the next utterance, about the Red Sox sweeping the series, I was baffled. I was committed enough to my interpretation of the sportscaster's ambiguous utterance that I couldn't resolve the inconsistency between a Red Sox loss and the potential for having won all the series' games. The conscious effort that I expended to reinterpret the newscast made the example very vivid.

My experience suggests that it might often be safer to leave an ambigous utterance uninterpreted until appropriate information becomes available for disambiguation. When there is insufficient knowledge preceding an ambiguity, it is only the speaker who can subsequently provide clarifying information. For a listener to hazard an immediate interpretation means risking an error. But consider a variation on the disaster-game utterance. Suppose a college classmate approaches me at my reunion and asks, "Were you here for the big game last fall? It was a disaster." My interpretation of that ambiguity would be relatively low risk, because of the knowledge we would share — that we both would be rooting for the same team. To minimize the overall risks of making errors, we might conditionalize ambiguity resolution by speaker: we'd only interpret an ambiguous utterance in circumstances where we'd have good reason to believe that our interpretation would be correct. Although this proposal seems plausible, it appears to be inconsistent with findings from other domains of linguistic ambiguity.

Researchers have studied the resolution of ambiguous words and synthetic structures. An utterance like "I looked at the bank" is indeterminate in meaning because of the lexical ambiguity of *bank*. An utterance like "They are baking apples" is indeterminate because of ambiguity in grammatical structure. In both domains, there is evidence that understanders resolve the ambiguity immediately, rather than maintaining multiple hypothesis about meaning or structures in working memory. For example, in a context without disambiguating information, a listener retains only the dominant or more frequent reading of an ambiguity (e.g., the *weight* sense of *scale*) in working memory (Simpson, 1981). Overall, ambiguity resolution is biased so that the dominant reading is the default interpretation (Simpson & Burgess, 1985). Similarly, theorists suggest only one synthetic structure at a time, even if the initial phrases of a particular utterance allow more than one potential grammatical analysis (cf. Ford, Bresnan, & Kaplan, 1982; Frazier & Fodor, 1978; Wanner, 1980; Wanner & Maratsos, 1978). Given a syntactic ambiguity, the parsing process takes as its hypothesis the higher frequency structure. This strategy will occasionally lead to momentary errors, as in "The horse raced past the car fell." However, because these processes are backed up by histories of use — without countermanding information they go with dominant or more frequent alternatives — so they minimize errors. We might, then, take it to be a design feature of comprehension that all ambiguities are interpreted immediately. The understander risks errors, but in doing so reduces the amount of information that must be kept active in working memory.

When we try to bring this perspective to pragmatically ambiguous utterances we are faced with a problem: there is no history of use to fall back on; there is no way for a comprehender to minimize errors by defaulting to a dominant interpretation. The two possible interpretations of *The game was a disaster* — a Red Sox or Yankee loss — are not ordered in memory. If comprehension is organized so that listeners immediately interpret all utterances, they will risk errors in an unprincipled fashion.

The seeming scarcity of such errors in interpretation may be a consequence of comprehension being adapted to the ways of conversation itself. When conversing, conversationalists appear to adhere to Grice's (1975) *cooperative principle*, which suggests that speakers only make utterances they believe their listeners will be able to understand correctly. In the current context, this principle suggests that a speaker ought not utter an ambiguous utterance unless he or she has good reason to believe that a listener will resolve the ambiguity appropriately. When a friend, Laura, and a stranger, Suzanne, approach me after a sporting event and both say, "The game was a disaster", my comprehension processes may be identical. If I err in interpreting Suzanne's remark, that is her fault. She ought not to have used this utterance if she wasn't reasonably certain that I would interpret it correctly. Similarly, the sportscaster is to blame for my original confusion. He should know that some segment of his audience doesn't share his loyalties. Thus, cooperative conversationalists allow the comprehension process to resolve ambiguities immediately while still being reasonably error free.

A type of ambiguity or uncertainty that we might not expect to be resolved moment by moment would be the determination of the sincerity of an utterance. Consider any evaluative statement that a speaker, Fred, utters in an interpersonal situation, for example, "This fettuccine alfredo is superb." In some narrow sense of *meaning*, the meaning of Fred's utterance is straightforward: he likes the food. In a broader communicative sense of *meaning*, the cook must know plenty about Fred to know what he really means. Perhaps Fred is an indiscriminate eater — he likes anything — or unfailingly polite — he compliments anything. The cook must also evaluate the overall context of the utterance — Fred's non-verbal responses to the food, his speed of eating, the size of his seconds — to determine the degree of fit between what he said and his true opinion. This example demonstrates again that understanders do not accomplish all of meaning recovery through comprehension. they must take time to puzzle out some aspects of what speakers mean. To explicate *comprehension* fully, we must identify the aspects of meaning recovery that listeners need not puzzle out.

## CONCLUSIONS

This chapter has been devoted primarily to the description of a variety of meaning recovery tasks. For each task, I have considered a series of questions: Is this aspect of meaning recovered in moment-by-moment comprehension? How? Is post-comprehension exploration needed? I chose three domains — contextual expressions, referring phrases, ambiguous utterances — to exemplify different challenges associated with answering these questions. At least one general theme spans the domains: each meaning recovery task reinforces the generalization that mutual knowledge — special shared information — must regularly be available to listeners in the course of comprehension. A process model of comprehension should incorporate that generalization.

By studying langauge as armchair theorists, we can determine what properties we would like comprehension to have — we can develop a sense of how comprehension might be structured to handle diverse phenomena with maximal generality. By studying language as empiricists, we can identify domains that allow tests of our theoretical predilections — we can examine the actual moment-by-moment processes that underlie efficient communication.

## ACKNOWLEDGEMENTS

Preparation of this chapter was supprted in part by BRSG S07-RR07015, awarded by the Biomedical Research Grant Progam, Division of Research Resources, National Institute of Health. I am indebted to Herbert Clark, Raymond Gibbs, Dana Kay, and Judith Suben for helpful comments on earlier drafts.

## REFERENCES

Clark, E. V. (1981). Lexical innovations: How children learn to create new words. In W. Deutsch (Ed.), *The child's construction of language* (pp. 299–328). London: Academic Press.

Clark, E. V. (1982). The young word-maker: A case study of innovation in the child's lexicon. In E. Wanner, & L. R. Gleitman (Eds.), *Language acquisition: The state of the art* (pp. 390–425). Cambridge: Cambridge University Press.

Clark, E. V., & Clark, H. H. (1979). When nouns surface as verbs. *Language*, **55**, 767–811.

Clark, E. V., & Hecht, B. F. (1982). Learning to coin agent and instrument nouns. *Cognition*, **12**, 1–24.

Clark, H. H. (1983). Making sense of nonce sense. In G. B. Flores d'Arcais & R. Jarvella (Eds.), *The process of understanding language* (pp. 297–331). New York: Wiley.

Clark, H. H., & Carlson, T. B. (1981). Context for comprehension. In J. Long & A. Baddeley (Eds.), *Attention and performance, IX* (pp. 313–330). Hillsdale, NJ.: Lawrence Erlbaum, 1981.

Clark, H. H., & Clark, E. V. (1977). *Psychology and language*. New York: Harcourt, Brace & Jovanovich.

Clark, H. H., & Gerrig, R. J. (1983). Understanding old words with new meanings. *Journal of Verbal Learning and Verbal Behavior*, **22**, 591–608.

Clark, H. H., & Marshall, C. R. (1978). Reference diaries. In D. L. waltz (Ed.), *Theoretical issues in natural language processing 2* (pp. 57–63). New York: Association for Computing machinery.

Clark, H. H., & Marshall, C. R. (1981). Definite reference and mutual knowledge. In A. K. Joshi, B. Webber, & I. Sag (Eds.), *Elements of discourse understanding* (pp. 10–63). Cambridge: Cambridge University Press.

Clark, H. H., & Sengul, C. (1979). In search of referents for nouns and pronouns. *Memory & Cognition*, **7**, 35–41.

Corbett, W., & Chang, F. (1983). Pronoun disambiguation: Accessing potential antecedents. *Memory & Cognition*, **11**, 283–294.

Donnellan, K. S. (1966). References and definite descriptions. *Philosophical Review*, **75**, 281–304.

Donnellan, K. S. (1978). Speaker references, descriptions and anaphora. In P. Cole (Ed.), *Syntax and semantics: Vol. 9. Pragmatics* (pp. 47–68). New York: Academic Press.

Downing, P. A. (1977). On the creation and use of English compound nouns. *Language*, **53**, 810–842.

Ehrlich, K. (1980). Comprehension of pronouns. *Quarterly Journal of Experimental Psychology*, **32**, 247–255.

Ehrlich, K., & Rayner, K. (1983). Pronoun assignment and semantic integration during reading: Eye movements and immediacy of processing. *Journal of Verbal Learning and Verbal Behavior*, **22**, 75–87.

Faulkner, W. (1929). *The sound and the fury*. New York: Vintage Books.

Fodor, J. A. (1983). *The modularity of mind*. Cambridge, MA: MIT Press.

Ford, M., Bresnan, J., & Kaplan, R. (1982). A competence-based theory of syntactic closure. In J. Bresnan (Ed.), *The mental representation of grammatical relations* (pp. 727–796). Cambridge, MA: MIT Press.

Forster, K. I. (1976). accessing the mental lexicon. In R. J. Wales & E. C. T. Walker (Eds.), *New approaches to language mechanisms* (pp. 257–287). Amsterdam: North Holland.

Forster, K. I. (1979). Levels of processing and the structure of the language processor. In W. E. Cooper & E. C. T. Walker (Eds.), *Sentence processing: Psycholonguistic studies presented to Merrill Garrett* (pp. 27–85). Hillsdale, New Jersey: Lawrence Erlbaum.

Frazier, L., & Fodor, J. D. (1978). The sausage machine: A new two-staged parsing model. *Cognition*, **6**, 291–325.

Gerrig, R. J., & Healy, A. F. (1983). Dual processes in metaphor understanding: Comprehension and appreciation. *Journal of Experimental Psychology: Learning, Memory, and Cognition*, **9**, 667–675.

Gibbs, R. W. (1979). Contextual effects in understanding indirect requests. *Discourse Processes*, **2**, 1–10.

Gibbs, R. W. (1983). Do people always process the literal meanings of indirect requests? *Journal of Experimental Psychology: Learning, Memory, and Cognition*, **9**, 524–533.

Gibbs, R. W. (1984). Literal meaning and psychological theory. *Cognitive Science*, **8**, 275–304.

Gildea, P., & Glucksberg, S. (1983). On understanding metaphor: The role of context. *Journal of Verbal Learning and Verbal Behavior*, **22**, 577–590.

Grice, H. P. (1957). Meaning. *Philosophical Review*, **66**, 377–388.

Grice, H. P. (1968). Utterer's meaning, sentence-meaning, and word meaning. *Foundations of Language*, **4**, 225–242.

Grice, H. P. (1975). Logic and conversion. In P. Cole & J. L. Morgan (Eds.), *Syntax and semantics: Vol. 3. Speech acts* (pp. 41–58). New York: Academic Press.

Grice, H. P. (1978). Further notes on logic and conversation. In P. Cole (Ed.), *Syntax and semantics: Vol. 9. Pragmatics* (pp. 113–128). New York: Academic Press.

Kay, P., & Zimmer, K. (1976). *On the semantics of compounds and genitives in English*. Paper presented at the Sixth Annual Meeting of the California Linguistics Association, San Diego, California.

Malt, B. C. (1985). The role of discourse structure in understanding anaphora. *Journal of Memory and Language*, **24**, 271–289.

Marslen-Wilson, W. D., & Tyler, L. K. (1980). The temporal structure of spoken language understanding. *Cognition*, **8**, 1–71.

Marslen-Wilson, W. D., & Welsh, A. (1978). Processing interactions and lexical access during word-recognition in continuous speech. *Cognitive Psychology*, **10**, 29–63.

McGuane, T. (1971). *The bushwhacked piano*. New York: Vintage Books.

Minsky, M. (1975). A framework for representing knowledge. In P. H. Winston (Ed.), *The psychology of computer vision* (pp. 211–277). New York: McGraw-Hill.

Morris, C. (1946). *Signs, language and behavior*. New York: Prentice-Hall.

Murphy, G. L.(1985). Process of understanding anaphora. *Journal of Memory and Language*, **24**, 290–303.

Ortony, A., & Anderson, R. C. (1977). Definite descriptions and semantic memory. *Cognitive Science*, **1**, 74–83.

Rumelhart, D. E. (1979). Some problems with the notion of literal meanings. In A. Ortony (Ed.), *Metaphor and thought* (pp. 78–90). Cambridge: Cambridge University Press.

Rumelhart, D. E. (1980). Schemata: The building blocks of cognition. In R. J. Spiro, B. C. Bruce, & W. F. Brewer (Eds.), *Theoretrical issues in reading comprehension: Perspectives from cognitive psychology, linguisitics, artificial intelligence, and education* (pp. 33–58). Hillsdale, NJ.: Lawrence Erlbaum.

Rumelhart, D. E., & Ortony, A. (1977). The representation of knowledge in memory. In R. C. Anderson, R. J. Spiro, & W. E. Montague (Eds.), *Schooling and the acquisition of knowledge* (pp. 99–135). Hillsdale, NJ: Lawrence Erlbaum.

Salasoo, A., & Pisoni, D. B. (1985). Interaction of knowledge sources in spoken word identification. *Journal of Memory and Language*, **24**, 210–231.

Sanford, A. J., & Garrod, S. C. (1981). *Understanding written language.* New York: Wiley.

Schank, R. (1982). *Dynamic memory.* Cambridge: Cambridge University Press.

Schank, R., & Abelson, R. (1977). *Scripts, plans, goals and understanding.* Hillsdale, NJ: Lawrence Erlbaum.

Searle, J. (1975). Indirect speech acts. In P. Cole & J. L. Morgan (Eds.), *Syntax and semantics: Vol. 3. Speech acts* (pp. 59–82). New York: Academic Press.

Seidenberg, M. S., Tanenhaus, M. K., Leiman, J. M., & Bienkowski, M. (1982). Automatic access of the meanings of ambiguous words in context: Some limitations of knowledge-based processing. *Cognitive Psychology*, **14**, 489–537.

Sidner, C. L. (1983). Focusing in the comprehension of definite anaphora. In M. Brady & R. C. Berwick (Eds.), *Computational models of discourse* (pp. 267–330). Cambridge, MA: MIT Press.

Simpson, G. B. (1981) Meaning dominance and semantic context in the processing of lexical ambiguity. *Journal of Verbal Learning and Verbal Behavior*, **20**, 120–136.

Simpson, G. B., & Burgess, C. (1985). Activation and selection processes in the recognition of ambiguous words. *Journal of Experimental Psychology: Human Perception and Performance*, **11**, 28–39.

Wanner, E. (1980). The ATN and the Sausage Machine: Which one is baloney? *Cognition*, **8**, 209–225.

Wanner, E., & Maratsos, M. (1978). An ATN approach to comprehension. In M. Halle, J. Bresnan, & G. A. Miller (Eds.), *Linguistic theory and psychological reality* (pp. 119–161). Cambridge, MA: MIT Press.

# 2

# Three ways of looking at memory

**John Morton** and **Debra Bekerian**

## I. INTRODUCTION

This chapter concerns the structure of theories of human memory. The unwary may imagine in advance, or after having read the first few paragraphs, that this chapter is about the structure of human memory. The perverse will continue to hold such opinion after having read what we have to say. Let us say again, this chapter concerns the structure of theories of human memory. We take three kinds of theory. Two of these are well established: associative network theories and schema theories.

Theories that are called network theories are related together in particular ways. That is to say they have certain features in common. For example, they all stress the way in which our knowledge is structured, focusing on nodes with links between them and using the concept of activation spreading along the network. A network theorist would never dream of performing experiments to test for the existence of nodes, nor would the concept of spreading activation be questioned. Rather, experiments would would focus on the precise nature of the network for a particular knowledge fragment and on the parameters of the spread of activation under particular experimental conditions. If such a theorist is forced to change her theory the result will be of the same family. Such a person would be said to work inside the associative network framework.

The same arguments apply to schema theories. The work of Minsky, Schank and Rumelhart may seem to be widely different, but they are alike in that they work inside the schema framework. As such their basic assumptions resemble each other in ways that differentiate them from the neoclassical network theories of Anderson or Bower.

One of the things we want to do in this chapter is to make the nature of these two frameworks clearer. They differ not only in the formulations and terminology used but also in the ease with which they handle different kinds

Cognition 85 23 1-23

of phenomena. We note that both Anderson and Bower can employ other notations with profit. Our focus, however, will be on some proposals concerning memory which fit neither with the associative network framework nor the schema framework (Morton, Hammersley & Bekerian, 1985). In addition, our proposals, termed *headed records*, contain sets of features that, if unconstrained, would be able to give an account of any data. In sum, our proposals constitute, in part, a new framework. We strongly recommend that you study the earlier paper before reading this chapter seriously.

A framework is to be contrasted with a *model* or *theory*. Models or theories are expressed within a framework, although this is not always apparent and is rarely made explicit. However, when a model is found deficient and is changed by its originator or a devotee, then the revision is almost invariably related to the original by virtue of being expressed within the same framework. Thus, the two versions of the logogen model (Morton, 1969, 1979) are related by virtue of being expressed inside a modular information-processing framework.

The important feature of a framework is that it is, in principle, not falsifiable. It may be limited in scope or it may become too cumbersome to use, but a proper framework has the resources to encompass any pattern of data within its domain. One example of this is Freud's psychoanalytic approach to personality. A second example is Piaget's notion of development change, where the terms 'accomodation' and 'assimilation' can jointly be used to cover all eventualities. Thirdly we can regard Skinner's proposals as having framework status. His failure was not that he was wrong in principle but that the scope of the framework was too unrestricted so that the accounts he gave of many phenomena were too cumbersome to be of interest (e.g. Skinner, 1957).

Within any interesting framework one can formulate theories or express models. It is these, and not the framework itself, that can be falisified. The consequence of confusing the two is often that supposed attacks upon a position can easily be refuted. Thus, Bekerian (1984) has argued that much of the recent work on learned helplessness has been misdirected because the original statement of learned helplessness (Maier & Seligman, 1976) had framework status. Attacks on the learned helplessness position that assumed it was a theory (e.g. Costello, 1978) were easily repulsed from within the framework (Abramson, Seligman & Teasdale, 1978).

The advantage of having a framework is to enable a coherent debate with prior agreement about the definition of terms. Progress can only be made ultimately, however, when specific models are formulated which can be empirically tested. It is thus of the greatest importance for theorists to distinguish between those aspects of their theories which have framework status and those which do not. We have attempted to do this for headed records by distinguishing *kernel assumptions*, which define the framework, from *additional assumptions,* which enable us to postulate a specific, falsifiable model.

We will attempt to contrast associative network and schema frameworks with our own approach. This contrast does not help us to perform critical experiments to decide among them; as we have already intimated, this is impossible. Rather, the contrast helps us to see how different assumptions can lead to different theoretical commitments for explaining behaviour. To give one example, all memory frameworks trade off structure and process to some extent. In schema framework everything is process (Rumelhart, 1980). Associative networks put a lot into the structures. Our own framework is intermediate in this respect. However, it would be improper to attempt a relative judgement of the framework in this regard. Structure and process can be seen simply as alternative ways of expressing the same underlying idea. However, the frameworks differ in the kinds of question which are easiest to address. Which framework is used will be determined in part by what one wants to know.

We should say a word about the utility of the comparisons we are about to make. So far as we were concerned, headed records started off as a model. We actually thought that we made predictions that schema theories and network models couldn't make. We then were made aware that it was only *particular* theories that made the wrong predictions. Change the theories slightly and they coped with the problem. This is perfectly normal science.

Given that the existing frameworks can cope with any data, why bother to put forward a new type of theory? The reason is because we wished to focus on certain properties of our memories illustrated in the following section. These properties could be captured in the existing frameworks but only by means of additional postulates. Each framework has its advantages as a viewpoint. What we wish to avoid is useless debate about which framework is correct. Inside each framework a particular model will be correct, and deciding on its form is the function of experiment.

### A. The motivation for headed records

The feature of memory we wish to stress is the distinction between information that can be used as a cue for recall and information that can be recalled but not used as a cue. The distinction is illustrated in the following three common memory experiences.

### Don't you remember?

Common experiences are that of trying to remember something or someone and being given a series of cues which fail to access the memorandum. The cues would all be considered to be important but yet were insufficient to help to retrieve the memory even though they uniquely defined it. The vital clue may well have been incidental. Here is an example taken from a dialogue between a husband and wife (H and W, respectively).

W:    I saw Mike M. today and he said ...
H:    Who's Mike M?
W:    You know, you met him at the pub about a fortnight ago.
H:    Nope, never did.
W:    Of course, you did. You remember, you have to, you were sitting

right next to him and Vince, right after you'd come from your meeting with your co-workers at ... You had a long conversation with him about the terrific late-night film that you were missing.

H:    No, I don't remember him. I do remember being at the pub, and I remember how disappointed I was to have to miss the film; but I don't think Mike M. was there, whoever he is.

W:    This is ridiculous. Look, not only did you talk to him, but you threatened to dance with him at the next ...

H:    Oh, now I remember. The juke-box was playing a really good song and I said how much I'd like a bop, to which Vince replied that Mike M. had just said the same thing and that maybe we should get together and have a bop when the next record came on. Funny, the only reason I remember him is because of that record ... what was it now?

W:    I shouldn't try to remember, if I were you.

### What was his name?

Most people admit to having experienced the situation of feeling able to recount virtually everything they know about a particular individual except their name. It was one such incident which initially led, while under the influence of Norman and Bobrow (1979), to the idea of a heading. Someone's research was being discussed. The main results were familiar to the two people involved. We knew where the man worked, where he lived, the name of his wife and the last time he had given a talk at the APU. But his name eluded us. When it happened the reasoning went as follows. The person's name must certainly be associated with all the information about him. If his name had been presented on another occasion, it would surely have led to recalling the information currently available. Suppose, then, his name is one means of access to the memory record containing all this information but is not itself actually in the memory record.

### Whatever made me think of that?

Rarer, but equally striking, is the experience of a memory being triggered spontaneously by something which was just a part of the background for an event but irrelevant to the content of the memory. Common triggers in our experience are specific places in a city, scents and certain pieces of music. Here is an example.

"A couple of years ago I changed my perfume. The perfume I wore before that I had worn during a very unhappy time in my life. A few months ago, I found this large bottle of perfume and thought 'I can't let this go to waste' and sprayed some on. Almost immediately I was back in hospital coming around after having my stomach pumped."

The particular fragrance of the perfume may well have been incidental to the unhappy experiences this person had to go through. Nonetheless, it was sufficient to retrieve a vivid collection of them.

These three types of experience illustrate the peculiar nature of the processes of memory. We can summarize them as follows:

(1) Information which is part of a memory does not necessarily serve as a cue for recall of that memory.

(2) Information which can be used as a cue for recall cannot necessarily itself be recalled.

(3) Some information that can be used as a cue is incidental to the content of the memory record.

The framework started with postulates which focused on the above distinctions. As other memory data and phenomena were considered, the framework was extended (see Morton *et al.,* 1985; Bekerian & Morton, in preparation). Our focus in this article is on the form of our proposals rather than their application.

## II. THE HEADED RECORD FRAMEWORK

The structure of this section is as follows. First we will outline the framework. Second we will make explicit what we consider the kernel assumptions of the framework to be. Next we will show how the set of kernel assumptions leads to a set of derived properties. Occasionally we make explicit contrasts between the assumptions of the headed record (HR) framework and other frameworks. Such contrasts will be made extensively in Section III.

### A. Summary of the framework

We regard memory as being split up into *records*. The record is the unit of storage. Either all of it is accessed or none of it. We make no assumptions as to the size of a record. To each record is linked a *heading*. The *headed record,* or HR, is the basic structural unit of the framework. We regard HRs as structurally independent of each other. Apparent associations between records are a result of the operation of the accompanying processes.

Search of the HR system can be initiated either as a result of our interaction with the perceptual world, or as a result of explicit interrogation of memory. In both cases a *description* is formed. This is the information which is used in the search process. Search proceeds until a heading is found which matches the description by some criteria. Following this, the linked record is made available to other processes. If the record which has been retrieved does not fulfil the current task demands then a new description is formed and the search cycle is repeated.

The framework can thus be seen as having the following components:

(1) A structure of independent headed records.
(2) Three devices:
    (a) An *encoder,* which creates the HRs.
    (b) A *describer,* which creates descriptions.
    (c) An *evaluator,* which assesses the retrieved record in the light of the task demands.
(3) A retrieval process which matches descriptions to headings and retrieves the associated records.

## B.  Kernel assumptions

the *kernel assumptions* (KAs) are the irreducible minimum independent set
of posulates. If any one of them were changed the framework would have
different properties. The *derived concepts* (DCs) are theoretically interesting consequences of the kernel assumptions.

The starting point for our framework was the paper by Norman and
Bobrow (1979). They define the <u>record</u> as the <u>basic structural unit of
memory</u>. The concept reflects the observation that memory seems to be
organised in chunks. Thus it is a defining property of records that at any one
time one either has access to all of it or none of it. However, the nature of the
post-retrieval processes may mean that not all of a retrieved record can be
used at any one time.

In Norman and Bobrow it is the records themselves that are searched in
retrieval from memory. The three classes of observation that led us to
propose a modification of their framework were illustrated in the introduction. The first observation was that key information concerning an episode
cannot always be found in a memory though it can lead to the memory.
Secondly, not all information in a memory can be used as a means of locating
that memory. Thirdly, irrelevances can cue recall. These three types of
phenomena suggest that of the information associated with a record, some
can only be used for access but cannot be retrieved, and some can be
retrieved but cannot be used for access. Our proposal focuses on this and
posits that all records are linked with their individual *headings,* and that it is
the headings which are searched and not the records.

## KERNEL ASSUMPTIONS (KA's)

### KA1.  Knowledge consists of heading–record (HR) pairs

The basic notion of a record follows that proposed by Normand and
Bobrow. Memory consists of a set of discrete records into which our
experience has been divided by some means.

The heading is made up of a number of distinct elements, not necessarily
related or of the same kind. Thus the heading for a record about a particular
individual may include his name, a representation of his face, a visual image
of the place he was last met, or a combination of these. The relationship
between the contents of a record and its heading does not form part of our
kernel assumptions. It is appropriate in the discussion of specific memory
phenomena (Morton *et al*, 1985). Equally, the structure and form of
information in a record is completely open. A particular record could be a
list, a network or a tree structure and could be coded verbally or visually, for
example.

### KA2.  HR pairs are independent

There are no direct associative connections between records. In this we
differ from Norman and Bobrow. We account for cases of apparent
association between records by reference to the operation of the basic
retrieval cycle. That is, when one record is retrieved, a new description can

be formed from it. This description is then used to retrieve another record. Regularities in this process will lead to regular sequencing of records in recall.

### KA3.  Headed records are unmodifiable
This assumption distinguishes the current framework from most others. We assume that once a headed record has been formed it cannot be deleted, changed, updated or linked to any more recent record. The only changes permitted to the memory structures are the addition of new headed records. In this respect the framework resembles some versions of production systems (Young, 1979).

### KA4.  Retrieval from memory first involves a match between a description and a single heading
The term *description* is taken from Norman and Bobrow. It refers to the information which is used in the search process. Given that search takes place, and given that retrieval from memory is at all selective, then there must be a description upon which the selectivity is based. Any model of retrieval must make a similar assumption. The nature of the description will be influenced by the current task demands.

We should note here that we are using the terms 'search', 'selective' and 'retrieval' in the most general senses possible. We explicitly do not mean to imply any particular mechanism.

The set of headings, then, are searched by some process until a particular match is found to the description that is currently being employed. Only one match can be successful (see KA6).

### KA5.  A record is made available for further processing only if its heading has been matched
The nature of the 'further processing' will be discussed later. We will see that it includes verification that the information is what is required, organisation of speech output, the use of the information to form a new description, and the creation of new records in combination either with other old records or with our perceptual experience.

### KA6.  Search with any description will only lead to the retrieval of one record
It is simplest to think of the system operating in such a way that once a match has been found to a description then the search process terminates (but see AA1 below).

### KA7.  Headings are not retrievable
This assumption, together with KAs 4 and 6 define the difference between information in the heading and information in the record. The headings are the sole means of accessing the memory structures but cannot themselves be retrieved. The records can be retrieved but can only be accessed through the headings. These assumptions were stimulated by (though not entailed by)

the memory phenomena recounted in Section I. Note that there is nothing preventing the occurrence of the same piece of information in both a heading and the linked record.

### KA8.  Perceptual experience is interpreted by reference to our knowledge

Specifically, this means that interpretation of perceptual experience involves the use of an existing record. This is an assumption founded in Norman and Bobrow and in many other theories. One difference between the HR framework and most other approaches is that we make no assumption about the nature of the record which is consulted. In Norman and Bobrow's account, and in schema theories in general, it is some kind of archetypal knowledge which is consulted (see Section III). In the HR framework it could just as well be the record of the most recent relevant experience. Which record would be consulted would depend upon the nature of the description which is set up from the perceptual data.

### KA9.  New records can be created from our perceptual experience, from old records or from some combination

With this assumption we maintain the possibility of records of different types. We see no reason to exclude the possibility of records consisting of relatively unprocessed perceptual experience or, indeed, of records of the perceptual processing itself or of action sequences. In addition we include records of interpreted experience. Since the interpretation of experience involves the use of existing records (KA8) the resulting new record may contain information which was present in the old record but not in the current perceptual environment. Finally we allow that new records can be created by extraction of information from an old record (as might occur when recounting an experience) or by combination of information which results when more than one old record is used in a particular task (as in creative thought).

### KA10.  There exists a task specification

The task specification normally guides the operation of the system in interpreting our perceptual experience. Equally the task specification could be based on a question asked by another person or an internally generated question. There may be more than one current task specification but at least one must be involved in guiding the course of any further processing of an accessed record (KA6).

Note that, in an experiment, the nominal task specification, as given by the experimenter, may not correspond to the actual task specification. The subject is free to modify the nominal instructions for strategic reasons. This may or may not lead to more successful retrieval.

### *The framework in operation*

The proposed framework is extremely powerful and, as stated, will allow for any contingency. We can illustrate the operation of retrieval with an example. Take the H–R illustrated in Fig. 1. The heading consists of four

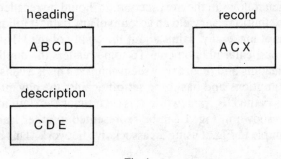

Fig. 1.

elements, A, B, C and D. The record consists of the elements, A, C and X. Suppose that the description contains the elements, C, D and E. The matching process may be satisfied with the equivalence of the elements C and D. The consequences would be that the record would be accessed, and elements A, C and X could be reported. Note that the element B, although in the heading, would not, in these circumstances, be accessed. Neither would the element D be reported as part of the record, although it appears both in the heading and the description.

We can now describe how the three classes of observation listed in the introduction fit into this framework.

*Don't you remember?* — The cues given to an incident need not be a part of the heading, but correspond to element X in the example. Given another cue which was part of the heading, the record could be retrived.

*What was his name?* — A person's name need not be a part of a record which concerns them. If the description contains other elements which are in the heading, the record could be accessed but the name would not be found. The name would thus correpond to element B in the example in Fig. 1.

*Whatever made me think of that?* — We have no reason for demanding that the heading for any record comprises all or any of what might be considered to be the significant aspects of the experience which was coded. Indeed, it seems to us that the conditions under which a particular feature of an experience will become a heading is an empirical question and one which is susceptible to experimental enquiry. This issue is discussed later.

To indicate the implications of even this simple formulation suppose that a part of the heading (B and D in Fig. 1) corresponded to the context in which the rest of the material (A, C) had been learned. Recall would then depend upon the context being reinstated i.e. B or D being part of the description. Recognition, involving the presentation of A or C, would not require the context to be reinstated since the presence of either of those elements in the description would be sufficient to match the heading. Thus, the context-dependent nature of recall and the context-free nature of recognition follow naturally (see Morton *et al.*, 1985, for a more detailed discussion).

We might here anticipate the comparison between different frameworks which follows in the next section. It should be recalled that any framework, by definition, can yield an account of any data. It follows that in principle we cannot make any claims about the ability of the HR framework to account for particular phenomena. To some readers the duplication of information in heading and record may seem clumsy. This is a consequence of our kernel assumptions and has to be set off against the advantages of viewing other data in the HR framework. It is clear that behaviour associated with the HR pair shown in Fig. 1 can be represented in other frameworks. We give an example in Fig. 2 using an associative network. This representation has the

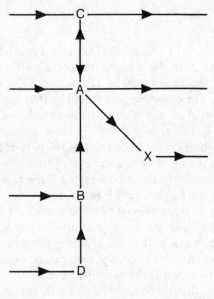

Fig. 2.

feature that elements are not duplicated. There are three kinds of node in Fig. 2, distinguished by whether they can be accessed and whether they give an output. With a few additional assumptions concerning the nature of the connections between nodes, the behaviour of the systems shown in Figs 1 and 2 are identical.

## DERIVED CONCEPTS (DCs)

The set of Kernel Assumptions (KAs) has a number of implications and consequences which are of theoretical interest. These we term *derived concepts*. All theories which can be expressed in the framework will have these features in common. It will be apparent that they do not all have the same logical status with respect to the KAs. However, we have grouped them together rather than increase the number of meta-theoretical entities.

## DC1.  There exists a describer

When memory is searched, the information used for the search, which we have termed the *description* (KA3), must be created. This must be based on the task specification, the available perceptual data and information in any record currently accessed. We assume in KA4 that currently available information need not all enter into a description and feel that the format of the available perceptual information need not be suitable for the search process. Thus, descriptions have to be created. The process or processes responsible for this we will term the *describer*. This is primarily for convenient of reference. As will be seen, it is an open question whether the describer is functionally distinct from all other processes.

## DC2.  There exists an encoder

Records can be created from experience using old records (KA2,9). Some processes will be necessary to effect this creation and the creation of headings. We will refer to these processes collectively as the *encoder*.

## DC3.  There exists a verifier

We have assumed a task specification which is used to guide the course of memory search (KA10). When any record is retrieved its contents must be compared with the task specification to determine whether it corresponds to the information sought. Equally, when a record is accessed in order to guide our interpretation of perceptual experience, some checks must be carried out to ascertain the continued relevance of the old record. These processes of verification we collectively refer to as the *verifier*.

## DC4.  The system effectively exhibits 'restricted content addressing'

The contrast here is with systems which exhibit unrestricted content addressing (Landauer, 1975; Collins and Quillian, 1972). In the HR framework it is possible that a piece of information which exists in a record or a number of records is absent from all the associated headings. Search with a description based on such a piece of information will give no result (KA4). In the extreme case, the content of a heading need bear no relation at all to the content of the record to which it is linked. It could, for example, be concerned solely with the environemental conditions under which the information in the record was encoded. It is easy to generate specific models with particular relationships between heading and record but there does not appear to be data currently available to support any restrictions.

## DC5.  What is retrieved need not be what one is looking for

We only gain access to a record through the heading. A particular piece of information, for example, BILL'S ADDRESS, need not be in a record headed by BILL. It might, for example, be in a record headed with NEARBY FRIENDS. Use of a description BILL may, then, come up with other information about Bill which is irrelevant for recalling his address.

A number of examples of such occurrences have been cited by Williams and Hollan (1981). It is clear from their examples, and from observations of our own behaviour, that there are two consequences of this. First, we are aware that the information we have retrieved is inappropriate. Secondly, we can go on looking.

**DC6. Successive retrieval attempts involve an iteration of the same process**
This principle of a retrieval cycle has been expanded upon and illustrated by Williams and Hollan (1981). It is a necessary part of any headed record model since there is no other way, given the kernel assumptions, of continuing the search process. Thus, if a record does not satisfy the task specification, either the description must be modified or a new description must be formed and the search process recycled. Note that within a different framework the further attempts could involve a completely different process from the initial search. Thus, within an associative network framework the initial access is 'direct', and subsequent search proceeds by traversing the network (see Section III).

**DC7. Accessibility of a record is partly determined by discriminability of its heading**
Records can only be accessed through their headings (KA4). This is effected through a match with the current heading. In any one retrieval cycle, only one record can be accessed. It follows that any records with similar headings will effectively be competing with each other. Thus the likelihood of accessing a particular record wil be determined by the distinctiveness of its heading.

**DC8. Apparent forgetting will occur as a result of the natural operations of the retrieval processes**
The separation of headings and records leads to retrieval being a two-stage operation. First, an appropriate heading must be located (KA4). Then the linked record must be retrieved (KA5). In the HR framework apparent forgetting can arise for a number of reasons. In general this would come about when the record was not headed with information reflecting the content (see DC4). First there may be no heading which matches the descriptions used. Secondly, the description may match a heading which is linked to a record with different but related content (e.g. the incident which followed the one sought). Thirdly, there need be no relationship between the content of a heading and the content of a record (cf. Landauer, 1975). In these three cases the evaluation procedures would report failure and the search process might be abandoned as fruitless. In a fourth option the evaluation procedures might report success but the record accessed may be the wrong one. This could occur if one was looking for the record of a film one had seen, but retrieved instead the record of the previous time one recounted the story of the film. There may be no indication that this was not the original record. If this recounting had been incomplete then the impression could be created that loss has occurred. In general, access to a record may be blocked by a more recent record with a similar heading. This

concept has been used by Bekerian and Bowers (1983, Bowers and Bekerian, 1984) to account for data by Loftus, Miller and Burns (1978) which purportedly demonstrated loss. Finally, there could be apparent forgetting as a result of post-retrieval procedures (see AA5, below). For example, the record may require editing before output, either as a consequence of its complexity of organisation or because the storage code needs translating (as with a visual image).

### DC9. Situational demands influence retrieval
In DC1 we observed that the situation at the time of memory search can influence the nature of the description that is set up. In DC6 we gave examples of apparent forgetting which are due to retrieval failure, i.e. due to the appropriate description not having been formed. We could expect, then, to find examples where a change in the situation following a failure to retrieve a memory will lead to the formation of a new description which leads to successful retrieval.

### DC10. There can be duplication of information
Since new records can be created from (a) the interaction of perceptual experience with information in an old record, or (b) as a result of the processing of one or more records (KA9), we have no reason for prohibiting duplication of information in records.

## ADDITIONAL ASSUMPTIONS (AA)

The kernel assumptions together with the derived concepts could serve to give an account of any pattern of data within the scope of the framework. In practice such accounts would be rather vague. In order to be more specific some *additional assumptions* have to be made. These are, in principle, falsifiable, unlike the kernel assumptions. The additional assumptions are a means of creating one of the many models possible within the framework set up by the kernel assumptions. The additional assumptions are strongly but not necessarily driven by the need to meet particular data.

Our strategy here will be to list the additional assumptions without too much justification.

### AA1. Search is effectively serial and backwards in time
The importance of this assumption is that if two or more records exist, the headings of which match the current description, then the most recent of these will be retrieved. The reason for making this assumption is the observation that when asked to recall an event, people often recall a previous recollection of that event and not the event itself (e.g. Bekerian and Bowers, 1983).

We would like to make it clear that we do not envisage a device which literally searches serially and backwards in time. This is merely a convenient way of regarding the operation of the system. If taken literally, the assumption could even be biologically impossible! There are, however, a number of ways of getting the same effect. One would be by means of some 'strength' notion — more recent headings being stronger and effecting the match with the description more rapidly, the search then being stopped. Or the headings which matched the description could be compared with each other, with the 'stronger' one winning. Alternatively there could be a 'time-stamp' included on each of the headings (cf. Morton, 1971). If a time-stamp appropriate to NOW were routinely included in the description, then this would match the more recent heading more closely.

While it is not our purpose here to produce a precise mechanism we could see a way of using Fahlman's (1981) NETL system to create the effects we need. Fahlman describes this system as a means of representing semantic knowledge. In the system all 'nodes' are connected to a 'Party-line bus'. Commands are sent down the bus by a serial control computer. Nodes can be selected by command and "selected nodes ... (can) ... queue up and report their serial numbers over the bus" (Fahlman, 1981, p. 154). In this way a quasi-parallel search mechanism can be made to behave in a serial fashion.

If the 'nodes' in Fahlman's system are equivalent to headings, if the information they report back is the address of the appropriate record and if the control computer only accepts the first item in the 'queue', then we have the behaviour we require.

We include this excursion into hardware simply to make the point that a description of the behaviour of a system does not put very strong constraints upon the detail of the underlying mechanism. For the purpose of analysing memory phenomena in the HR framework, then, we will continue with the convenience of representing HR pairs as a linear array which is searched serially, backwards in time.

### AA2. The encoder, the describer and the verifier have overlapping functions

The three kinds of process required to handle the HR system need to be interconnected. We will assume that they are in fact the same device, which we will call the *characterizer*. The overlapping functions can be seen as follows. Before the encoder can operate, a referent record has to be found. For this to be achieved a description must be formed from the available information. This may be contextual, e.g. you may know you are about to go into a restaurant. With unexpected events, however, some feature of the environment must be selected to form a description. We would expect the criteria for selection in this case to be simlar to the criteria used in memory search. Thus, encoder and describer functions must overlap. While a record is being used to interpret the current experience, i.e. as a referent, the evaluation function will have to operate continuously to check that the current referent is still appropriate. This evaluation will resemble the processes carried out to verify that a retrieved record satisfies task criteria in a situation demanding memory search. It would be simpler, then, to assume that they are the same process and that they are closely linked to the encoding function.

### AA3. All characterizer activity leads to the creation of new records

We assume that if we recount a prior experience then a new record will be set up, consisting of those parts which were recouned plus, perhaps, material which was retrieved but rejected as being unsuitable or inappropriate for the particular occasion. The assumption is an extreme one that has a least two major contrasts. The first contrast would be with a framework which allowed experience to change an old record (e.g. Loftus & Loftus, 1980). This is already ruled out by our KA6, i.e. unmodified records. The second contrast is within our own framework. We could allow instead that experiences need not always lead to new records. We could assume that only experiences evaluated as 'important' lead to new records being formed.

### AA4. There are basic recognition and response processes operating outside the HR structures

We assume that basic object recognition, word recognition, speech ouput and similar processes operate in a largely data-driven fashion without recourse to information in the knowledge structures. This assumption is shared by schema theory (Rumelhart, 1980). The information received by the encoder will thus be interpreted to some extent. In the case of object recognition we would envisage the use of HR structures for identification below the 'basic level' (Rosch *et al.*, 1976). The interpretation of a perceptual experience would begin with such categorization as the basic recognition processes had managed to effect. These could decide that there was a dog in front of you, but the headed records system would be needed to decide that it was a poodle, or Spot, the next door's dog.

### AA5. Post-retrieval processes are imperfect

We assume that if a complex record is available for further processing (KA6) then the whole of its contents might not be accessed by the relevant processes. Thus, in telling a story, we assume that parts of a particular record may be omitted. This could be caused by problems of place-keeping or the limited capacity of a short-term buffer store.

### AA6. The conditions on a heading–description match are variable

The status of this AA is marginal. In some cases we assume that a match between part of the description and part of a heading will suffice. This will require the setting of some criterion and possibly the weighting of information in the description for importance. In addition we anticipate some descriptions might require an exact match. This is effectively the condition used in the production system framework (Newell & Simon, 1972; Young, 1979). This might be the case when getting the definition of words. Further, we could envisage the criterion for a match being influenced by task specifications. The range of possibilities is large. Each option constitutes a theory inside the framework which is subject to empirical test. The consequences of the alternatives are likely to be important, but at the present stage of outlining the framework we can leave the options until they can be constrained by data.

## III.  ALTERNATIVE FRAMEWORKS

In the course of developing this new framework we were forced eventually to ask the crucial question: what does this 'new' framework provide that other already established frameworks lack? This turns out to be a relatively difficult question to answer for a number of reasons. First, frameworks can only be compared in terms of their kernel assumptions. As pointed out in the Introduction, all associative network models must have some common assumptions in order to be categorized as 'associative network models', and these would comprise kernel assumptions. However, kernel assumptions are not data-driven, i.e., are unfalisifiable. So, a comparison of two frameworks will never be resolved in terms of one being more correct than the other by virtue of examing 'the data'. A second and related problem concerns the application of a framework to specific classes of memory behaviour. In principle a number of frameworks could address (more or less efficiently) a general class of behaviour like memory phenomena. This means that any two frameworks (given equivalent completeness) can address the same empirical issues. However, it may be easier to discuss certain phenomena within one framework than in others. This means that, in practice, specific models using the kernel assumptions and terminology of a particular framework tend to be limited with respect to the paradigms and behaviour they discuss. It also means that models in different frameworks tend to address different issues. Finally, there is no reason to suppose that two different frameworks could not be further classified under a superordinate 'meta-framework'. Some of the kernel assumptions may be similar, others not. In comparing two frameworks, then, it may be rather difficult to know whether their dissimilarities should be given more weight, or their similarities.

We will attempt to divide the statements about other frameworks into kernel assumptions, derived concepts, and additional assumptions. We doubt that our account will satisfy the proponents of any particular model we subsume under these frameworks (though we doubt whether any two objectors would agree with each other as to our shortcomings). Two points might be made. The division between kernel assumptions and derived concepts is dificult to establish from the available literature. However, as long as we accurately characterize the contrast with the HR framework this need not matter. Secondly, we have been sparing with the number of additional assumptions we list. The reason for this is that it is the additional assumptions which distinguish the different exemplar models; and the detail of operation of a particular model is beyond our current purpose, even though the originator may stress this detail in his writing.

### A.  Association/semantic frameworks

The associative or semantic (network) framework (ASF) means somewhat different things to different people; and the range of models utilizing an ASF notation is wide. Nonetheless we will try to provide statements which can be applied to all models of human memory search falling under the general category of ASF. We will maintain the convention of referring to kernel assumptions, derived concepts and additional assumptions as used in our presentation of HR. In practice the KAs will resemble the features of prototype theory: all ASF theories subscribe to most of the KAs but not necessarily to all of them.

### Kernel assumptions in ASF

(1) Information in memory is represented discretely by nodes and links. Nodes correspond to concepts and/or ideas and/or propositions; links reflect relationships between nodes.

(2) Duplication of information in nodes is avoided, i.e. each node is unique (though there are some exceptions, e.g. Collins & Loftus, 1975).

(3) Links connect nodes to form an associative network. The relationships established between nodes by the links may either be direct or indirect via an intervening or mediating node. Thus, one could have the indirect relationship (*A spaniel is an animal*) from a combination of two direct relationships (*A spaniel is a dog*) and (*A dog is an animal*).

(4) Links are labelled in accordance with the information they represent. Nodes may have means identifying them, but need not.

(5) Networks are modifiable. This means that new experiences can result in the formation of new links, or in the additional marking of already existing connections.

(6) Retrieval from an associative network involves two stages: first, initial access into the network; and secondly, search through the network by spreading activation which is related to some input description of the information sought.

(7) Initial access to a named node or nodes is non-problematic and is automatic. This is often referred to as *direct access* and accounts for the first stage of retrieval. The actual use of direct access is somewhat ambiguous in practice since not all named nodes are addressable directly.

(8) During the second stage of retrieval a partial description of the sought-after information may guarantee access of that information, as for example, the access of higher-order propositional nodes through the access of its constituent members. This is often referred to as *content addressing*.

(9) In the event that the input description fails to find a match, retrieval can become an iterative process by modifying the input description until a match is found to some part of the network.

### Derived concepts in ASF

(1) Type-token distinctions of information represented in nodes are provided by labelled links. This follows as nodes are unique (KA2) and links serve to establish relationships between nodes (KA3).

(2) Parsers (linguistic and perceptual) convert external information into a form congruent to that of the network. This follows from the assumption that an input description is used to search the network (KA6).

(3) Search through the network involves traversing links or having markers passed along links. This follows as links connect all nodes in the network (KA3).

(4) *In principle* any named node can serve as an initial access point for the search process. This must be assumed given that access into the memory network is accomplished by direct access using names (KA7).

(5) After search has produced a candidate match some verification processes might be required. However, verification procedures are not mandatory since attempts to retrieve particular information can be expected to succeed through content addressing (KA8).

(6) The network is passive, therefore some process or processes are necessary to read the information reflected in links. This follows since nodes and links are represented as structural units upon which the search procedure operates (KA3, KA8). In some models processes are identified as *procedural knowledge* to be contrasted with the *declarative knowledge* represented by nodes and links (e.g. Anderson, 1976).

In addition to the above, it also seems that most ASF models make a few additional assumptions. These latter assumptions are not logical consequences of kernel assumptions stated earlier.

### Additional assumptions

(1) Links have values which correspond to or reflect the associative strength between nodes. This property enables different associated concepts to be unequal in their ability to act as retrieval cues.

(2) The traversing of links between nodes may not be bidirectional. This means that the access of one node, A, can lead to the access of node B, but not necessarily vice versa.

(3) The time taken to traverse links may be in part a function of the associative strength between nodes.

(4) During search some part of the associative network is 'activated'. In some instances activation delimits the search area (e.g. Anderson & Bower, 1973). In others, the notion of 'activation' is more dynamic and data-driven (e.g. Anderson, 1980; Collins and Quillian, 1972).

### Comparison of ASF with the headed records framework (HRF)

Perhaps the most notable distinction between ASF and HRF is the relative emphasis each places on assumptions of structure or on assumptions of processes. The strongest assumptions of ASF are concerned with the representation of information in a semantic network (see Ross & Bower, 1981). In contrast, the HRF makes only two assumptions about structural components of memory; more are made about the nature of encoding and retrieval processes. We feel this difference in emphasis has consequences in the types of questions which can be conveniently addressed by both frameworks. First, however, we will attempt to compare both frameworks directly.

(1) Both ASF and HRF assume discrete memory units, i.e. links and nodes and records respectively. However, nodes are atomistic, whereas records can be arbitrarily complex.

(2) ASF assumes uniqueness of nodes as a starting postulate; thus, information can only be represented in one place. HRF is not explicit with respect to the uniqueness of records. However, the processing assumptions of HRF require that information at the level of concepts (e.g. BILL) is represented in more than one record.

(3) ASF assumes that all nodes in the network are connected. In contrast, HRF is explicit in stating that there are no direct connections between memory units. However, indirect connections can be effectively mimicked by forming a new description from one record and then accessing a second record which contains related information. The absence of links between records does not preclude the possibility of links between elements within a record.

(4) ASF assumes that information is conveyed in the labelling of links. This enables, for example, a type–token distinction to be implemented. As HRF assumes no direct connections there is no comparable assumption. However, effective type-token distinctions can occur in the HRF. This would occur if a particular record was always used in interpreting a particular class of situation (e.g. a typical evening in the pub). However, such use is not obligatory (the record of a specific evening could be used) and the 'typical' record could not contain any reference to the individual events unless it had been re-created after these events had occurred. This follows from the unchangeability of records in the HRF.

(5) Both HRF and ASF characterize retrieval as an iterative search with some memory description. However, in ASF initial access into the network can be achieved by a direct access procedure and is, consequently, distinguishable from the search process. In contrast, HRF assumes that initial access and extended search involve similar processes.

(6) Both HRF and ASF assume that a search–match process occurs in retrieval. In most versions of ASF, any named node can serve as an entry into the network and, therefore, as an initiation of the search––match process. In the second strage, the search–match process is theoretically unrestricted, i.e. through access of all nodes and links. In HRF only headings are searched for and matched.

(7) Successful retrieval in ASF is accomplished by content addressing. The most common reading of this assumption is that any constituents of the input description can be used in the search process. In HRF search proceeds only through matches between description and heading. In the latter case, even if the input description contains information directly represented in a record, search may fail unless the description contains

information represented in the heading. Thus, successful search is restricted to the contents of the heading.

The essential differences between ASF and HRF can now be summarized. One issue concerns the assumptions of direct connections between memory units. Another concerns the differentiation of memory units into types. In ASF, type nodes are labelled explicitly. In HRF, records have no formal distinctions, except by use. Yet another difference between the two frameworks arises over issues of search processes. In ASF an initial direct access is followed by a search by content addressing. In HRF there is just the search of headings with a description. Finally, ASF postulates unique nodes whereas the HRF is forced to allow duplication of information. There are of course advantages and disadvantages of holding different positions on these issues. We will now try to illustrate what a few of these might be.

### Direct connections in memory
There are some distinct advantages from the point of view of efficiency and economy of having direct connections between memory units even in an HR framework. For example, take the representation of our knowledge about a personal friend, let's call him BILL. We might have a record BILL which contains personal information like physical appearance, addresses, etc. Connected to the BILL record would be other HRs representing other kinds of information about BILL, e.g. events in which BILL appeared, events in which BILL was a topic of conversation. The most striking advantage in this system is that, in principle, we can rapidly discover all there is to know about BILL by travelling along the appropriate links. We can also direct our search rather expediently by only considering links which are labelled appropriately given the input description.

However, there are some distinct difficulties with this system. First, it requires very sophisticated support processes, ones that can specify "... the types of nodes and links ... the rules for their possible combinations ... (and) the import of the various types of links and structures — what is meant by them ..." (Woods, 1975, p. 49). For example, we would have to have some way of distinguishing those HRs where we were stating some information about BILL (e.g. BILL was at the wrestling match), from those where we were providing a description of BILL (e.g. the record of the event in which BILL was referred to as an avid sports fan). These and other requirements would be necessary not only for retrieval but also for establishing new connections in the network; they force a great deal of notational complexity and result in a rather cumbersome network (cf. Kintsch, 1974). The question is not whether such complexity should be avoided, but rather whether the particular approach is desirable, given such complexity.

With discrete records we avoid these structural problems. The burden is instead on expanding the processes of description formation and the evaluation process. This is because we maintain that apparent associations between records are the result of the operation of the basic retrieval cycle (see Section II, KA2). That we prefer this option is, at the moment, a matter of taste.

### Extent of content addressing

According to ASF, retrieval is accomplished by content addressing. In principle this gives great flexibility: virtually any constituent part of the information to be retrieved can be used to access it. However, it is suggested that in practice content addressing is much more restricted, i.e. not all parts of the information sought can be used as a cue to retrieve the rest. Many specific models within the ASF have attempted to accommodate this fact; yet, it should be remembered that in doing so, the strong assumption about content addressing is always weakened, for example by use of probabilisitic pathways. Since a weakened version of content addressing seems to be necessary, it seems better to maintain the position of restricted content addressing from the outset.

It should be mentioned that our position has certain costs associated with it. For example, we maintain that information must be in the heading in order for it to be a potential retrieval cue. However, we have also asserted that information in the heading is not retrievable. At the extreme, this means that information that can serve as a cue should never be recalled! Of course, this is not the case. To get around this problem, we are forced to assume the possibility of information being duplicated. That is, information contained in a heading can be represented either in its corresponding record or in another record. The occasions on which such duplication will occur are as yet unspecified.

### Uniqueness of memory units

Any system which does not allow for duplication of structural units is efficient and encomomical. There would be minimal inconsistency at encoding and minimal redundancy. As we have already sated, one of the kernel assumptions of ASF is the uniqueness of nodes. So, generally speaking, ASF offers a way of representing an economic memory.

In contrast, information at the level of concepts is assumed to be duplicated in HRF. Thus, more than one record could contain the concept BILL. We admit that such a system is redundant. Also the system would undoubtedly be susceptible to inconsistencies at encoding, which could then pose problems of 'decoding' ambiguous information, e.g. if more than one BILL were known.

Nonetheless, we prefer the latter system for two reasons. First, the economy of an uniqueness assumption is most striking only when the information being represented is rather finite and well defined, e.g. unique category membership. However, human memory represents a domain of discourse where knowledge can also extend in all directions at once. Given this, the economy gained by node uniqueness is simply replaced by a different type of inefficiency — namely, the issue of linking related nodes together.

Secondly, we would argue that human memory is indeed redundant and uneconomical in its operations. Our suggestion that conceptual information is duplicated forces us to specify eventually how encoding and retrieval processes cope with redundancy and ambiguity. The problem we confront revolves round determining the nature of the processes involved in description formation, description–heading matching, characterizer functions, and so on.

### Scale of operation

As we have remarked, the basic unit of ASF is the node and that for HRF is the record. These units differ in their size, and the relative strengths of the frameworks reflects this. Models within the ASF framework have gone a long way in accounting for memory performance at the lower levels, items in lists, elements of propositions, propositions within texts. They have not yet addressed the kinds of issues which the HRF is designed to address. There is no principled reason why the ASF models should not address these issues; it is just that the expression of them is more complex than in HRF. On the other hand, it will be seen that we have only the most general statements to make about the microstructure of recall. This, too, is not a principled restriction.

In short, ASF does not differ dramatically from HRF in terms of the static representation of knowledge. In fact, ASF seems more complete in its discussion of the structural characteristics of memory. However, we suggest that while ASF entertains important questions about knowledge representation, it provides only limited understanding of the processes responsible for the encoding and retrieval of information outside a rather rigidly defined set of circumstances. Questions about processes will prove crucial, we feel, in gaining a more complete understanding of how human memory works, be it in the experimental setting or in a natural one.

### B.  Schemata framework

"... I strongly dislike the term 'schema'. It is at once too definite and too sketchy. The word is already widely used in controversial psychological writing to refer generally to any rather vaguely outlined theory." (Bartlett, 1932, p. 201)

The schema framework (SF) has been used to describe how people go about interpreting sensory data, retrieving information from memory, organizing actions, determining goals or behaviour, allocating processing resources and, generally, directing overall processing in attentional, perceptual and memorial systems. Rumelhart (1980) states "... because our understanding of none of these tasks ... has reached maturity, it is little wonder that a definitive explication of schemata does not yet exist and that sceptics view theories based on them with some suspicion" (p. 34). Nonetheless, in this section we will attempt to give an overview of the SF and make comparisons between it and the HR framework. Of course, as with network theories, there are a number of variants. In La Jolla, even married couples have been known to disagree about the nature of schemata (or schema) (Mandler & Mandler, personal communication). While our overview will please none of the practitioners it should sufficiently reflect all their views (so far as we can see) in contrast with other frameworks.

### Kernel assumptions

(1) Schemata are discrete, abstract knowledge structures which represent past actions or experiences. They do not, however, map directly on to any single event, i.e. schemata represent generic concepts and are types rather than tokens.

(2) Schemata are unique. In the limit, no information is duplicated, e.g. "... you have to find one and only one place to store general information ..." (Schank, 1980, p. 272). For some schema theories there can be duplication of subparts — thus, for some theorists, 'paying the cashier' would be found in the restaurant script, the catching-a-train script, and so on. However, information about particulars is, universally, stored in a single place.

(3) The regular elements of an event type are represented as slots in the corresponding schema, e.g. steretyped scriptal actions (Schank & Abelson, 1977). Schemata thus provide an organization for the typical aspects of events, actions and concepts.

(4) Schemata organize information at different levels of abstraction. This allows schemata to be embeded in one another (Rumelhart, 1980), e.g.meta-scripts or MOPS (Abelson, 1981; Schank, 1980).

(5) At the lowest level of abstraction there are specific, fragmentary representations of aspects of specific events. These are sometimes called 'memory traces' and are conceptualized as distinct from schemata (Schank, 1980); other schema theorists regard them as 'spatio-temporal instantiations' which are 'part of the schema' (Mandler, G., personal communication). This seems to be a matter of taste. We will use the term 'memory trace' without prejudice. The memory traces are labelled with pointers that serve to establish reference to the relevant schemata (Rumelhart & Ortony, 1977; Schank, 1980). These memory traces are created only when particular aspects of an event are irregular with respect to the expected values and when the irregularities have consequences on the overall organization of actions or features in schemata (Schank, 1980).

(6) Schemata may be modified or new schemata may be abstracted as a consequence of new experiences.

(7) Schemata are involved in all processing that is required for perception and memory.

(8) Schemata are always receptive to relevant information from the sensory receptors and from other schemata.

(9) When a schema receives information it becomes 'activated'. The consequence of this is that it then 'seeks' further information relevant to its own appropriateness.

(10) In perception, the instantiation of a schema (i.e. the filling in of empty slots) can arise either perceptually, from other schemata (Schank & Abelson, 1977), or from the schema itself (Rumelhart, 1980; Schank, 1980). In the latter case, default values will be used (Mandler, 1979).

(11) The schema which offers the best match to the information being processed eventually 'switches off' other schemata at the same level.

(12) All remembering (as well as comprehension) is constructive. The highly regular aspects of specific events are reconstructed from schemata. To these are added the deviant or irregular aspects of events which are represented directly in specific memory traces (cf. KA5). Default values are used for any slots which are not specifically filled (Mandler, 1979).

### Derived concepts

(1) Aspects of an event which conform to a particular slot are evaluated to determine whether they are sufficiently deviant or important to warrant direct storage in a memory trace (KA5).

(2) There are constraints on the values that schematic variables (slots) can take and, consequently, on the mechanism by which things may be perceived or remembered. (This follows from KA 3–5.)

(3) As DCs 1 and 2 indicate, there are three ways in which aspects of an event can be stored.
   (a) Regular, predictable aspects will not be represented. There will be representations during perception, but these are transitory.
   (b) deviant aspects which nonetheless conform to a slot may be represented as specific memory traces.
   (c) Aspects which do not fit into a slot will not be represented at all unless they have specific consequences, in which case a new schema will be created (KA6).

(4) Recollected information about an event can be drawn from a number of different data structures at different levels of abstraction (KAs 4 and 11).

(5) Recollection is a dynamic activity, not an automatic one: that is, the combination of information from different levels of abstraction will require evaluation procedures. (This follows from KA11.)

(6) Errors in remembering specific events can have multiple loci. Errors may result if inferences are based on information reconstructed from schemata (KA11). Errors may also be due to loss of information resulting from modifications of schemata (KA6).

### Additional assumptions

(1) Event-specific information which conforms to typical instances of schemata are more readily processed (Rosch et al., 1976); these typical instances may or may not be readily retrieved (Graesser et al., 1980).

(2) Instantiation of higher-order schemata involves non-serial processes (Abelson, 1981; Rumelhart, 1980; Schank, 1980).
(3) The notion of loss of stored information can be accommodated in the framework. Such effects would be restricted to the level of the memory trace (Schank, 1980).

### Comparison of frameworks

(1) Both SF and HRF emphasize a structural basis of memory as opposed to a process basis, e.g. Hinton (1981).
(2) In SF different types of information are represented by different structures. Schemata represent only abstracted information, while memory traces represent information that is specific to an event. Further, different schemata contain different levels of abstracted information. In HRF, there is only one type of representation, HR pairs.
(3) In SF, traces of specific events are connected to these schema used during the processing of the event, e.g. "At the end of each [MOP] strand are particular experiences (i.e., scripts" (Schank, 1980, p. 273). In HRF no direct connections are allowed between HR pairs although a new record may contain elements of the old record which was used in interpreting an experience.
(4) Traces of specific events are attached to only one schema, i.e. they are unique. As already discussed, HRF is unprincipled in this respect.
(5) In SF forgetting may result from errors in reconstruction, or loss of event-specific memory traces. In HRF all forgetting is assumed to be the result of retrieval failures.
(6) In SF event-specific information must be reconstructed by accessing a number of schemata in addition to accessing a specific memory trace. In HRF information about a specific event may be represented in more than one record, but need not be.
(7) Although both SF and HRF assume a 'matching' procedure, they are functionally dissimilar. In SF schemata appear to match incoming information by unrestricted content addressing. In HRF only Headings are matched to a description. Futher, while SF allows the possibilty of schemata determining their own 'goodness' of match, HRF assumes that decisions about description–heading matches are made by independent processes. We will now go into more detail about the last two points.

### Reconstructive processes

The assumption most often associated with the SF is that perception and remembering involve processes of reconstruction. This assumption warrants very careful consideration in order to appreciate fully the consequences it holds for the SF.

Perhaps the best place to start is to define what the notion of reconstruction might mean in the context of memory. When one postulates the need for reconstruction, one implies that 'something' is missing in the memory trace. The nature of memorial incompleteness will have direct consequences on the nature of the reconstructive processes. For example, one could have a memory trace where all of the task-relevant details of an event are represented in a uniform code at the time of storage, but the details are in a form that is unsuitable for output. Higher-order structures (or processes) might then be required to interpret the code. These auxiliary structures might serve to verify the information, decode the 'meaning' behind the memorial information (as in hash-coding) or both. Rumelhart (1980) implies the use of schemata for these opertions when he states "... memorial fragments [present] themselves to the memory system for interpretation ... the processes of interpretation [select] potential configurations of schemata and [verify] that they are consistent with the stored data ... sometimes ... the interpretation of this fragment of memory is enough to respond to the question at hand" (p. 51). If we define memory in this way, the reconstructive process is somewhat similar for both SF and HRF. We have chosen to describe it under characterizer functions.

A very different sense of reconstruction is implied when one suggests that any memory trace lacks a substantial amount of event-specific information needed to complete the task at hand. Here all the relevant information is not to be found by simply accessing the memory. Thus, if the memory trace is only a fragmentary copy of an event-type, only limited information will be available (Rumelhart, 1980). The same holds true if a memory trace contains only unusual or deviant information plus a reference 'pointer' (Schank, 1980). Once one is committed to such impoverished memorial representations, processes of reconstruction take on a new meaning (although processes of the former type may still occur). Reconstruction now becomes a necessity for 'filling in' or providing a substantial amount of envent-specific information needed for the task. In some sense, of course, event-specific information is still contained in the trace: pointers, for example, do convey information. However, the information sufficient to recollect the specific event does not reside in one location, i.e. in the memory trace. Various higher-order structures must be consulted for the task of recollection to continue. If the reconstructed information were congruent with the specific event features not present in the trace, then recall would be accurate. If this reconstructed information were not congruent with the event-specific details, reconstructive errors would occur. This type of reconstruction is implied in SF.

In contrast, HRF assumes that a record may or may not contain enough event-specific information with respect to the task at hand. If the record is incomplete, then further iterations of the retrieval cycle will be necessary, starting with the formation of a new description, in order to obtain sufficient task-relevant information. If the record provides sufficient information for the task, no further retrieval question would be necessary.

We have tried to show that a commitment to fragmentary memory traces requires the kind of reconstructive processes assumed by SF, namely those which fill in missing information. What are the benefits of this position? At least one advantage is economy of storing otherwise repetitive information: given the necessary schemata exist, it would be sufficient to store only atypical, event-specific information. However, such a system requires a number of additional assumptions. For one, there must be some way of deciding 'deviancy'. Although this problem has been attacked in the implementations of SF (e.g. Schank & Abelson, 1977), its resolution hinges critically on defining the invariances of schemata — a job which is difficult due to the nebulous nature of schemata themselves (cf. Bartlett, 1932). Further, it is not clear that the economy in storage is not offset by the additional processing required for the retrieval of information.

In HRF we make no a priori claims about the completeness of the record. This means hat we cannot specify the general cases under which successful retrieval will involve accessing only one record as opposed to more than one. However, we can suggest how such questions might be approached. For example, task demands should detemine how 'complete' a record will be, in addition to the conditions existing at the time of retrieval.

### Schemata require instantiation

A simple way of viewing the problem of instantiation is to consider it as a problem of determining which schemata best account for the current input. Type–token relationships are determined in this way, for example. HRF also must deal with a similar sort of problem. However, in HRF the problem is in the creation of the initial description and in determining which heading matches the description. Also, in SF it is assumed that some features, e.g. memorial fragments (Rumelhart, 1980), will trigger the activation of certain schemata. In HRF, these 'cues' are restricted to being elements of the heading. Another nominal distinction between the two frameworks concerns the locus of procedures responsible for instantiation. In SF, processes such as these are either contained within the schemata or are external to them. In HRF we are committed to the latter. At this time there would seem to be no obvious consequences of either position on the behaviour of the systems.

### Coda

Let us repeat that we believe that all three frameworks can, in principle, account for any pattern of data. If any kernel assumption turns out to be falsifiable, then we have mischaracterized it. Each framework has its strengths. We feel we should be able to use all of them as appropriate and work out the mapping relationships among them. At least we hope that our discussions will help in avoiding sectarian conflict.

## REFERENCES

Abelson, R. P. (1981). Psychological status of the script concept. *American Psychologist*, **36**, 715–729.

Abramson, L., Seligman, M., & Teasdale, J. (1978). Learned helplessness in humans. Critique and reformulation. *Journal of Abnormal Psychology*, **87**, 49–74.

Anderson, J. A., & Bower, G. (1973). *Human associative memory*. Washington, DC: Winston.

Anderson, J.A. (1976). *Language, memory and thought*. Experimental Psychology Series. Hillsdale, NJ: Lawrence Erlbaum.

Anderson, J. A. (1980). On the merits of ACT and information-processing psychology: A response to Wexler's review. *Cognition*, **8**, 73–88.

Bartlett, F. C. (1932). *Remembering*. London: Cambridge University Press.

Bekerian, D. A. (1984). Learned helplessness theory: a framework in disguise. *Current Psychological Research and Reviews*, **1**, 19–37.

Bekerian, D. A., & Bowers, J. M. (1983). Eyewitness testimony: Were we misled? *Journal of Experimental Psychology. Learning, Memory and Cognition*, **9**, 139–145.

Bekerian, D. A., & Morton, J. (in preparation) *The book on memory they tried to stop us from publishing*.

Bowers, J. M., & Bekerian, D. A. (1984). When will post-event information distort eyewitness testimony? *Journal of Applied psychology*, **69**, 3, 466–472.

Collins, A. M., & Loftus, E. F. (1975). A spreading activation theory of semantic processing. *Psychological Review*, **82**, 407–428.

Collins, A. M., & Quillian, M. P. (1972). How to make a language user. In E. Tulving & W. Donaldson, (Eds.), *Organisation and memory*. New York: Academic Press.

Costello, C. (1978). A critical review of Seligman's laboratory experiments on learned helplessness and depression in humans. *Journal of Abnormal Psycholoy*, **87**, 21–31.

Fahlman, S. E. (1981). Representing implicit knowledge. In G. E. Hinton & J. A. Anderson (Eds.), *Parallel models of associative memory*. Hillsdale, NJ: Lawrence Erlbaum.

Graesser, A., Woll, S. Kowalski, D., & Smith, D. (1980) Memory for typical and atypical action in scripted activities. *Journal of Experimental Psychology: Human Learning and Memory*, **6**, 503–575.

Hinton, G. E. (1981). Implementing semantic networks in parallel hardware. In G. E. Hinton & J. A. Anderson (Eds.), *Parallel models of associative memory*. Hillsdale, NJ: Lawrence Erlbaum.

Kintsch, W. (1974). *The representation of meaning in memory*. Hillsdale, NJ: Lawrence Erlbaum.

Landauer, T. K. (1975). Memory without organisation: properties of a model with random storage and undirected retrieval. *Cognitive Psychology*, **7**, 495–553.

Loftus, E. F., & Loftus, G. R. (1980). On the permanence of stored information in the human brain. *American Psychologist*, **35**, 409–420.

Loftus, E. F., Miller, D. G., & Burns, H. J. (1978). Semantic integration of verbal information into visual memory. *Journal of Experimental Psychology: Human Learning and Memory*, **4**, 19–31.

Maier, S., & Seligman, M. (1976) Learned helplessness: Theory and evidence. *Journal of Experimental Psychology: General*, **105**, 3–46.

Mandler, J. (1979). Categorical and schematic organization in memory. In
    R. C. Puff (Ed.), *memory, organization and structure*. New York:
    Academic Press.

Morton, J. (1969). The interaction of information in word recognition.
    *Psychological Review*, **76**, 165–178.

Morton, J. (1971). What could possibly be innate? In J. Morton (Ed.),*Biological and social aspects of psycholinguistics*. London: Logos Press.

Morton, J. (1979). Facilitation in word recognition experiments leading to
    changes in the logogen model. In P. Kolers, M. Wrolstad, & H. Bouma
    (Eds.), *Processing of Visible Language*, **1**. New York: Plenum Press.

Morton, J., Hammersley, R. H., & Bekerian, D. A. (1985). Headed
    records: A model for memory and its failures. *Cognition*, **20**, 1–23.

Newell, A., & Simon, H. (1972). *Human problem solving*. Englewood
    Cliffs, NJ: Prentice Hall.

Norman, D. A., & Bobrow, D. G. (1979). Descriptions: An intermediate
    stage in memory retrieval. *Cognitive Psychology*, **11**, 107–123.

Rumelhart, D. (1980). The building of blocks of cognition. In R. Spiro, B.
    Bruce, & W. Brewer (Eds.), *Theoretical issues in reading comprehension*. Hillsdale, NJ: Lawrence Erlbaum.

Rosch, E., Mervis, C., Gray, W., Johnson, D., & Boyes-Braem, P. (1976).
    Basic objects in natural categories. *Cognitive Psychology*, **8**, 382–439.

Ross, B. H., & Bower, G. H. (1981). Comparison of models of associative
    recall. *Memory and Cognition*, **9**, 1–16.

Rumelhart, D., & Ortony, A. (1977). The representation of knowledge in
    memory. In R. C. Anderson, R. J. Spiro, & W. E. Montague (Eds.),
    *Schooling and the acquisition of knowledge*. Hillsdale, NJ: Lawrence
    Erlbaum.

Schank, R. C. (1980). Language and memory. *Cognitive Science*, **4**,
    243–284.

Schank, R. C., & Abelson, R. P. (1977). *Scripts, plans, goals & understanding: An inquiry into human knowledge structures*. Hillsdale, NJ: Lawrence Erlbaum.

Skinner, B. F. (1957). *Verbal behaviour*. London: Methuin.

Williams, M. D., & Hollan, J. D. (1981). The process of retrieval from very
    long term memory. *Cognitive Science*, **5**, 87–119.

Woods, W. A. (1975). What's in a link: Foundations for semantic networks.
    In D. Bobrow & A. Collins (Eds.), *Representation and understanding*.
    New York: Academic Press.

Young, R. M. (1979). Production systems for modelling human cognition.
    In D. Michie (Ed.), *Expert systems in the micro-electronic age*.Edinburgh: Edinburgh University Press.

# 3

# Summarization in the Small

**Richard Alterman**

## INTRODUCTION

In artificial intelligence human understanding of text is modeled by programs which construct representations of text. These representations are used as a basis for performing question answering and summarization tasks. The idea is that a representation of a piece of text is adequate if a machine can use it to answer questions and summarize text in a manner consistent with the performance of a human understander. Hence these tasks act as a feedback to the text representation problem.

Historically summarization has been used to investigate the adequacy of a representation in characterizing the overall understanding of a piece of text. The problem is that artificial intelligence systems can produce representations that characterize, perhaps, one aspect of the text, but not a complete understanding. Consequently there appears to be a mismatch between summarization tasks, and the types of representation that artificial intelligence programs can produce.

In this chapter I will argue that summarization is a much more diverse phenomenon than has been previously recognized. The argument will be that summarization based on overall understanding is only one way in which a text can be summarized. By considering other kinds of summaries it becomes possible to use summarization as a test for a representation which characterizes only certain features of text.

In this chapter I will roughly divide summarization tasks into two groups: in-the-large and in-the-small. I will argue that in-the-small summarization tasks can be used to investigate particular features of text. I will describe a method for representing one aspect of text structure: the underlying structure of the event concepts invoked by the text. I will show how this representation can be used as a basis for performing summarization-in-the-small.

Summarization-in-the-large refers to summarization tasks that require that the text be dealt with as a whole. In-the-large summaries view the pieces of a text in relation to the whole and select, for inclusion in the summary, the critical points in the composition of the text. In-the-large summaries must necessarily deal with complex issues concerning importance, interest, and salience. Examples of summarization-in-the-large tasks are: abstracts, epitomes, and overviews.

Summarization-in-the-small tasks apply local summarization techniques. They do not require an understanding of the text as a whole, but instead preserve the text's message and proportions by means of systematic abbreviations. They consider each piece of text in relative isolation and attempt to summarize it. Much of in-the-small summaries is based on an analysis of the underlying conceptual structure of the text. Examples of summarization-in-the-small tasks are: abridgements, digests, and recapitulations.

Consider the following piece text from 'William Tell, The Archer' (Protter, 1961).

Just then the clatter of horses' hooves was heard. And Gessler, the governor general, galloped into the square. His military retinue followed him. He reined his horse to a stop before the pole.

An in-the-large summary would require that the importance of this passage to the message of the text as a whole be determined. An in-the-small summary applies local techniques to reducing the volume of this piece of text while maintaining its central content. A reasonable summarization-in-the-small of this text would be:

The governor general rode into the square.

The summary includes the cultural event concept of this piece of text while deleting that fact that the clattering of hooves could be heard and the details of the riding. Notice that the event of 'riding' that is mentioned in the summary is not explicitly mentioned in the original text.

Imagine two sets of experiments. In the first set a subject is given an entire story and asked to summarize it. In a second set of experiments, subjects are given the same story a paragraph at a time, perhaps in random order, and asked to summarize each paragraph in isolation. One would expect the two groups of subjects to produce different sorts of summaries. Moreover, one would expect that these experiments were aimed at investigating different aspects of understanding. The first group would be using their overall understanding. The second group would be closely tied to the task of exploiting, for summarization purposes, the structure and content of individual concepts. According to the distinction I am making here, the first group would be producing in-the-large summaries and the second group in-the-small summaries.

Admittedly an in-the-large/in-the-small distinction is an idealization (since any kind of summary undoubtedly involves both kinds of techniques to varying degrees). But by emphasizing one or the other it becomes possible to use summarization as a vehicle for studying different aspects of cognition. The importance of summarization-in-the-large is that is can be used as a vehicle for modeling memory and understanding, or alternatively global text structures. But summarization-in-the-small has a much more analytic flavor, and its importance is that it can be used to directly study underlying conceptual structure.

This chapter will use summarization-in-the-small tasks as an aid to investigating the structure of individual event concepts and their inter-relationships. Its emphasis will be on summarization-in-the-small as it applies to narrative text. It develops local techniques that exploit the underlying event conceptual structure of the narration. In particular, this analysis will be based on the coherence of event concepts (Alterman 1983, 1985a,b). Given the event concept coherence analysis, as produced by a program called NEXUS, the in-the-small techniques will fall into two groups. A computer program called SUM has been used to help develop the summarization techniques described in this paper.

The first group of in-the-small techniques effect the *granularity* of the text. I use the term 'granularity', alternately 'shift in granularity', to refer to the amount of detail included in the description of a single event concept. For example, the text:

John mounted his horse. He trotted through the woods and galloped along the beach, reining when he reached the bluffs.

is part of a single riding event, and it can be abbreviated

John rode his horse to the bluffs.

The second description removes some of the details of the original text (it is a shift of granularity), but maintains its essential content.

Narrative text is composed of a number of embellished text descriptions that are enmeshed together. A change in textual granularity is achieved by systematically going through the text to identify and bundle together little pieces of text that conceptually form a larger event and then describing these concepts by their core. The shift in granularity is accomplished by a process of *delineation* and *extraction*. Delineation untangles the mesh of concepts by delineating the boundaries of the larger events and from these larger events the core concept is extracted. For example, the more detailed description of John riding his horse could be part of a text concerning a romantic encounter with a mysterious woman. During its delineation phase, SUM delineates the above detailed description as a single large concept. During extraction, SUM achieves a shift in granularity by extracting the core concept of 'riding'. The approach to delination and extraction that is developed in this chapter is based on the event concept coherence analysis produced by NEXUS.

The shift in granularity does not effect flow of the text: the same events are there, only in less detail. The second group of in-the-small techniques reduce the text by identifying the major narrative thread and *pruning* those streams which either diverge from or join in with it. Where a change in granularity effects the density of the text, pruning streamlines it.

The relationships between the larger concepts created by delineation and extraction will be characterized by one of six types of connections. Each type of connection provides information on the flow of the narration at a particular juncture. This information can be used as a basis for deleting ancillary developments while identifying and preserving the major narrative thread. The types of connections also result from the event concept coherence analysis produced by NEXUS.

The next section of the chapter will explore the in-the-large/in-the-small distiction in the context of the literature. The remainder of the chapter will introduce the notion of event concept coherence and show how this analysis can be used to perform local summaries.

## ARTIFICIAL INTELLIGENCE SUMMARIZATION LITERATURE

My plan is to discuss the artificial intelligence summarization literature in terms of the in-the-large/in-the-small distinction. In many cases, I take this to be a task of clarification and not criticism.

Research on story trees and schemas have characterized the text by a syntax of narrative form. Typically they include story categories such as episode and setting. Both Rumelhart (1975) and Simmons and Correira (1980; Correira, 1980) summarized text by level of the tree. Rumelhart worked with two trees: one contains the syntactic structue of the story, the other its semantic structure. His system summarized the text by simultaneously descending both trees, deleting subtrees according to a set of semantic summarization rules. Simmons & Correira worked with a single tree which represented a combination of the syntactic and semantic structure of the story. Any level of their tree represented a summarization of the story. No extra rewrite rules were required.

The work of Rumelhart and Simmons and Correira is an attempt to summarize text by taking advantage of global structure as characterized by the story tree. Such techniques are in-the-large summary techniques that benefit from an analysis of the structure of the story syntax. Summarization-in-the-small trechniques take just the opposite approach, summarizing the text by a series of local decisions about the underlying conceptual structure.

Wilensky has suggested a theory of summarization based on the identification of *story points* (Wilensky, 1980, 1982). Story points roughly correspond to the essential tension points of a story, i.e. what the story is about. The idea is that points represent what is interesting in a story and therefore likely to be included in a summary. Wilensky suggests some rules for recognizing points. The rules are based on his theory of goal interaction (Wilensky, 1983). If a character plans to go outside to get the newspaper and discovers it is raining outdoors, a *goal conflict* occurs between the goal to get a newspaper and the goal to stay dry. If an educator is offered a thousand dollars to give a student a high grade that he or she did not deserve, a goal conflict occurs between the goal to be ethical and the goal to increase wealth. Wilensky argues that situations where goal interactions occur are potentially dramatic and consequently likely candidates as story points. In themselves goal interactions are not sufficient for determining story points. For example, if both of the above goal conflicts appeared in the same story the goal interaction analysis does not help us to decide which of the interactions is more important. Moreover, there are situations which are inherently interesting (e.g. a character in a story may discover a chest of gold in his backyard), but do not involve goal interactions. Wilensky appears to have a theory of summarization-in-the-large implemented using in-the-small techniques. One could argue that a goal interaction analysis is a step towards making an in-the-large summary, but in itself it is only sufficient for doing in-the-small summaries.

DeJong (1979) produces representations of text by applying in a top-down fashion sketchy scripts (e.g. accidents and terrorist acts). His system, called FRUMP, extracts from wire-service newspaper stories just enough facts to fill in the arguments of a sketchy script. Because the stories that DeJong works with are so steretoyped, he can summarize text by using a set of fill-in-the-blank type summarization statements attached to each sketchy script. These techniques are by definition limited to stereotypical situations. Moreover, as has been pointed out previously (Lehnert & Loiselle, 1985) sketchy script summarization techniques cannot deal with unusual events that occur in the context of a script. For example, within the restaurant context, if while bringing the food to the table the waiter drops his tray, no summarization techniques are proposed for dealing with this kind of situation. Clearly sketchy script-based summarization is a summarization-in-the-small technique.

Lehnert (1981, 1985) has developed a scheme for summarizing text based on plot units. Plot units represent affect-state patterns. Lehnert identifies a number of primitive plot units (e.g. motivation, success, preserverance) which can be combined into more complex plot units (e.g. fortuitous problem resolution, fleeting success, giving up). Narrative text is represented by interconnected plot units. Summaries are based on the identification of pivotal plot units, i.e. the plot units which are maximally connected.

Since the psychological evidence Lehnert cites for plot unit summarization techniques is based on recall summarization experiments (Lehnert, 1981), it is clear that the plot unit summarization work is intended to model memory-based summarization. Her argument is that an affect analysis of character reactions reflects the priorities and perspective of the reader, and that the key points in the summary should correspond to the centrally connected plot units. As an analysis of the underlying affect structure of a piece of text, Lehnert's work is most interesting. As a method for summarization-in-the-large, it does have some problems. In particular, the summarization that is produced is disproportionately affected by the depth of analysis of each character's reactions. As in the case of Wilensky's work, it appears that Lehnert is trying to use an in-the-small anlaysis for an in-the-large summary.


## EVENT CONCEPT COHERENCE

This section of the chapter will briefly describe the theory of event concept coherence. A program called NEXUS produces event concept coherence representations of narrative text. Latter sections of the chapter will show how these representations of an underlying event conceptual structure are used as a basis for doing summarization-in-the-small.

Event concept coherence interpretations of narrative text are achieved by matching the text against its underlying event structure as represented in a network. The coherence of the event descriptions of the text are determined on the basis of a property of the network, i.e. the proximity of the event concepts invoked by the text. As a representation, event concept coherence shows which of the events are connected.

For this theory the meaning of a concept is represented by its position in a network. For example, the concept 'carry' is defined in part by its relationship to concepts like 'travel' and 'hold', which are in turn related to concepts like 'arrive' and 'drop' (see Fig. 1). When an object is 'carried' it is 'held'. The agent that 'carries' the object 'travels'. When one 'travels' one eventually 'arrives' someplace. If something was 'dropped' it was first held.


Given the text,

   While carrying the tray to the table, the waiter dropped it

the two event/state descriptions used in the text are event concept coherent due to the close interrelationship between the concepts 'carrying', 'holding' and 'dropping'. Similarly, given the text,

   The messenger carried the package to the company. He arrived before
   noon

the two event state descriptions used in the text are event concept coherent because the concepts 'carry', 'travel', and 'arrive' are all part of a nexus of meaning.

The point of an event concept coherence representation of text has to do with the difficulty of establishing meaning representations. The idea is to capture only some of the properties of the text's meaning, to organize the text for further interpretation without losing any of the information of its original form. Event concept coherence allows the text to be structured not so much on the basis of its meaning, but on the bnasis of a property of its meaning, the connectivity of interdefining concepts. NEXUS is a system

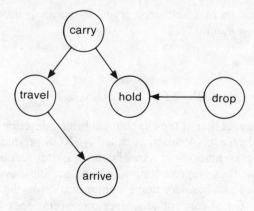

Fig. 1 — Coherence of some concepts.

which computes such a representation using a spreading activation algorithm (Alterman, 1985a). Its knowledge-base is a network of event/state concepts. The representation it produces is essentially a copy of the relevant portion of the network.

### Seven concept coherence relations

NEXUS uses seven event concept coherence relations (see Fig. 2). There is one taxonomic relation, two partonomic relations, and four temporal relations. The taxonomic relation is used to indicate property inheritance. The partonomic relations are used for indicating the relationship between an event and its component sub-events. The temporal relations are used to connect streams of events which commonly co-occur. In this paper I will emphasize the importance of these relations from the vantage point of informativeness.

The taxonomic relation is *class/subclass*. A subclass concept adds properties to its parent concept. For example, 'snatching' is a kind of 'taking' and with regards to informativeness it is more informative because it adds information to the concept of 'taking'. Consequently given the test (see Fig. 3)

John took the cash, snatching it from the dealer

the summary

John snatched the cash from the dealer

is a better summary than

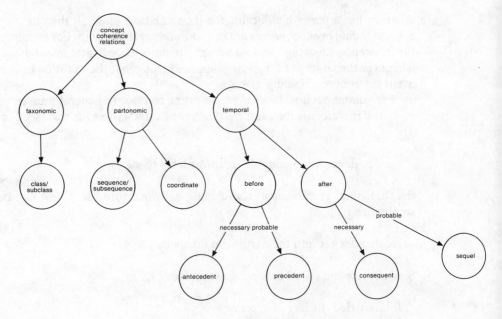

Fig. 2 — Seven event concept coherence relations.


John took the cash from the dealer

because it is more informative. The former implies the latter, but visa versa
is not the case.

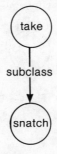

Fig. 3 — Snatching.


If one event is a part of another event, and it occurs for a sub-interval of
time, then the corresponding concepts are in a *sequence/subsequence*
relationship. For example, the concepts 'digging' and 'breaking' are in a
sequence/subsequence relationship; whenever the concept of 'digging earth'
applies the concept 'breaking earth' applies for a sub-interval of that time. If

an event has a part which occurs for the same time interval, then the two corresponding event concepts are in a *coordinate* relationship. For example, the concepts 'carrying' and 'holding' are in a coordinate relationship; whenever the concept of 'carrying' applies throughout the duration of that event the concept 'holding' applies.

   For summarization tasks a whole event concept in general implies its parts and therefore is the preferred summarization. Given the text (see Fig. 4)

   He dug deeper, breaking the earth with his spade

the 'breaking' is implicit in the digging and therefore the above can be summarized

   He dug deeper into the earth with his spade.

Simlarly, for the coordinate related text (see Fig. 5)

   John carried the bag of groceries
   He held the bag in his hands

can be summarized

   John carried the bag of groceries.

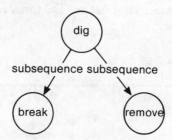

Fig. 4 — Digging in the earth.

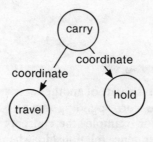

Fig. 5 — Carry.

The temporal relations are used to connect events which typically co-occur in event streams. NEXUS uses both before and after relations. One might think that having before and after relations is redundant since they are isometric. Suppose only the temporal relation 'before' is used. Given the text

John cleaned the laundry
He carried it home

or the text

The ball moved
It hit the wall

either one of these could be represented by either relation 'before' or 'after' (see Fig. 6). But the problem is that for summarization purposes a single temporal relation is inadequate for distinguishing between *core* and *peripheral* concepts. For example, the core of the first of these examples is that John cleaned his laundry and that he carried it home is a highly likely sequel that lies on the periphery of this episode. And in the case of the ball hitting the wall just the opposite is the case; if the two things hit it was necessarily the case that one of them was moving. Consequently for summarization purposes, when two events are related using one of the 'before' relations it is intended to indicate that the event which came before is on the periphery and at least highly predictable from the core. Similarly, when two events are related using one of the 'after' relations it is intended to indicate that the event which came after is on the periphery and at least highly predictable from the core.

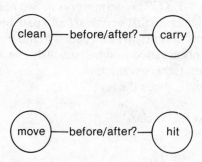

Fig. 6a — (a) Undifferentiated 'before' and 'after'.

Furthermore, in NEXUS, the 'before' and 'after' relations are differentiated by their probability. An event which necessarily comes 'before' another event is an *antecedent*. An event which necessarily comes 'after' a

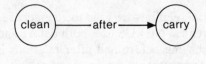

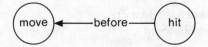

Fig. 6b — (b) Differentiated 'before' and 'after'.

seond event is a *consequent*. Similarly an event which probably comes before another event is a *precedent*, and an event which probably comes after another event is a *sequel*. For the purposes of this paper these refinements will be dropped and just the temporal relations 'before' and 'after' will be used.

**Some details on how NEXUS computes the coherence representation**

NEXUS uses a spreading activation mechanism to compute the event concept coherence representation (Alterman, 1985a). Text is considered an event description at a time. The input to NEXUS is the text in case notation form; therefore the head of each unit is an event/state concept. The NEXUS base of knowledge is a network of mutually defining event state terms. Associated with every edge in the network are a set of constraints on the matching of case arguments. The representation that NEXUS produces is basically a copy of the relevant portion of its network with various case slots filled in. The NEXUS program works in two phases. In phase one it does a bidirectional breadth first search to find a path between the old concepts and the new event concepts. When a path is found the constraints on matching of case arguments are used to simultaneously check that the path is consistent and perform reference resolution.

For example, given the text

John threw the brick
It hit Mary

NEXUS gets as input the following case representation:

(throw agent John object (brick determiner the))
(hit object1 it object2 Mary)

The case representation states that "John was the agent of throwing and the object he threw was a brick. Two objects hit: one of them was 'it' and the other was 'Mary' ". The path it finds between the event concepts 'throwing' and 'hitting' is:

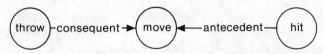

Constraints:
The object of the throwing
must match the object moving.

Constraints:
The object moving must match
an object involved in hitting.

Roughly the above diagram reads' "As a consequence of throwing an object that object necessarily moves. If two objects hit, it is necessarily the case that one of them must have been moving". NEXUS uses the relationships shown above, and their associated constraints, to produce the following representation.

    (consequent (throw agent John object (brick determiner the))
        (move object (brick determiner the)) )
    (antecedent (hit object1 (brick determiner the) object2 Mary)
        (move object (brick determiner the)) )

The above linear notation can be read: "As a consequence of John throwing the brick, the brick moves. An antecedent of the brick hitting Mary is that the brick was moving." Pictorially the above linear representation will be depicted in this chapter as follows.

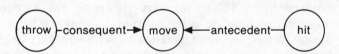

## DELINEATION AND EXTRACTION

The event concept coherence produced by NEXUS is the input to SUM. SUM uses the representation to delineate from the mass of concepts in a narration the boundaries of individual event concepts. Furthermore, SUM uses the representation to extract from these bundles of little events a core concept from which the bulk of the encompassing event concept is largely determinable.

The event concept coherence rrepresentation produced by NEXUS is composed of multiple interconnected event concept trees. A concept tree is recursively composed of all its subclass, part, and before/after descendants (see Fig. 7). Each tree represents a delineated concept. Because of the hierarchical organization of the concept tree extracting the central concept is relatively straightforward. With one exception SUM summarizes single concept trees by extracting the top node in the concept's tree. Before

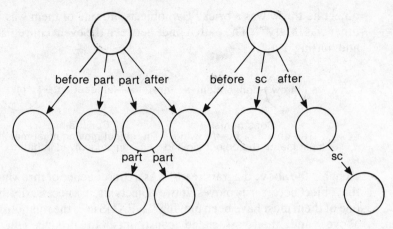

Fig. 7 — Two interconnected concept trees.

considering the exception consider an example of the rule. For "The Restaurant Story" (Schank & Abelson, 1977) NEXUS produces a single concept tree. The text of this story reads:

> John went to a restaurant. The hostess seated John. The hostess gave John a menu. The waiter came to the table. John ordered a lobster. He was served quickly. He left a large tip. He left the restaurant.

Fig. 8 shows SUM's handling of this story. The input to SUM is the output produced by NEXUS for this story (see Fig. 9). The story does not explicitly mention that John ate at the restaurant, nor that if he did eat that he ate lobster, yet the representation that NEXUS builds is a tree whose top node is 'eating lobster'. Consequently, when SUM extracts the top node in the tree it correctly summarizes the story as an 'eating at a restaurant' event.

```
(working on example rest)
(delineation (eat)) ; delineated concept = top of concept tree
(doing promotion)
(extraction (eat)) ; extracted concept
(summary (eat))
(john ate lobster at a restaurant)
```

Fig. 8 — Trace of 'The Restaurant Story'.

The exception is not much harder to handle. The exception occurs because NEXUS uses property inheritance to represent the net. In a class/ subclass relationship the subclass concept is preferred because more is inferable from it than the parent class. A subclass inherits all the properties of its parent class. If the parent class is in an antecedent relationship with a

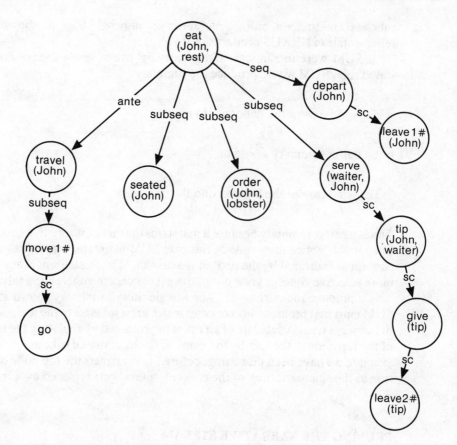

Fig. 9 — 'The Restaurant Story'.

'having', then the subclass concept inherits this relationship. But vice versa is not the case. If a summary mentions an instantiated subclass concept the reader can predict all its relationships as well as the relationships it inherits from its ancestors. If a summary mentions the parent class instead of the subclass then the reader of the summary has lost the relationships which the subclass makes available. So the subclass concept is preferred over the class concept with regards to extraction because it is more informative. The term *promotion* is used to refer to the cases when SUM substitutes a subclass concept for its parent concept.

Consider the case of "The Margie Story" (Rumelhart, 1975). Margie is holding on to the string of a balloon. A gust of wind carries Margie's balloon into a tree, where it hits a branch and bursts. Part of the text of the Margie story reads:

... The wind carried it into a tree. The balloon hit a branch and ...

To connect the 'carrying' to the 'catching' and 'hitting' NEXUS climbs up a subclass arc to to a more general sense 'moving'. Fig. 10 shows the representation NEXUS produces of it.

If SUM were to summarize the 'carrying' event, given the previously stated rule, SUM would produce the summary:

The wind *moved* the balloon into the tree.

But a better summary would be:

The wind *carried* the balloon into the tree.

This is a better summary because it maintains the more informative concept. In contrast, notice that while in this case SUM maintains a more selective concept as indicated by the text, in the case of "The Restaurant Story" the more selective concept grew out of the event concept coherence analysis.

To produce the portion of "The Margie Story" summary shown above SUM must first promote any concepts which are a subclass to the top node in the concept tree. A subclass of an event in promoted by replacing the name of the top node in the tree by the name of the instantiated subclass. For the example we have been discussing, before SUM extracts the top node of the tree as the summarization of the concept, 'move' gets replaced by 'carry'.

## PRUNING THE NARRATIVE STREAM

SUM achieves delineation and extraction by exploiting the event concept coherence representation. Each concept tree, in the event concept coherence analysis, represents a delineated event/state concept. The internal organization of each of these trees suggests the critical concept for extraction; after promotion the top node of the tree is chosen as the concept to be extracted. After delineation and extraction there has been a shift in the granularity of the text: the same events are described but in less detail.

SUM continues the in-the-small summarization process by pruning the text's narrative stream. Pruning consists of deleting narrative streams that branch from, join with, or embellish the major narrative thread. The recognition of what is, and is not, part of the major thread involves the event concept coherence analysis. Each type of connection between concept trees is a juncture in the flow of the narration. The junctures characterize the narration at a given point. They provide information that aids in the determination of the narrative thread.

There are six types of junctures (see Fig. 11). The junctures result from a combination of the part and temporal relations that exist between the concept trees. The first of these types is where a pair of concepts are temporally related, that is one temporally follows the other. I will refer to

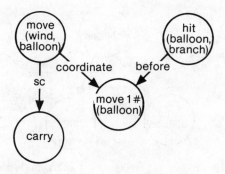

Fig. 10 — The wind carried the balloon.

this as *temporal sequence*. Temporal sequence indicates that two event concept trees are in the same stream. A case of this occurs in "The Margie Story" (see Fig. 12).

... The wind caught the balloon and carried it into a tree ...

Because the wind 'caught' the balloon it 'had' it, which is a necessary

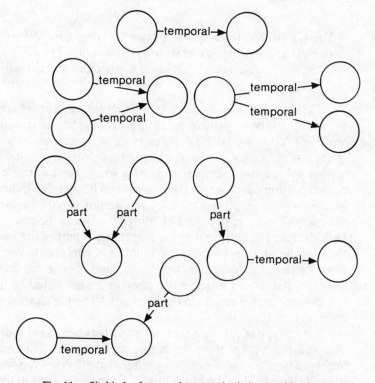

Fig. 11 — Six kinds of part and temporal relation combinations.

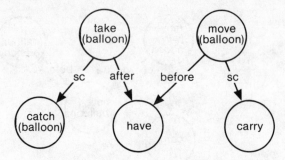

Fig. 12 — Catching the balloon.

condition for 'carrying'. The event concept coherence representation results in two concept trees connected by temporal relations. For summarization purposes, two concept trees in a temporal sequence are deleted only if they turn out to be part of an ancillary narrative stream.

A second type of juncture which can occur between event concept trees are *joins*. In text this occurs when two events described by the author meet at a future point. For example, a join occurs in the following text adapted from the "The Tale of the Pig" (Protter, 1961).

The pig trotted towards the stream carrying a bundle of clothes. The animal expertly soaked and scoured the laundry. The pig hung the clothes in the sun to dry. The pig gathered her laundry and trotted home.

Fig. 13 shows the relevant portion of the event concept coherence (most of the underlying concept turns out to be part of the 'cleaning' concept tree). A sequel of 'cleaning laundry' is 'carrying it home', and a consequent of 'gathering' is 'having', which is a condition of 'carrying'. The 'cleaning' and 'gathering' are two temporal sequences which meet at the 'carrying'. For summarization purposes, of the two streams being joined, the one with the greatest emphasis placed on it by the author should be included in the summary. There are two ways of doing this. One is the count the length of each stream, and assume that the longer one is part of the major narrative thread. The other is to count the number of concepts in each stream that were explicitly indicated by the author and choose for inclusion in the summary the stream which is described in greater detail by the author. In this case, emphasis results in the summary "The pig cleaned clothes at the stream" (see Fig. 14).

A third type of juncture that can occur between event concept coherent chunks are *splits*. Splits are the mirror image of joins. They occur when the author describes sequences of events that diverge at some points. In identifying the major narrative thread, heuristics similar to those that were used for joins can be employed for splits.

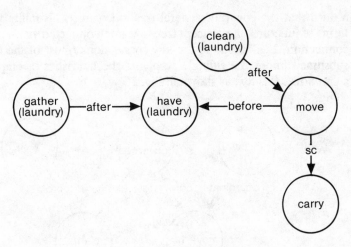

Fig. 13 — Cleaning the laundry.

(working on example pig2)
(delineation (clean gather)) ; Delineated Concepts
(doing promotion)
(extraction (clean gather)) ; Extracted Concepts

. 
. 
. 

(the junctures are ((tsj clean gather))) ;
          TSJ = Temporal Stream Join
Summary (clean))
(the pig cleaned clothes at the stream)

Fig. 14 — Trace of cleaning laundry.

A fourth type of juncture between concept trees is where concept
coherent trees are related via parts, i.e. *shared parts*. In text this occurs
when the author is providing the reader with multiple interpretations of a
single event. For example, the text from "William Tell, The Archer"
contains a multiple interrpretation.

Just then the clatter of horse hooves was heard. And Gessler, the
governor general, galloped into the square. His military retinue followed
him. He reined his horse to a stop before the pole.

One interpretation of the event was that the governor general was riding into
the town square, a second that the sound of clattering hooves was heard. and

a third that the governor general was followed by his military retinue. In terms of junctures the concept trees are interconnected via the shared parts connection. Fig. 15 shows the key connections (most of the concepts are subsumed under the riding). Applying the heuristics of emphasis, SUM summarizes this text as shown in Fig. 16.

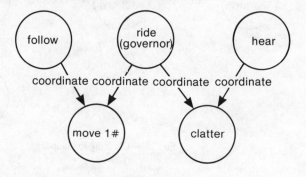

Fig. 15 — Clattering and riding.

(working on example wtell))
(delineation (follow hear ride)) ; delineated concepts
(doing promotion)
(extraction (follow hear ride)) ; extracted concepts

.
.
.

(the junctures are ((sp follow ride) (sp hear ride))) ;
        SP = Shared Parts
(summary (ride))
(the governor-general rode his horse to the square)

Fig. 16 — Trace of riding.

The last two types of junctures between concept trees that can occur concern the intersection of a temporal sequence with a part of some concept tree. The first of these I will refer to as a *part-to-temporal* juncture. A part-to-temporal juncture occurs when a part of one concept tree leads to a temporal sequence. This type of juncture is an unusual event sequence because normally when one event temporally follows another the connection is that the expected after-effects of the first event lead to second event. When it is the after-effects of a *part* of the first event that leads to the second event it is unusual. An example of a part-to-temporal juncture comes from "The Peasant and the waterman" (see Fig. 17).

A peasant was chopping a tree in the woods. He dropped his axe into the lake ...

A part of 'chopping a tree' is 'holding the axe', which is a condition of 'dropping'. When an unusual event sequence of this sort occurs both events of the jucture should be described in the summary (see Fig. 18).

The second kind of connection between temporal sequence and parts is what I will refer to as *temporal-to-part*. This type of juncture occurs when the text describes a temporal sequence which connects to another concept tree via a part of the second concept tree. Usually this means the first stream is a preparation for the second, and consequently, assuming it correlates with emphasis information, it should be pruned.

## SUMMARY AND CONCLUSIONS

In-the-large summaries attempt to understand the parts in relation to the whole and select, for inclusion in the summary, those events which are the most critical and important. In-the-small summaries preserve the message and proportions of the text by making a series of local reductions. Each of these approaches produces a different sort of summary. In-the-large techniques must rise above the text to grasp its global structure, and consequently have the flavor of memory and understanding. In-the-small techniques directly exploit the underlying conceptual structure of the text, and consequently have the flavor of problem solving. Human readers are undoubtedly capable of producing either kind of summary. When asked to produce a summary of their understanding of a piece of text, one would suspect that both sorts of techniques are utilized.

Previously researchers have treated summarization as a single task. They use it as method for investigating representations of the reader's overall understanding of a piece of text. By making a distinction between in-the-large and in-the-small summaries, it becomes possible to investigate representations of specific aspects of text (as opposed to overall content and salience).

In this chapter I have explored in-the-small techniques that take advantage of the underlying event structure of a piece of text as represented by event concept coherence and produced by NEXUS. A computer program called SUM has been used as a vehicle for exploring these summarization techniques. The techniques SUM uses fall into two groups: those that change the granularity of the text and those that prune the narration. Changing granularity involves delineating the boundaries of encompassing concepts and extracting from them the core event concept. Each event concept tree in the event concept coherence analysis represents a delineated concept. After promotion, the top node in the tree represents the concept that should be extracted. Pruning the text is primarily based on recognizing the type of connection between the larger delineated events. The relation-

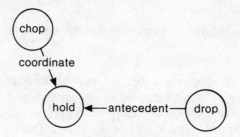

Fig. 17 — Chopping and dropping.

```
(working on example waterman)
(delineation (chop1 drop follow seek)) ; delineated concepts
(doing promotion)
(extraction (chop1 drop follow seek)) ; extracted concepts
     .
     .
     .
(the junctures are ((ues chop1 drop) (tp drop follow) (sp follow seek)))
     ; UES = part-to-temporal
(summary (chop1 drop seek))
(a peasant was chopping a tree in the woods)
(a peasant dropped his axe into the lake)
     .
     .
     .
```

Fig. 18 — Trace of dropping.

ships between the larger delineated events can be characterized in terms of the part and temporal relations provided by the event concept coherence analysis. Six types of junctures have been described. Each juncture characterizes the flow of the narration and can be used as an aid to ferreting out the major narrative thread.

## ACKNOWLEDGEMENTS

I would like to thank Noel Sharkey for his detailed reading and commenting on an earlier version of this manuscript.

This research was sponsored in part by Defense Advance Research Projects Agency (DOD), Arpa Order No. 4031, Monitored by Naval Electronic system command under Contract No. N00039-C-0235.

## REFERENCES

Alterman, R. (1983). Event concept coherence of narrative text. In *Proceedings of the Fifth Annual Conference of the Cognitive Science Society*.

Alterman, R. (1985a). A dictionary based on concept coherence. *Artificial Intelligence*, **25**, 2, 153–186.

Alterman, R. (1985b). Event concept coherence. In D. Waltz (Ed.), *Advances in natural language understanding*. Hillsdale, NJ: Lawrence Erlbaum (forthcoming).

Correira, A., (1980). Computing story trees. *American Journal of Computational Linguistics*, **6**, 135–149.

DeJong, G. (1979) Skimming stories in real time: an experiment in integrated understanding. Technical Report #158, Yale University.

Lehnert, W. (1981). Plot units and narrative summarization. *Cognitive Science*, **5**, 4, 293–331.

Lehnert, W., Black, J., & Reiser, B. (1981). Summarizing narratives. In *Proceedings of the Seventh International Joint Conference on Artificial Intelligence*.

Lehnert, W., & Loiselle, C. (1985). An introduction to plot units. In D. Waltz (Ed.), *Advances in natural language understanding*. Hillsdale, NJ: Lawrence Erlbaum (forthcoming).

Protter, E. (1961). *A children's treasury of folk and fairy tales*. New York: Beaufort Books.

Rumelhart, D. E. (1975) Notes on a schema for stories. In D. G. Bobrow & A. Collins (Eds.), *Representation and understanding*. New York: Academic Press.

Schank, R. C., & Abelson, R. P. (1977). *Scripts, plans, goals, and understanding*. Hillsdale, NJ: Lawrence Erlbaum.

Simmons, R. F., & Correira, A. (1980). Rule forms for verse, sentences, and story trees. In N. Findler (Ed.), *Associative networks: The representation and use of knowledge in computers*. New York: Academic Press.

Wilensky, R. (1980). What's the point? In *Proceedings of the Third National Conference of the Canadian Society for the Computational Studies of Intelligence*.

Wilensky, R. (1982). Points: A theory of the structure of stories in memory. In W. Lehnert & M. Ringle (Eds.), *Strategies for natural language processing*. Hillsdale, NJ: Lawrence Erlbaum.

Wilensky, R. (1983). Planning and understanding. Reading, MA: Addison-Wesley.

# 4

# Understanding actions in relation to goals

Carolyn L. Foss and Gordon H. Bower

## INTRODUCTION

We assume that people understand the actions of others by viewing those actions as purposive, as goal-directed. People use their knowledge of human intentionality, of the types of goals people have and of the types of plans they devise in service of those goals, to understand action sequences that are described in narratives or observed directly. Many recent approaches to comprehension emphasize the role of goal-planning knowledge when understanding narratives (e.g. Cullingford, 1978; Schank & Abelson, 1977; Wilensky, 1978, 1983) and conversations (e.g. Perault, Allen, & Cohen, 1978; Schank *et al.*, 1982), and when remembering observed sequences and goal-directed actions (Lichtenstein & Brewer, 1980; Brewer & Dupree, 1983).

According to these approaches, understanding involves inferring the intentions (i.e. the plans and goals) of the characters, speakers, or actors. Such inferences are ubiquitous because narratives frequently provide only sketchy descriptions of the character's actions and goals; speakers rarely state their intentions directly; and observers rarely see all the events preceding or following the action to be explained. Therefore, people are forced to use their general knowledge of human intentionality to fill in the missing information; they do this by generating expectations and drawing inferences in order to come up with a plan that explains an actor's behavior. Although the importance of this type of knowledge for understanding natural discourse and action sequences has been recognized, only recently have cognitive scientists begun examining the psychological processes involved in drawing inferences about human intentionality. In this paper we examine what people know about goal–action relationships, and how they retrieve this knowledge to make sense of goal-directed actions.

We will assume that information about plans, goals, and actions is retrieved in much the same way as is other information from memory. The classic experiments on retrieval of information from semantic memory assume that information is organized in a semantic network of concepts and relations, with certain concepts organized hierarchically (e.g. Collins & Loftus, 1975; Holyoak & Glass, 1975). For example, properties are stored at the most general level possible. Thus, in an animal hierarchy where a canary is a bird which is an animal, a property like "has skin" would be stored only at the most superordinate level (attached to "animal" only), whereas a unique, distinguishing property like "canaries are yellow" would be directly attached to the subconcept of canary. The model assumes that to answer such queries as "Do canaries have skin?" a person derives the relationship between the subject and predicate by retrieving and combining individual facts. Thus, because a canary is a bird, and a bird is an animal, and animals have skin, it follows that a canary has skin. Allegedly, the longer the derivation, the more elementary facts that have to be retrieved and combined to connect the subject and predicate, and the longer the time people need to answer such questions.

This paper concerns the connecting-up processes involved in understanding actions described in narratives. Although we will deal exclusively with subjects understanding actions stated in text, we assume that similar processes occur when subjects comprehend actions they observe directly (see Lichtenstein & Brewer, 1980). A plausible proposal is that similar linking-up processes will be involved in interpreting the goal-directed actions of real-life actors as well as in filling in missing information while trying to understand events described in narratives. In both cases understanding involves generating explanations and predictions related to the actor's plans.

When understanding narratives, an important step in generating predictions is to know or guess a character's goals, because these can predict actions. For instance, if a reader knows that a character's goal is to go on an overseas trip, then actions such as packing or going to the airport are expected and readily understood. Similarly, actions can imply their underlying motives. We try to explain an action by linking it to one of the actor's known goals or to a goal-generating theme or role for that actor (see Schank & Abelson , 1977, for a detailed discussion of this approach to comprehension).

Let us briefly consider what people might know about goal relationships and how that information may be organized. Goals are typically arranged in a hierarchy of subgoals. Goals and subgoals can be represented in a goal reduction tree, which is constructed by decomposing a top-level goal into a conjunction or disjunction of subgoals which may in turn be decomposed further. The decomposition ends when only immediately attainable goals (or executable actions) are left. The goals, subgoals, and actions so generated may be represented as nodes in a tree linked by branches. The relationships among goals are revealed by their placement along the branches. For any given node, we can designate all its ancestors (items above and on the same branch) as "goals", and all its descendants (items below the node and on the same branch) as "actions". Thus, any node in the tree, except the top node and the terminal nodes, can be a "goal" or an "action", depending upon whether it is viewed from "below" or "above", respectively.

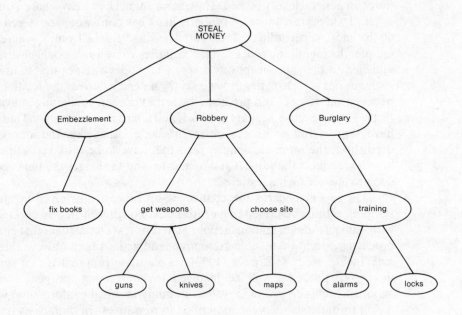

Fig. 1 — An example of goal reduction tree, also referred to as a goal hierarchy.

To illustrate, the top goal of the goal reduction tree schematized in Fig. 1 is to steal money. For the person whose limited knowledge is represented by this tree, this top goal can be achieved by either of three means or subgoals. To steal money, he believes only that he can either embezzle or rob or burglarize. Nodes that stem from such *or* branches are *not* preconditions or subgoals for one another. For instance, performing a robbery is not a precondition for embezzlement. The vertical links in the tree represent the "is a subgoal of" relationship. This relationship is transitive for nodes that lie along a single vertical branch; this relationship thus imposes a partial ordering on to the nodes. For example, "fixing the books" is a subgoal of the top goal "stealing money" because it is directly linked to "embezzlement" which in turn is directly linked to "stealing money"

We began our investigations with the intuition that goals and actions would vary in their "psychological distance" from one another. We will coordinate this notion of "psychological distance" to the distance in the goal-reduction tree (the number of links) separating the action from the goal state. Notice in Fig. 1 that the same action (e.g. getting a gun) can be *near* to one goal (e.g. finding a weapon), but *far* from another goal (e.g. stealing money) that lies along one branch of a goal-reduction tree.

We hypothesize further that people will often understand the relationship between a goal and an action by finding, retrieving, or computing a link between the intervening subgoals. For instance, understanding a sentence like, "John wanted to go overseas; so he caught a bus" involves guessing that John is probably taking a bus to the airport so he can catch a flight overseas.

Wilensky (1978, 1983) created a computer simulation program that understands simple plan-based episodes by applying knowledge about goals and actions and how they fit in with plans. Although no experimental evidence was offered for the program as a psychological model, it does produce explanations (answers to *why* questions about human-action episodes) somewhat similar to those of human understanders. Wilensky's story understanding program, called PAM for Plan Applier Mechanism, follows a specific algorithm for understanding each action as it occurs in a story. The program begins by using the first few lines to guess at a plan or goal for the actor. If a goal is stated, then an action which will lead to that goal is expected to follow in the next few story statements. If no goal is stated, then it is assumed that the statement will suggest a plan, so that the plan's goal will be inferred. If actions or goals mentioned in the next few story statements match the inferred plan, then the plan is taken to be the explanation for those actions. Consider these statements:

(1)  The company accountant wanted to steal some money.
(2)  He fixed the company's books.

The first step in understanding (2) would be to infer a plan from the action (fix company's books). A guess is that the plan is to embezzle from the company. The plan is instrumental to a known goal, of stealing money. Thus, the explanation of the action is assumed to be that the accountant fixed the books because he wanted to embezzle from the company.

Some episodes are more difficult to understand than others because they may contain actions or goals that are difficult to incorporate into any plan. One way this difficulty arises is when the goals and actions in an episode are psychologically distant and so require many inferences to associate them. If understanding an action involves linking it with a known goal, then we would expect comprehension of an action statement to take longer the greater the psychological distance between the goal and action. In terms of our goal reduction tree in Fig. 1, we may conceive of the listener linking up the action (e.g. "fix books") to the stated goal (e.g. "steal money") by a memory search process. The greater the link distance, the longer the search for an intersection point in the tree, and hence the longer it will take the reader to understand the action in the light of the goal. The same reasoning would apply if the action is stated first and we measure how long the reader requires to understand the goal statement.

In the experiments below, we set out to find such "distance effects" in people's comprehension of actions in the light of the actor's goals. We are not the first ones to search for a "distance" effect in comprehension of narratives. Bower, Black, and Turner (1979, Exp. 6) used stereotypic, script-based narratives, and measured how quickly a critical script-action description was read as a function of its hypothetical "distance" from the script-action mentioned in the prior sentence. The distance was either one, two, or three steps back in the underlying script. For example, a restaurant story might have the target action sentence: John ordered lambchops. Its reading time would be measured immediately following the reading of a context sentence, either (a), (b), or (c):

(a)  He decided what he wanted to eat.
(b)  He took up the menu.
(c)  He sat down at a table.

In the underlying script, the target action is closest to event (a), intermediate to event (b), and farthest from event (c), both in terms of temporal distance and in terms of chains of causes or enablements. Although they expected a monotonic distance effect on the basis of spreading activation from the context event to the target event, Bower et al. observed a non-monotonic trend: target actions at the intermediate distance were understood more slowly than the closest actions, but the farthest actions were as fast as the closest actions. Thus, the "distance" hypothesis received only equivocal support.

Abbott, Black, and Smith (1985, Exp. 2) hypothesized that the non-monotonic distance effect observed by Bower et al. could have arisen from the way they constructed their script narratives. Specifically, scripts are hierarchically structured, so that certain actions name larger, higher chunks of the script ("Script headers" such as "the customer ordered"), whereas other actions specify lower, more detailed aspects of the scene ("actions" like "the customer read the menu"). Some of the script narratives written by Bower et al. used target and context actions that came from different levels of the script hierarchy. Such texts are stylistically somewhat "choppy" and require the reader to shift levels, and this may have obscured a simple distance effect. When Abbot et al. repeated the Bower et al. experiment with script actions in a narrative all at the same level (all scene headers, or all detailed actions), a monotonic distance effect was observed: a given target action took longer to comprehend the greater the scripted distance ("gap") between it and the prior action mentioned in the text.

Recall that we are interested in how rapidly an action is understood in the light of its "psychological distance" from its goal. Thus, the aforementioned script distance studies are not directly relevant, since early events in a scriptal sequence only rarely name the goal of a later event (action). For example, "He sat down" is not a goal satisfied by "The waitress took his order". Rather, the earlier context statement may refer to a temporally preceding event and/or an enabling precondition of the target event. Thus, an experiment is needed in which explicit goal–action distances are investigated.

A directly relevant study was reported at the 1981 Cognitive Science Conference by Smith and Collins (1981). They studied the time subjects took to understand an action that seemed near or far to an earlier stated (or implied) goal. An example of their material is:

John needed money to pay for his wife's operation.
(a) He decided to borrow money from his Uncle Harry.
(b) He would give his Uncle Harry a quick call.
(c) He had to find out Uncle Harry's phone number.
John reached for the most recent suburban directory.

Subject's reading times were measured for the first sentence, then for either (a), (b), or (c), and then for the final sentence. Based on a goal-subgoal analysis, the authors note that sentence (a) is close to the top goal (need money) but far from the last sentence (get directory); that sentence (b) is intermediate; and that sentence (c) is far from the top goal but near to the final sentence. Smith and Collins predicted that reading time for the second sentence would be faster the "nearer" its action was to the top goal sentence, i.e. (a) fastest, (c) slowest, but that the reading time for the final common sentence (get directory) would show the reverse trend, i.e. slowest after (a), fastest after (c). They reported that their results generally confirmed these predictions, whether the story statements emphasized the character's intentions (like "decided" or "would give") or emphasized his actions (e.g. "he called" or "he asked for a loan"). Thus, these results support the goal–action distance hypothesis that we stated in the Introduction.

Our experiments, which were completed before the Smith and Collins report, avoid one inelegancy of the Smith and Collins design, and attempt to extend the distance effect to new domains. The inelegancy of their design is that the critical "gap size" variable was manipulated by varying which of three target sentences (a), (b), or (c) subjects read, and so the actual target material was confounded with the gap size. This "materials confound" may have created problems, since Smith and Collins noted that the magnitude of the gap-size effect varied considerably across different lines and episodes. In our experiments, the crucial target sentence was fixed within a given narrative and the prior context-sentences were varied, so that the distance variable was not confounded with the actual target sentence.

The first experiment examined how distance between goals and actions in natural episodes about familiar situations affects comprehension. We worried about a potential problem with the use of naturalistic materials, however. "Distance" is not always easy to estimate for familiar plans because of people's differing experiences; therefore, the second experiment drew on subject's knowledge about a newly learned artificial goal hierarchy, for which we could calculate the distance between any goal and action. Experiment 3 returned to a more naturalistic reading procedure: subjects first casually read over an actual folktale, and then performed a goal–action verification task similar to that in Experiment 2.

## EXPERIMENT 1

Wilensky's (1983) story understanding algorithm is a useful hypothesis about the steps people follow when filling in missing information in order to understand narratives. If the relationships between story events are not stated, the reader has to infer the necessary connections. Readers search for explanations of story events by successively matching actors' goals to their actions. If an action does not fit an inferred goal, then it is necessary either to establish a new goal for the character, to redefine the character's old goal, or to decompose an old goal into one or more subgoals that may match the action better. Different goal–action pairs may require differing numbers of steps to link them together. Consider these goal–action sequences:

(3) A *far* pair
Goal: Marge wanted to stop construction of a nuclear power plant.
Action: She made a sign.

(4) A *near* pair
Goal: Marge wanted to participate in an anti-nuke protest rally.
Action: She made a sign.

Compared to the *far* goal–action sequence, the *near* pair would probably require fewer inferential steps to integrate. Some sequences will be easier to understand than others depending on the transparency of the goals and subgoals. Sequences with clearly stated or easily inferred goals that lead to close ("obvious") actions should be relatively easy to comprehend.

Our hypothesis is that comprehension will be more difficult the greater the number of intervening subgoals between the stated goal and its actions. This will be called the distance hypothesis, where "distance" refers to the number of subgoals in a chain of subordinates separating a goal and an action. Distance will be used here in a comparative manner, with comparisons restricted to two *nested* goals and an action, all of which lie along the same branch of a goal reduction tree. Hence, the second sequence in the example is *near* (closer) compared to the first (*far*) sequence.

If the two goal–action sequences in the example were charted in a goal reduction tree, the goal (stop construction) would be at the top; below that would be several subgoals, including goal 2 (participate in rally). The action (make a sign) would lie further along the same branch; hence, the action is a descendant of both goals. Since goal 1 is a greater distance in the tree from the action, the distance hypothesis predicts that this sequence would take longer to understand than the goal 2–action sequence. The distance hypothesis will be tested by constructing a collection of short episodes that contain both a *far* event sequence and a *near* subgoal sequence nested within it. As in the example, we tried to select sequences of top goal–subgoal–action that would be nested along one branch of a goal reduction tree, so that the *near* event sequences (subgoal–action) were embedded within the *far* sequences (top goal–action).

So far we have discussed the case where the goal is stated first, followed by the action. But a distance effect should also occur in situations where the action is mentioned *before* the goal is stated, as in sequences such as "John caught a bus; he wanted to go overseas." The same linking up processes should be taking place, so we expect that *near* action–goal sequences will take less time to understand than *far* action–goal sequences. However, the goal-then-action sequences may be understood quicker than its action-then-goal mate, since the former follows the canonical order of antecedent-then-consequent in most causal schemata.

The distance hypothesis was tested in Experiment 1 with a set of episodes written to exemplify *near* and *far* event sequences. We measured reading time for a critical goal or action statement when it was embedded in a *near* or *far* episode.

## Method
We constructed a base of 48 episodes similar to this example:†

> Opening (O): Marge was concerned about the environment.
> Goal (G): She wanted to stop construction of a power plant.
> Subgoal (S): She participated in an anti-nuclear rally.
> Action (A): She made a sign.
> Closing (C): Marge believed atomic power plants are harmful.

Every episode presented began with an opening, ended with a closing, and presented two of the three G, S, or A statements in some order. The critical statement whose reading time was measured was always located in the third position. Four experimental conditions were created by varying the second (context) statement in the episode and its relation to this critical third statement. For 24 of the 48 base episodes, the critical third sentence was always the action, A (e.g. "She made a sign"), which was preceded by its near goal (S) half the time and by its far goal (G) the other half of the time. For the other 24 base episodes, the critical third sentence was always the goal, G (e.g. "She wanted to stop construction of a power plant"), which was preceded by its far action (A) half the time and by its near action (S) otherwise. With respect to the critical third sentence, these materials permitted us to record twelve reading times for each of four episode types — near goal–action, far goal–action, near action–goal, far action–goal.

Subjects read the episodes one line at a time on a computer screen by pressing a button that cleared the screen and caused the next sentence in the episode to appear. They were told to read each line in the episode, and to push the button when they were sure they understood the sentence; they were not told that their reading time was being measured. They were also told to read each episode carefully, in preparation for a comprehension test to follow after reading the entire set of episodes. The subjects were 14 Stanford University students who participated in the experiment for extra credit in their Introductory Psychology class. Each subject was run individually; the session lasted 45 minutes.

† The materials used in these experiments can be obtained by writing the first author.

**Results and discussion**

The critical measure is the reading time on the third sentence of each four-line episode. To check for possible performance differences between the two sets of episodes, an overall subject by episode set analysis of variance (ANOVA) was performed on the average reading times. Since no reliable differences were found, the data from the two sets of episodes were combined for the following analyses.

Our first question is whether subjects take longer to comprehend action statements when they are preceded by "distant" goals. The results, shown in Fig. 2, reveal that target sentences were indeed easier to comprehend when preceded by near rather than far context sentences. A three-way ANOVA,

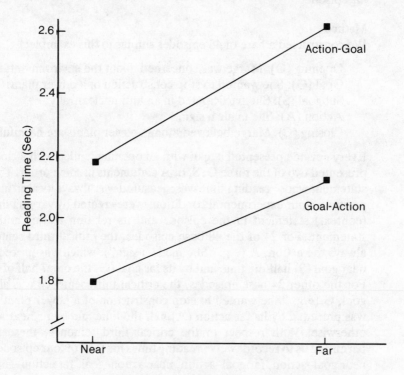

Fig. 2 — Mean reading times for target sentences when preceded by either near or far context sentences in Experiment 1.

with factors of subjects, distance (near or far), and episode-type (goal–action or action–goal), was performed on the target comprehension times. This yielded a significant main effect for distance ($F(1, 12) = 13.34$, $p < 0.01$). As illustrated in Fig. 2, the differences in reading time were in the predicted direction for all conditions: when preceded by a near versus far goal, reading time for an action target sentence was 1.80 sec. versus 2.10 sec., respectively. Similarly, a goal target sentence was read faster when it followed a near action (2.19 sec.) rather than a far action (2.61 sec.). Each mean cited is based on approximately 168 observations.

The distance hypothesis was supported by these data. Subjects needed more time to integrate a target sentence into an episode as its inferential distance from the context sentence increased. This was true for both goal–action and action–goal episodes. That is, it took more time to integrate an action target statement when it was preceded by a far goal rather than a near goal. Similarly, more time was needed to understand a goal target statement when it was preceded by a far rather than near action. This suggests that subjects understood the episodes by inferring plausible connections between the context and target statements. Our hypothesis says that this reading time was quicker for near episodes because fewer inferential steps were needed to relate the goals and actions to each other.

As can be seen in Fig. 2, target sentences were read faster in goal–action episodes (mean = 1.95 sec.) than in action–goal episodes (mean = 2.40 sec.), $F(1, 12) = 16.99, p < 0.001$. Furthermore, examining reading time for the second or context sentences revealed that they were read faster in goal–action episodes (mean = 2.15 sec.) than in action–goal episodes (mean = 2.39 sec.), $F(1, 12) = 6.79, p < 0.02$. We may relate this order effect to the fact that goals are typically followed by actions in episodes. For example: "John wanted to go downtown, he caught a bus" is more conventional in text than the reverse order. This order also follows the rule of "tell the cause first, then the effect." This may explain why episodes containing action–goal sequences are read slower. This effect was probably heightened by the "one-line-at-a-time" presentation, since that forced subjects to comprehend each sentence as it appeared on the screen. Normally, unusually ordered statements in an episode can be re-read until their relationship is uncovered. As expected, there were no significant effects for distance in the context sentences. In other words, time to read the goal statement, for goal–action episodes and time to read the action statement, for action–goal episodes, was not reliably affected by being near to or far from the target statement which followed. Similarly, the reading times for opening and closing statements were not affected by distance (near or far) or episode-type (goal–action of action–goal) nor was there a distance by episode-type interaction.

The comprehension and recall test was only given to motivate the subjects to read the episodes carefully. As expected, no differences between conditions were found in number of target sentences recalled on the 24-item comprehension test. The mean number of correct items based on goal–action episodes was 22.36 and 22.57 for far and near episodes, respectively. Similarly, scores for items taken from far action–goal episodes (21.78) did not differ from scores for near action–goal episodes (21.93).

This experiment provided evidence for the distance hypothesis. However, as alluded to earlier, several problems arise from the use of short naturalistic episodes. One problem stems from assumptions about subjects' pre-experimental knowledge. There is no way of assuring that the episodes activate the same goal structure for every subject. We do no know how accurate we were in guessing at culturally prototypical goal trees. Related to this problem is the "functional inequality" of different subgoals, which surely affects the ease of linking up actions with them. Some actions such as "look into the yellow pages" are appropriate for a vast number of long-range goals, while others may have narrower ranges of application. Additionally, different goals may have varying numbers of subgoals and actions beneath them. Thus, necessary subgoals may enjoy priority over other subgoals.

Another problem stems from generation and selection of the episodes. In this first experiment, there was no formal way of determining near versus far event sequences beyond our judgement that they appeared to lie nested along one branch of a goal reduction tree. The problem of selection can be compounded by pre-experimental associations that subjects may have between various goals and actions. Experiment 2 used an artificial goal structure to overcome some of these problems.

## EXPERIMENT 2

Experiment 1 found that difficulty of comprehension increased with psychological distance separating goals and actions in a goal hierarchy. However, "distance" was relative since it was determined only within a triad of goal–subgoal–action elements judged to lie along the same branch of a goal hierarchy. Goal-to-action distance or number of links could be manipulated with more precision if the goal hierarchy in question was created by the experimenter and taught to the subjects prior to the comprehension study.

Experiment 2 used an artificial goal hierarchy to circumvent the difficulties associated with the test episodes in Experiment 1. An artificial goal hierarchy minimizes the likelihood that pre-experimental knowledge will introduce unwanted variability between subjects and materials. An advantage of using an artificial goal hieracrchy is that the experimenter determines exactly the number of subgoals or distance between goals and actions. Thus, since we can select goal–action pairs of varying distances with certainty, we can study the effects of distance between goals and actions on comprehension in a carefully controlled way.

Experiment 2 used the time to verify a true–false assertion as a dependent measure rather than reading time. Although reading time was used successfully as a measure on comprehension in Experiment 1 and has been used extensively in many classic experiments (e.g. see Haviland & Clark, 1974), the measure is not without its problems. From the subjects' point of view, the task of simply presenting themselves with sentences on a computer screen has uncertain goals and criteria. Surely, subjects' criteria for reporting their "comprehension" varies in uncontrolled ways. Further, reading time varies with task demands. A subject instructed to skim the sentences for gist approaches a reading task differently than will one instructed to learn the sentences for recall. Thus, reading time itself can be a complex measure.

The time to verify a statement (decide whether it is true or false) was used in Experiment 2 to avoid some of these problems associated with reading times. Since comprehension is a precondition for making a correct verification, we assume verification time is composed of comprehension time plus the time to verify or disconfirm a statement.

The statements to be verified in Experiment 2 were phrased similarly to test questions used in a verification task studied by Farley and McCarty (1981). They presented subjects with some single-episode short stories and asked them to rate the acceptability of statements in the following form: "The protagonist did *Action 1* in order that the protagonist could do *Action 2*". They found that subjects' acceptability judgements decreased with greater distances in the goal-tree analysis of the narrative episodes. That is, the closer *Action 1* was to *Action* along a branch of a goal reduction tree, the higher was the acceptability rating for the pair. Following the lead of Farley and McCarty, the statements in our experiment consisted of two-part questions containing a goal phrase and an action phrase. An example test item is, "In order to do Goal X, the protagonist did Action Y". The goal phrase was selected to be either near or far from the action in the artificial goal hierarchy the subject had just learned.

We expected that subjects would verify or disconfirm the questions by inferring the subgoals between the goal and action phrase. Assuming that inferences take time, we predict that verification time should increase as "distance" between the goal phrase and action phrase increases in the artificial goal hierarchy. In order to build up the sample size, the test questions were repeated a second time. We expected the verification times to shorten from both a general practice effect and due to storage of answers to earlier questions that originally required slow derivation of the answer.

**Method**
An artificial goal hierarchy was constructed that depicted a lengthy procedure for becoming a member of the "Top Secret Club". This goal hierarchy is illustrated in Fig. 3. The goal hierarchy consisted of 18 subgoals nested along six branches below the top goal. In actuality, the subjects never saw a representation of the goal hierarchy such as that in Fig. 3. Rather, they read a 600-word description of the procedure for joining the Top Secret Club, which embodied the goal–subgoal relationships represented in the hierarchy.

A set of 32 true and 24 false "in order to" statements were constructed as possible plans for individuals to become members of the Top Secret Club. The subjects decided whether each plan was correct (true) or incorrect (false). False statements were needed as foils in the verification task. An "In order to do X, John did Y" statement is false either if X is a descendant of Y, or X is on a branch to the side of Y. An example of a false "plan" is: "In order to spy on the Zero Club, John did the initiation rites".

The questions were constructed from a base set of triplets sampled from the tree. A triplet consisted of three randomly spaced goals or actions nested

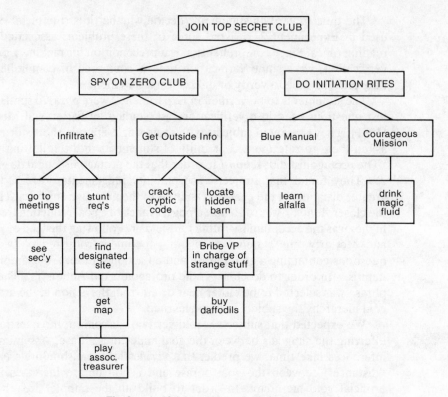

Fig. 3 — Artificial goal hierarchy from Experiment 2.

along one branch of the tree. None of the triplets contained the top goal. Referring to Fig. 3, an example of a "nested" triplet is: (1) spy on the Zero Club, (2) find the location of the hidden barn, (3) buy daffodils. Four types of questions were created from such triplets: true–near, true–far, false–near, and false–far. True–near and true–far questions were constructed by designating the lowest element in the triplet as the action and the two higher members (up the branch) as near or far goals. The question sets contained 32 trues (16 near, 16 far) and 24 falses (8 near, 8 far, and 8 lateral).

To illustrate, a true–near question from the triplet described above (see Fig. 3) is: "In order to find the location of the hidden barn, John bought some daffodils" and the true–far version is: "In order to spy on the Zero Club, John bought some daffodils." False–near and false–far items were constructed by reversing the two clauses in the question, thereby altering the truth of the assertion. An example of a false–near question is: "In order to buy some daffodils, John located the hidden barn"; its false–far counterpart is: "In order to buy daffodils, John spied on the Zero Club". Lateral falses, the third type of false question, were constructed by using a goal and action selected from completely different branches of the tree. An example is: "In order to buy daffodils, John drank the magic fluid". Lateral falses were identical in both sets of questions. Note that the three types of false questions differ in their second clause. The questions were presented in a new random order for each subject.

Distance, defined as the number of links between the goal and action phrase in a question, was computed by subtracting the height of the action phrase from the height of the goal phrase (see Fig. 3). Setting the top goal in the tree to a height of 1, any subgoal or action has a height equal to the height of its immediate goal plus 1. For example, the test item "In order to do the initiation rites, John drank the magic fluid" has a distance of $4 - 2 = 2$ (see Fig. 3). The questions tested distances ranging from 1 to 5, since no questions contained the highest goal ("Join the Top Secret Club"). The average distance for nears was 1.2 and for fars was 2.77.

Subjects learned the goal hierarchy by working through some training materials. The entire goal hierarchy had to be thoroughly memorized to assure the subjects' low error rates on the verification task. To help them memorize all the goal–action relationships described in the manual, a questionnaire was prepared containing short-answer "why" and "how" questions that could be answered by moving one step up or down the goal hierarchy. The questionnaire was designed so that the subjects could work through it at their own pace and receive immediate feedback.

The experiment consisted of a training phase followed by a test phase. After reading introductory instructions, subjects began the training phase, which involved reading the "Top Secret" manual, recalling its contents, re-reading the manual, filling out the questionnaire and, finally, re-reading the manual a third time. The testing phase began by giving subjects instructions to read that familiarized them with the "in order to" phrasing of the questions, gave examples of true and false items, and that asked them to respond as fast and accurately as possible to the test questions. Next, subjects were seated before a computer screen where a "warm-up" instruction paragraph appeared that they read one line at a time by pressing a button after they read each sentence. There followed four practice questions and then the 56 test questions for which verification time was measured. After this, the 56 questions were re-randomized and presented a second time, making a total of 112 test questions per subject.

Subjects presented themselves with the two-phrase questions, one phrase at a time on the computer screen. One second after the prior trial, a new trial began with the goal phrase ("In order to do Goal X") of the next question appearing automatically. When subjects finished reading this phrase, they pressed a button labeled "Next" to clear the screen, start the clock, and present the action phrase ("John did Action Y"). Subjects decided whether or not this second phrase named an action that was part of those needed to achieve the stated goal, i.e. whether the action was a "direct descendant" of the goal named in the first phrase. If subjects agreed with the plan they pressed a button labeled "True" with their dominant hand; if they judged the plan to be incorrect, they pressed the "False" button with the other hand. Either button press cleared the screen, stopped the clock, and presented feedback (four stars for correct, or the word "error" for incorrect responses), which remained on the screen during the inter-trial interval of 1 second. Verification time was recorded for the target (action) phrase, and reading time was recorded for the context (goal) phrase. Twelve Stanford University students participated for credit in their Introductory Psychology class. Each subject was tested individually; the session lasted 1.5 hours.

**Results and discussion**
Subjects understood the phrasing of the "in order to" questions as evidenced by a low overall error rate of 7%, with no reliable differences in error rate across types of question. To check for possible performance differences between the two matched sets of questions, an initial five-way ANOVA (subjects by run by question set by distance by question type) was performed on the verification times and no differences involving the question sets were found. Thus, data from the two sets were combined in subsequent analyses. Very long reaction times greater than 10 seconds were removed (about 1% of the observations). Only error-free data were used in the following analyses.

*The distance effect*
Our first question is whether subjects used the organization of the goal hierarchy to answer the questions. If so, then verification times should be positively related to distance between the goal phrase and action phrase in the artificial goal hierarchy. Fig. 4 shows that the predicted relation is strongly upheld in the true data. The data for the false questions will be discussed shortly.

For the first run through the 56 questions, mean verification time was 1.89 seconds for true–near questions, and 2.96 seconds for true–far questions, a 58% increase. (Each mean is based on approximately 192 observations.) Decision times for the second run were shorter and differences were again in the predicted direction. Mean verification times were 1.32 seconds for true–nears, and 1.94 seconds for true–fars, an increase of 47%. In a four-way ANOVA, with factors of subjects, run, distance, and answer (true versus false, excluding lateral falses), the distance effect was highly reliable ($F(1, 11) = 16.18, p < 0.002$).

Turning to the differences between Run 1 and Run 2, we see two types of practice effects. Recall that Run 2 consisted of the same questions (re-randomized) that appeared in Run 1. First, Run 2 verification times were shorter than Run 1. Mean verification time for Run 2 was 1.74 seconds compared to 2.38 seconds for Run 1 ($F(1, 11) = 30.38, p < 0.001$). Second, the distance effect was reduced slightly in Run 2. This run by distance interaction ($F(1, 11) = 5.92, p < 0.032$) could result either as a "scaling effect" of lowered times or if subjects remembered some of the answers to the inference questions they saw in Run 1, making it unnecessary to recompute the answer in Run 2. Although the distance effect was weakened

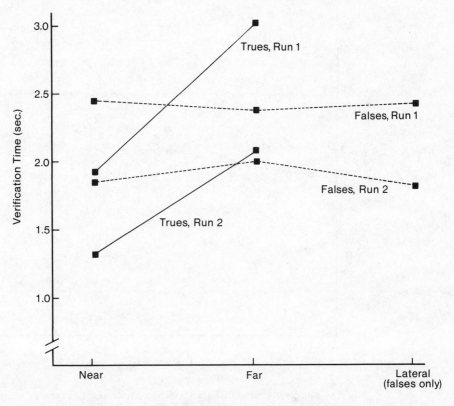

Fig. 4 — Mean verification time for action phrases when preceded by either near, far,
or lateral goal phrases in Experiment 2.

slightly by practice, the general finding is that for the trues, questions
involving more distant goal–action relationships take more time to confirm.

We examined this relationship between distance and verification time in
more detail and found it to be quite orderly. Recall that distance between
the goal and action phrases ranged from 1 to 5. Mean verification times
grouped according to distance are displayed in Fig. 5 (combining data for
distances 4 and 5 due to the small samples). Since the pattern of results was
the same for Run 1 and Run 2, the data from both runs were combined for
the following analyses. For the trues, verification time increased linearly
with distance between the goal and action phrases in the questions ($F(1, 44)$
$= 37.73, p < 0.001$).

These results suggest that subjects used the goal hierarchy in a systematic
way to verify the questions in Experiment 2. Decision times were largely
determined by the positions of the goal and the action in the hierarchy. As
distance between the goal and action statements increased, more inferential
steps were needed to relate them. So far, then, the results for the true
questions strongly suggest a simple, linear relationship between verification
time and distance. However, data for the false questions indicate otherwise.

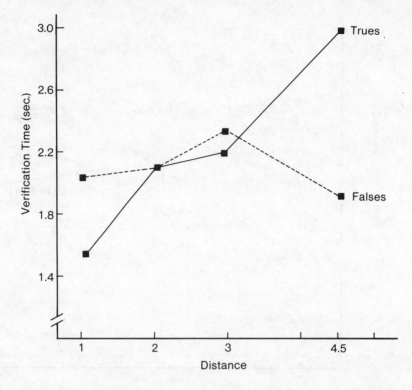

Fig. 5 — Mean verification time for the action phrase as a function of distance separating the goal and action phrases in Experiment 2, collapsed over both runs.

Although a reliable distance effect occurred for the true questions, Figs. 4 and 5 show its complete absence for the falses. The interaction between question type (true versus false) and distance (near versus far) was highly significant ($F(1, 11) = 12.06, p < 0.005$). A three-way ANOVA (subjects by run by distance) on the false data alone revealed no reliable effects of distance on verification times. Each mean for the false questions is based on approximately 96 observations. As expected, the time to reject false plans shortened with practice, from 2.32 seconds for Run 1 to 1.82 seconds for Run 2, ($F(1, 11) = 16.21, p < 0.002$).

One may ask how we could observe such a robust distance effect for trues but no effect at all for falses. Rather than an embarrassment, this difference in outcome strongly implies a consistent strategy by which our subjects verified the conjectured plans. We call this the downward search model, to which we now turn.

### A downward search model

We hoped that the strategies subjects used to link the goal and action statements in the verification task would be similar to those they use to make sense of events in narratives. In both tasks, relationships between the goal and the action have to be figured out by calling to mind the connecting subgoals. However, people are rarely faced with the problem of detecting absurd goal–action relationships. For this reason, we were primarily interested in the way people verified the true questions and did not plan to focus on how they disconfirmed the falses. Those questions were mainly included as foils for the trues.

But the false data can help us develop a more precise description of the inference strategy used by our subjects. First, the strategy used has to fulfill the dual requirement of verifying true goal–action relationships as well as disconfirming false relationships. Second, the strategy must not only produce a robust distance effect for the trues, but also the absence of an effect for the falses. These constraints narrow the possibilities substantially. The downward search model meets these requirements.

In the downward search model, a goal–action plan would be verified by entering memory at the node stipulated by the first ("goal") phrase, and successively retrieving the chain of subgoals beneath the goal statement, looking for the action mentioned in the plan. The more subgoals separating the goal and action of a "true" plan, the more memory retrieval required, and so the longer it should take to connect the goal to the action statement in the goal hierarchy. On the other hand, plans can be rejected when the action is not among the descendants of a goal phrase. To understand the expected outcomes for trues and falses in our experiment, let us first review how true and false questions were constructed.

In the actual hierarchical tree, (Fig. 3), goal nodes are ancestors of action nodes (higher up), so this was the case for the true questions in the experiment; the first (goal) phrase was logically above the second (action) phrase. For the false questions, though, this relationship was violated. The first (alleged goal) phrase (e.g. "In order to drink the magic fluid") was either *below* the second (action) phrase ("John carried out a courageous mission") or on a side ("lateral") branch.

A downward search model would decide about a statement such as, "In order to locate the hidden barn, John bought some daffodils" by entering the tree at the first goal phrase node ("Locate hidden barn") and then searching down the branch for the second, action phrase. If the action phrase is found, then the conjectured plan is verified; if the action is not uncovered in the downward search, then the plan is disconfirmed.

This model predicts that, for the true questions, verification time increases with distance. Recall that near and far true questions were constructed by fixing the action phrase and moving the goal phrase up or down one branch of the tree. The model assumes that (1) the tree is always entered at the node corresponding to the first (goal) phrase, and (2) search time is proportional to the distance searched downward in the tree. Thus we expect true–far questions to take longer because the tree is entered at a point farther from the action than is the case for a true–near question.

However, for false statements, this model predicts that verification time will not be affected by distance separating the first and second phrases. To explain the absence of differences among false items, recall that the false

questions were constructed differently from the trues. The first (goal) phrase
(rather than the action phrase) was held constant and the second (action)
phrase was selected to be near or far from it in the tree. The action phrase
was always *above* the goal phrase. This arrangement has consequences for
the downward search model, in which a plan is evaluated by entering the tree
at the first-named node and searching down among its descendants until
either the second-named node of the plan is found or the terminal node is
hit. Since the second phrase named a node *above* that named by the first
phrase, a downward search from the first-named node would terminate
when it reached the bottom of the tree. Moreover, the time it takes to reach
the bottom of the tree is independent of how far the second-named node is
above the first-named node. Therefore, this model predicts no difference
between the near and far falses, because in both cases *the tree is entered at
the same point*, so the search distance to the bottom of the tree will average
the same for both false–near and false–far questions.

In general, the downward search model accounts for the interaction
between distance and question type, but since the experiment was not
originally designed to test this model *per se*, certain factors (e.g. sentence
length) that are important for testing its implications were not counterba-
lanced in a controlled way. It is proposed here only as one possible avenue of
exploration and future experiments could refine this model better.


### The fan effect

Earlier we mentioned that retrieval of information about goals probably
proceeds in the same way as retrieval of other information from memory.
One well-known effect produced in many sentence verification experiments
is an associative interference effect (also called a "fan" effect by Anderson
& Bower, 1973; Anderson, 1976). As more facts are learned about a
concept, the more time it usually takes to retrieve any particular fact.

In this experiment we observed similar interference effects. A node in
the goal hierarchy can have one or two immediate descendants (subgoals).
For example (see Fig. 3), the node "Do intitiation rites" branches to two
immediate descendants, "Read blue manual" and "Do courageous mission" (i.e. one branch point). On the other hand, the node "Locate hidden
barn" has only a single immediate descendant (i.e. no branching). If
subjects verify the "in order to" questions by searching down the tree for a
link between the action and the goal, then verification time should increase if
there are branching subgoals between the goal and action phrases.

The questions in this experiment could span either 0, 1, or 2 branching
points. Referring again to Fig. 3, a question with distance between the goal
and action phrase equal to, say, two links can span either two branching
points (e.g. "In order to do the spy on the Zero Club, John went to the
meetings"); one branch (e.g. "In order to do the initiation rites, John drank
the magic fluid"); or zero branchings (e.g. "In order to locate the hidden
barn, John bought some daffodils"). For a given distance, reaction time
increased with the number of branch points in 83% of the cases for the trues

and 80% of the cases for the falses. We expect a fan effect for the false questions since falses with higher branching factors (downward from the node mentioned in the first phrase) are more likely to contain goal phrases that are distant from the terminal nodes. Thus, for both the trues and the falses, as the branching factor increases, so does the difficulty of deciding how the goal and action are related. As the number of subgoals branching off the goal increases, retrieval time increases, which is consistent with the fan effect found in other fact retrieval studies (e.g. Anderson, 1974; Hayes-Roth, 1977; Thorndyke & Bower, 1974).

## EXPERIMENT 3

In Experiment 2 verification time increased almost linearly with the number of subgoals needed to be inferred in order to link the action with the goal. The purpose of Experiment 3 was to extend these results to a situation where the information about the goal–action relationships had been acquired in a more naturalistic situation. In this experiment subjects casually read a folktale, much as they would do in an everyday situation. By reading a story, without instructions emphasizing the character's goals and actions, subjects are expected to arrive at a "naturalistic" representation of the goal relationships. For this naturalistic representation, we asked whether the subjects would still verify the "in order to" questions by recalling the connecting subgoals mentioned in the story, thus causing them to take more time to verify the far questions.

This follow-up study was conducted using a Grimm fairy tale, which was read in a natural manner. Rather than memorizing the material extensively, the subjects in this experiment simply read the fairy tale and wrote a short summary of it. We did not emphasize memorizing or paying special attention to the goal–action relationships in the story.

This experiment retained several of the methodological advantages of Experiment 2. A goal hierarchy could be inferred from the story, since the story described the characters' plans and actions carried out in service of their top goals. Thus, distance between goals and actions could be computed, as with the artificial goal structure experiment. Also, the story had a novel goal structure (e.g. the wolf, who wanted to eat the baby goats, disguised himself as their mother by eating chalk to soften his voice). This unusual content controls for pre-experimental associations and knowledge about goals.

A second aim of Experiment 3 was to examine more closely the rejection of false sentences. In Experiment 2 the near and far false targets were varied, while the context sentence was fixed. In this experiment, we held constant the false target phrase and varied the context sentences to be near or far. If subjects use a downward search strategy, then the far context sentence is closer than the near context sentence to the bottom of the goal tree and so we should observe a *reverse* distance effect for near versus far false targets.

**Method**

The goal structure used as a basis for questions in this experiment was extracted from a Grimm fairy tale, *The wolf and the seven little kids*. The story describes a mother goat trying to protect her seven kids from being eaten by a wolf. The goal structures, which differ for the two main characters (the wolf and the mother), are depicted in Fig. 6. Only actions which were

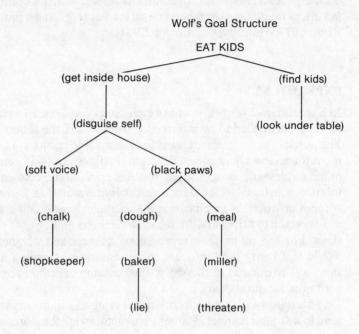

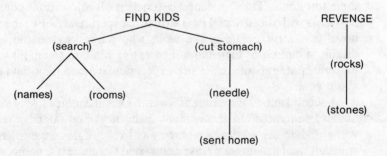

Fig. 6 — Goal hierarchies used in Experiment 3 to construct questions, taken from a Grimms' fairy tale, "The wolf and the seven little kids".

explicitly stated in the story appear in the goal hierarchy. The actions in the hierarchy are a subset of all the story events. The wolf's goal structure consisted of 15 nodes, representing actions, nested along four brances and the mother's consisted of 10 nodes along 4 branches.

The method of constructing questions closely resembles that used in Experiment 2. Thirty true (15 near, 15 far) and 30 false (10 near, 10 far, 10 lateral) "in order to" questions, containing a goal and an action phrase, were constructed from a base set of triplets sampled from the goal hierarchies. An example of a nested triplet, which as before consists of three randomly spaced actions nested along one branch of the tree, is: (1) disguise self; (2) make voice soft; (3) eat chalk. The true questions were constructed as in Experiment 2, by designating the lowest element in the triplet the action and the two higher members as near and far goals. Thus a true–near question from this triplet is: "In order to make his voice soft, the wolf ate some chalk", and a true–far question is: "In order to diguise himself, the wolf ate some chalk".

Recall that in Experiment 2 false questions had been constructed by reversing the order of the two clauses in the question, thus altering the truth of the decision. The *lowest* element in the triplet was designated as the goal, the middle element as a near action and the highest element as a far action. Thus, false–near and false–far questions were created in Experiment 2 by holding the *goal* phrase constant and following it by near or far actions. In contrast, in Experiment 3, false questions were created in the same way as the true questions: false–near and false–far questions were produced by holding the *action* phrase constant and preceding it by a near or far goal. For true questions, the action phrase is below the goal phrase in the tree, but for false questions, the action phrase is *above* the goal phrase. A false–near question from the triplet described above is: "In order to make his voice soft, the wolf tried to disguise himself", and a false–far question is: "In order to eat chalk, the wolf tried to disguise himself". In both cases the action phrase, "The wolf tried to disguise hemself", is above the goal phrase in the tree.

The probability of a question being true was not related to the height of its first phrase. The questions were randomized for each subject. Distance between goal and action phrases varied from 1 to 5, with 1.12 the average distance for nears and 2.48 the average distance for fars.

As in Experiment 2, this experiment had two phases, a training and a testing phase. The training phase was simplified considerably. During this phase, subjects read the 1112-word fairy tale, wrote a two-sentence summary without referring back to the story, then re-read the fairy tale. This process was paced by the subjects and usually lasted about 15 minutes. None of the subjects were familiar with the fairy tale prior to the experiment.

After completing the training, the subjects read preliminary instructions like those in Experiment 2, which familiarized them with the "in order to" wording of the questions. The testing proceeded as in Experiment 2. Subjects were presented with 4 practice questions and 60 test questions for which decision time was measured. After this, the 60 questions were re-randomized and presented a second time, making a total of 120 test questions per subject. Fifteen Stanford University undergraduate students participated for credit in their Introductory Psychology class. Each subject was tested individually and each session lasted about 45 minutes.

## Results and discussion

The error rate was slightly higher in this experiment than in Experiment 2 (10& versus 7% in Experiment 2). The higher error rate was probably a result of the short training period since in an earlier pilot study, nearly identical except for a more elaborate training sequence, errors were 5%. There were no reliable differences in error rate across types of questions. As in Experiment 2 there were no performance differences between the two matched sets of questions, so they were combined in these analyses. To clean up the data, all reaction times less than 0.5 sec. and greater than 10 sec. were removed. This procedure reduced the data set by less than 4%. All means reported below are based on errorless trials.

Our first question is whether subjects used the organization of the goal hierarchies that were implicit in the story to verify the "in order to" questions. The results suggest that this was the case, even with minimal training. The results, collapsed across both runs, are depicted in Fig. 7. Each

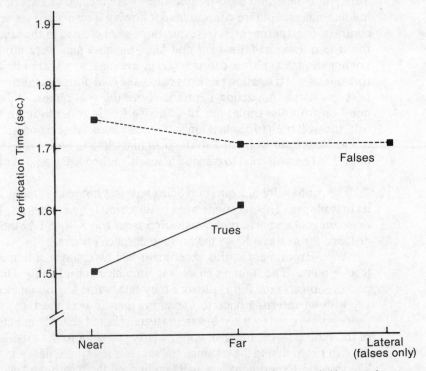

Fig. 7 — Mean verification time of the action phrase when preceded by near, far, or lateral goal phrases in Experiment 3.

point is based on approximately 450 observations for the trues and approximately 300 observations for the falses. The true–far questions took about 100 msec. longer to verify than the true–near questions, a 7% increase. This difference was significant in a subjects by distance ANOVA on the verification time for the true questions ($F(1, 14) = 5.8$, $p < 0.03$).

An overall subjects by run by distance by question type (true versus false) ANOVA showed the expected practice effects. Run 2 decisions were faster (mean = 1.67 sec.) than Run 1 decisions (mean = 1.77 sec., $F(1, 14) = 7.32$, $p < 0.02$). As discussed earlier, the faster verification times in Run 2 would result if the subjects memorized some of the goal–action linkages they computed in Run 1, thus circumventing the need to recompute them in Run 2.

We next analyzed the data for the link distance between the goal and action. Unlike the aggregated near versus far comparisons in Fig. 7, this link distance analysis is not at all controlled for the target phrase that is being timed. Consequently, the results do not plot as an orderly function (see Fig. 8). In this uncontrolled comparison, the true means do not plot as a linear

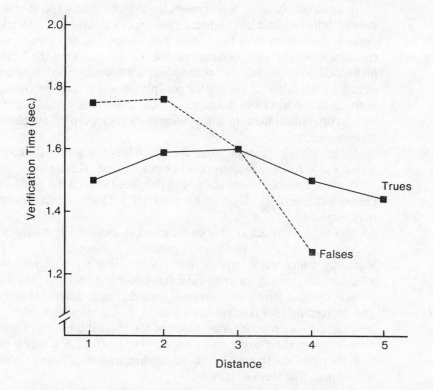

Fig. 8 — Mean verification time for the action phrase as a function of the distance separating the goal and action phrases in Experiment 3.

function of link distance. We expect a weakening of the distance effect when the data are regrouped by distance, since recall that the target sentence is controlled for (i.e. held constant as distance is varied) only in the near versus far comparisons displayed in Fig. 7. In addition, as will be discussed later, some unexpected factors resulting from using a natural story are probably responsible for the weakened distance effect found here.

Let us now turn to the false data. The downward search model assumes that a question is verified by entering the tree at the goal phrase and then searching down the branch for the action phrase. For false questions, the action phrase is always above the goal phrase, so the search stops at the terminal node, before intersecting the action phrase. There was no distance effect for the falses in Experiment 2 because the goal phrase was identical for both near and far false questions, so the tree was entered at the same point for both types of questions. Recall that the model assumes a question is disconfirmed if only terminal nodes are reached without finding the action phrase node. Thus, there was no distance effect for the falses in Experiment 2 because the distance to the terminal node was the same for near and far versions of a given question.

In contrast, falses in Experiment 3 were constructed so that a reverse distance effect would be produced. We expected false–nears to take more time to disconfirm than false–fars. The action (target) phrase was held constant while the goal (context) phrase was moved down the hierarchy to make it either near or far. Since the goal phrase was always below the action phrase for the falses, the closer the goal phrase was to the terminal node, the more distant it was from the action phrase. False-fars should thus take less time to disconfirm than the false–nears since they were always closer to the terminal node.

When the verification times for the falses are grouped according to distance, we see a reliable reverse distance effect. As displayed in Fig. 8, verification time decreases linearly as distance between the goal and action phrase increases ($F(1, 42) = 26.84, p < 0.001$). This confirms the downward search model.

The primary result of this experiment is that time to verify questions about goal–action relationships depends on the organization of the goal hierarchy, which was inferrable from reading the story. It appears that even with minimal training on a natural folktale, subjects link the goal and action phrases by successively inferring subgoals that were described in the story. The pattern of results is similar to those in Experiment 2, although less striking. Although verification time for the trues did not increase linearly with distance when target materials were uncontrolled, subjects generally took longer to verify true–far questions than true–near questions when the crucial materials were controlled.

Some unexpected factors arising from use of a natural story are probably responsible for the weaker distance effect found in this experiment. Inherent in the use of natural materials are various extraneous factors that can affect the outcome of an experiment. A goal hierarchy is surely only one of many possible determinants of the memory a reader has of a story. Other factors such as the importance of an action, its interestingness, salience, and unusualness contribute to how story events are processed.

Suppose, for instance, that a reader pays greater attention to the more important elements of the story. If so, then it would be possible for some of the near questions to be actually more difficult than the fars, because the near items require knowledge of small details of the story; and such details would normally be discounted as unimportant to the main story line. To illustrate, one of the true–near questions used in the experiment was: "In order to have some meal strewn on his feet, the wolf went to the miller", and its matched true–far question was: "In order to disguise himself as the mother, the wolf went to the miller". In this example, the true–near question may actually have been more difficult to verify or disconfirm because it tapped some easily confusable story details. It is hard to remember whether the wolf went to the miller, the baker, or the shopkeeper to get the meal to disguise his feet. These details can be ignored when answering the true–far question because the only knowledge needed is that the wolf went to a series of proprietors to buy items for his disguise. It is not necessary to know that the wolf bought chalk from the storekeeper, dough from the baker, and meal from the miller. Given these factors that could affect the inferencing processes, it is encouraging that any distance effect was produced at all in this experiment.

## GENERAL DISCUSSION

Taken together the results of the experiments described in this chapter indicate that goal relationships are understood by inferring subgoals which connect the action with the goal. A consistent finding was that as distance increased between the goal and action, ease of understanding decreased. Psychological distance between goals and actions was characterized as the number of intervening subgoals in a goal-reduction tree.

Each experiment required subjects to comprehend goal–action sequences, based on their knowledge of goal relationships. Experiment 1 tapped the subjects' general knowledge about goal relationships by measuring comprehension time for episodes dealing with everyday events. Ease of comprehension was affected by the "intuitive" distance separating the goals and actions in the episodes. In Experiments 2 and 3 subjects used newly acquired knowledge about goal relationships, which enabled a better measure of psychological distance between the goals and actions that appeared in the verification tasks. Again distance effects were produced, indicating the necessity of inferring the connecting subgoals when comprehending goal–action sequences.

Decision time did not increase with distance for the false questions in either experiment. In Experiment 2 there was no relationship between distance and verification time, and in Experiment 3 verification time decreased with distance. A downward search model was proposed to account for this pattern of results. The model described how subjects searched their recently learned goal hierarchies to verify goal–action relationships. Although this downward search model accounted for our true and false results, we propose it tentatively because (1) we expected search to be bidirectional, and (2) the false questions in Experiment 2 were not carefully controlled for question length and complexity throughout the hierarchy. We would have more confidence in our false results, and hence the downward search model, if future experiments were designed to control for these extraneous factors.

### Future extensions

Of the several issues suggested by our results, we choose for discussion possibly fruitful directions for future research on plans and goals in understanding actions. We find that the "artificial hierarchy" task of Experiment 2 is most easily extended into new research questions. Let us consider several of these research questions.

In Experiment 2, our subjects judged the well-formedness of small plans in the true–false format "in order to achieve goal G, actor performed action A". Time to decide whether the action in the second clause was a descendant of the goal stated in the first clause increased linearly with the distance (G–A) in the goal hierarchy. A first simple extension of this task is to look at the reading time for the action clause in the context of the prior goal clause. Presumably the action should be read and comprehended more readily the closer it is to the goal just stated for the actor. This outcome could be examined by having the subject memorize a goal tree and then either read a series of short vignettes about different characters going through parts of the plan, or by measuring reading time directly for a number of unrelated goal–action pairs.

Another converging measure would examine the *priming* of recognition memory judgements. After memorizing a goal-tree, the subject would be tested by presentation of a number of goal (or action) phrases, some from the tree, some from outside it. The subjects judge whether the phrase mentions an element of the tree they studied. A distance effect would be expected in a shorter time to recognize as "old" a target action of the tree when it closely follows in the test sequence a test of a goal that is close to the target action in the tree.

An interesting variation to the plan judgment task of Experiment 2 would alter the question, so that one asks for "sufficiency" judgments rather than "necessity" judgments. To elaborate, the goal tree of Experiment 2 asserted that each action in the tree was necessary in order to achieve the goal (or subgoal) above it. The implicit question that subjects answered during testing was: "Is action X one of the necessary acts I must do in order to achieve goal G?" One could alter the task so as to get at sufficiency judgments, asking, "Are acts X and Y (and Z) jointly sufficient to achieve goal G?" Depending on the branching of the tree, more or less acts would be required to achieve the goal. True sufficiency judgments would surely be slower the more necessary acts required to achieve the goal, whereas false judgments would be slower the closer the set of test actions came to a sufficient set.

The tree studied in Experiment 2 was an "unordered-AND" tree. That is, the subgoals listed under a given node were all necessary and jointly sufficient to attain the goal; however, the subgoals did not have to be attained in any specified order—any order was admissible. Clearly, there are many other kinds of goal–action relationships and goal trees. One modification is to have several alternative ways to achieve a goal; this is called an "OR tree", in that the goal can be achieved by actions A or B or C. An example was the "steal money" tree shown in Fig. 1. In such a tree, an action is sufficient but not necessary to achieve its parent goal. A given goal tree may have any pattern of AND nodes and OR nodes. Presumably OR nodes are searched in memory in the same fashion as AND nodes—they differ mainly in the criteria for judgments regarding goal–action questions. However, that conjecture awaits experimental testing.

An interesting task to examine in AND/OR trees is how the person propagates through the tree the implications of temporary disablement information. Suppose that a person believes that a goal can be achieved by plans A or B or C (each with its subtrees), and then he learns that a minor but necessary component of plan C is temporarily unattainable. He should now disqualify plan C, and only choose between A and B to achieve the goal. Presumably, it would require some time for the subject to infer that plan C is temporarily disabled. And this disablement inference time should vary directly with the distance between the goal of plan C and the sub-action that is said to be temporarily disabled. For example, in the "stealing" hierarchy of Fig. 1, a person should more quickly judge that robbery (a top goal) is unattainable if told that "choosing a site to rob" is unattainable than if told that "getting maps to find a robbery site" is unattainable. In an experiment to realize these arrangements, the subject would first memorize an AND/OR goal tree and would then be timed as he was tested repeatedly with a variety of temporarily disabled actions, at varying levels. Disablement affects AND and OR branches differently. Each subgoal of an AND node is necessary to goal attainment, so that disabling one part will disable its immediate subgoal and all the remote ancestors which depend on that subgoal. Disabling a subgoal of an OR node has less impact on higher goals except in cases where all the subgoals are disabled.

Another type of goal tree we are investigating has orderd subgoals, at least in some parts. Goal nodes which have two or more subgoals which must be attained in a specified order will be called AND-THEN trees. AND-THEN trees can have numerous levels, with each level requiring an ordered set of subgoals to be achieved. Thus, a top goal may require attainment of subgoal A and the subgoal B and the subgoal C, where each subgoal such as A requires attainment of ordered subgoals such as $a_1$ and then $a_2$ and then $a_3$ (and similarly for subgoals B and C).

A number of interesting questions arise in considering how people retrieve parts of AND-THEN trees and make judgments about them. For example, the subject may be asked to judge whether subgoal X must be attained (at some time) before subgoal Y is attained. The simplest search algorithm would be to locate element X and search for Y among its successors (THEN links) and simultaneously locate element Y and search for X among its ancestors (inverse-THEN links). This algorithm implies that the time to verify that $a_1$ precedes $a_3$ *within* a subgoal chunk (A) would be shorter than the time to verify that $a_3$ precedes $b_2$ across a chunk boundary (from A to B). There is some doubt whether subjects would learn a lengthy serial list of AND-THEN as a series of one-step associations (which by itself would imply strict distance effects in verifying "X must precede Y" questions). A more plausible hypothesis is that learning subjects will convert a series of AND-THEN nodes into an internal location on a time-line, so that the relative times of two subgoals (events) would be assessed by a kind of internal psychophysical judgement. In such judgments, subjects more readily verify the ordering of two subgoals that are very far apart (on the internal time line) then subgoals that are close together in time. This "reverse distance" is a well-known phenomenon that arises in judgments of stimuli that people have encoded and ordered along a one-dimensional continuum (e.g. Holyoak & Walker, 1976; Moyer & Bayer, 1976; Woocher, Glass, & Holyoak, 1978). Probably the subgoals in our hypothetical AND-THEN tree would be so encoded during learning, which would imply that the subject would show a reverse distance effect when asked to verify statements of the form "X must be achieved before Y". An interesting question is whether order information about higher-level nodes in the tree can be retrieved directly, or whether intervening subnodes must be visited during the search. In terms of our earlier illustration, in verifying that subgoal A must precede C, can memory search directly from A through B to C, or must our memory fruitlessly search all the subparts of A and B before it arrives at C and verifies the test statement?

Clearly, many interesting variations of the experimental task yield both meaningful goal tree structures as well as practical questions which probe different kinds of information from the tree and judgment criteria. The spreading activation theory is a useful place to start theorizing about how pieces of the goal tree are retrieved and combined to make judgments. We hope that continued exploration of these tasks will provide us with a fuller description and more complete understanding of the process by which memorized plans are retrieved, guide comprehension, and are used to answer questions.

## ACKNOWLEDGEMENTS

This research was supported by a research grant, MH-13950, to Gordon Bower from NIMH. Address correspondence to Carolyn Foss, Department of Psychology, Jordan Hall Bldg. 420, Stangord University, Stanford, CA 94305, USA.

## REFERENCES

Abbott, V., Black, J. B., & Smith, E. E. (1985). The representation of scripts in memory. *Journal of Memory and Language*, **24**, 179–199.

Anderson, J. R. (1974). Verbatim and propositional representation of sentences in immediate and long-term memory. *Journal of Verbal Learning and Verbal Behavior*, **13**, 149–162.

Anderson, J. R. (1976). *Language, memory, and thought.* Hillsdale, NJ: Lawrence Erlbaum.

Anderson, J. R., & Bower, G. H. (1973). *Human associative memory.* Washington, DC: Winston.

Bower, G. H., Black J. B., & Turner, T. J. (1979). Scripts in memory for text. *Cognitive Psychology*,**11**, 177–220.

Brewer, W. F., & Dupree, D. A. (1983). Use of plan schemata in the recall and recognition of goal-directed actions. *Journal of Experimental Psychology: Learning, Memory, & Cognition*, **9**, 117–129.

Collins, A. M., & Loftus, E. F. (1975). A spreading activation theory of semantic processing. *Psychological Review*, **82**, 407–428.

Cullingford, R. E. (1978). *Script application: Computer understanding of newspaper stories.* (Tech. Rep. 116). New Haven, CT: Yale University, Department of Computer Science.

Farley, A. M., & McCarty. D. L. (1981). Representing problem-solving episodes. *Proceedings of the 3rd Annual Conference of the Cognitive Science Society.* Berkeley, CA.

*The complete Grimm's fairy tales.* (1944). New York: Pantheon Books.

Haviland, S. E. & Clark, H. H. (1974). What's new? Acquiring new information as a process in comprehension. *Journal of Verbal Learning and Verbal Behavior*, **13**, 512–521.

Hayes-Roth, B. (1977). Evolution of cognitive structures and processes. *Psychological Review*, **84**, 260–278.

Holyoak, K. J., & Glass, A. L. (1975). The role of contradictions and counterexamples in the rejection of false sentences. *Journal of Verbal Learning and Verbal Behavior*, **14**, 215–239.

Holyoak, K. J., & Walker, J. H. (1976). Subjective magnitude information in semantic orderings. *Journal of Verbal Learning and Verbal Behavior*, **15**, 287–299.

Lichtenstein, E. H., & Brewer, W. F. (1980). Memory for goal directed events. *Cognitive Psychology*, **12**, 412–445.

Moyer, R. S., & Bayer, R. H. (1976). Mental comparison and the symbolic distance effect. *Cognitive Psychology*, **8**, 228–246.

Perault, C. R., Allen, J. F., & Cohen, P. R. (1978). Speech acts as a basis for understanding dialogue coherence. In *TINLAP-2: Theoretical issues in natural language processing—2.* ACM, University of Illinois at Urbana-Champaign.

Schank, R. C., & Abelson, R. P. (1977). *Scripts, plans, goals, and understanding.* Hillsdale, NJ: Lawrence Erlbaum.

Schank, R. C., Collins, G. C., Davis, E., Johnson, P. N., Lytinen, S. & Reiser, B. J. (1982). What's the point? *Cognitive Science*, **6**, 255–275.

Smith, E. E., & Collins, A. M. (1981). Use of goal-plan knowledge in understanding stories. *Proceedings of the 3rd Annual Conference of the Cognitive Science Society*, Berkeley, CA.

Thorndyke, P. W., & Bower, G. H. (1974). Storage and retrieval processes in sentence memory. *Cognitive Psychology*, **5**, 515–543.

Wilensky, R. (1978). *Understanding goal-based stories*. (Research Report No. 140). New Haven, CT: Yale University, Department of Computer Science.

Wilensky, R. (1983). *Planning and understanding: A computational approach to human reasoning*. Reading, MA: Addison-Wesley.

Woocher, F. D., Glass, A. L., & Holyoak, K. J. (1978). Positional discrimination in linear orderings. *Memory and Cognition*, **6**, 165–173.

# 5

# The construction of knowledge structures and inferences during text comprehension

**Arthur C. Graesser, Keith K. Millis, and Debra L. Long**

### The Czar and His Daughters

Once there was a Czar who had three lovely daughters. One day the three daughters went walking in the woods. They were enjoying themselves so much that they forgot the time and stayed too long. A dragon kidnapped the three daughters. As they were being dragged off, they cried for help. Three heros heard the cries and set off to rescue the daughters. The heros came and fought the dragon and rescued the maidens. Then the heroes returned the daughters to their palace. When the Czar heard of the rescue, he rewarded the heroes.

We have analyzed how college students comprehend short narrative passages such as the *The Czar and His Daughters*. The critical questions guiding our research have focused on the construction of passage structures, the generation of knowledge-based inferences, and world knowledge. Problems of sentence syntax and text linguistics have taken a back seat in our investigations. In this chapter we describe the highlights of our psychological model of text comprehension and some of the evidence that supports the model. A more detailed discussion of an earlier version of this model is reported in Graesser and Clark (1985).

According to our model, many types of knowledge structures get constructed during story comprehension. There are knowledge structures associated with the episodes in the plot, with the spatial settings, and with the physical properties of the story characters. There is a knowledge structure that captures the point or moral of the story, and yet another knowledge structure that represents the pragmatic/social context motivating the speaker to tell the story to the listener. The knowledge structures at each level are very rich conceptualizations that contain many inferences. When the Czar story is comprehended by a college student, hundreds of knowledge-based inferences are generated. For example, the comprehender infers that the story characters have traits (e.g. the dragon is evil, the daughters are weak), that characters have goals (the daughters wanted someone to rescue them, the Czar wanted to repay the heroes), and that characters experience emotions (the daughters were frightened). These knowledge-based inferences are not logically derived according to some formal theory in propositional calculus or text linguistics. Instead, they are inherited from generic knowledge structures that embody world knowledge. The Czar story activates generic knowledge structures (GKSs) associated with animate agents (HERO, DAUGHTER, CZAR), spatial regions (FOREST, PALACE), events (CRYING, HEARING), intentional actions (KIDNAPPING, WALKING), and abstract ideas (FAIRYTALE, EVILNESS). The GKSs get activated and furnish the knowledge-based inferences in specific passages.

The Czar story is a very boring story for adults to comprehend. In fact, it is difficult to imagine a natural conversation in which an adult would tell this story to another adult. It is even challenging to imagine a situation in which an adult would tell the Czar story to a child. One problem with this story is that the points or morals of the story (i.e. good overcomes evil, children should not stay out too late) are much too banal to inform or to entertain the listener. Adults normally convey more sophisticated points, with clever or humorous plots that require many episodes to be fleshed out. Nevertheless, we have learned a great deal about comprehension by having adults comprehend short boring narrative passages in psychology experiments. Adults are quite familiar with the words and ideas conveyed in the passages. They agree on how the text should be interpreted. We were able to observe systematic trends by focusing on situations in which comprehension is easy.

The model presented in this chapter attempts to provide answers to a number of difficult questions that have confronted investigators of text comprehension. A sample of these difficult questions is listed below.

What knowledge structures are constructed during passage comprehension?
What knowledge-based inferences are generated during comprehension?
How are the inferences and knowledge structures constructed during comprehension?
How do generic knowledge structures (GKSs) particitate in comprehension mechanisms?

This chapter concentrates on the distinctive properties of the model, i.e. the properties that make our model different from other psychological models (van Dijk & Kintsch, 1983; Mandler, 1984; Trabasso, Secco, & van den Broek, 1983). We will occasionally describe psychological research that supports some assumptions and predictions of the model. Nevertheless, our intent is to convey our theoretical framework rather than to present convincing and definitive empirical data. Empirical support for our model is presented in other published studies (Graesser, 1981; Graesser & Clark, 1985; Graesser, Haberlandt, & Koizumi, in press; Graesser, Robertson, & Anderson, 1981; Graesser & Murachver, 1985).

Before we launch into a description of our model, we need to say a few words about the methods we have adopted in our investigations of text comprehension. We have adopted a rather unique set of methodological tools.

## MULTIPLE METHODOLOGICAL PERSPECTIVES

In the spirit of cognitive science, we adopted several methodological tools in our investigations of text comprehension. One set of tools consists of the traditional behavioral methods that experimental psychologists use to test existing hypotheses, models, and theories. A second set of tools consists of the computer simulation techniques and computational methods in artificial intelligence. A third set of tools is perhaps the most distinctive to our research program. We systematically analyzed verbal protocols (i.e. think-aloud protocols and question-answering protocols) which were collected while individuals comprehended text. We took advantage of all of these methodological tools in order to converge on a satisfactory psychological model.

### Behavioral methods in experimental psychology

Most cognitive psychologists seriously endorse the traditional behavioral methods in experimental psychology. They present carefully controlled stimulus passages to human subjects and measure responses that are easy to scale and code. They systematically manipulate independent variables, hoping to pin down causal relationships among variables. They agonize over the validity and reliability of their independent variables and dependent variables.

There are several measures that may be collected *after* a passage has been comprehended. Subjects may recall the passages, summarize the passages, or judge whether test statements are true or false. The experimenter normally segments the text into idea units (such as propositions) and computes the likelihood that each idea unit is included in a recall protocol or in a summary protocol. A good theory of text organization would predict the likelihood that explicit idea units in the text are included in recall protocols and in summarization protocols (Black & Bower, 1980; Graesser & Clark, 1985; Kintsch, 1974; Meyer, 1975). Regarding truth verification tasks, the subjects give truth ratings to idea units that were explicitly mentioned in the text or merely inferred. Alternatively, the experimenter measures the time it takes for subjects to decide whether a test statement is true or false (Graesser, Robertson, & Anderson, 1981: Reder, 1982; Singer, 1981). If a particular class of inferences was actually constructed during text comprehension, then the truth ratings and decision latencies for these "comprehension-generated" inferences should be equivalent to the ratings and latencies of the explicit text statements (all things being equal).

There are several measures which tap comprehension mechanisms *during* comprehension. The experimenter may measure the amount of time it takes for comprehenders to read text segments. Researchers have collected reading times for words (Haberlandt & Graesser, 1985; Just, Carpenter, & Woolley, 1982), sentences (Clark & Haviland, 1977; Graesser & Riha, 1984), phrases (Mitchell & Green, 1978), and entire passages. A model of comprehension should be able to predict reading times for text segments. Other measures of on-line processing require subjects to make specific decisions about the text as it is comprehended. For example, in a phoneme-monitoring task, subjects may be asked to push a button whenever an incoming word begins with the letter "b" (Swinney, 1982; Foss & Jenkins, 1973). In a lexical decision task, the subject judges whether an incoming stimulus string is a word versus a non-word (Sharkey & Mitchell, 1985). There are also priming tasks (McKoon & Ratcliff, 1981) and experiments which collect response latencies to secondary tasks (Britton *et al.*, 1983). By observing patterns of response latencies or reading times, the researcher can assess the cognitive processing load at different points in the text. A good theory of comprehension should be able to predict these patterns.

There is one major shortcoming with the behavioural methods in experimental psychology. These methods are not suited for *discovering* mechanisms of comprehension. Whereas the methods are appropriate for *testing* (*verifying*) existing theories and hypotheses, the data are not rich enough for discovering new mechanisms (see Graesser, 1981; Black, Galambos, & Reiser, 1984). A dozen mean latencies are not distinctive enough for the investigator to discover mechanisms at the level of detail and sophistication that is typical in modern cognitive science. After inspecting data from hundreds of experiments, a researcher might in principle be able to infer mechanisms by induction; but not in practice. Consequently, many experimental psychologists have ended up testing theories that have been transported from other disciplines, such as linguistics, philosophy, or artificial intelligence. What is needed is a behavioral methodology which is rich and distinctive enough for researchers to discover psychological mechanisms during a comparatively short time span.

### Simulation techniques and computational methods in artificial intelligence and linguistics

Researchers in artificial intelligence (AI) have developed computer models which simulate comprehension mechanisms (Dyer, 1983; Lehnert, 1982; Schank & Abelson, 1977; Waltz, 1982; Winograd, 1972). The researcher demonstrates that the computer system comprehends text by asking the computer to summarize the text, to paraphrase the text, and to answer questions about statements in the text. A good simulation of human comprehension would generate output that matches human responses. Of course, a good simulation of comprehension would be a challenging and ambitious achievement. Researchers in AI have not developed a computer system that would impress most critics and non-scientists.

Computer simulation techniques are particularly useful for identifying limitations and errors in an existing model of comprehension. Researchers can assess the impact of theoretical assumptions on the comprehension system as a whole. Researchers can test whether specific knowledge representations, planning routines, algorithms, and heuristics are sufficient for generating the desired behaviour in a complex system. These capabilities add some rigor in theory testing and some flexibility in theory construction. When a researcher attempts to simulate a mechanism, the researcher must make specific and tractable assumptions about each component in the system. When the researcher has gaps in his theory and makes logical leaps, the computer simulates either a monster or nothing at all. The ability to generate a phenomenon is a powerful demonstration that a researcher understands the phenomenon.

AI, philosophny, and linguistics have contributed many insights and ideas on how knowledge *might* be represented and utilized in humans. However, the structures and procedures of the human mind either may or may not correspond closely to the structures and procedures that are discussed in non-psychological theories. Therefore, psychologists must carefully scrutinize and test theories that proliferate in the sister disciplines. AI, philosophy, and linguistics furnish theoretical constructs, formalisms and architectures that have potential relevance to psychology, so they are sometimes a source of inspiration. However, many ideas in the sister disciplines have been quite off the mark when it comes to being psychologically plausible.

### Collecting verbal protocols during text comprehension

In recent years, cognitive scientists have appreciated the value of collecting verbal protocols while individuals perform behavioral tasks. The individuals "think aloud" or answer questions while they perform the tasks under investigation. The verbal protocols uncover many of the knowledge states and some of the processes that underly the psychological mechanisms. The verbal protocols constitute a rich and detailed database that is suited for discovering properties of psychological mechanisms. Researchers have applied verbal protocol methods in order to investigate problem solving (Newell & Simon, 1972; Ericcson & Simon, 1980), scientific reasoning (Chi, Glaser, & Rees, 1982), mathematical reasoning (Ginsburg *et al.*, 1983; Lewis, 1981), writing (Hayes & Flower, 1980), text comprehension (Graesser, 1981; Graesser & Clark, 1985; Olson, Duffy, & Mack, 1984, 1985), and the operation of computers or other technological devices (Carroll & Mack, 1983; Graesser & Murray, in press; Kieras, 1982; Mack, Lewis, & Carroll, 1982).

In the past, many psychologists have been skeptical about the validity of verbal protocols as a database for discovering or testing psychological mechanisms (Nisbett & Wilson, 1977). However, cognitive scientists have acquired a more fine-grained understanding of the conditions in which verbal protocols are valid windows into the mysteries of psychological states and processes (Ericcson & Simon, 1980; Graesser & Clark, 1985; Graesser, Haberlandt, & Koizumi, in press; Olson *et al.*, 1984, 1985). For example, consider text comprehension. Researchers have assessed whether the data and insights from the verbal protocols can predict reading times for text in a separate group of subjects who do not supply verbal protocols. Olson *et al.* (1984) reported that sentence reading times in narrative text increased as a function of the number of inferences generated by the sentences; the inferences were manifested in think-aloud protocols that another group of subjects had supplied. It is informative to note that the same trend did not exist in expository passages, perhaps because few inferences are generated in expository text. Graesser, Haberlandt, and Koizumi (in press) reported that end-of-clause word reading times could be predicted by the number of goal, action, and event inferences that are generated by the clause; these inferences were manifested by answers to why-questions that a separate group of subjects supplied as they read the passages. In contrast, word reading times were not predicted by (a) the number of inferences that were states (as opposed to events, actions, and goals) and (b) the number of inferences tapped by other categories of questions (how-questions and what-happened-next-questions). In summary, there is ample evidence that some, but not all, types of the verbal protocols are valid windows into comprehension mechanisms.

Graesser developed a question answering (Q/A) methodology for investigating comprehension mechanisms. Comprehenders answer questions (why, how, what-happened-next) about each explicit statement in the text as they incrementally read the text, statement by statement. The answers to these kinds of questions expose knowledge-based inferences that the comprehenders generate during comprehension of narrative plot (see Grasser, 1981; Nicholas & Trabasso, 1980). Graesser could also trace the evolution of the knowledge structures as passages were comprehended, statement by statement. A *constructive history chart* was prepared for each knowledge-based inference. The chart recorded the explicit clause in the passage that first activated the inference. The chart specified whether the inference was preserved versus disconfirmed by virtue of the information in the subsequent passage context.

Graesser attempted to be very systematic, detailed, and rigorous when the Q/A methodology was developed and applied. It is important to discuss the Q/A methodology in a bit more detail in order to convey an adequate picture of what the methodology has to offer.

Graesser manipulated the passage context that comprehenders had available when they answered the questions. Some subjects read the entire passage before they were probed with questions (i.e. a full context condition). For other subjects, questions were probed on-line as each explicit statement in the text was incementally presented in the passage (i.e. a prior context condition). Still other subjects were probed with questions after the comprehenders read passage statements in isolation, with no passage context (i.e. a no context condition). By manipulating passage context,

Graesser could observe which text statement or groups of statements activated each of the inferences.

Graesser mapped out the generic knowledge structures which furnished the knowlege-based inferences in the text. For example, the GKS for KIDNAPPING would obviously be activated when the Czar story is comprehended. The GKS for KIDNAPPING contains states, goals, actions, and events which typically occur in kidnappings. Graesser used a *free generation plus question answering* method in order to extract the content of GKSs relevant to the passages. In this method a "free generation" group of subjects write down the typical states, actions, goals, and events that exist or occur in a typical kidnapping. Each proposition generated in the free generation phase is submitted to a "question answering" phase where subjects answer why- and how-questions about the free generation propositions. The total set of propositions of KIDNAPPING consists of all propositions generated by at least two subjects in either the free generation phase or the question-answering phase (or both). The average GKS contained 166 propositions. Graesser empirically mapped out the content of the GKSs associated with the passages. For example, there were 35 GKSs associated with the Czar story. Most of these GKSs were word-activated in the sense that the GKS was activatd by a noun, verb, or adjective which was explicitly mentioned in the text. Some GKSs were pattern-activated instead of word-activated. Pattern-activated GKSs (e.g. FAIRYTALE, CONFLICT) are activated by fragments of knowledge that are inferred during comprehension rather than by explicit linguistic elements in the text. The pattern-activated GKSs had been identified by at least two out of five researchers and research assistants.

Graesser observed that most passage inferences came from GKSs that are associated with the text. Approximately 72% of the inferences in the text matched a proposition in one or more GKSs that were relevant to the text. Once again, this claim was based on a detailed analysis of content that was extracted empirically. When a constructive history chart was prepared for each inference, Graesser specified which GKSs contained a propostion that matched the inference. When a GKS contained a propostion that matched the inference, then the GKS was scored as an information source for the inference.

In order to illustrate the data available for each passage inference, consider the constructive history chart for the inference *The heroes did not want the dragon to keep the daughters*.

Inference: *The heroes did not want the dragon to keep the daughters*
Inference category: *Goal*
Text statement that first elicited the inference: *The heroes fought the dragon*
Scope of text that elicited the inference: *Text statement together with the prior passage context*. The above text statement alone would not generate the inference
Type of question that elicited the inference: *Why-question*

Is the inference preserved in the final passage structure or disconfirmed
by subsequent passage context? *preserved*
GKSs that contain a proposition which matches the inference: *KIDNAP-
PING, FIGHTING, HERO*

Constructive history charts were prepared for thousands of knowledge-
based inferences that were associated with the passages under investigation.
An analysis of these constructive history charts led to several discoveries
about comprehension mechanisms and inference processes.

In addition to the content analyses described above, Graesser structurally organized the content according to a theory of knowledge representation. According to the representational theory, specific knowledge structures (such as a structure for a passage) and generic knowledge structures
(GKSs) are represented as conceptual graph structures. A conceptual graph
structure is a set of categorized statement nodes that are interrelated by
categorized, directed, relational arcs. Fig. 1 shows a subgraph associated
with the Czar story. Explicit passage statements are in the squares, whereas
inferences are in ovals. Each statement node is numbered and categorized
(state, event, goal). The arc categories include reason arcs (R), outcome
arcs (O), initate arcs (I), consequence arcs (C), manner arcs (M), and
implies arcs (Im). It is beyond the scope of this chapter, however, to discuss
the details of this representational theory. The details of the Graesser's
conceptual graph structures are discussed in Graesser and Clark (1985). The
representational theory incorporates properties of Schank's conceptional
dependencey theory (Schank & Abelson, 1977), Sowa's conceptual graph
structures (Sowa, 1983), and several other representational theories that
have been proposed in modern cognitive science.

Organizing the content into conceptual graph structures provided an
additional level of sophistication to Graesser's analyses. Graesser observed
how the knowledge structures interacted during comprehension. The available structures included (a) incoming clause C, (b) the passage structure
available after text clauses 1 to C-1 were interpreted, and (c) the GKSs that
were activated and available in working memory. Two structures (A and B)
"communicated" when statement nodes from structure A intersected
(matched, overlapped) with statement nodes in structure B. The content of
one structure would often modify the content of another structure during
comprehension. For example, structure A imposed constraints on structure
B whenever the semantic properties of structure A pruned out nodes from
structure B. Structure A embellished structure B when it added nodes to
structure B. Structure A had priority over structure B when more statement
nodes were preserved from structure A than from structure B. Graesser
could observe structure mapping mechanisms by overlaying structures
and inspecting nodes that ended up being preserved in the passage structure.
Graesser observed "slices of structured descriptions" that dynamically
grew or receded as statements in the text were incrementally interpreted
during comprehension. The database was a gold-mine for

discovering comprehension mechanisms that had never been introduced in the available theories of comprehension.

The Q/A methodology (and other verbal protocol analyses) provide an important window to psychological mechanisms. However, these methods do have their shortcomings. First, the analyses are exceedingly tedious and time-consuming. Therefore, many psychologists are quickly bored and frustrated with the amount of work involved in systematic application of verbal protocol methods. Second, the investigator must constantly evaluate whether the content of the verbal protocols truly reflects the knowledge states and procedures in the human mind. Graesser assessed which inferences were actually generated during comprehension by (a) conducting several follow-up analyses of the Q/A protocols, (b) conducting experiments involving on-line behavioral measures (i.e. word-reading times), and (c) considering the research and theories of other investigators. Of course, researchers who pursue all behavioral methods must cross-validate their measures and findings.

We are convinced that there are important virtues and advantages to adopting multiple methodological perspectives. Indeed, the proposed model of comprehension would never have been developed without the insights and constraints imposed by all three major methodological perspectives. Insisting that only one of these methodologies is "scientifically valid" is akin to inbreeding. A single methodology spawns bizarre offspring.

## SPECIFIC KNOWLEDGE STRUCTURES THAT GET CONSTRUCTED AT MULTIPLE LEVELS OF DISCOURSE ANALYSIS

When text is comprehended, knowledge structures are constructed at many different levels. The knowledge structures are specific in the sense that they apply to the specific text that the individual comprehends. The number and types of knowledge structures depend on both the text and the social context of the communicative interchange. For illustration, consider stories. The following knowledge structures would be constructed when most stories are told.

### Social-pragmatic structure

When a speaker tells a story, there is a social context that motivates the story (Shiffrin, 1984). For example, the speaker might feel paternalistic and want to teach the listener an important lesson. Alternatively, the story-teller might want to boast, so he tells a story that shows how clever or humorous he is. In most conversations, story-tellers must preface the story by giving out cues and negotiating for an extended turn in the conversation (e.g., "Did I tell you what happened the other day? ..."). The social-pragmatic structure represents the social context within which the story is embedded.

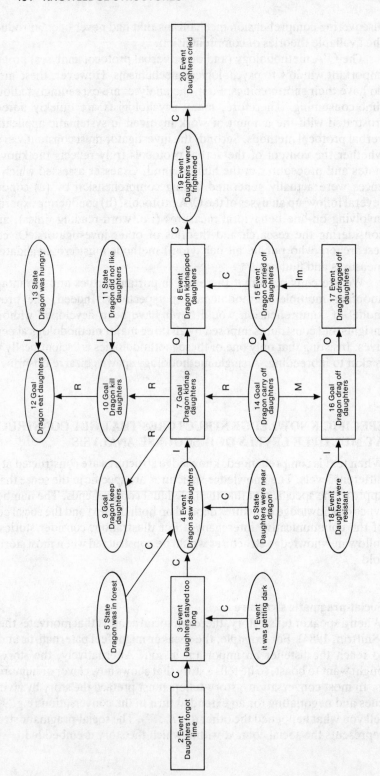

Fig. 1 — A substructure from *The Czar and his Daughters*. The statement nodes in squares were explicitly mentioned in the text. The statement nodes in ovals are knowledge-based inferences that were uncovered empirically by the question-answering methodology.

**Point or moral of the story**

There is a knowledge structure that succinctly captures the point or moral of the story. During the last few years, cognitive scientists have analyzed how points are computed or derived from the story plot. In artificial intelligence, the primary focus has been on the goal structures and planning of characters (Dyer, 1983; Lehnert, 1982, Wilensky, 1983). In the plot of most stories, the characters have goals, they select planning strategies to achieve goals, their goals are sometimes blocked, and they emotionally react. The point of many stories addresses the selection and nature of the planning strategies. For example, the point of a story might be that a single action sometimes achieves two goals (i.e., "Killing two birds with one stone").

We recently read a large corpus of stories and identified the factors or dimensions that influence effective planning strategies of story characters. These factors included conservation, rationality, caution, cooperation, competition, foresight, consistency, ingenuity, perserverance, competence, coordination, timing, flexiblility, organization, common sense, intelligence, resourcefulness, ambition, and leadership. There clearly are many dimensions that contribute to effective planning. Stories are told to transmit these dimensions in a culture.

In the field of literature, there is a greater emphasis on the idea that story points convey values, virtues, and social norms in a society. Foster-Harris (1974) asserts that all good fiction conveys a parable (truth, moral lesson), with a plot that contains a problem, a solution, and an answer. When we read and analyzed the corpus of stories, we found that many stories bolster the social norms of equity, equality, justice and reciprocity. The virtues transmitted in the stories included sincerety, honesty, temperance, trust-worthiness, loyalty, honor, bravery, mercy, selflessness, humor, strength, humility, responsibility, modesty, conscience, independence, and good grace in the face of adversity. In addition, we found that certain virtues (e.g. honesty, humility) tended to cluster with particular planning strategies (e.g. cooperation). In other words, the virtues constrain the choice of planning strategies. When story characters follow these norms and virtues, they usually end up getting their goals achieved or rewarded. Thus, story outcomes serve to reward characters who act in accordance with the norms and virtues and to punish characters who violate them. On the other hand, a few of the stories suggested that luck, fate, or coincidence are responsible for the outcomes in stories.

Knowledge of effective planning strategies, virtues, and social norms would be useful to all members of a culture. Consequently, there are stories to convey these points that have general utility to members of a culture. However, when individuals convey stories in naturalistic conversations, the points may be very specific and personal (Shiffrin, 1984). For example, Shiffrin discusses a conversation in which the story point is that a particular famous comedian has a dry wit. The significance of this story point can only be appreciated when the social-pragmatic context is known. The story-teller wanted to boast. One way to boast is to show that you hang out with famous people. In order to prove that you hang out with a famous person, you tell a story conveying a personal fact about the famous person (i.e. that the person has a dry wit). It should be noted that the point of the story did not address a planning strategy, social norm, virtue, or value. The point was personal and specific. It should be noted that this story point is appropriate for the specific conversation, but not for general consumption to all members of a culture. Shiffrin's story would not make the list of best sellers.

Computing the point of a story has been a challenge not only for researchers. Members of a culture also find it difficult. Individuals quibble over the actual point of a story. Children often miss the point of a story or fail to arrive at any point at all (Goldman, 1985). The points of some stories cannot be computed unless the listener is privy to the social-pragmatic context that inspired the story. Other stories are more self-contained. They can be told out of context, conveying a point that would be of interest to most members of a culture.

## Story plot

The story plot consists of a sequence of episodes that unfolds chronologically. The episodes are not randomly selected by the story-teller. The episodes either satisfy or block the goals and plans of the story characters. Episodes include actions that are intentionally performed by characters, events that activate the goals, and events that are emotional reactions of characters. Characters experience negative emotions when their goals are blocked and positive emotions when difficult goals are accomplished. The emotions of characters are substantially explained by the configuration of goals, outcomes, and social interactions (see Lehnert, 1982). Once again, the episode structure is composed in order to convey a major point.

The construction of an interesting story plot is very complex. The plot may elicit an emotion in the listener, such as suspense or surprise (Brewer & Lichtenstein, 1982). According to Foster-Harris, the plot has a problem, a solution, and an answer (which is the reverse of the problem). Moreover, the method of solution invariably is to invert, to reverse, to "twist" the problem picture so that a new picture abruptly emerges. In the new picture, the seemingly irreconcilable elements of the problem suddenty are reconciled, combined, and unified. Composing a story with an interesting twist in the plot is clearly non-trivial.

## Story setting

The story setting includes (a) traits of the characters, (b) the time frame of the story (c) the objects and properties of the spatial scenario, and (d) the situation which invokes the problem and the characters' major goals in the plot. In most stories, the characters have traits which are congruent with their goals, their planning strategies, and their virtues. For example, heroes are strong, victims are innocent, and villains are ugly. The components of the spatial scenario enable actions and events to occur in the plot. When the setting is embellished with ornate detail, the reader constructs a more concrete image of the story. Sometimes information in the setting leads the reader to expect certain episodes in the plot. Suppose that a character in a fairy-tale is beautiful on the inside, but physically ugly at the beginning of the story. We would expect that the character would become physically beautiful by the end of the story.

## Rhetorical structure
Researchers have developed story grammars which capture the conventional rhetorical patterns in the oral tradition (Mandler, 1984; Rumelhart, 1977a; Stein & Glenn, 1979). For example, when stories are normally told, the setting is described before the plot. In a story episode, the following components are either explicitly stated or inferred: (a) the character's goal, (b) event or state that initiates the goal, (c) an attempt to achieve the goal, (d) an outcome that specifies whether or not the goal is achieved, (e) the character's cognitive or emotional reaction to the outcome, and (f) a consequence of c, d, or e. Stories can be translated into tree structures which cater to the constraints (rewrite rules) of the story grammars.

## Additional issues about the different levels of structure
When an incoming clause is comprehended, the content of the clause contributes information to one or more of the above knowledge structures. Thus, clauses are crafted with a great deal of sophistication in order to satisfy multiple goals and different levels of knowledge. Satisfaction of multiple goals and multiple knowledge structures is perhaps the rule rather than the exception when stories are written (Appelt, 1985). Stated differently, when a story-teller composes a clause, the content of the clause must address the constraints imposed by multiple goals and multiple knowledge structures. Writing mechanisms and comprehension mechanisms are extremely complex.

According to our comprehension model, it would be a serious mistake to assert that any one type or level of knowledge structure constitutes the true psychological representation of the passage. A psychological theory of text representation is incomplete when it restricts its scope to only one level. An adequate psychological theory of text representation would generate organized representations for each of the above types of knowledge. An adequate theory would also specify how each level of knowledge is integrated with the other levels. Simiarly, an adequate psycholgical theory of text comprehension would specify how the comprehender constructs knowledge structures at each level during comprehension, how the comprehender integrates these structures, and how the cognitive processing resources are distributed among the different levels.

The Q/A methodology provides a useful vehicle for studying the different knowledge structures. Of course, it is important to choose the appropriate questions when probing the comprehender. The following questions are useful for tapping the social-pragmatic structure and the story point:

Why did the story-teller tell this story?
What does this story mean?
What is the point of telling this story?

What is the significance of this story?
What is the significance of this fact/episode in this story?
So what?

The following questions are useful for tapping the story plot:

Why/how did the character do action X?
Why/how did event X occur?

The following questions tap properties of the setting:

Why/how does a particular state exist?
What are the properties of person/object/location X?

However, the Q/A methodology is not well suited to tapping the conventions and properties of rhetorical knowledge structures, such as those associated with story grammars. Rhetorical structures are too abstract.

## GENERIC KNOWLEDGE STRUCTURES (GKS)

Generic knowledge structures are summaries or abstractions of several specific knowledge structures (i.e. exemplars). For example, there is a GKS for KIDNAPPING which embodies general knowledge of kidnapping. The GKS would contain typical characters (kidnapper, victim), properties of characters (the kidnapper is evil, the victim's relative is rich), a setting (room, warehouse), properties of the setting (the room is dirty), props (rope, money), intentional actions (the kidnapper ties up the victim), events (the victim becomes frightened), goals (the kidnapper wants money), different methods of achieving goals (calling the rich relative by phone versus sending a note), and rules of social etiquette (the kidnapper should not beat the victim before the kidnapper contacts the rich relative). GKSs are very rich data structures! Whenever a specific exemplar is interpreted (e.g. the Czar story), a subset of the GKS nodes is passed to the specific knowledge structure. A major goal of our comprehension model is to specify what subset of GKS nodes gets passed to the passage structure during comprehension.

When a passage is comprehended, GKSs are activated through pattern recognition mechanisms. The activated GKSs subsequently guide interpretive mechanisms and supply inferences. There are different categories of GKS and cognitive scientists have developed a rich terminology for categorizing them. There are schemata (Mandler, 1984; Rumelhart & Ortony, 1977), frames (Minsky, 1975), scripts (Bower, Black & Turner, 1979; Graesser & Nakamura, 1982; Schank & Abelson, 1977), and memory organization packages (Schank, 1982), just to name a few. However, we will spare the reader an extensive discussion of the similarities and differences of these GKS categories.

As we discussed earlier, Graesser and Clark (1985) developed an empirical method of extracting the content of GKSs. This method was called the free generation plus question answering method. This method was used to extract the content of 128 GKSs that were relevant to the passages they investigated. An average GKS was a very rich structure containing 166 idea units, called statement nodes. Graesser and Clark organized the empirically generated content into conceptual graph structures. The construction of the conceptual graph structures followed a set of quasiformal rules of composition. Thus, the "wiring" of these knowledge structures was driven by a theory rather than being based entirely on the investigator's subjective intuition.

After Graesser and Clark mapped out the content and structure of the GKSs associated with the passages, they could observe which GKS nodes were passed to the passage structures in the form of inferences. They could identify those GKSs which were rich information sources, supplying many of the passage inferences. Their detailed analyses of the GKSs and of the constructive history charts for inferences (see earlier discussion) permitted them to observe directly the interaction between text and world knowledge during comprehension.

Graesser and Clark reported that the vast majority of passage inferences matched a statement node in at least one GKS. Stated differently, very few passage inferences were "novel" inferences, matching no GKSs in working memory. A passage structure is best viewed as a unique combination of GKS substructures rather than an "emergent" conceptualization which bears little resemblance to the relevant GKSs. Given that the passage inferences are transported from the GKSs, Graesser and Clark subsequently analyzed which GKSs were major information sources. They found that the word-activated GKSs were substantially more prolific information sources than were the pattern-activated GKSs. In fact, nearly all of the passage inferences matched a statement node in at least one word-activated GKS. Thus, the passage inferences normally come from the world knowledge associated with the explicit content words in the text. Graesser and Clark predicted that text comprehension would be difficult when comprehenders are expected to derive critical inferences from pattern-activated GKSs or when the critical inferences are novel inferences.

## WORKING MEMORY

Comprehension proceeds in an active, limited capacity working memory (see Anderson, 1983; Thibadeau, Just, & Carpenter, 1982; van Dijk & Kintsch, 1983). Working memory is equivalent to what other researchers have called a cognitive workbench (Britton, Glynn, & Smith, 1985), a message center (Rumelhart, 1977b), or a blackboard (Reddy, 1980). As knowledge structures flow in and out of working memory, they communicate and interact in parallel. The constraints of one knowledge structure are broadcast to some, or all other knowledge structures in working memory. Some knowledge structures enter working memory in a data-driven fashion. For example, word-activated GKSs are data-driven. Other knowledge structures enter working memory because they are actively consulted in a conceptually driven fashion. For example, when the comprehender reads a novel and tries to retrieve information from several pages earlier, the reinstatement of the information into working memory is conceptually driven.

Graesser and Clark (1985) offered specific assumptions about the content of working memory at particular points in the text. They called these assumptions the working memory occupancy (WMO) assumptions. Graesser and Clark measured time spans in clause increments. When a given clause C is interpreted, working memory contains the following structures and passage nodes:

(1) The word-activated GKSs corresponding to clause C and clause C-1.
(2) A set of pattern-activated GKSs that get recycled in working memory (see Graesser & Clark, 1985). For example, the GKSs for FAIRY-TALE would get recycled when all of the clauses in the Czar story are interpreted.
(3) The explicit statement nodes associated with clause C.
(4) The new and recycled statement nodes that are associated with clause C-1 (including inferences).

Graesser and Clark reported data which supported their WMO assumptions. For example, they found that nearly all of the inferences associated with clause C came from GKSs that were in working memory; virtually none of the inferences came from GKSs outside of the scope of working memory. Approximately 90% of the inferences came from the word-activated GKSs triggered by clause C, whereas the other 10% required pattern-activated GKSs or word-activated GKSs associated with clause C-1. According to Sharkey and Mitchell (1985), GKSs do not exit working memory according to a simple decay function. Instead, GKSs are deactivated systematically by control cues in the text. Graesser and Clark's WMO assumptions are consistent with this active view of working memory.

It is important to acknowledge that hundreds of statement nodes reside in working memory during any given time span. When a single GKS is activated, for example, approximately 100 to 200 nodes are automatically dragged into working memory. Some colleagues have wondered whether such an assumption is inconsistent with the idea that working memory has a limited capacity. It could be argued, however, that there is no inconsistency. A GKS is an automatized knowledge structure. When a knowledge structure is automatized, hundreds of nodes can be activated at very little cost to working memory (Britton *et al.*, 1983; LaBerge & Samuels, 1974; Posner & Snyder, 1975; Swinney, 1982). According to Swinney's (1982) model of sentence comprehension and word processing, when a word is initially perceived by the comprehender, all possible meanings and senses of the word are activated, even when the sentence context has a strong bias toward one meaning or sense; there is a convergence toward a single meaning or sense during a later, integrative stage of processing. Thus, comprehension starts out with an activation of many nodes, meanings, and senses of a word, whereas later stages of comprehension converge on a smaller set of relevant information. Graesser and Clark's model is quite compatible with Swinney's data and model of comprehension.

## CONVERGENCE MECHANISMS

According to the model of comprehension discussed so far, elaborate knowledge structures are constructed at different levels of analysis, and hundreds of nodes vigorously interact in a limited capacity working memory. Some cognitive psychologists would be amazed that comprehension could succeed under these conditions because there would be a staggering number of codes and processes. Once again, however, these mechanisms would not appreciably tax working memory if the structures and procedures were overlearned and automatized. The mechanisms are indeed overlearned and automatized as long as the text has familiar words and the ideas interrelate in a sensible way. According to the proposed model, it is inappropriate to assess comprehension difficulty by counting the number of nodes constructed and processes executed in working memory. Instead, text is difficult to comprehend when the reader has a problem converging on an "explanation" of the text which successfully integrates the different types and levels of knowledge structures (Collins, Brown, & Larkin, 1980; Graesser & Clark, 1985). Metaphorically speaking, successful comprehension is akin to an elaborate puzzle that successfully falls into place. When the GKSs associated with the text are rich conceptualizations, there is a higher likelihood of integrating the different pieces of the puzzle.

One of the major goals of Graesser and Clark's model of comprehension is to explain the convergence problem. They performed detailed analyses on the constructive history charts for inferences in narrative text. According to these analyses, a short passage like the Czar story contains 25 explicit statement nodes and 125 inference nodes. It is important to mention that these 125 inferences would include those inferences that are usually generated during comprehension; their estimate excluded those inferences that were extracted by the Q/A task, yet theoretically were unlikely to have been generated during comprehension. As we discussed earlier, the vast majority of the inferences come from GKSs that get activated during text comprehension. Consequently, we know where the inferences come from. Given that there were 35 GKSs associated with the Czar story (23 word-activated and 12 pattern-activated GKSs) and an average GKS contains 166 nodes (according to Graesser and Clark's analyses), there were 5810 nodes among the GKSs that could serve as potential inferences for the passage. The question arises as to how the node space converges from 5810 nodes in the generic node space to 125 nodes that end up being passage inferences. This question was addressed and to some extent answered in the analyses that Graesser and Clark reported.

In order to discover the convergence mechanisms in story comprehension, Graesser and Clark observed the GKSs and the specific passage

structures that evolved dynamically as clauses were incrementally interpreted during comprehension. They found that three principles accounted
for most of the convergence. We will call these principles the intersection
principle, the principle of constraint propagation, and the principle of
structural priority.

### The intersection principle

According to this principle, nodes that intersect (overlap, match) between
knowledge structures in working memory have a high likelihood of being
passage inferences. Regarding the non-intersecting nodes, there is a pro-
gressively lower likelihood of there being passage inferences as the non-
intersecting nodes radiate further and further from the nearest intersecting
node. When they observed the non-intersecting GKS nodes that were one
arc from an intersecting node, 19% of these non-intersecting nodes ended
up being passage inferences. The non-intersecting GKS nodes with arc
distances of 2, 3, and 4 had percentages of 1%, 6%, and 3%, respectively.
Therefore, there is an exponentially decreasing function when inference
likelihood scores are plotted as a function of distance from the nearest
intersecting node. This exponential function produces a robust convergence
from the generic node space to the passage inferences.

### Constraint propagation

The exponentially decreasing function discussed above could perhaps be
explained by a principle of spreading activation with a dampening process
(Anderson, 1983; Sharkey & Bower, 1984). Dampening occurs because
activation strength is divided among different paths of arcs which radiate
from a given node. For example, suppose that an intersecting GKS node
received 100 units of activation and that four nodes directly radiated from
the intersecting node. Each of the four nodes would receive 25 units of
activation. As GKS nodes radiate further and further from the intersecting
node, they would receive fewer units of activation. According to spreading
activation models, dampening occurs because a limited amount of activation
strength is distributed among the nodes in the structure.

An alternative explanation of the exponentially decreasing function
appeals to constraint propagation (Winston, 1984). The dampening process
may be a product of qualitative contextual constraints that block intersecting
nodes and non-intersecting nodes. The nodes in a GKS are blocked by
contextual constraints because such constraints are imposed by GKSs and
passage structures in working memory that have higher priority. An exponentially decreasing function would occur if it is assumed that *pruning* occurs
whenever a node in a GKS is blocked by contextual constraints. That is,
whenever node N is pruned (i.e. disconfirmed), then all nodes that radiate
from node N (away from the nearest intersecting node) are also pruned.

Graesser and Clark performed some analyses which assessed the constraint propagation principle. They inspected the total set of "chains" in the GKSs that were within five arcs from the nearest intersecting node. The source of each chain was the intersecting node. In the next step of the analysis, they observed the constraints that pruned out erroneous nodes in each chain. For each chain, they started at the source node and radiated outward until they encountered an erroneous node (from the perspective of the passage statement's meaning). Whenever an erroneous node was identified, all nodes radiating beyond that node were also assumed to be erroneous. Thus, only one type of constraint was scored for any given chain. After observing all of the chains in the GKSs, Graesser and Clark categorized and tabulated the various constraints.

Graesser and Clark identified five major constraints in their analysis of the GKS node chains. The first constraint category involved a direct contradiction, such that the erroneous node in a chain contradicted a node in another structure that had higher priority. For example, an erroneous node was *The child is strong*; this node contradicted another node, *The daughers were weak*. Among all of the constraints that were scored, 35% of the constraints involved a direct contradiction. The second constraint category involved a problem with an argument slot in a statement node. For example, one erroneous node in the GKS for DAUGHTER was *The daughters rode a car*; it is impossible to have a car when the passage statement is *Daughters walked in the woods*. Argument slot incompatibilities comprised 29% of the constraints. The third constraint category involved temporal incompatibilities and comprised 14% of the observations. For example, the GKS node *Daughter was born* is quite outside of the time frame of the Czar story. The fourth constrtaint category involved goal incompatibilities. *The daughters set up camp* is incompatibile with the passage statement *The daughters walked in the woods* because it is impossible to walk in the woods and set up camp simultaneously. Goal incompatibilities constituted 9% of the pruned nodes. The fifth constraint category was more difficult to specify and constituted 8% of the pruned nodes. According to this relevance constraint, the GKS node (e.g. *daughters play with dolls*) is irrelevant to the text statement (e.g. *Daughters walked in the woods*) but the node would not be pruned on the basis of the other four categories. Overall, the five constraint categories accounted for 95% of the erroneous GKS nodes in the sample.

The above data provide encouraging support for the constraint propagation principle. When GKSs are activated during comprehension, there is not an exponential explosion of inferences. Instead, potential inferences are blocked by qualitative conceptual constraints imposed by other structures in working memory. When knowledge structures of higher priority post constraints in working memory, then many nodes in a GKS get pruned out because they are incompatible with the posted constraints. Constraint propagation mechanisms provide a robust convergence to a comparatively small set of passage inferences. Text comprehension is difficult when the constraints posted in working memory are contradictory or extremely restrictive, making it impossible for GKS nodes to satisfy the constraints.

**Principle of structural priority**

Whenever there is a constraint, there is a priority among knowledge structures. If node X in structure A is pruned because of a constraint imposed by structure B, then structure B has priority over structure A. Graesser and Clark identified some of the priorities among structures in working memory. They proposed five priority assumptions that apply to narrative text. They also reported data which supported all five priority assumptions. It should be noted that these five priorities constitute regularities rather than absolute rules:

(1)  Word-activated GKSs have priority over pattern-activated GKSs.
(2)  GKSs that are activated by clause C have priority over GKSs associated with clause C-1.
(3)  The old passage structure (constructed via clauses 1 through C-1) and clause C have priority over the GKSs. Without this priority assumption, the comprehender would end up discounting information in the text.
(4)  The new passage structure (that is constructed when clause C is interpreted) has priority over the old passage structure. Without this assumption, the passage structure would not get revised when new statements are comprehended.
(5)  Among the word-activated GKSs, GKSs in the activity and event families (normally associated with active verbs) have priority over GKSs in the animate, concrete, and abstract families (normally associated with nouns and adjectives). Thus, the reader tries to explain the actions and events in the plot.

We suspect that these priority assumptions would generalize to the plot in most narrative passages. However, they would probably not hold up for text in other genres, such as expository text or persuasive text. More research is obviously needed in order to assess the generality of these priority assumptions. Nevertheless, Graesser and Clark have developed an empirical method for discovering these priorities.


## THE MATCHING-BRIDGING-PRUNING-PROJECTION (MBPP) MECHANISM

The MBPP mechanism specifies the procedures that are executed when a clause is comprehended on-line and when the passage structure gets updated. Fig. 2 summarizes the MBPP mechanism. Similar mechanisms have been proposed by other researchers who have investigated the dynamic construction of passage structures (Collins, Brown, & Larkin, 1980; Glowalla & Colonius, 1982; Sowa, 1983).

When an explicit statement C is comprehended, the MBPP mechanism initially evaluates whether there is a direct connection between statement C and the old structure. The old structure is the passage structure (with inferences) that was constructed after passage statements 1 to C-1 were comprehended. A direct connection would occur, for examaple, if passage

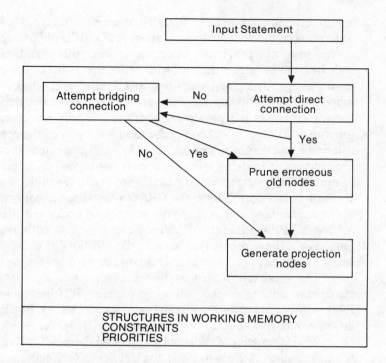

Fig. 2 — The matching-bridging-pruning-projection (MBPP) mechanism of constructing passage structure when an incoming clause is comprehended.

statement C was *The heroes rescued the daughters* and one of the nodes in the old passage structure was ‹X› *rescue daughters*. A direct connection occurs whenever an expectation is eventually confirmed later in the passage.

According to Fig. 2, if a direct connection is established, then the mechanism proceeds to the pruning component. Alternatively, additional connections between statement C and the old passage structure may be established by proceeding to the bridging component. If a direct connection was *not* established, then the MBPP mechanism attempts to build one or more bridges between statement C and the old passage structure. Bridges are constructed by transporting nodes and chains from the GKSs that are active in working memory. The convergence mechanisms (see previous section) determine the selection of nodes and chains from the GKSs.

If a bridging connection is established, then the MBPP mechanism proceeds to the pruning component. The pruning procedure deletes erroneous nodes in the old passage structure in light of the new information. If a bridging connection and a direct connection was not successfully achieved, then statement C is either irrelevant or begins a new episode (or scene or topic); the mechanism then proceeds to the projection component.

The projection component generates elaborations and expectations about subsequent occurrences in the plot. Projection inferences are different to bridging inferences. Bridging inferences fill gaps and establish conceptual connectivity between statement C and the old passage structure. In contrast, the projection inferences (elaborations and expectations) embellish the passage structure, with nodes that radiate outward from the main passage structure. According to Graesser and Clark's model and supporting data, bridging inferences are normally generated during comprehension, whereas the projection nodes are usually not comprehension-generated. The goals and comprehension strategies of the comprehender determine whether or not projection nodes are generated. In contrast, the construction of bridging inferences tends not to vary as a function of the comprehender's strategies and goals. In any event, the projection nodes and chains are transported from the GKSs in working memory, with convergence mechanisms orchestrating the selection of nodes and chains.

The MBPP mechanism offers predictions for data collected in reading time tasks. These predictions address the difficulty of constructing inferences when conceptual graph structures are constructed during comprehension. The mechanism predicts that reading times for explicit passage statements will have the following pattern: RT(direct connection) < RT(bridging connection) < RT(no bridging connection). Reading time studies have indeed confirmed these comparisons (Bellezza, 1983; Clark, 1977; Graesser, Haberlandt, & Koizumi, in press; Haberlandt & Bingham, 1982; Keenan, Baillet, & Brown, 1984; den Uhl & van Oostendorp, 1980).

The MBPP mechanism also offers several predictions for data collected using the Q/A methodology. For example, passage statements that involve a bridging connection should generate more new inferences than passage statements that involve a direct connection. Graesser and Clark reported data that confirmed this prediction.

Perhaps the most interesting analyses emerged when Graesser and Clark observed the incremental updating of passage structures as statements were comprehended. They inspected the dynamic growth of conceptual graph structures as explicit passage statements were incrementally comprehended. If a passage contains 25 explicit statements, then there are 25 passage structures to examine: S(1), S(1-2), S(1-2-3), and so on. Graesser and Clark examined how structure S(1 to C) is transformed to structure S(1 to C+1) by virtue of comprehending statement C+1. They found that virtually all of the structural modifications involved simple transformations of *appending* and *pruning*. Appending occurs when a chain of new nodes is adjoined to a node in the old passage structure. Pruning occurs when (a) a node in the old passage structure is deleted and (b) all nodes radiating from the deleted node (away from the main passage structure) are also deleted. Virtually none of the modifications involved comparatively complex transformations of *inserting, deleting+compressing*, and *reordering*. In the inserting transformation, a new node is inserted in between two nodes in the old passage structure. In the deleting+compressing transformation, a node in the old passage structure is deleted and then nodes adjacent to the deleted node are compressed. In the reordering transformation, nodes in the old structure are "rewired". It should be noted that the complex transformations involve a reorganization of the old structure whereas the simple transformations simply add or subtract nodes from the old structure. The fact that there were very few complex transformations confirms the layered architecture of the MBPP mechanism (i.e. pruning occurs after bridging). According to Graesser and Clark, text comprehension is very difficult when the comprehender must reorganize the old structure while they comprehend an incoming clause.

Graesser and Clark reported dozens of other observations when they performed the detailed analyses of the passage structures, constructive history charts, and GKSs. The Q/A methodology was a gold-mine for discovering properties of comprehension mechanisms that would not be anticipated by available research and theory. However, it is beyond the scope of this chapter to discuss all of their informative findings.

## INFERENCE GENERATION DURING COMPREHENSION

Graesser and Clark identified those categories of inferences which are usually generated during comprehension, versus those that are not usually comprehension-generated. Their conclusions were based on several sources of evidence. First, there were detailed analyses of the data collected in Q/A tasks, recall tasks, and summarization tasks. Second, there were experiments which collected reading times for the words in the passages; they identified those categories of inferences which predicted the word-reading times. Third, there were studies and conclusions by other cognitive psychologists who used behavioral methods to study inference processes. Fourth, there were rational considerations, including insights in artificial intelligence and linguistics. Therefore, the conclusions were based on several sources of data, involving multiple methodological tools.

According to Graesser and Clark, comprehenders have a much higher likelihood of constructing bridging inferences than projection inferences during text comprehension. The bridging inferences fill the conceptual gaps that exist in the explicit text and also enable a sensible interpretation of the explicit text. In contrast, projection inferences (elaborations, exceptions) are not very critical for interpreting clauses, for establishing conceptual connectivity, and for formulating global conceptualizations. Bridging inferences are part of the guts of the meaning structure whereas the elaborative inferences are expendable ornaments.

Graesser and Clark reported that answers to why-questions tend to include bridging inferences while other question categories (how, what-happened-next, where, etc.) tend to produce elaborative inferences and expectations. According to their estimates, 86% of the answers to why-questions were bridging inferences, whereas the other question categories yielded very low percentages (less than 20%). Therefore, researchers can uncover many of the bridging inferences in narrative plot by having comprehenders answer why-questions. However, referential inferences are one class of bridging inferences that why-questions do not uncover. When a pronoun is read, for example, the reader must determine the referent of the pronoun. The reader constructs a bridging inference when referents of pronouns are computed (e.g. "they" refers to "daughters"). Although referential bridging inferences are not directly manifested by answers to why-questions, there are some sophisticated theories of reference resolution that go a long way in computing these bridging inferences (see Clark, 1977; Clark, Schreuder, & Buttrick, 1983; Sanford & Garrod, 1981; Webber, 1983).

### What inferences are comprehension-generated?
In order to illustrate what inferences are comprehension-generated, consider the Czar story and the following excerpt:

(1) A dragon kidnapped the daughters.
(2) As they were being dragged off,
(3) they cried
(4) for help.

We list below some different categories of inferences, along with examples that should be construed in the context of the Czar story.

### Referential inferences
As discussed above, the reader constructs a bridging inference when pronouns are interpreted. The bridging inference specifies the referent of the pronoun. For example, the pronoun *they* in statements (2) and (3) refers to the daughters; the bridging inference is *"they" refers to daughters*. Pronouns are not the only category of referring expressions that require referential bridging inferences. The nouns in definite noun-phrases require referential bridging inferences. For example, *the maidens* in the Czar story refers to the daughters.

### Superordinate goals and motives of characters
When characters perform intentional actions, the actions are motivated by superordinate goals. Some goals that are superordinate to statements (1) and (2) are *the dragon wanted to keep the daughters* and *the dragon wanted to eat the daughters*. Goals that are superordinate to actions in text are elicited when comprehenders answer why-questions (e.g. why did the dragon kidnap the daughters?). As characters in stories perform intentional actions, they all have their separate goal hierarchies which motivate their actions. The goal hierarchies of different characters clash in interesting stories.

### Events and actions that trigger goals of characters
An event in the social or physical world may trigger a character's goal hierarchy. For example, the heroes' hearing the daughters' cries triggered their goal of going to the daughters. Sometimes the action of one character ends up triggering a goal hierarchy in another character. These triggering events and actions are manifested in answers to why-questions.

### Event sequences that connect an explicit action/event with a subsequent event

An example event chain that connects statements (2) (the dragon dragged off the daughters) and statement (3) (the daughters cried) is *the daughters were hurt* and *the daughters were frightened*. These intermediate event inferences are bridging inferences that provide conceptual connectivity between explicit statements (2) and (3). These event chains are manifested in answers to why-questions (e.g. why did the daughters cry?).

Graesser and Clark (1985) reported several findings that supported the conclusion that the above categories of inferences are comprehension-generated. First, compared to other categories of inferences (discussed below), the above bridging inferences had three to four times the likelihood of being produced in a variety of different tasks that involve the collection of verbal protocols. Such data included (a) intrusions in recall protocols, (b) statements in summary protocols, and (c) answers produced from different question categories (how, when, where, what-enabled X, what are the consequences of X, what is the significance of X). Second, the above inference categories predicted word reading times whereas other inference categories failed to predict word reading times (Graesser, Haberlandt, & Koizumi, in press). Third, other researchers have confirmed that some of the above inference categories are comprehension-generated (Clark, 1977; Robertson, Black, & Lehnert, 1985; Walker & Yekovich, 1984).

### What inferences are usually not comprehension-generated?

According to Graesser and Clark (1985), projection nodes tend not to be comprehension-generated. Elaborations and expectations are not generated during comprehension unless the GKSs that supply the inferences are so automatized that generating the inferences imposes zero cost to working memory. Although these inferences are not generated during comprehension, they can be exposed during question answering after comprehension has been completed.

### Goals/actions that are subordinate to an explicit intentional action

When a character performs an intentional action, the character executes a subordinate plan of goals and actions. For example, consider statement (2) (the dragon dragged off the daughters). Goals/actions that are subordinate to this action are *the dragon grabbed the daughters* and *the dragon lifted the daughters*. These subordinate goals/actions embellish *how* an intentional action is executed and are elicited when individuals answer how-questions.

### Style specifications

These elaborative inferences specify the manner in which actions and events occur. They specify speed (X occurred *slowly*), intensity (X occurred *forcefully*), and qualitative properties of motion (X occurred *in circles*). Style specifications also include instrumental objects, body parts, and resources (e.g. X did something *with a hammer*, *with his hand*). Style specifications are elicited from how-questions and are usually not comprehension-generated.

### States that enable events and actions
Most events and actions are enabled by the existence of supporting states. For example, the state *daughters have eyes* enables the event of the daughters crying. The state *heroes are near daughters* enables the event of the heroes hearing their cries. Although enabling states are necessary for actions and events to occur, they tend not to be comprehension-generated.

### States that ascribe properties to entities
Properties can be ascribed to characters in a story (the dragon is evil, the daughters are short), to spatial regions (the forest is dark), and to objects and artifacts (the dress is pink). These traits and properties are elaborative inferences which are not normally comprehension-generated. For example, most readers do not inferentially construct a detailed spatial scenario because constructing such a scenario is too time-consuming (Kosslyn, 1980). Most readers settle for a primitive topological representation with predicates specifying containment and proximity (e.g. the characters are somewhere in the forest).

### Expectations about subsequent occurrences in the plot
Some early models of comprehension in artificial intelligence emphasized the importance of expectations (DeJong, 1979; Schank & Abelson, 1977). According to these models, the comprehender is constantly generating expectations about subsequent occurrences and many of these expectations are substantiated when the subsequent plot unfolds. The expectations are manifested in answers to what-happened-next questions and what-are-the-consequences questions. However, according to Graesser and Clark's model and available data, expectations do not have a large explanatory role in comprehension. Readers normally accommodate and explain unpredicted test statements rather than formulating and verifying predictions. Graesser and Clark identified only two classes of expectations that are sometimes comprehension-generated. First, there are expectations that correspond to achieved superordinate goals; if there is a superordinate goal that the dragon wanted to eat the daughters, then the expectation would be *the dragon ate the daughters*. Second, there are expectations that constitute the second part of a reciprocity module; if character A intentionally hurts character B, then the reader expects B to retaliate and hurt A. Other types of expectations have a low likelihood of being confirmed in the subsequent plot and are normally not comprehension-generated.

### Other elaborative inferences
There are other categories of elaborative inferences which are not comprehension-generated. There are generalizations (e.g. heroes usually save people) and evaluative inferences (the reader does not like the dragon)

which are often elicited by "significance" questions (i.e. what is the significance of X?). There are quantitative expressions that can be derived from mathematical, statistical, or logical reasoning strategies.

### The relationship between reading time and inference generation

Graesser, Haberlandt, and Koizumi (in press) reported that there is not a unidimensional relationship between reading time and the number of inferences generated by clauses in text. They used multiple regression techniques in order to assess the extent to which end-of-clause word reading times can be predicted by the number and types of inferences generated by the clause. For referential inferences, there was a positive correlation between number of inferences and reading time (when extraneous variables were controlled for). Indeed, there is an extensive body of psyhological research which confirms that reference resolution takes a measurable amount of processing time (Clark, 1977; Clark & Sengul, 1979; Sanford & Garrod, 1981), particularly when there is some ambiguity.

The relationship between reading time and number of inferences is altogether different when other categories of bridging inferences are considered. Graesser, Haberlandt, and Koizumi reported multiple regression analyses showing a negative correlation between end-of-clause reading times and the number of non-referential bridging inferences (i.e. superordinate goals, events/actions that trigger goals, and causal event chains). When a clause generates many bridging inferences, there are many GKSs and nodes that serve as a database for sampling bridging inferences and chains. End-of-clause reading times are long when the reader is desperately trying to establish a conceptual bridge from an impoverished database. Clauses are demanding on cognitive resources to the extent that (a) few GKSs are in working memory, (b) the GKSs have very few nodes, (c) the nodes in the GKS are not automatized, and (d) the GKS nodes and passage structure nodes fail to converge on a structure that explains the text.

Consider the following three sentences from the perspective of the model that is being proposed here:

(1)  When the animal did something to the girl, she cried.
(2)  When the goat slapped the princess, she cried.
(3)  When the dragon kidnapped the princess, she cried.

The model predicts that sentence (3) would generate the most knowledge-based inferences and would be read the fastest. Sentence (1) generates few inferences because the GKSs in the first clause (ANIMAL, DOING, GIRL) are not as conceptually rich as the GKSs in sentence (3) (DRAGON, KIDNAPPING, PRINCESS). It is a struggle to construct bridging inferences from a meager knowledge base so reading times for sentence (1) will be comparatively long. Sentence (2) would generate few bridging inferences because there is a lack of convergence among the structures associated with the GKSs; there are few intersecting nodes among the GKSs for GOAT, SLAPPING, and PRINCESS. These GKSs are richer than those in sentence

(1), but the GKSs do not converge on a sensible set of bridging inferences. Sentence (3) would be read the fastest because there is a rich knowledge base to sample bridging inferences and there are many intersecting nodes among the GKSs.

The proposed model explains why technical expository text takes so long to read compared to narrative text (Graesser & Riha, 1984; Haberlandt & Graesser, 1985). The words in expository text tend to be less familiar to the reader, tend not to be overlearned, and tend to be abstract. Thus, there are fewer nodes in the GKSs and fewer inferences are generated. According to Graesser and Goodman (1985), four times as many inferences are generated in narrative text as in expository text. It is difficult to establish conceptual connectivity between explicit text statements when there is such a scanty database (among the GKSs) from which to transport bridging inferences and chains.

When expository text is written, the writer needs to compensate for the difficulty in generating bridging inferences. The writer should explicitly mention critical ideas rather than leaving them to be inferred. The writer should explicitly present connectives (*therefore*, *but*, *because*, etc.) in order to clarify how ideas are conceptually and structurally related. Indeed, Britton, Glynn, and Smith (1985) have reported that explicit presentation of connectives and signaling devices (headers, subtitles) facilitates comprehension speed.

## FINAL COMMENTS

In the spirit of cognitive science, we have adopted several methodological tools in order to investigate inference generation and the process of constructing knowledge structures during text comprehension. We were particularly impressed with the Q/A methodology. It provided a rich database for discovering mysteries of comprehension that were not handed down from available research and theory. However, it was important to assess the validity of the Q/A protocols by conducting follow-up research which adopted traditional behavioral methodologies (i.e. reading time, recall, inference verification tasks). It was also important to keep abreast of work in text linguistics, Artificial intelligence, and the experimental findings of other psychologists. We are firmly convinced that an interdisciplinary perspective is extremely healthy in cognitive research. It keeps us from developing psychological models that are paradigm-ridden and inadequate.

## REFERENCES

Anderson, J. R. (1983). *The architecture of of cognition*. Cambridge, MA: Harvard University Press.

Appelt, D. E. (1985). Planning English referring expressions. *Artificial Intelligence,* **26**, 1–33.

Bellezza, F. S. (1983). Recalling script-based text: The role of selective processing and schematic cues. *Bulletin of the Psychonomic Society,* **21**, 267–270.

Black, J. B., & Bower, G. H. (1980). Story understanding as problem-solving. *Poetics,* **9**, 223–250.

Black, J. B., Galambos, J., & Reiser, B. J. (1984). Coordination discovery and verification research. In D. S. Kieras & M. A. Just (Eds.), *New methods in reading comprehension research.* Hillsdale, NJ: Lawrence Erlbaum.

Bower, G. H., Black, J. B., & Turner, T. J. (1979). Scripts in memory for text. *Cognitive Psychology,* **11**, 177–220.

Brewer, W. F., & Lichtenstein, E. H. (1982). Event schemas, story schemas, and story grammars. In J. Long & A. D. Baddeley (Eds.), *Attention and Performance IX.* Hillsdale, NJ: Lawrence Erlbaum.

Britton, B. K., Glynn, S. M., & Smith, J. W. (1985). Cognitive demands of processing expository text: A cognitive workbench model. In B. K. Britton, & J. B. Black (Eds.), *Understanding expository text.* Hillsdale, NJ: Lawrence Erlbaum.

Britton, B. K., Graesser, A. C., Glynn, S. M., Hamilton, T., & Penland, M. (1983). Use of cognitive capacity in reading: Effects of some content-factors of text. *Discourse Processes,* **6**, 39–58.

Carroll, J. M., & Mack, R. (1983). Actively learning to use a word processor. In W. Copper (Ed.), *Cognitive aspects of skilled typewriting.* New York: Springer-Verlag.

Chi, M. T. H., Glaser, R., & Rees, E. (1982). Expertise in problem-solving. In R. J. Sternberg (Ed.), *Advances in the psychology of human intelligence.* Hillsdale, NJ: Lawrence Erlbaum.

Clark, H. H. (1977). Bridging. In P. N. Johnson-Laird & P. C. Wason (Eds.), *Thinking: Readings in cognitive science.* London: Cambridge University Press.

Clark, H. H., & Haviland, S. E. (1977). Comprehension and the given-new contract. In R. O. Freedle (Ed.), *Discourse production and comprehension.* Norwood, NJ: Ablex.

Clark, H. H., Schreuder, R., & Buttrick, S. (1983). Common ground and the understanding of demonstrative reference. *Journal of Verbal Learning and Verbal Behavior,* **22**, 245–258.

Clark, H. H., & Sengul, C. J. (1979). In search of referents for nouns and pronouns. *Memory and Cognition,* **7**, 35–41.

Collins, A. M., Brown, J. S., & Larkin, K. M. (1980). Inferences in text understanding. In R. J. Spiro, B. C. Bruce, & W. F. Brewer (Eds.), *Theoretical issues in reading comprehension.* Hillsdale, NJ: Lawrence Erlbaum.

DeJong, G. (1979). Prediction and substantiation: A new approach to natural language processing. *Cognitive Science,* **3**, 251–273.

den Uhl, M., & van Oostendorp, H. (1980). The use of scripts in text comprehension. *Poetics,* **9**, 275–294.

Dyer, M. G. (1983). *In-depth understanding: A computer model of inte-*

*grated processing for narrative comprehension.* Cambridge, MA: MIT Press.

Ericsson, K. A. & Simon, H. A. (1980). Verbal reports as data. *Psychological Review,* **87,** 215–251.

Foss, D. J., & Jenkins, C. J. (1973). Some effects of context on the comprehension of ambigious sentences. *Journal of Verbal Learning and Verbal Behavior,* **12**, 577–589.

Foster-Harris, W. (1974). *The basic pattern of plot.* Norman, Oklahoma: University of Oklahoma Press.

Ginsberg, H. P., Kossan, N. E., Schwartz, R., & Swanson, D. (1983). Protocol methods in research on mathematical thinking. In H. P. Ginsberg (Ed.), *The development of mathematical thinking.* New York: Academic Press.

Glowalla, H., & Colonius, S. H. (1982). Toward a model of macrostructure search. In A. Flammer & W. Kintsch (Eds.), *Discourse processing.* Amsterdam: North-Holland.

Goldman, S. R. (1985). Inferential reasoning in and about narrative texts. In A. C. Graesser & J. B. Black (Eds.), *The psychology of questions.* Hillsdale, NJ: Laurence Erlbaum.

Graesser, A. C. (1981). *Prose comprehension beyond the word.* New York: Springer-Verlag.

Graesser, A. C., & Clark, L. F. (1985). *Structures and procedures of implicit knowledge.* Norwood, NJ: Ablex.

Graesser, A. C., & Goodman, S. M. (1985). Implicit knowledge, question-answering, and the representation of expository text. In B. Britton & J. B. Black (Eds.), *Understanding expository text.* Hillsdale, NJ: Lawrence Erlbaum.

Graesser, A. C., Haberlandt, K., & Koizumi, D. (in press). How is reading time influenced by knowledge-based inferences and world knowledge? In B. Britton (Ed.), *Executive control processes in reading.* Hillsdale, NJ: Lawrence Erlbaum.

Graesser, A. C., & Murachver, T. (1985). Symbolic procedures of question-answering. In A. C. Graesser & J. B. Black (Eds.), *The psychology of questions.* Hillsdale, NJ: Lawrence Erlbaum.

Graesser, A. C., & Murray, K. (in press). An analysis of verbal protocols to explore the acquisition of a computer environment. In S. P. Robertson, W. Zachary, & J. B. Black (Eds.), *Cognition, computing and interaction.* Norwood, NJ: Ablex.

Graesser, A. C., & Nakamura, G. V. (1982). The impact of a schema on comprehension and memory. In G. H. Bower (Ed.), *The psychology of learning and motivation,* Vol. 16. Hillsdale, NJ: Lawrence Erlbaum.

Graesser, A. C., & Riha, J. R. (1984). An application of multiple regression techniques to sentence reading times. In D. Kieras & M. Just (Eds.), *New methods in comprehension research.* Hillsdale, NJ: Lawrence Erlbaum.

Graesser, A. C., Robertson, S. P., & Anderson, P. A. (1981). Incorporating inferences in narrative representations: A study of how and why. *Cognitive Psychology,* **13**, 1–26.

Haberlandt, K., & Bingham, G. (1982). The role of scripts in the comprehension and retention of texts. *Text,* **2**, 29–46.

Haberlandt, K., & Graesser, A. C. (1985). Component processes in textcomprehension and some of their interactions. *Journal of Experimental Psychology: General,* **114**, 357–374.

Hayes, J. R., & Flower, L. S. (1980). Identifying the organization of writing processes. In L. W. Gregg & E. R. Steinberg (Eds.), *Cognitive processes in writing.* Hillsdale, NJ: Lawrence Erlbaum.

Just, M. A., Carpenter, P. A., & Woolley, J. D. (1982). Paradigms and processes in reading comprehension, *Journal of Experimental Psychology: General,* **111**, 228–238.

Keenan, J. M., Baillet, S. D., & Brown, P. (1984). The effects of causal cohesion on comprehension and memory. *Journal of Verbal Learning and Verbal Behaviour,* **23**, 115–126.

Kieras, D. E. (1982). *What people know about electronic devices: A descriptive study.* Tech. rep. No. 12). Tucson: University of Arizona.

Kintsch, W. (1974). *The representation of meaning in memory.* Hillsdale, NJ: Lawrence Erlbaum.

Kosslyn, S. M. (1980). *Image and mind.* Cambridge, MA: Harvard University Press.

LaBerge, D., & Samuels. S. J. (1974). Toward a theory of automatic information processing during reading. *Cognitive Psychology,* **6**, 293–323.

Lehnert, W. G. (1982). Plot units: A narrative summarization strategy. In W. G. Lehnert & M. H. Ringle (Eds.), *Strategies for natural language processing.* Hillsdale, NJ: Lawrence Erlbaum.

Lewis, C. (1981). Skill in algebra. In J. R. Anderson (Ed.), *Cognitive skills and their acquisition.* Hillsdale, NJ: Lawrence Erlbaum.

Mack, R., Lewis, C., & Carroll, J. (1982). *Learning to use word processors: Problems and prospects.* (Research Rep. No. 42887). New York: IBM Thomas Watson Research Center.

Mandler, J. M. (1984). *Stories, scripts, and scenes.* Hillsdale, NJ: Lawrence Erlbaum.

McKoon, G., & Ratcliff, R. (1981). The comprehension processes and memory structures involved in instrumental inferences. *Journal of Verbal Learning and Verbal Behavior,* **20**, 671–682.

Meyer, B. J. F. (1975). *The organization of prose and effects on memory.* New York: Elsevier.

Minsky, M. (1975). A framework for representing knowledge. In P. H. Winston (Ed.), *The psychology of computer vision.* New York: McGraw-Hill.

Mitchell, D. C., & Green, D. W. (1978). The effects of content on immediate processing in reading. *Quarterly Journal of Experimental Psychology,* **30**, 609–636.

Newell, A., & Simon, H. A. (1972). *Human problem-solving.* Englewood Cliffs, N J: Prentice-Hall.

Nicholas, D. W., & Trabasso, T. (1980). Towards a taxonomy of inferences. In F. Wilkening, J. Becker, & T. Trabasso (Eds.), *Information integration by children*. Hillsdale, NJ: Lawrence Erlbaum.

Nisbett, R. E., & Wilson, T. D. (1977). Telling more than we can know: Verbal reports on mental processes. *Psychological Review,* **84**, 231–279.

Olson, G. M., Duffy, S. A., & Mack, R. L. (1984). Thinking-out-loud as a method for studying real-time comprehension proceses. In D. E. Kieras & M. Just (Eds.), *New methods in the study of immediate processes in comprehension*. Hillsdale, NJ: Lawrence Erlbaum.

Olson, G. M., Duffy, S. A., & Mack, R. L. (1985). Question asking as a component of text comprehension. In A. C. Graesser, & J. B. Black (Eds.), *The psychology of questions*. Hillsdale, NJ: Lawrence Erlbaum.

Posner, M. I., & Snyder, C. R. (1975). Attention and cognitive control. In R. L. Solso (Ed.), *Information processing and cognition: The Loyola symposium*. Hillsdale, NJ: Lawrence Erlbaum.

Reddy, D. R. (1980). Machine models of speech perception. In R. A. Cole (Ed.), *Perception and production of fluent speech*. Hillsdale, NJ: Lawrence Erlbaum.

Reder, L. M. (1982). Elaborations: When do they help and when do they hurt? *Text,* **2**, 211–224.

Robertson, S. P., Black, J. B., & Lehnert, W. G. (1985). Misleading question effects as evidence for integrated question understanding and memory search. In A. C. Graesser & J. B. Black (Eds.), *The psychology of questions*. Hillsdale, NJ: Lawrence Erlbaum.

Rumelhart, D. E. (1977a). Understanding and summarizing brief stories. In D. LaBerge & S. J. Samuels (Eds.), *Basic processes in reading: Perception and comprehension*. Hillsdale, NJ: Lawrence Erlbaum.

Rumelhart, D. E. (1977b). Toward an interactive model of reading. In S. Dornie (Ed.), *Attention and performance VI*. Hillsdale, NJ: Lawrence Erlbaum.

Rumelhart, D. E., & Ortony, A. (1977). The representation of knowledge in memory. In R. C. Anderson, R. J. Spiro, & W. E. Montague (Eds.), *Schooling and the acquisition of knowledge*. Hillsdale, NJ: Lawrence Erlbaum.

Sanford, A. J., & Garrod, S. C. (1981). *Understanding written language: Explorations in comprehension beyond the sentence*. New York: Wiley.

Schank, R. C. (1982). Reminding and memory organization: An introduction to MOPs. In W. G. Lehnert & M. H. Ringle (Eds.), *Strategies of natural language comprehension*. Hillsdale, NJ: Lawrence Erlbaum.

Schank, R. C., & Abelson, R. P. (1977). *Scripts, plans, goals, and understanding*. Hillsdale, NJ: Lawrence Erlbaum.

Sharkey, N. E., & Bower, G. H. (1984). The integration of goals and actions in text understanding. *Proceedings of the Sixth Annual Cognitive Science Society Conference,* Boulder, Colorado.

Sharkey, N. E., & Mitchell, D. C. (1985). Word recognition in a functional context: The use of scripts in reading. *Journal of Memory and Language,* **24**, 253–270.

Shiffrin, D. (1984). How a story says what it means and does. *Text,* **4**, 313–346.

Singer, M. (1981). Verifying the assertions and implications of language. *Journal of Verbal Learning and Verbal Behavior,* **20**, 46–60.

Singer, M. (1985). Mental processes in question answering. In A. C. Graesser & J. B. Black (Eds.), *The psychology of questions.* Hillsdale, NJ: Lawrence Erlbaum.

Sowa, J. F. (1983). *Conceptual structures: Information processing in mind and machine.* Reading, MA: Addison-Wesley.

Stein, N. L., & Glenn, C. G. (1979). An analysis of story comprehension in elementary school children. In R. O. Freedle (Ed.), *New directions in discourse processing* (Vol. 2). Norwood, NJ: Ablex.

Swinney, D. A. (1982). The structure and time-course of information interaction during speech comprehension: Lexical segmentation, access, and interpretation. In J. Mehler, E. C. T. Walker, & G. M. Garrett (Eds.), *Perspectives on mental representation,* Hillsdale, NJ: Lawrence Erlbaum.

Thibadeau, R., Just, M. A., & Carpenter, P. A. (1982). A model of the time cause and content of reading. *Cognitive Science,* **6,** 157–203.

Trabasso, T., Secco, T., & van den Broek, P. (1983). Causal cohesion and story coherence. In H. Mandl, N. L. Stein, & T. Trabasso (Eds.), *Learning and comprehension of text.* Hillsdale, NJ: Lawrence Erlbaum.

van Dijk, T. A. & Kintsch, W. A. (1983). *Strategies of discourse comprehension.* New York: Academic Press.

Walker, C. H., & Yekovich, F. R. (1984). Script-based inferences: Effects of text and knowledge variables on recognition memory. *Journal of Verbal Learning and Verbal Behaviour,* **23,** 357–370.

Waltz, D. L. (1982). The state of the art in natural-language understanding. In W. G. Lehnert & M. H. Ringle (Eds.), *Strategies for natural language processing.* Hillsdale, NJ: Lawrence Erlbaum.

Webber, B. L. (1983). So what can we talk about now? In M. Brady & R. C. Berwick (Eds.), *Computational models of discourse.* Cambridge, MA: MIT Press.

Wilensky, R. (1983). *Planning and understanding.* Cambridge, MA: Addison-Wesley.

Winograd, T. (1972). *Understanding natural language.* New York: Academic Press.

Winston, P. H. (1984). *Artificial intelligence* (2nd ed.) Reading, MA: Prentice-Hall.

# 6

# Neural Nets, Routines, and Semantic Networks

**Lokendra Shastri and Jerome A. Feldman**

## 1. INTRODUCTION

The past few years have witnessed a significant reawakening of interest in massively parallel computation, often portrayed as neural nets. Rapid advances in computational, behavioral theories have brought about a new and much more sophisticated effort to model cognition and perception in physiologically plausible terms. Most of the detailed work has been concerned with relatively peripheral (low conceptual level) activities such as early vision, word recognition, speech and motor control. Higher mental functions such as language comprehension, logical inference and planning have not been treated effectively with massively (brain-scale) parallel techniques and many scientists believe that it is impossible to do so. In this chapter we introduce a set of (connectionist) mechanisms for representation of and inference about conceptual information. We suggest that these mechanisms form an adequate base for the study of problems of higher-level vision and language understanding.

The representation of complex knowledge and associative access to it lie at the core of intelligence. Semantic networks — graph structures with "concepts" as nodes and "associations" as arcs — have became a standard way of envisioning knowledge representation schemes. This chapter suggests a unified approach to semantic network representations, which has a number of advantages over previous schemes.

Semantic network models of various kinds have been used in a wide range of studies in artificial intelligence and cognitive science. One line of work uses "spreading activation" in concept networks to model contextual effects in, e.g., word perception (McClelland & Rumelhart, 1981) disambiguation (Quillian, 1968; Cottrell & Small, 1983), speech production (Dell, 1985) and memory retrieval (Anderson, 1983). Most other work using semantic network models assumes that the network is passive and is *interpreted* by a control program. Interpreted semantic networks can be futher divided into recognition and deduction applications of networks. Recognition of complex visual scenes is almost universally based on network models at the higher conceptual levels (Ballard & Brown, 1982; Marr & Nishihara, 1978) and speech recognition work often has this character (Lowerre & Reddy, 1979). Deduction models employing semantic networks are generally employed in natural language and related research (Walker, 1978; Findler, 1979).

All of these various uses of semantic networks make somewhat different demands on the representation and have evolved to the point where they have distinct computational characteristics. the salient point for our purposes is the presence or absence of a distinct interpreting program that can examine and modify the network. For a variety of reasons to be outlined below, we will consider only systems with no interpreter and attempt to show how such systems can support all the existing applications of semantic networks. The only computational primitives in our models will be the calculation and transmission of activity states. This is the computational characteristic of neural net models — hence the title of the chapter. The underlying thesis of the chapter is that semantic networks have a natural realization in neural nets.

In addition to the general virtues of uniformity we have several technical reasons for exploring activation (or value passing (Fahlman, 1982)) models of semantic networks. One technical problem arises when the information to be captured contains apparently inconsistent statements. A well-known example is given below. The four facts:

Dick is a Quaker
Quakers are pacifists
Republicans are not pacifists
Dick is a Republican

could well arise in real life without causing difficulty. In standard semantic network models using conventional logic as a basis, the four statements entail a contradiction which, in the worst case, could render the system useless. More sophisticated non-monotonic logical treatments (Reiter, 1980), suggest that the system must choose a consistent subset of the four assertions, but this entails making arbitrary choices and amounts to ignoring some of the information provided. There is no denying that Dick could be a Quaker and a Republican at the same time. There is some evidence that Dick is not a pacifist (because he is a Republican and Republicans *tend* to be non-pacifists); at the same time there is some evidence that he is a pacifist (he is a Quaker and Quakers tend to be pacifists). Our semantic network model should be able to incorporate such evidential statements and to draw appropriate inferances from them. The Republican-Quaker example is typical of a large number of evidential conflict situations.

Another technical point that we address in the current model is the specification of 'natural kind' terms. There is no way to specify exactly what conditions are necessary and sufficient to have something be deemed an "elephant" or "chair" or "fight" (Smith & Medin, 1981). We will treat this issue also as one of evidence. The idea is seen most clearly in the realm of visual input, where various features are recognized with varying degrees of confidence. There is an enormous variety of conditions under which one would be willing to assert the presence of a chair. In our treatment, chair legs are evidence for the presence of a chair in the same way that Republicanism is evidence for non-pacifism. The major difficulty with evidential approaches has been the absence of an adequate mathematical theory of evidential reasoning; we say more about this elsewhere (Shastri & Feldman, 1984; Shastri, 1985).

An evidential framework is useful for both characterizing entities and for dealing with conflicting assertions, but one could pursue evidential formulations without abandoning the intepretive version of semantic nets (Lowrance, 1982). Abandoning the interpretive model has several distinct benefits which will be discussed at appropriate places in the chapter. For now, we will be content with one consideration which has led us and others to concentrate on massively parallel, active networks for modelling intelligent behavior.

Psychological and biological results suggest that many cognitive tasks like visual recognition, categorization and associative retrieval do not take more than 100 sequential steps. This follows because typical neuronal firing rates are a few milliseconds and the response time of cognitive agents during numerous experimental tasks is a few hundred milliseconds. This observation imposes a major contraint on the manner in which conceptual information may be organized and accessed and is one reason for our rejection of an interpreter. Other motivations for the choice of spreading activation models include their good fit with human data on retrieval (Dosher, 1983), on errors (Dell, 1985) and the natural mapping to the underlying physiological substrate.

The massively parallel (connectionist) formulation of semantic networks avoids the interpreter bottleneck, but brings in a whole range of new problems in representation, stability, learning, etc. There is a growing literature dealing with these issues. We will concern ourselves in this chapter only with representation questions, using a particular computational model outlined below and presented in detail elsewhere (Feldman & Ballard, 1982). There is enough experience with the theoretical and experimental properties of this formulation to convince us that the key compuatational questions can be resolved. The machine examples in this chapter were built using a general-purpose simulator (Small et al. 1982) which has also been used in a variety of other domains (Addanki, 1983; Cottrell & Small, 1983). By suppressing the computational issues, we are able to focus on the many questions of representation and use of knowledge. The central issue addressed in this chapter is the efficacy of a self-activating semantic network as the vehicle for conceptual reasoning.

## 1.1 The connectionist model

The connectionsit model provides a plausible view of computations carried out in neuronal networks and, independent of any such consideration, is a powerful model of massively parallel computation. The details of the connectionist model in its current state of development have been laid out by Feldman & Ballard (1982), and Feldman (1982). We present the salient features below.

Connectionist networks are made up of *active* elements that are capable of performing simple processing. These units have very high fan-ins and fan-outs and communicate with the rest of the network by transmitting a simple value. A unit transmits the same value to all units to which it is connected. The output value is closely related to the unit's internal potential and is best described as a level of activation. A unit's potential is a function of the amount of activation the unit has been receiving from other units. All inputs are weighted and combined in a manner specified by the *potential function* in order to update a unit's potential. A more technical description follows.

A network consists of a large number of units connected to a large number of other units via links. The units are computational entities defined by:

$\{q\}$:   a small set of states, (fewer than 10)
$p$      a continuous value called potential, roughly the internal level of activation
$v$      an output value, approximately 10 discrete values
$i$      a vector of inputs $i_1, i_2, \ldots i_n$.

together with functions that define the values of potential, state and output at time $t+1$, based on the values at time $t$:

$$p_{t+1} \longleftarrow \mathbf{P}(i_t, p_t, q_t)$$
$$q_{t+1} \longleftarrow \mathbf{Q}(i_t, p_t, q_t)$$
$$v_{t+1} \longleftarrow \mathbf{V}(i_t, p_t, q_t)$$

A unit does not treat all inputs uniformly. Units receive inputs via links (or connections) and each incoming link has an associated *weight*. A weight may have a *positive* or *negative* value. A unit weighs each input using the weight on the appropriate link. Furthermore, a unit may have more than one "input site" and incoming links are connected to specific sites. Each site has an associated site-function. These functions carry out local computations based on the input values at the site, and it is the result of this computation that is processed by the functions $\mathbf{P}$, $\mathbf{Q}$ and $\mathbf{V}$. The notion of sites is useful in defining interesting unit behavior like OR-of-AND. For example, a unit might become active if any one of a number of conditions hold (OR), where each condition requires several simultaneous inputs (AND). The functions **P**, **Q** and **V** are arbitrary, but in keeping with the underlying philosophy of these models it is desired that these functions be "simple."

In our formulation, a semantic network (SN) is an information retrieval mechanism with a limited amount of built-in inference (cf. Allen, 1983). The first issues to be addressed are how a query is presented to an SN and how an answer is returned. In order to keep the treatment uniform, we require that the query be presented and the answer be received in connectionist fashion. This is achieved by introducing simple kinds of routines expressed as connectionist networks. Sequencing in routines is described below. A query arises from a point in a routine where information is needed and answers are returned by activating appropriate units in the inquiring routine. Our routines are like schemas and scripts. Although they are not adequate to model the full range of plans and actions (Schank, 1982) they suffice for our present purposes.

We will start with a trivial example to introduce the notation and general framework of our treatment. Fig. 1 shows a fragment of a simple restaurant routine for a person who always orders one of two lunches depending upon how much the special appeals. A routine is represented as a sequence of nodes (units) connected so that activation can serve to sequence through the routine. Stepping from one node in a routine to its successor will depend on a completion signal which will not be shown explicitly in the figures. We depict action steps as oval-shaped nodes, queries as hexagonal nodes and answers as circular ones. In this routine, ordering a meal gives rise to a query about the agent's desire for ham, directed to the sematic network which this chapter is attempting to characterize. Answers are returned from the semantic network by sending activation to the [yes] and [no] units in the routine. The [yes] and [no] nodes are primed by the question unit to be responsive to activation and are connected in a WTA (winner-take-all) fashion to force a decision. Whichever answer node dominates will activate its successor and thus trigger the appropriate speech act. We will obviously be dealing with more complex routines, queries and answers, but the basic structure of this example will be meaintained throughout the chapter.

Even this simple example raises the question of parameterized routines. The query to the semantic network must include some situational information, namely the special featured that day. Routines will generally include several such parameters that must be specified in the extraction of the routine. We call these *roles*. Roles will play a central part in our treatment. A role will be *bound* to a *concept* for the execution of its routine. In Fig. 1, the [special] role might be bound to [ham]. We assume that this binding is implemented by a dyanamic link network (cf. Feldman, 1982) so that activating either end of the [special ~ ham] link will activate the other end. Notive that the binding will permit parameterized actions such as ordering ham when ham is the daily special. Roles correspond to typed or sorted free variables in a formulation based on mathematical logic.

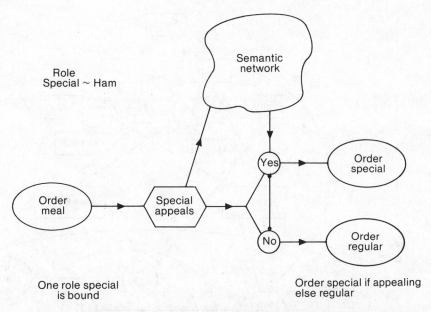

Fig. 1. — Simplified view of a query: a query is posed by activation of the hexagonal node, which activates semantic nodes. These trigger an appropriate response (round) node which can then enable an action (oval) node.

World knowledge, such as one's taste for ham, is encoded in the semantic network (SN) which is the main focus of this chapter. We now give a crude overview of how the SN and the luncheon routine would interact in choosing what to order. The various concepts in the SN will be represented by individual nodes, which will be depicted by rectangular boxes. Since there is no interpreter, the links between concepts will have to be highly specific in their spreading of activation. The oversimplified network gvien in Fig. 1 has each kind of food directly linked to the answers for which it is appropriate. In this case, activating the question [special appeals?] activates the role node for [special] which activates its binding [ham]. The [ham] unit in the role network would directly activate the [ham] node in the SN which would send activation to the particular [yes] node of this routine (as well as to many other places). Since this routine and the particular [yes] node are enabled, activation continues to the appropriate response. The dynamic link [special ~ ham] will then cause the word "ham" to be spoken when the [order special] action is carried out.

The remainder of the chapter is concerned with the details of this process. Fig. 2 gives a more accurate indication of the knowledge representation mechanism. The network in Fig. 2 encodes the following information:

HAM and YAM are two types of objects in the domain.

Objects in the example domain are characterized by two properties, *HAS-TASTE* and *HAS-FOOD-KIND*

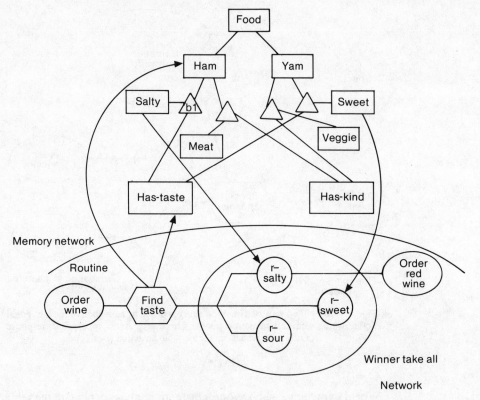

Fig. 2. — A more detailed query example: each triangular node links attributes,
objects and values and becomes active when any two of its inputs are active.

HAM is SALTY in taste and is a kind of MEAT.
YAM is SWEET in taste and is kind of VEGETABLE.

Each arc in the network represents a pair of links, one in either direction.
We are using an arc in place of a pair of links to improve the readibility of
these diagrams. The triangular nodes in the network associate objects,
properties and property values.

Each node is a computing element and, when in an "active" state, sends
out activation to all the nodes connected to it. A node may become active on
receiving activation from another node or an external source. Triangular
nodes behave slightly differently in that they become active only on
receiving simultaneous activation from two nodes.

The crude description given above is sufficient to demonstrate how
simple recognition and retrieval tasks may be outlined by such networks. To
find an object in the network with a salty taste one would activate the nodes
*HAS-TASTE* and SALTY. The triangular node linking *HAS-TASTE* and SALTY

will receive coincident activation along two of its links and become active. As a result, it will transmit activation to HAM which will ultimately become active (have high potential and output).

Alternatively, assume that one is interested in finding out the taste of HAM. This could be done by activating the nodes *HAS-TASTE* and HAM. This will cause the same triangular node to become active and transmit activation to SALTY. The time course of this query in the system of Shastri & Feldman (1984) is shown in Fig. 3. The nodes for HAM and HAS-TASTE were activated

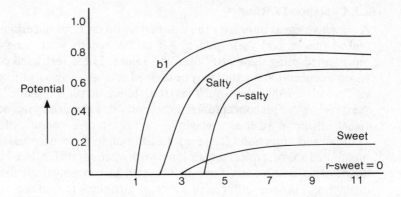

Fig. 3. — The activation of selected nodes in Fig. 2 for the query "HAM HAS-TASTE?" The binder node b1 activates the knowledge unit "salty" which triggers the response "r-salty".

at time = 0 and the response network (r-nodes) was enabled. Since node b1 has two active inputs, its activity rises quickly and spreads to the SALTY node. This in turn activates the r-salty node in the enabled response work. There is an indirect path from HAM through FOOD to YAM allowing some activation through b2 of SWEET, but the corresponding response node r-sweet never overcomes the inibition from r-salty so the answer is unequivocal. The details of two different computational models of this behavior are given elsewhere (Shastri & Feldman, 1984; Shastri, 1985). Here, we will focus on issues of representation and inference, supressing computational details.

## 2. STRUCTURE OF KNOWLEDGE

In developing a framework for representing conceptual knowledge we will concern ourselves with the *internal* representation that a cognitive agent may have of the external world. We are not interested in the external world *per se* but rather in an agent's conceptualization of the external world. The knowledge embodied in the agent's internal representation is highly *structured* and *interrelated* and is less a collection of "facts" than an intricately woven fabric of interrelated items which fit together to form a **conceptual structure**. In this section we will develop a vocabulary to decribe the conceptual strucute and to specify the interactions that occur within it. This chapter does not address all the relevant issues and although some important problems are analysed in depth, some others are merely identified. The framework shares features with other semantic network (Brachman, 1982; Fahlman, 1979) and frame-based (Minsky, 1975; Roberts & Goldstein, 1977) schemes, but differs from all of these in several fundamental respects.

### 2.1 Conceptual attributes

A cognitive agent interprets the external world in terms of certain conceptual attributes and their *values*. All of the agent's world knowledge is represented using these attributes and values. In the restricted context of vision a conceptual stucture may be defined in terms of visual attributes such as "color" (with values such as red, blue, purple), "shape", "size", "texture", etc. This conceptual structure may be extended by including non-visual attributes such as "weight", "temperature", "odor", "location", "utility" and "function" (i.e. use). In addition to the conceptual attributes mentioned above, typical semantic network relations such as *is-a-kind-of*, *is-a-part-of*, *is-an-element-of* are also treated as conceptual attributes. The distinction between differerent kinds of attributes is dicussed in Section 2.3.1.

The explicit identification of attibutes and their values is a crucial step in extracting the structure of knowledge. All the components of the conceptual structure are defined in terms of these attributes and values. Hereafter we use the term attribute to mean conceptual attribute.

Attributes need not be primitive. For example, a complex attribute like "shape" may have finer structure consisting of several "sub" attributes such as "length to breadth ratio" or "relations between subparts", Similarly, "physical property" may be regarded as an attribute is some domain but may be composed of more specific attributes like "size", "weight", "color", etc.

### 2.2 Conceptual entities

The primary level of organization in the conceptual structure centers around the notion of **conceptual entities**. These are *labelled* collections of coherent <attribute, value> pairs. For instance, an entity labelled FIDO may partially consist of the following <attribute, value> pairs: "*is-an-instance of* DOG, *is-an-instance-of* ANIMAL, *has-body-part* LEGS, *has-body-part* TAIL, *has-coat-type* FURRY ...". The values of attibutes are conceptual entities and hence conceptual entities may be arbitrarily complex. This definition does not suggest circularity because some conceptual entities are grounded in preception. Conceptual entities are like **concepts** in semantic networks and will often be referred to as such.

Entities may denote different sorts of things in the domain such as objects categories, events, locations and relations. For instance, entities may denote "my dog Fido", "the color red", "dog", "color", "the Sox Phillies game", "the concert tonight" or "John's passing of the ball to Leo".

Different classes of entities may have different sorts of <attribute, value> pairs associated with them. Thus, physical objects may have attributes mentioned earlier such as "*is-an-instance-of*", "*has-color*", "*has-shape*" and "*has-size*", whereas attributes associated with events may be "*has-location*", "*has-agent*", "*has-time-of-occurrence*" etc.

We do not suggest that all knowledge can be usefully captured as attribute–value pairs. It is technically true that a multi-place relation like *between* could be broken down into properties; such a representation would not yield the rapid inferences that we require. This chapter concentrates on knowledge that is effectively treatable as semantic networks.

### 2.2.1 What distinguishes a conceptual entity

Although any possible collection of <attribute, value> pairs is a potential entity, *only explicitly labelled collections are entities*. Which collections of <attribute, value> pairs will be grouped together to form entities will primarily depend on an underlying *theory of learning or concept formation*; and, with less import, on the domain being modelled. We develop these ideas further in Section 4.4.

### 2.3 CONCEPTUAL STRUCTURE

### 2.3.1 Properties and structural links

Conceptual entities were described above as collections of <attribute, value> pairs wherein each <attribute, value> pair related the entity being described to another entity. Attributes are classified into two broad categories: *PROPERTIES* and *structural links*. This is a crucial distinction which forms the basis of controlled interactions that may occur between entities. Italicized lower case will be used to refer to structure link names and italicized upper-case to refer to property names.

Structural links provide the coupling between structure and inference. They reflect the epistemological belief that world knowledge is highly organized and that much of this structure can be factored out to provide general **domain independent** inference rules. Structural links are attributes that have this quality and are used to provide built-in inference paths. The most representative structural link is the *is-an-instance-of* link that is used for "inheritance" in semantic networks. We employ an extended notion of property inheritance and include other structural links such as the *is-a-part-of* links used to infer values of attributes such as *HAS-LOCATION*, and *occurred-during* links (Allen, 1983) (used to make inferences pertaining to time). Each structural link has an associated set of properties that may be inherited along the link and this information is used to perform inferences.

Properties correspond to the intrinsic features of concepts and thus may vary from domain to domain. When describing physical objects the relevant properties may be *HAS-WEIGHT*, *HAS-SHAPE* and *HAS-COLOR*, while events may have properties like *HAS-LOCATION*, *HAS-AGENT* and *HAS-TIME-OF-OCCURRENCE*. Properties roughly correspond to the notion of "roles" of KL-ONE (Brachman, 1982). "role nodes" of NETL (Fahlman, 1979) and "slots" of FRL (Roberts & Goldstein, 1977).

### 2.3.2 Types and Tokens

An entity may be classified as either a **Type** or a **Token**. Elements of the physical world that are interpreted as *instances* by the agent are represented as Tokens in his conceptual structure. For example, Tokens may represent "Fido the Dog", "the table in my office" and "the location that is the top of my table". Types refer to *abstractions* defined over Tokens. A Type, when instantiated or individual, maps into a Token, but by itself does not represent an instance in the external world. Types are summary descriptions that may be viewed as encoding the agent's belief that there are objects in the physical world that *conform* to these descriptions and that these descriptions may be used to make inferences about objects. Examples of Types are "Apple" and "Dog". Types serve two important purposes: they help structure and organize the knowledge about Tokens so that the "quantum" of knowledge remains within manageable bounds and, more importantly, they provide the basis for inductive learning and the encoding of abstractions.

The *is-an-instance-of* relation expresses the relationship between Tokens and Types while the inverse relationship between Types and Tokens is expressed by the *"is-instantiated-by"*. Thus, FIDO *is-an-instance-of* DOG and DOG *is-instantiated-by* FIDO. Henceforth, we will use small capitals to denote Tokens and Types.

Contrary to many standard interpretations, our framework does not define a Type to be a set of Tokens. Both Types and Tokens are entities and hence have a similar syntactic structure, namely a collection of <attribute, value> pairs. They differ in that *a value owned by a Type describes the value of a property shared by a large number of its Tokens* (This notion will be refined in due course). Thus, the Type ELEPHANT may own the *value* GRAY for the *property HAS-COLOR* to represent the fact "most elephants are gray". However, the Type ELEPHANT would not own any value for the property *HAS-AGE* because the instances of elephants would not have any characteristic value for this property.

### 2.3.3 Hierarchies

The process of abstraction need not stop at one level. Abstractions over Types may yield more abstract Types (or a Type may be differentiated to produce more refined Types). This leads to a hierarchical structure. In general, multiple hierarchies may be defined over the same set of Tokens. For example, a dog is a kind of animal but is also a kind of pet; similarly, a friend of mine is human, a graduate student, male, a classical music aficionado and, of course, a friend. The result of having multiple hierarchies is that each Token may be related to more than one Type via the same structural relation. The formulation developed here allows any number of hierarchies to be defined on the underlying tokens as long as the resulting structure is acyclic. An example of such an acyclic structure is shown in Fig. 4. Note that DOG is related to two Types via the *is-an-instance-of* relation, namely, ANIMAL and PET.

The heirarchies are not limited to those defined by the relation *is-an-instance-of*. Other structural relations like *is-a-part-of* and *is-a-member-of* also define hierarchies over the tokens. These hierarchies differ in the nature of inheritance that may occur along them, as described earlier in Section 2.3.1.

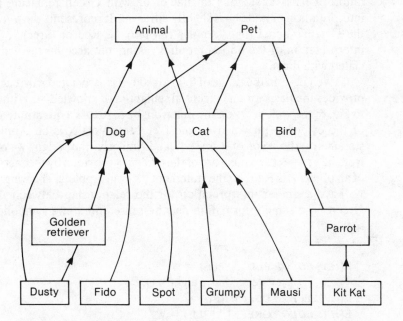

.Fig. 4. — Simplified *is-an-instance-of* acyclic network.

## 2.4 A REPRESENTATIONAL NOTATION

We employ a graphical notation in order to present the role of evidence in the representational framework. Fig. 5 displays a sample network encoding the following information: "Fruits are a kind of Thing, Apple is a kind of Fruit, Things have the property Color, Apples are generally Red or Green, and Red and Green are instances of Color. Arcs in the figure are simplified representations of links. There exists a simple mapping between networks depicted in this section and the actual connectionist network implementation as described by Shastri & Feldman (1984). Recall that the major goal of this research is to construct networks that perform simple inferences without an interpreter.

The representation uses three kinds of nodes: the Type node, the Token node and the Binder node. Type and Token nodes label collections of <attribute, value> pairs. Properties and values are associated to concepts via Binder nodes and structural links are encoded directly as links. The framework permits associating properties as well as property values with concepts. For example, the binder node b1 in the above network associates the property of having color with Things (and hence Fruits and Apples) without specifying any particular color values. On the other hand the Binder node b2 represents "the value of the property color for Apples may be Red" and also "something that has color Red may be an Apple". The interpretation of b3 is analogous to that of b2 with Green replacing Red. The interpretation of node b4 is slightly different. It represents the *uncertainty* in the system's belief that "Apples can *only* be Red or Green". The exact interpretation of the notion requires taking into account the weights associated with links.

A weight — in the range of 0.00 to 1.00 — is associated with each link and provides the basis for an evidential semantics of knowledge. With reference to Fig. 5, the weight W1 on the link from b2 to RED is a quantitative measure of the evidence provided by the fact "an object X is an Apple" to the statement "the color of X is Red" and similarly, the weight W4 on the link from b2 to APPLE is a measure of the evidence provided by the fact "the color of an object X is Red" to the statement "X is an Apple". The weights W2 and W5 have a similar interpretation for the relationship between Apple and Green. The same information may be represented in a symbolic notation such as:

$$E(\textit{HAS-COLOR} \text{ RED} | \text{ APPLE}) = W1$$
$$(\text{evidence has weight } W1).$$
$$E(\text{APPLE} | \textit{HAS-COLOR} \text{ RED}) = W4.$$
$$E(\textit{HAS-COLOR} \text{ GREEN} | \text{ APPLE}) = W2.$$
$$E(\text{APPLE} | \textit{HAS-COLOR} \text{ GREEN}) = W5.$$

The weights are not independent. For instance, the weights on links from Binders that relate RED to Concepts that are red in color add up to 1.0, and similarly the weights on links from Binders relating APPLE to its various color value nodes should also add up to 1.0 ($W1 + W2 + W3 = 1.0$). The weight W3 is a measure of the "ignorance" or "uncertainty" in the information about Apples and their color and is equal to: $1.0 - (W1 + W2)$. W6 is equal to W3 but encodes negative evidence for APPLE which comes into play *only if the value specified for color is neither Red nor Green*. If no color value is specified or if the specified value is Red or Green, the negative evidence is disabled.

We would like to point out some salient features of the representation.

i.     Necessary properties and sufficient properties: The weights on links

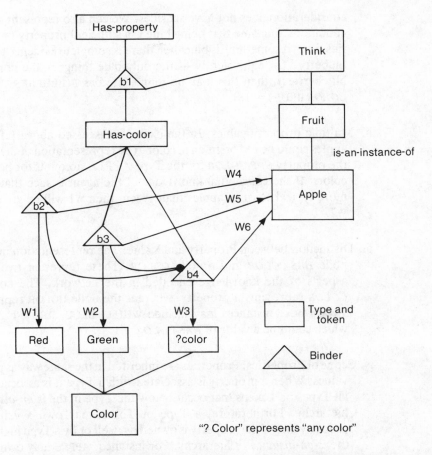

Fig. 5. — Evidential links in the semantic network: for example, the node b2 and weight w4 encode the evidence that a thing is an apple, given that it is red.

from owners to binders provide a mechanism for encoding the differences in the strength of the generalizations represented by a Type. Consider the following assertions about Types and properties.

(a)  Hexagons have six sides.
(b)  Dogs have four legs.
(c)  Birds fly.
(d)  Apples are red.

(a) and (b) are examples of assertions with the highest evidential weights, followed by weights of assertions (c) and (d). In particular, (a) is a statement about a necessary property of hexagons. The use of negative evidence permits the representation of necessary property value. Because a hexagon necessarily has six sides (a) will be encoded as $E(HAS\text{-}NUMBER\text{-}OF\text{-}SIDES \ 6| \ HEXAGON) = 1.0$ and hence HEXAGON would receive an extremely high negative evidence if the object under consideration does not have six sides. We can also represent sufficient conditions. Imagine that being blue is a sufficient property of blueberries, i.e. "if something is blue then there is complete evidence that it is a bluberry" (or equivalently — the only blue things in the domain are blueberries), then this may be represented as E(BLUEBERRIES| *HAS-COLOR* BLUE) = 1.0.

ii. Multiple property values: In the example discussed above (cf. Fig. 5) apples could be red or green in color. The representation of the value of the property *HAS-COLOR* for the Type APPLE accounts for both these colors. If the conceptual knowledge of the agent is such that red is a more typical color of apples than green, then w1 will be greater than w2.

iii. Distinction between Property and Value: The representation includes a node *HAS-COLOR* and a node COLOR. These represent two distinct aspects of the knowledge encoded in the network. The node *HAS-COLOR* represents a property, whereas the node COLOR represents a Type whose instances may include WHITE, BLUE, RED etc., each of which could be a value of *HAS-COLOR*.

iv. Scope of Properties: Properties are inherited in the same way as property values. When a property is associated with a Type it is associated with all Types or Tokens that occur below the Type in the *is-an-instance-of* hierarchy. Furthermore, a Type or Token may own a value for a property only if the property is owned by itself or by a Type higher up in the *is-an-instance-of* hierarchy. For instance, APPLE may own a value for *HAS-COLOR* because that property is owned by FRUIT which is a superType of APPLE.

## 2.4.1 Representation of exceptions

In standard representation schemes, attaching a value V1 for the property P1 to a Type T1 is considered equivalent to declaring that for all x, if the type of x is T1, then P1 of x has value V1, or in formal logic:

$$\forall x \; \text{TYPE}(x, T1) \Rightarrow P1(x, V1)$$

for instance,

$$\forall x \; \text{TYPE}(x, \text{APPLE}) \Rightarrow \text{COLOR}(x, \text{RED})$$

The representation of a Token of T1 which does not agree with the value of the property P1 causes problems. This problem is referred to as the problem of exceptions and cancellation in AI (Touretsky, 1984; Etherington & Reiter, 1983).

There would indeed be a problem if one were to interpret the following two assertions together:

(1) $\forall x$ TYPE$(x, T1) \Rightarrow P1(x, V1)$
(2) TYPE$(A, T1)$ & P1$(A, V2)$
(3) V1 $\neq$ V2

There cannot be any satisfactory interpretation of these two statements: they are simply inconsistent (assuming P1$(x,y) \Rightarrow (\forall z$ P1$(x,y) \Rightarrow z=y))$.

The explicit distinction between Types and properties and the evidential semantics of our representation provides a natural representation of "exceptions" and gives a clean semantics to the *is-an-instance-of* link. In this framework, *all exceptions are stated in terms of property values* and not Type memberships. Thus, either a Token is an instance of a Type or it is not and the *is-an-instance-of* link states this unequivocally (The same applies to subTypes and superTypes).

Our evidential framework allows the representation of a range of "quantifications" — universal quantification being a limiting case — and at the same time rules out genuinely meaningless statements. In this framework, one cannot say both

"All Swans are white" and
"Giselle is a Swan whose color is Black".

However, one may say,

"Most Swans are white" and
"Giselle is a Swan whose color is Black".

The following example illustrates the way exceptions are handled:

Let us assume that SWAN is a Type represented in the conceptual structure and that one of the abstractions it encodes is: "all Swans are white", i.e. "if something is a Swan then there is absolute evidence that its color is white". Fig. 6 depicts SWAN along with an instance HANSA — notice that the weight from b1 to WHITE equals 1.0. If a new instance (GISELLE) is introduced such that all its properties match those of SWAN except that it is black, the network modification rules would have to choose between three alternatives: (1) lower the weight W1 therby redefining SWAN and attach the new instance below SWAN, **or** (2) classify the new instance as something other than SWAN and represent it seprately, **or** (3) split SWAN into subTypes on the basis of the property *HAS-COLOR* and attach the instance to the appropriate subType. The first case corresponds to representing exceptions and is illustrated in Fig. 7. The crucial point is that GISELLE may not be

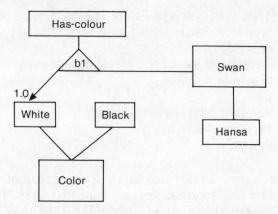

Fig. 6. — A Semantic network fragment that believes all swans are white.

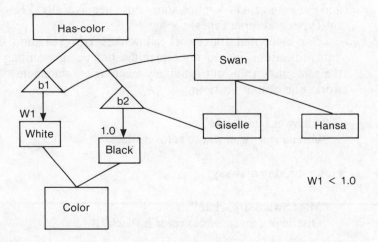

Fig. 7. — Upon Learning of a black swan (Giselle), the network would have to revise
its belief that all swans are white.

attached as an instance of SWAN unless the weight of the link from b1 to
WHITE is reduced to a value less than 1.0. No such implementation of
learning and network modification has been yet implemented.

Not making this distinction between properties and Types leads to
confused interpretations of the *is-an-instance-of* link (the "infamous" IS-A
link). The cancellation of IS-A links to handle exceptions is symptomatic of
this confusion. For a discussion of these problems see Brachman (1982).

### 2.4.2 Types and Prototypes

The use of weighted links leads to an interesting consequence. What would happen if the network were to "imagine a Type"? For a moment assume that this is akin to activating the Type node and letting activation spread to the binder nodes. The weights on the links from owners to binders will select the most typical values of each of the properties owned by the Type (it is assumed that typical values have higher weights than less typical ones). Thus, the resulting imagined instance of a Type will correspond to a maximally typical instance of the Type (not necessarily an actual instance). This observation suggests that treating links between owners and binders as weighted links obviates the need to store exemplars and prototypes in the representation of Types in order to explain certain behavioral results. The representation of a Type does double duty and acts as if it were a prototypical representation besides being an abstract representation of a class of Tokens.

## 2.5 EVIDENTIAL BASIS OF CATEGORIZATION (RECOGNITION)

In Section 2.4 we observed that weighted links provide a mechanism for discriminating between different levels of confidence in the generalization made by Types. In this section we consider the obverse namely *categorizing* an occurrence (assigning a Type to a collection of <property, value> pairs) on the basis of the property values.

It is possible to make the process of categorization entirely symmetrical to the process of retrieval by using the weights on links from binders to owners. With the weights taken into account, a match between property values of a Token and the property values of a Type can be assigned a metric. This process may be described as that of collecting weighted votes: each Type receives some "evidence" from its binders if a value of the Token's property matches that of the Type's. This evidence is combined and each Type ends up with a quantitative measure for the goodness of its match with the Token. The Type with the highest number wins. Furthermore, the metric can be used to explain what is meant by a Token being a stereotypical or prototypical instance of a category. If a Token has property values that match the most of the typical values of the Type then this Token appears to be more stereotypical. This is a simplified version of the visual categorization model presented in (Feldman, 1982); this paper supplies the elaborated semantic net model promised there. In terms of Rosch's work on prototypicality (Rosch 1975; Smith & Medin 1981), a Robin matches most of the properties of the representation of the Type Bird whereas a Penguin matches only a few.

## 3. INFERENCE IN MEMORY NETWORKS

Section 2 described a notation for representing conceptual knowledge and also provided a partial specification of active networks capable of performing limited inferences on the information represented in them. In this section we define the inferences computable within these networks and describe how these can be extended by the use of routines.

The basis for the built-in inference mechanisms is controlled spreading of activation. Unlike conventional semantic networks, our networks are not accessed by an interpreter. Consequently, the limited inference mechanisms have to be hardwired into the network. This makes these networks more complicated than typical semantic networks. Additional machinery is needed to control the spreading of activation. In order to keep the exposition clear, we will introduce these additions. The method we have adopted is that of presenting a number of examples that illustrate the various mechanisms involved. The exact rules governing the spreading of activation are given by Shastri & Feldman (1984).

As discussed in Section 1, questions for the Memory Network arise from routines and the answers are assumed to be conveyed to Answer Networks which form part of the routines. We will first specify the types of queries the Memory Network can answer and then describe the mechanism for posing a query to and receiving an answer from the Memory Network.

### 3.1 Nature of queries

The questions to the Memory Network are framed in terms of conceptual entities (concept), conceptual attributes (attribute) and the values of conceptual attributes (value). There are three classes of basic queries that may be posed:
060
#### Class I queries

These queries specify a concept and one of its attributes and seek the value of the specified attribute for the concept. An example of such a query is, "What is the taste of Ham?" For the sake of brevity and uniformity we will express all queries of this class as ?$v(o\ a)$, which may be read as, "What is the value of the <u>attribute</u> **a** of the <u>concept</u> **o**?" Thus,

"What is the taste of Ham?" becomes:

?**v** (HAM *HAS-TASTE*).

"What is the color of an Apple?" maps to:

?**v** (**APPLE** *HAS-COLOR*).

As another example, consider the query:

"What is the nose a part of?" which is expressed in this notation as:

?**v** (NOSE *is-a-part-of*).

#### Class II queries

These queries specify one or more attributes along with their values and seek an entity that best matches this description. In our notation these queries are expressed as ?$o\{(a\ v)\}$, which may be read as, "Which object **o** is described by the following attribute value pairs $\{(a\ v)\}$?" Some examples follow:

"Find a red fruit" →

?**o** {(*is-a-subtype-of FRUIT*) (*HAS-COLOR* RED)}

"Name an animal that flies, is white and quacks" →

?**o** {(*is-a-kind-of ANIMAL*)  (*HAS-MODE-OF-LOCOMOTION* FLYING)
(*HAS-COLOR* WHITE) (*HAS-SOUND* "quack-quack")}

### Class III queries

Class III queries seek the attribute that corresponds to an attribute value of
an entity. These queries are represented as ?**a**(**o v**). For instance:

"What property of Apple has the value Red?" →

?**a** (APPLE RED)

### Queries as multiple choice questions

In this formulation we will assume that all questions posed to the memory
network are multiple choice questions. For present purposes, this may be
treated as a restriction on the kinds of queries that the network can answer.
A wide variety of access to the network essentially consists of dealing with
multiple choice questions in the sense that the process of accessing the
information in the network may be viewed as selecting the best among a set
of hypotheses on the basis of the evidence provided by the network and the
query.

Besides including the choices specified in the question, the set of
hypotheses being evaluated explicitly includes two additional choices that
correspond to the answer "do not know". The additional choices are:

(1) "unable to pick a clear winner because of conflicting evidence".
(2) "unable to decide because none of the hypotheses is receiving supporting evidence".

The idea of an explicit set of answers fits in well with the routine networks
described in Section 1 (recall the use of [yes] [no] nodes in the example
routine shown in Fig. 1). The use of "do not know" option allows us to
account explicitly for uncertainty; Section 3.4 describes how the "do not
know" response may be used for controlling inference. Some situations may
require handling questions that are not multiple choice; such cases are
discussed in Section 4.2.

In the light of the assumption that all questions are multiple choice, all
queries (at least implicitly) include an enumeration of the possible answers.
Thus, the queries corresponding to the above examples would look like:

?**v** {SALTY SWEET SOUR} (HAM *HAS-TASTE*)

?**v** {RED BLUE GREEN} (APPLE *HAS-COLOR*)

?**o** {APPLE PEAR BLUEBERRY} {(*HAS-COLOR RED*)(*is-a-kind-of* FRUIT)}

?**p** {*HAS-TASTE HAS-SHAPE HAS-COLOR*} (APPLE RED).

## 3.2 Query interface to the Memory Network

We now describe how routines pose queries to and receive responses from the Memory Network.

Queries originate from hexagonal nodes in routines called Query nodes. Each Query node is connected to the appropriate nodes in the Memory Network. If the routine includes roles that need to be bound during excution, the links between the Query nodes and the appropriate nodes inthe Memory Network are established via the Role Network. When a Query node is activated is sends activation to all the nodes it is connected to.

The multiple choices that make up the possible answers to the query are encoded within the routine in the form of a WTA network and are referred to as the Answer Network. These networks contain a node for each of the possible responses to the query and two special purpose nodes called the [?-conflict] node and the [?-no-info] node. The Answer Networks are designed such that the [?-conflict] nodes win the competition if there is a lack of decisive evidence and none of the possible responses is a clear winner, while the [?-no-info] nodes dominate the competition if none of the possible responses are supported by the Memory Network.

Consider a routine that decides whether some food goes well with red wine. One may imagine such a routine to include the following query: "Which of these best describes the taste of the food: Sweet, Sour or Salty"? The above routine fragment includes a role "food" that becomes bound to the appropriate food item when the routine is invoked. For instance, if the routine were to be invoked to decide, "Does Ham go well with red wine?", the role "food" would be bound to "Ham" via a dynamic link. The connections are depicted in Fig. 8 which we explain below.

The query denoted by the routine in this example is of the form ?v {SWEET SOUR SALTY} (HAM HAS-TASTE). This is encoded by *direct* links from the Query node TASTE-OF-FOOD in the routine to HAS-TASTE, O-ENABLE and P-ENABLE nodes, and via *dynamic* links to the HAM node. The function of the enable nodes is explained below. Following the Query node, the routine includes an Answer Network with a node assigned to each of the three candidate responses, SWEET, SALTY and SOUR (as a matter of convention, we will label these units r-SWEET, r-SALTY, and r-SOUR). The nodes thus assigned are connected, one to one, to the nodes representing the entities SWEET, SALTY and SOUR in the Memory Network. These links are directional: the activation flows from nodes in the Memory Network to nodes in the Answer Network. The latter accumulate activation arriving from the Memory Network and compete with each other to decide on the correct answer. The first node in the Answer Network to cross a preset threshold is considered to be the answer. As explained earlier, the Answer Network also includes the [?-conflict] and [?-no-info] nodes and any of these may dominate under the specified conditions.

## 3.3 Inference in the Memory Network

We now present examples that illustrate the inference process. The dynamics of these networks and the computational details pertaining to the

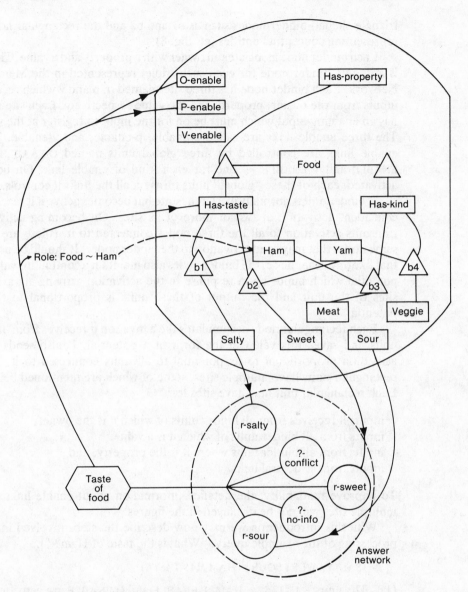

Fig. 8. — Details of the activation and enabling links for a query "HAM HAS-TASTE?"

implementation of these machines are described by Shastri & Feldman (1984).

### Example I

As the first example we consider the query:

?v {SWEET SALTY SOUR} (HAM *HAS-TASTE*)

We have seen the way this query is set up in the networks in Fig. 8. To see how the query is processed we need to examine the functioning of the triangle-shaped binder nodes such as b1 and b2 and the rectangular nodes representing conceptual entities (cf. Fig. 8).

Each binder node associates an owner with a property and a value. There is a unique binder node for each such triplet represented in the Memory Network. Each binder node has three sites named o, p and v which receive inputs from the owner, property and the value respectively. Each site also has an enabling input which must be on for the input to register at the site. The three enable links are called o-enable, p-enable, and v-enable. The enable links are controlled by three global units named O-ENABLE, P-ENABLE and V-ENABLE — one for each kind of enable link. On being activated, each of these "global" units turns on all the links it controls.

A binder unit is normally in a latent state but becomes active if it receives coincident activation at two or more of its sites. On becoming active it transmits activation to all the three nodes connected to it. (these are the same nodes that may send activation to the binder node.) It should be noted that like any other node, the binder nodes also maintain a continuous valued potential which builds up in response to the activation arriving at various sites of the unit and the output of these units is proportional to their potential.

Each rectangular node accumulates the activation it receives from other units and saves this value in the form of a potential. It also sends out activation proportional to its potential to all units connected to it. The rectangular units have multiple sites, some of which are mentioned below. Each rectangular unit may have sites for:

inputs it receives from all binder units of which it is the owner,
inputs from all binder units of which it is a value.
inputs from all binder units where it is the property, and
inputs from structural links.

To improve readability, the detailed information about enable links and multiple sites will not be displayed in the figures.

With this introduction we may now describe the steps involved in the processing of the example query: "What is the taste of Ham?" i.e.

?v {SALTY SWEET SOUR} (HAM HAS-TASTE)

(1)   The units HAS-TASTE, HAM, P-ENABLE and O-ENABLE are activated.
(2)   The activation spreads and results in the node b1 (cf. Fig. 8) becoming active as two of its sites — o and p — receive simultaneous activation (along with the enable signals).
(3)   b1 in turn activates SALTY.
(4)   In the next few time steps, the potential of r-SALTY builds up and as there is no competition it soon reaches a high value, indicating that the answer to the query is SALTY. A trace of the potential of selected units is shown in Fig. 9.

More examples can be based on the Memory Network shown in Fig. 10. (The links from the property node HAS-COLOR to the various Binder nodes

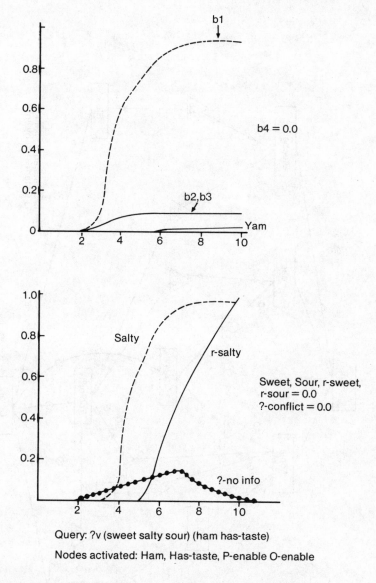

Fig. 9 — Activation trace of selected nodes for the query "HAM HAS-TASTE?"

and the enable signals are not shown in the figure.) The information encoded in the network may be summarized as follows:

"Apples, Pears and Blueberries are three kinds of Fruits. Apples are generally Red or Green, Pears are generally Green and Blueberries are always Blue. Most Red things are Apples, most Green things are Pears but some are also Apples and all Blue things are Blueberries. MAC6 and YEL1 are two instances of Apples".

In terms of the evidential semantics the information encoded is as follows:

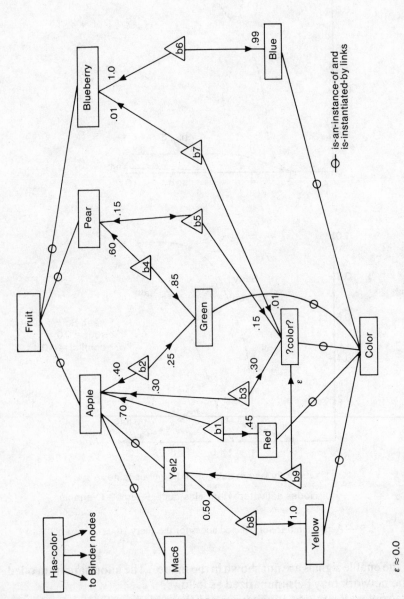

All binder nodes have an input from Has-color and inputs from enable nodes

⊖ is-an-instance-of and
is-instantiated-by links

ε ≈ 0.0

Fig. 10. — Another network, showing details of evidential weights involving fruits and colors.

E($HAS\text{-}COLOR$ RED| APPLE) = 0.45
E($HAS\text{-}COLOR$ GREEN| APPLE) = 0.25
E($HAS\text{-}COLOR$ ? | APPLE) = 0.30
E($HAS\text{-}COLOR$ GREEN| PEAR) = 0.85
E($HAS\text{-}COLOR$ ? | PEAR) = 0.15
E($HAS\text{-}COLOR$ BLUE| BLUEBERRY) = 0.99
E($HAS\text{-}COLOR$ ? | BLUEBERRY) = 0.01
E($HAS\text{-}COLOR$ YELLOW| YEL2) = 1.0

and

E(APPLE| $HAS\text{-}COLOR$ RED) = 0.70
E(APPLE023 $HAS\text{-}COLOR$ GREEN) = 0.40
E(PEAR| $HAS\text{-}COLOR$ GREEN) = 0.60
E(BLUEBERRY| $HAS\text{-}COLOR$ BLUE) = 1.0
E(YEL2| $HAS\text{-}COLOR$ YELLOW) = 0.50

For each of the following examples we will state the query, list the nodes in the Memory Network activated by it, specifying the structural links that it enables and trace the potential of a select set of nodes.

### Example II
Query:

?v {RED GREEN BLUE YELLOW} (MAC6 $HAS\text{-}COLOR$)

Nodes Activated:

$HAS\text{-}COLOR$, MAC6, P-ENABLE and O-ENABLE

Structural Link enabled:

*is-an-instance-of*

Response Nodes:

r-RED r-GREEN r-BLUE r-YELLOW [?-conflict] [?-no-info]

Fig. 11 traces the potential of the nodes: APPLE, the four instances of COLOR, and the corresponding nodes in the Answer Network. In brief, the activation moves up the *is-an-instance-of* link to APPLE. Now both b1 and b2 become active and send activation to RED and GREEN. The stronger evidence for RED results in its dominating GREEN in the Answer Network.

### Example III
In this example we demonstrate how information about exceptions plays a

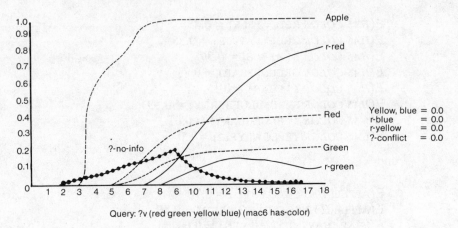

Fig. 11. — Activation trace of nodes from Fig. 10 given the query "MAC6 HAS-COLOR?"

role in retrieval from the Memory Network. Graphs like that given for Example II can be found elsewhere (Shastri & Feldman, 1984).

Query:

?v {RED GREEN BLUE YELLOW} (YEL2 *HAS-COLOR*)

The only difference in this query and the previous one is that YEL2 is activated instead of MAC6. The potentials of selected nodes are plotted in Fig. 12. This example illustrates how the dynamics of the network behavior

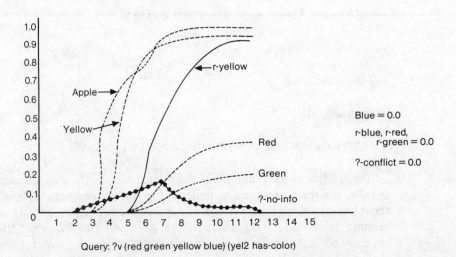

Fig. 12. — Activation trace from the same network (Fig. 10) presented with a query
"YEL2 HAS-COLOR?"

causes the value of Token's property to override the value stored at the Type. The computation of exception was affected by two factors: strength of evidence (the higher evidence from YEL2 to YELLOW compared to that from APPLE to RED and GREEN), and the proximity of information (the Binder local to YEL2 became active before the Binders associated with APPLE). The structuring of knowledge is an integral part of the evidential semantics; neither of these may be treated in isolation. The structuring affects the dynamics of spreading activation and hence the computation of evidence.

### Example IV

Query:

> ?o {APPLE PEAR BLUEBERRY} {(*HAS-COLOR* BLUE)(*is-an-instance-of* FRUIT)

Nodes Activated:

> *HAS-COLOR*, BLUE, FRUIT, P-ENABLE, V-ENABLE

Structural Link enabled:

> *is-instantiated-by*

Response nodes:

> r-APPLE r-PEAR r-BLUBERRY [?-conflict] [?-no-info]

This in an example of a Class II query. All instances of FRUIT receive activation along the *is-instantiated-by* links. BLUEBERRY gets additional evidence from b6 while APPLE and PEAR get negative evidence. Notice that PEAR decays faster than APPLE. This is because the uncertainty about the color of PEAR is less than that about the color of APPLE and hence PEAR receives more negative evidence.

### Example V

Query:

> ?o {APPLE PEAR BLUBERRY} {(*HAS-COLOR* RED)(*is-an-instance-of* FRUIT)}

Nodes Activated:

> *HAS-COLOR*, RED, FRUIT, P-ENABLE, V-ENABLE

Structural Link enabled:

*is-instantiated-by*

Response nodes:

  r-APPLE r-PEAR r-BLUEBERRY [?-conflict] [?-no-info]

The difference between this and the previous example is that the evidence from RED to APPLE was not as strong as that from BLUE to BLUEBERRY. As a result the time response of the network was slower in this example.


### Example VI

As the last example of this subsection, we see how the question, "Is Dick a Pacifist?" is answered by a network which encodes the assertions, "Quakers are Pacifists", "Republicans are non-Pacifists", "Dick is a Quaker" and "Dick is a Republican". The Memory Network in Fig. 13 encodes this information. The weights w1 and w2 encode the strength of evidence E(*HAS-BELIEFS* PACIFIST| QUAKER) and E(*HAS-BELIEFS* NON-PACIFIST| REPUBLI-CAN) respectively. Needless to say, the encoding is a simplification but we can claim that it indicates the manner in which such information is encoded.

Query:

  ?v {non-PACIFIST PACIFIST} (DICK *HAS-BELIEFS*)

Nodes activated:

  DICK, *HAS-BELIEFS,* P-ENABLE, O-ENABLE

Structural Links enabled:

  *is-an-instance-of*

Response Nodes:

  r-PACIFIST r-non-PACIFIST [?-conflict] [?-no-info]

The activation moves up the *is-an-instance-of* links to QUAKER and REPUB-LICAN units and both PACIFIST and non-PACIFIST receive activation in proportion to the weights w1 and w2 respectively.

An example trace with a particular choice of weights is shown in Fig. 14. Conflicting evidence is treated in much greater detail by Shastri (1985).

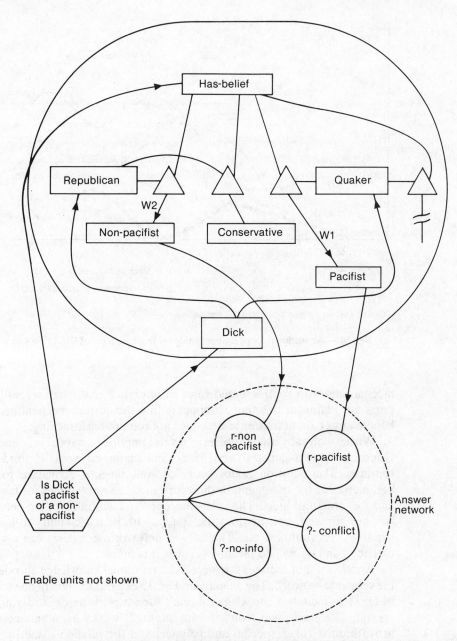

Fig. 13 — An example with conflicting evidence: both pacifist and non-pacifist will
get support, depending on the relative strengths of w1 and w2.

### 3.4 Routine-based inferences

The previous subsection showed how a number of different kinds of basic
inference could be captured within our connectionist semantic network. We
can greatly extend the class of supported inferences by augmenting these

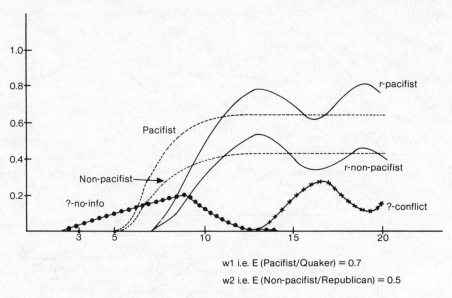

w1 i.e. E (Pacifist/Quaker) = 0.7

w2 i.e. E (Non-pacifist/Republican) = 0.5

Query: ?v (pacifist non-pacifist) (Dick has-belief)

Fig. 14 — Activation trace of the conflicting evidence example of Fig. 13 with w1 = 0.7 and w2 = 0.5.

mechanisms with routine-based rules of inference. Although we will not press any claims at this time, it appears that the currect mechanisms can handle any chain of inference that does not require backtracking.

We have already used routines in several important ways in inferencing. Questions were assumed to arise from, and answer networks to reside in, routines. The question nodes provided simultaneous activation to the parameters of the query and to the appropriate ENABLE nodes for binders and for structural links. The role~concept dynamic-link binding network was not stressed, but provides the system with its basic ability to handle variables, subroutines, etc. The answer network mechanism can also be extended and we will do this first because it is simple.

Another use of routines is to access the relational knowledge encoded in the semantic network. The example in Fig. 15 extends the luncheon routine of Fig. 1 to include a check against one's supper plans before ordering the special. The new node [conflict with supper?] works by simultaneously activating the roles [special] and [supper] and the relation name [not on same day]. This (in a few steps) would cause activation of [instance 6214] which is a postive instance of conflict between foods and thus linked into the r-yes node in the routine. Similar mechanisms will work for any query of the form R(A,B) where any of R, A, B can be variables (roles) bound to particular concepts. Another routine could provide activation to, e.g., all foods that shouldn't be eaten after ham by activating [ham], [first], and [not on same day] to make instances active and then activating [second] and [not on same day] to route activation to foods such as [pork]. We have not yet said how one could then make use of this diffuse activation in the network (cf. Section 4.2).

Another question that might arise is how the binding [supper~pork] came about. It could be that the binding remained from the morning as a kind of intermediate term memory, but would only handle a restricted set of cases. Fig. 16 suggests a general way that such a binding might be computed by an embedded (sub)routine. The important point for us is that the [role~concept] mechanism provides a natural way of linking together routines, similar to the binding mechanisms in logic or programming. The (somewhat fanciful) routine in Fig. 16 has our hero employing the strategy of imagining the situation (cf. Feldman, 1982) of his kitchen that morning and focusing on the traditional defrosting counter.

This class of problem has not yet been worked out as carefully as some earlier examples, but the basic ideas are similar. Activation of the appropriate situation node and relation query would lead to activation of the appropriate unit in the network. The difference here is that the "answer" is being used to establish a binding in the role network of supper~pork. There would have to be enabling links to facilitate such bindings, but this is straightforward. The general idea is that any route network can both take and return role~concept bindings, significantly broadening the range of inferences computable with our networks.

The use of multiple role~concept bindings in a routine gives rise to a computational problem that is particular to and ubiquitous in connectionist models (Feldman & Ballard, 1982). By depending on parallel spreading activation, we become subject to the possibility of false coincidences or cross-talk producing false responses. This is particularly tricky since a role can be occupied by different concepts, but the knowledge is all encoded by concepts. An example situation is one where John loves Mary, Mary likes John and John has been transferred. We suppose that this event makes John sad and Mary relieved. The technical problem here is that the roles of John and Mary could be reversed and the mechanism must support either binding. The routine fragment of interest simply activates [lover is sad] and [lovee is relieved] sequentially. Each person is assumed to have several affective states including [happy], [sad] and [relieved]. Consider the spread of activation caused by the first action of the script. Activating [lover is sad] causes activity to spread to the [sad] node of everyone, including John and Mary. At the same time, the [lover] role in the dynamic link network is triggered and this causes activation of [John]. This, in turn, activates [John's affect] and all its possible values. Now in the entire SN, there is only one unit — [sad] of [John's affect] — which is receiving coincident activation. We assume that this coincident activation raises the potential of John's [sad] unit; this is the mechanism proposed for capturing the sadness of John in our SN.

The second action [lovee is relieved] will, of course, lead to coincident activation of the [relieved] node of Mary. It is important to notice that it is *not* possible to do these two actions in parallel. If both [lover is sad] and [lover is relieved] were simultaneously activated, then both the [lover] and

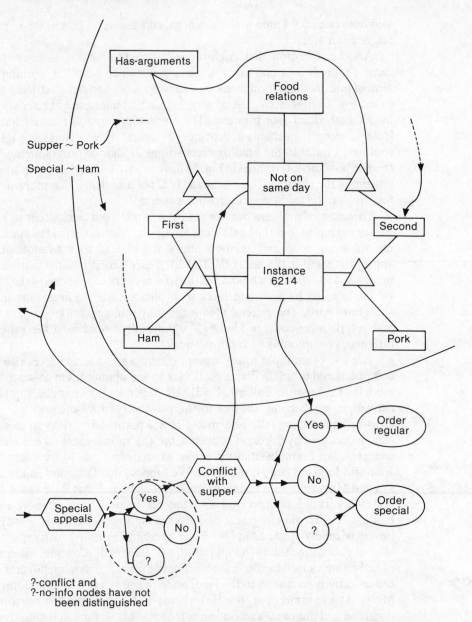

Has-arguments

Food relations

Supper ~ Pork
Special ~ Ham

Not on same day

First

Second

Instance 6214

Ham

Pork

Yes → Order regular

Conflict with supper

No

Order special

?

Special appeals

Yes

No

?

?-conflict and
?-no-info nodes have not
been distinguished

Fig. 15 — A hypothetical extension to relational knowledge and its probing by a routine.

[lovee] roles would become active. This would lead, for example, to coincident activation of the [relieved] node of John as well as to the desired coincidences. This problem is an instance of the general *cross-talk* problem in connectionist networks (Feldman & Ballard, 1982). Whenever one uses coincidences for inference, care must be taken to ensure that no false

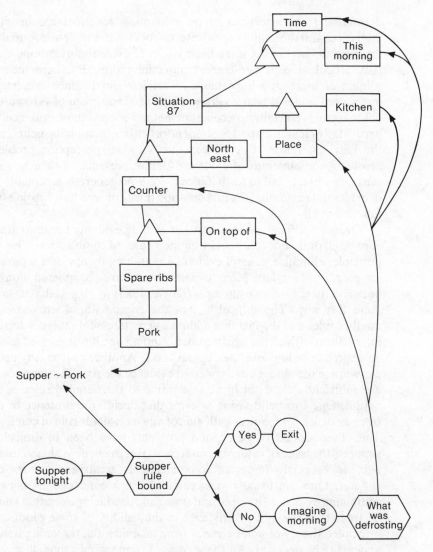

Fig. 16 — A routine and network combination that could be used to bind a role for
use in a subsequent routine.

coincidences arise. This is most often done by sequential execution of
separate steps. The formation of role~concept bindings itself is one such
case. At least for our formulation, sequential processing is required whenever bindings are being established (cf. Anderson, 1983).

## 4.  RELATED ISSUES

### 4.1 Evidence, energy and convergence
Throughout the earlier sections of the chapter we have referred informally
to our treatment of representation and inference as "evidential". The

determining characteristics of an evidential treatment are quantitative inferences and the ability to deal effectively with incomplete information. In this section, we discuss some basic issues of evidential reasoning and how they articulate with our current implementation. Evidence theory is a subject of increasing importance in artificial intelligence and has many unresolved issues. From a certain point of view, much of AI and related fields depends crucially on a coherent method of combining evidence. This is particularly clear in Expert Systems efforts where combining beliefs is often the basic operation. But we can also view all perception problems as involving combinations of evidence for the presence of an edge, a word sense, an object, and so forth. Since there is no generally acceptable theory of evidential reasoning, the first question must concern how existing systems function at all.

Over-simplifying, one can say that existing evidential systems are either very small or do not rely heavily on their rules of combination. One can, in principle, eliminate general evidential reasoning by having a separate rule for each combination. Many expert systems are constructed along these lines and there are some attempts (Doyle, 1983) to suggest that it should be done this way. The difficulties are the combinatorial explosion in the number rules and the fact that adding a new statement involves deciding its interactions with all the existing ones. And no one has suggested using such an approach in low-level perceptual tasks. Another reason why programs can work in the absence of a coherent evidence theory is that many decisions are sufficiently clear-cut to be insensitive to the detailed rules of combination. One can build vision systems that decide the presence of objects from evidence for features with almost any monotonic rule of combination. The other aspects of perception problems have been so difficult as to suppress the issue of evidential inference. But the issue is always there, and becomes especially important in connectionist treatments like the current chapter. One can usually view each unit in a connectionist network as combining evidence (its input and state) and producing an output which can be treated as the unit's confidence in the validity of some production. A principled theory of unit behavior from an evidential reasoning standpoint appears to be necessary for the success of connectionist modelling.

The examples presented in this chapter were carried out in a system that was loosely based on Dempster–Shafer evidence theory (Lowrance, 1982). Our more recent efforts (Shastri & Feldman, 1985; Shastri, 1985) employ a rigorous formulation based on the maximum-entropy principle. There has been considerable recent progress in understanding evidential methods in cognitive science but a great deal remains to be done.

A related technical problem concerns mathematically establishing the correctness of network computations. One does not expect to be able to prove the correctness of complex connectionist networks any more than we can prove large programs or other complex designs. On the other hand, formal analysis of particular structures and systems has proven to be an invaluable source of insight in other complex domains and will clearly be needed here. One useful technique for establishing properties of networks derives from computer science work on distributed algorithms. This style is employed by, e.g., Shastri (1985). Another currently popular methodology relies upon the metaphor of statistical mechanics (Ackley *et al.*, 1985; Hopfield, 1982). Some connectionist networks can be expressed in a way that allows classical energy minimization to predict their behavior. An analysis and comparison of these techniques can be found in Feldman (1985c).

## 4.2  Extracting answers from the Memory Network

In Section 3 we restricted the kinds of queries handled by the system to be multiple choice questions. We now re-examine some important issues underlying this restriction.

Queries are posed to the Memory Network (network) by activating certain nodes and enabling specific links in the network. Once the state of the network is thus initialized, the inference process proceeds independently in the network according to the built-in rules of propagation and evidence accumulation. The ensuing state of the network (primarily the levels of activation of concept nodes), in a sense, *is the result of the inference* performed in response to the query. However, the set of active nodes in the network resulting from a query not only includes nodes that correspond to the answers being sought, but also includes other nodes that take part in the inference process. For instance, in a query involving property inheritance many nodes along the Type hierarchy may get activated before the node that represents the answer.

The presence of other active nodes besides the ones representing the answer raises the fundamental question of how to extract the final answer from the resulting state of the network. In the framework described in this chapter we have finessed the problem of answer extraction by employing Answer Networks in routines. Routines always pose queries with reference to an explicit frame of discernment (the set of possible answers). The frame of discernment is encoded in the form of an Answer Network. The final answer is determined by the Answer Network node that receives the strongest support from the Memory Network.

Assuming the availability of an explicit set of answers is consistent with the notion of routines. Routines pre-wired (compiled) networks dedicated to specific tasks and hence it may be assumed that the possible answers to queries originating from routines are known in advance and encoded as Answer Networks within the routines. However, it is easy to visualize situations in which one cannot assume advance knowledge of the frame of deiscernment (in the present context, the existence of a routine with an appropriate Answer Network). A query such as "What does John like most?" does not have an obvious frame of discernment. The answers could be as varied as "ice-cream" (a kind of food), "science fiction" (a kind of literature), "tennis" (a sport) or even something such as "a glorious sunset" or "freshly fallen snow". The problem is further confounded in situations where the answer does not correspond to a specific node in the Memory Network but must be expressed by interpreting the relations between a number of active nodes. An example of this could be an answer such as: "the tall man wearing the black tie ...", which would involve many active nodes; a probable set being nodes that represent MAN, *HAS-HEIGHT*, TALL, TIE, *HAS-COLOR*, BLACK and *IS-WEARING*.

In its most general form, the problem of answer extraction is related to and seems at least as complex as the problem of natural language generation. We feel that the work of other researchers in this area (McDonald, 1983; Dell, 1985; Simmons & Slocum, 1972) will provide us with valuable insights. Though at present we have not directed much effort towards solving this problem, we propose a possible way of dealing with some restricted case of answer extraction in the absence of an explicit frame of discernment (*fod*).

It is possible to extend the preceding ideas to handle queries that have a very diffuse *fod*, if any. This is accomplished by using routines to perform a heirarchically organized search. If no *fod* is suggested by a query then the *fod* associated with the most general concept in the Memory Network is taken as the initial *fod*. As the computation progresses, the *fod* is refined incrementally by moving down the Type hierarchy until an acceptable answer is found.

Under this proposal the routines essentially perform a breadth first search in parallel and the number of steps taken by even the most general query are proportional to the depth of the conceptual hierarchy. Admittedly the proposal needs to be refined and we hope to do this in the near future.

### 4.3 Extending the representational framework

Our approach to the problem of semantic information requires us to treat the traditionally distinct issues of knowledge representation, inference and computational framework simultaneously. In order to keep the overall complexity within manageable bounds while being honest to the approach, our strategy has been to consider only a restricted class of representational issues. This has allowed us to devote requisite attention to issues related to inference and the development of a connectionist system that embodies our solutions. In terms of purely representational issues we have thus far focused primarily on developing a framework that is best suited for representing simple concepts and natural kind terms. There are several important issues that we have not addressed as yet. These include representation of complex information such as description of actions, events, complex shapes, definition of composite relations, finer structure of properties and constraints between property values (structural descriptions, Brachman, 1982). An open question is the division of knowledge between the Memory Network and the routines. Eventually, some of the information referred to above may be represented in the form of routines rather than in the Memory Network. Needless to say, many problems remain to be solved, but on the basis of our experience so far we are hopeful that it will be possible to extend the framework to solve most of the open questions.

In Section 2 we over-simplified and used values such as red and green for the colors of apples and pears. However, we expect to represent these values by concepts that are much more fine-grained. In developing representations it is important to bear in mind that the normal use of language often belies the complexity of the information being communicated. In some cases detailed information may not be articulated as it is not relevant to the situation. However, a speaker often will not make certain distinctions because he relies upon the hearer to make these by using his world knowledge. For instance, while refering to the color of an apple and that of a brick as "red" one seldom means that they are the one and the same color. One assumes that the hearer is aware of the difference between the two colors and hence will be able to interpret the two uses of "red" appropriately. In view of the above we intend to use color values such as APPLE-RED, ROSE-RED and BRICK-RED. It is important to make these distinctions in a knowledge representation scheme in spite of the surface uniformity of language. Traditional knowledge representation systems do not have to represent these distinctions explicitly as they can shift the burden to the interpreter; the interpreter may be programmed to treat differently the value "red" when it is associated with distinct objects. The absence of an interpreter in our formulation, however, makes it necessary explicitly to represent concepts at a finer grain. We envisage the relationship between concepts such as APPLE-RED and RED to be the same as that between RED and COLOR. The properties associated with color — *HUE, BRIGHTNESS* and *SATURATION* — may be used to make classifications like RED and GREEN and also to make finer distinctions like BRICK-RED and APPLE-RED.

The function of exploded concepts acquires added importance in the representation of semantic information about events and actions. Finer case roles like *HAS-LOVE-AGENT, HAS-BUY-AGENT* and *HAS-PROPEL-AGENT* are needed to represent detailed information about the differences in predicates such as LOVE, BUY and PROPEL (Cottrell, 1985). Furthermore, distinct case roles make it possible to represent possible constraints on values of case roles. The hierarchical organization of concepts of varying granularity gives the ability to perform general inferences about COLOR and *HAS-AGENT* as well as specific inferences about APPLE-RED and *HAS-LOVE-AGENT*.

We also wish to pursue the representation of other ontological categories such as events, sets and situations. Different ontological categories have different sorts of attributes associated with them. For example, the representation of events could be based on properties such as *TIME-OF-OCCURRENCE, LOCATION-OF-OCCURRENCE, CAUSE-OF-OCCURRENCE* and *DESCRIPTION-OF-OCCURRENCE*. In modelling actions and events we hope to take advantage of the work by other researchers in AI and linguistics (Jackendoff, 1983; Bruce, 1975; Schank, 1973).

Sets and situations may also be represented in a manner similar to that of other concepts. By sets we mean a finite and unordered collection of entities where the members of the set are explicitly enumerated. This corresponds to a naive notion of sets and is not equivalent to that of formal set theory. Like all other conceptual entities, sets also represented as collections of <attribute, value> pairs. This collection includes a pair for each member of the set where the property in the pair is *HAS-MEMBER* and the value is one of the member concepts of the set. The collection of <attribute, value> pairs defining a set may also include structural links such as *is-a-subset-of* and *is-a-superset-of*. Inferences on sets will be controlled by specific routines that will compute set-membership, union and intersection.

A situation is a special kind of set consisting of entities, a set of relations on these entities and associated location and time. Examples of situations are: "Harvard Square on a Friday night" or "an auction at Sotheby's". Feldman (1985a) describes how knowledge encoded as situations may be used during visual recognition. Situations may be represented in our formulation by extending the properties associated with sets to include the attributes *HAS-LOCATION* and *HAS-TIME-OF-OCCURRENCE*, and restricting the members of the set to be relations and entities occurring in these relations. The interactions between routines and situations remain to be worked out.

### 4.4 Learning

A major issue in connectionist models is the mechanism for the acquisition of knowledge. The problem of learning has not been solved for systems with a central interpreter and data structures, but there is clearly enough mechanism in such formulations to support learning. For connectionist modelers the problem is made more difficult by the biological constraint that new connections cannot be grown nearly rapidly or extensively enough to account for everyday learning. The only mechanism available appears to be the change in the effectiveness (weight) of existing connections (synapses). Fortunately, there does seem to be adequate biological support for learning through weight change and there is a considerable literature on the mathematics of various possible alteration schemes. But all of this is focused on problems that are structurally much simpler than our routines and memory networks. The key technical issue is how a connectionist network could have a pre-existing structure rich enough to allow for learning the representations described in earlier sections of this chapter, Although we are far from solving this problem, we have a general idea of how learning may occur in the Memory Network. We have not yet seriously addressed the learning of routines.

The proposed mechanism for learning in the Memory Network is based on the notions of recruitment and chunking (Feldman, 1982; Wickelgren, 1979) and we will discuss these in brief before outlining a plausible mechanism of concept formation. Broadly speaking, the idea of chunking may be described as follows. At a given time, the network consists of two classes of nodes:

(1) *Committed* Nodes. These are nodes that have acquired a distinct "meaning" in the network. By this we mean that given any committed node, one can clearly identify sets of other committed nodes, whose activation will result in the former becoming activated. Committed

nodes are connected to other committed nodes by "strong" links, and to a host of other *free* nodes (see below), via "weak" links.

(2) *Free* Nodes. These are nodes that have a multiplicity of weak links to other nodes, both free and committed. These form a kind of "primordial network" of uncommitted nodes within which the network of committed nodes is embedded.

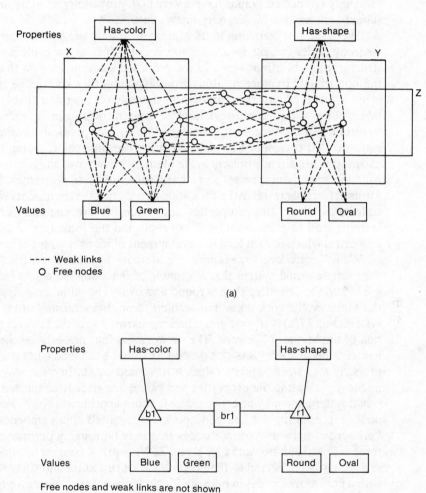

Fig. 17 — (a) A fragment of the semantic network potentially able to learn about shapes and colors of objects. (b) Nodes b1 and r1 have been "recruited" to link the properties and values of br1.

Chunking involves strengthening the links between a cluster of committed nodes and a free node. Thereafter, the free node becomes committed and functions as a chunking node for the cluster, i.e. the activation of nodes in the cluster results in the activation of the chunking node and, conversely, the activation of the chunking node activates all the nodes in the cluster. The process by which a free node is transformed to a committed node is called *recruitment*. The mechanics of recruitment in connectionist networks is described in detail by Feldman (1982). The basic insight in the solution to the problem of learning through weight change is that certain classes of randomly connected graphs have a very high probability of containing the subnetwork needed for learning a new concept.

The notion of chunking in its generic form only suggests a mechanism whereby nodes can be assocaited and is not sufficient for explaining how structured relationships arise. In the proposed solution we wish to exploit the non-trivial structure resulting from assuming that knowledge is organized in terms of properties and values thereof. We postulate that learning takes place within a network that is already organized to reflect this structure. For instance, in the context of vision, we specifically assume that concepts that correspond to primitive properties like color, shape, texture and motion are already present in the Memory Network of an agent together with concepts that represent some basic values of these properties. Simple forms of learning result in the formation of concepts that represent coherent collections of existing properties and values. More complex forms of learning lead to generalization of concepts and the formation of complex properties which in turn lead to development of more complex concepts.

We will consider a toy example of a Memory Network interacting with a very simple visual system that is capable of detecting the colors blue and green and the primitive shapes round and oval. The initial organization of the Memory Network takes into account these characteristics of the visual system. Fig. 17(a) is an over-simplified representation of the initial organization of the Memory Network. The network has four pre-existing concepts, namely, the property HAS-COLOR and its values BLUE and GREEN and the property HAS-SHAPE and its values ROUND and OVAL. In other words, the nodes representing the properties and values are already connected to the visual system and may be activated by it under appropriate conditions. The nodes representing the four concepts are committed nodes embedded in a "primordial network" of free nodes that may be roughly partitioned into three diffused sub-networks X, Y and Z. Network X consists of nodes that are primarily connected to the nodes HAS-COLOR, BLUE and GREEN along with a host of free nodes in network Z. Nodes in network Y receive most of their connections from the nodes HAS-SHAPE, ROUND and OVAL and also from numerous free nodes in network Z. Finally, the nodes in network Z are connected to a large number of nodes throughout the Memory Network. The existence of networks X and Y indicates that the Memory Network is pre-wired to "know" that the BLUE and GREEN are values of HAS-COLOR while ROUND and OVAL are the values of HAS-SHAPE.

Fig. 17(b) depicts the result of learning an instance of a blue and round object. The figure only shows the committed units and their interconnections. Learning an instance involves two stages of recruitment; the binder nodes B1 and R1 are recruited first, followed by the concept node BR1.

When the visual system detects the color blue in the stimulus it activates the node *HAS-COLOR* and BLUE. This coincident activation results in the recruitment of a free node (B1) from the pool of free nodes in network X. The node R1 is recruited in an analogous manner from the pool of nodes in network Y. The simultaneous activity in B1 and R1 leads to the recruitment of the node (BR1) from network Z. Thereafter, the nodes B1 and R1 act as binder nodes and BR1 represents the newly acquired concept. B1 is activated by the coincident activity of *HAS-COLOR* and BLUE while R1 is activated by the coincident activity of *HAS-SHAPE* and ROUND. The activity of the concept node BR1 is strongly correlated with the activity of B1 and R1.

The working of the scheme depends on the assumptions we made about the pre-existing structure of the Memory Network. It was crucial to assume the existence of property and value nodes with appropriate connections to the visual system. The organization of free nodes as networks, X, Y and Z was equally important. Networks X and Y provided binder nodes in order to associate properties with their values, and the networks Z provided a pool of nodes that could be recruited to "chunk" binder nodes in order to form concepts.

We have only provided a crude description of how recruitment of free nodes and release of committed nodes gives rise to representation of new instances and development of concepts that are generalizations of existing concepts. The latter kind of concept formation is accompanied by substantial reduction in the number of committed nodes and links. There are several quite different approaches to learning in connectionist models and each has interesting strengths (Ackley, *et al.*, 1985; Barto & Anderson, 1985; Rumelhart & Zipser, 1985).

We expect that we will not require major changes in the *basic* design of our networks in order to support learning. The connectionist implementation described in this chapter uses complex unit types but it is possible to implement the same basic design in terms of simpler unit types that are more likely to fit into a learning scheme. The primary reason for not using the simpler unit types was to keep the simulations simple. The use of simpler unit types would result in larger networks because more than one simple unit would be required to perform a function currently porformed by a single unit. Probably the best way to view this subsection on learning and the other parts of Section 4 is as plasusibility arguments suggesting that there are no insuperable barriers to a complete connectionist theory of semantic memory.

## REFERENCES AND BIBLIOGRAPHY

Ackley, D. H., Hinton, G. E., & Sejnowki, T. J. (1985). Learning and communication in Boltzmann machines. *Cognitive Science*, **9** (1), 147–169.

Addanki, S. (1983). *Applications of connectionist modeling for motor control systems*. PhD Dissertion, Computer Science Dept., Univ. of Rochester.

Allen, J. F. (1983). Maintaining knowledge about temporal intervals. Commun. ACM, **26**, 832–843.

Allen, J. F., & Frisch, A. M. (1983). What's in a semantic network? *Proc. 20th Annual Meeting, Assoc. of Computational Linguistics.* Univ. of Toronto.

Anderson, J. R. (1983). *The architecture of cognition.* Cambridge, MA: Harvard University Press.

Ballard, D. H. & Brown, C. M. (1982) *Computer vision.* Englewood Cliffs, NJ: Prentice Hall.

Barto, A. G., & Anderson, C. W. (1985) Structural learning in connectionst systems. *Proceedings, 7th Annual Conf. of the Cognitive Science Society.* Irvine, CA, August.

Bobrow, D. G., & Winograd, T. (1976). *An overview of KRL: A knowledge representation language.* CSL-76-4. Xerox Palo Alto Research Centre.

Brachman, R. J. (1982) What "ISA" is and isn't. *Proceedings, Fourth National Conference of the Canadian Society for the Computational Studies of Intelligence.* Saskatoon, Canada, pp. 212–221.

Brachman, R. J., Fikes, R. E., & Levesque, H. J. (1983). KRYPTON: A functional approach to knowledge representation. *IEEE Computer*, **16**, (10).

Bruce, B. C. (1975). Case systems for natural language. *Artificial Intelligence*, **6**, 327–360.

Collins, A. M., & Loftus, E. F. (1975). A spreading activation theory of semantic processing. *Psych. Review*, **82** (6), 409–428.

Cottrell, G. W. (1985). A connectionist approach to word-sense disambiguation. PhD Dissertation, Computer Science Dept., University of Rochester.

Cottrell, G. W., & Small, S. L. (1983). A connectionist scheme for modeling word sense disambiguation. *Cognition and Brain Theory*, **6** (1), 89–120.

Crick, F., & Mitchison, G. (1983). The function of dream sleep. *Nature*, **304**, 5922, 111–114.

Dell, G. S. (1985). Positive feedback in hierarchical connectionist models: Applications to language production. *Cognitive Science*, **9** (1), 3–23.

Dosher, B. A. (1983). Effect of sentence size and network distance on retrieval speed. *Journal of Experimental Psychology: Learning, Memory, and Cognition*, **8** (3), 173–207.

Doyle, J. (1983). *Some theories of reasoned assumptions: An essay in rational psychology.* Tech. Report CS-83-125, Carnegie-Mellon University, Pittsburgh, PA.

Etherington, D. W., & Reiter, R. (1983). On inheritance hierarchies with exceptions. *Proceedings, AAAI-83.* Washington, DC.

Fahlman, S. E. (1979). *NETL: A system for representing and using real-world knowledge.* Cambridge, MA: MIT Press.

Fahlman, S. E. (1982). Three flavors of parallelism. *Proceedings of the 4th National Conference of the Canadian Society for Computer Studies of Intelligence,* Saskatoon, Saskatchewan, May.

Fahlman, S. E., Touretzky, D. S., & van Roggen, W. (1981). Cancellation in a parallel semantic network. *Proceedings, 7th International Joint Conference on Artificial Intelligence*. Vancouver, BC.

Feldman, J. A. (1982). Dynamic connections in neural networks. *Biological Cybernetics*, **46**, 27–39.

Feldman, J. A. (1985a). Four frames suffice: A provisional model of vision and space. *Behavioral and Brain Sciences*, June.

Feldman, J. A. (1985b). Connectionist models and parallelism in high level vision. *Computer Vision, Graphics and Image Processing* (in press).

Feldman, J. A. (1985c) *Energy and the behavior of connectionist models*. TR155, Computer Science Dept., Univ. Rochester.

Feldman, J. A., & Ballard, D. H. (1982). Connectionist models and their properties. *Cognitive Science*, **6**, 205–254.

Feldman, J. A., & Shastri, L. (1984). Evidential inference in activation networks. *Proceedings, Cognitive Science Society Conference*. Boulder, CO.

Fillmore, C. J. (1968). The case for case. In E. W. Bach & R. T. Harms (Eds.), *Universals in linguistic theory*. New York: Holt, Rinehart & Winston, pp. 1–88.

Findler, N. V. (1979). (Ed). *Associative networks: Representation and use of knowledge by computers*. New York: Academic Press.

Fox, M. S. (1982). Reasoning with incomplete knowledge in a resource-limited environment: Integrating reasoning and knowledge acquisition. *Proceedings, Seventh International Joint Conference on Artifical Intelligence*. Vancouver, BC, pp. 313–318.

Frisch, A. M., & Allen, J. F. (1982). Knowledge retrieval as limited inference. In D. W. Loveland (Ed.), *Lecture notes in computer science: 6th conference on automated deduction*. New York: Springer-Verlag.

Garvey, T. D., Lowrence, J. D., & Fischler, M. S. (1981). An inference technique for integrating knowledge from disparate sources. *Proceedings, 7th International Conference on Artificial Intelligence*. Vancouver, BC.

Geman, S., & Geman, D. (1983). *Stochastic relaxations, Gibbs distribution and the Baysian restoration of images*. Unpublished manuscript.

Goldschlager, L. M. (1984). A computational theory of higher brain function. Unpublished manuscript, Computer Science Dept., Stanford University, CA.

Halpern, J. Y., & McAllester, D. A. (1984). Likelihood, probability and knowledge. *Proceedings, AAAI-84*. Austin, TX.

Hinton, G. E., & Anderson, J. A. (1981). (Eds.) *Parallel models of associative memory*. Hillsdale, NJ: Lawrence Erlbaum.

Hinton, G. E., & Sejnowski, T. (1983). Analyzing cooperative computation. *Proceedings, Fifth Annual Conference of the Cognitive Science Society*. Rochester, New York.

Hopfield, J. J. (1982). Neural networks and physical systems with emergent collective computational abilities. *Proceedings, National Academy of Sciences USA*, **79**, 2554–2558.

Jackendoff, R. (1983). *Semantics and cognition.* Cambridge, MA: MIT Press.

Jaynes, E. G. (1979). Where do we stand on maximum entropy? In R. D. Levine and M. Tribus (Eds.), *The maximum entropy formalism.* Cambridge, MA: MIT Press.

Keil, F. D. (1979). *Semantic and conceptual development.* Cambridge, MA: Harvard University Press.

Kyburg, H. (1974). *The logical foundations of statistical inference.* Dordretch, Holland: Reidel.

Levesque, H. J. (1984). A fundamental tradeoff in knowledge representation and reasoning. *Proceedings, CS-CSI-84,* London, Ontario, Canada.

Lowerre, B. T., & Reddy, R. (1979). The HARPY speech understanding system. In W. A. Lea (Ed.), *Trends in speech recognition.* Englewood Cliffs, NJ: Prentice Hall.

Lowrence, J. D. (1982). *Dependency-graph models of evidential support.* PhD thesis, Department of Computer and Information Science, University of Massachusetts, Amherst, MA.

Marr, D., & Nishihara, H. K. (1978). Representation and recognition of the spatial organization of three-dimensional shapes. *Proceedings, Royal Society of London,* **200**, 269–294.

McClelland, J. L., & Rumelhart, D. E. (1981). An interactive activation model of context effects in letter perception. Part I, an account of basic findings. *Psych. Review,* **88**, 375–407.

McDonald, D. D. (1983). Natural language generation as a computational problem: An introduction. In M. Brady, & R. C. Colby (Eds.) *Computational models of discourse.* Cambridge, MA: MIT Press.

Minsky, M. A. (1975). A framework for representing knowledge. In P. H. Winston (Ed.), *The Psychology of vision.* New York: McGraw-Hill, 211–280.

Quillian, R. M., (1968). Semantic memory. In M. Minsky (Ed.), *Semantic information processing.* Cambridge, MA: MIT Press.

Quinlan, J. R. (1983). Consistency and plausible reasoning. *Proceedings Eight International Joint Conference on Artificial Intelligence.* Karlsruhe, West Germany, pp. 137–144.

Reiter, R. (1980). A logic for default reasoning. *Artifical Intelligence,* **13**, 81–132.

Rich, E. (1984). Default reasoning as likelihood reasoning. *Proceedings, AAAI-84.* Washington, DC, pp. 348–351.

Roberts, B., & Goldstein, I. (1977). *The FRL manual.* AI Memo 409, Massachusetts Institute of Technology.

Rosch, E. (1975). Cognitive representations of semantic categories. *Journal of Experimental Psychology: General,* **104**, 192–233.

Rumelhart, D. E., Hinton, G. E., & Williams, R. J. (1985) *Learning internal representations by error propagation.* ICS Report 8506, Institute for Cognitive Science, Univ. of Calif., San Diego.

Rumelhart, D. E., & Zipser, D. (1985). Feature discovery by competitive learning. *Cognitive Science,* **9** (1), 75–112.

Sabbah, D. (1985). Computing with connections in visual recognition of origami objects. *Cognitive Science*, **9** (1), 25–50.

Schank, R. C. (1973). Identification of concenptualization underlying natural language. In R. C. Schank, & K. Colby (Eds.), *Computer models of thought and language*. San Francisco, CA: Freeman.

Schank, R. C. (1982). *Dynamic memory: A theory of reminding and learning in computers and people*. New York: Cambridge University Press.

Schubert, L. D. (1975). Extending an Expressive power of semantic networks. *Proceedings, Fouth International Joint Conference on Artificial Intelligence*.

Schubert, L. K., Papalaskaris, M. A., & Taugher, J. (1983). Determining type, part, color, and time relationships. *IEEE Computer*, **16** (10), 55–60.

Shafer, G. (1976). A mathematical theory of evidence. Princeton, NJ: Princeton University Press.

Shastri, L. (1985). Knowledge representation in a parallel evidential framework. PhD Dissertation, Dept. of Computer Science, University of Rochester.

Shastri, L., & Feldman, J. A. (1984). *Semantic networks and neural nets*. TR131, Computer Science Dept., Univ. of Rochester.

Shastri, L., & Feldman, J. A. (1985). Evidential reasoning in semantic networks: A formal theory. *Proceedings, 9th Int'l. Joint Conf. on Artificial Intelligence*. Los Angeles, CA, pp. 465–474.

Simmons, R. F., & Slocum, J. (1972). Generating English discourse from semantic networks. *Comm. of the ACM 15*, **10**, 891–905.

Small, S. L., Shastri, L., Brucks, M. L., Kaufman, S. G., Cottrell, G. W., & Addanki, S. (1982). *ISCON: An interactive simulator for connectionist networks*. TR 109, Dept. of Computer Science, University of Rochester.

Smith, E. E., & Medin, D. L. (1981). *Categories and concepts*. Cambridge, MA: Harvard University Press.

Touretzky, D. S. (1984). The mathematics of inheritance systems. PhD Thesis, Carnegie Mellon University, CMV–CS–84–136.

Walker, D. E. (1978). (Ed.), *Understanding spoken language*. New York: American Elsevier.

Wickelgren, W. A. (1979). Chunking and consolidation: A theoretical synthesis of semantic networks, configuring in conditioning, S-R versus cognitive learning, normal forgetting, the amnesic syndrome, and the hippocampal arousal system. *Psych. Review*, **86** (1), 44–60.

Woods, W. A. (1975). What's in a link: Foundations for semantic networks. In D. G. Bobrow, & A. M. Collins (Eds.), *Representation and understanding: Studies in cognitive science*. New York: Academic Press, 35–82.

# 7

# Formal modeling of subsymbolic processes: An introduction to harmony theory

**Paul Smolensky**

## INTRODUCTION

### The theory of information processing

At this early stage in the development of cognitive science, methodological issues are both open and central. There may have been times when developments in neuroscience, artifical intelligence, or cognitive psychology seduced researchers into believing that their discipline was on the verge of discovering the secret of intelligence. But a humbling history of hopes disappointed has produced the realization that understanding the mind will challenge the power of all these methodologies combined.

The work reported in this chapter rests on the conviction that a methodology that has a crucial role to play in the development of cognitive science is *mathematical analysis*. The success of cognitive science, like that of many other sciences, will, I believe, depend upon the construction of a solid body of theoretical results: results that express in a mathematical language the conceptual insights of the field; results that squeeze all possible implications out of those insights by exploiting powerful mathematical techniques.

This body of results, which I will call the *Theory of Information Processing,* exists because information is a concept that lends itself to mathematical formalization. One part of the Theory of Information Processing is already well developed. The classical Theory of Computation provides powerful and elegant results about the notion of *effective procedure,* including languages for precisely expressing them and theoretical machines for realizing them. This body of theory grew out of mathematical logic, and in turn contributed to computer science, physical computing systems, and the theoretical paradigm in cognitive science often called *the [von Neumann] computer metaphor.*

In his paper *Physical symbol systems,* Allen Newell (1980) articulated the role of the mathematical theory of symbolic computation in cognitive science, and furnished a manifesto for what I call *the symbolic paradigm.* The present chapter explores an alternative paradigm for cognitive science, the *subsymbolic paradigm,* in which the most powerful level of description of cognitive systems is hypothesized to be lower than the level that is naturally described by symbol manipulation. (For further explorations of this paradigm, see Rumelhart & McClelland, forthcoming; McClelland & Rumelhart, forthcoming; Hofstadter, 1983; Hinton & Anderson 1981; Grossberg, 1982; Feldman & Ballard, 1982; *Cognitive Science,* 1985, **9**, no. 1: Special issue on connectionist models and their applications.)

The fundamental insights into cognition explored by the subsymbolic paradigm do not involve effective procedures and symbol manipulation. Instead they involve the "spread of activation", relaxation, and statistical correlation. The mathematical language in which these concepts are naturally expressed are probability theory and the theory of dynamical systems. By dynamical systems theory I mean the study of sets of numerical variables (e.g. activation levels) that evolve in time in parallel, and interact through differential equations. The classical theory of dynamical systems includes the study of natural physical systems (e.g. mathematical physics) and artificially designed systems (e.g. control theory). Mathematical characterizations of dynamical systems that formalize the insights of the subsymbolic paradigm would be most helpful in developing the paradigm.

## A top-down theoretical strategy

How can mathematical analysis be used to study the processing mechanisms underlying the performance of some cognitive task?

One strategy, often associated with David Marr (1982), is to characterize the task in a way that allows mathematical *derivation* of mechanisms that perform it. This *top-down* theoretical strategy is pursued in harmony theory. My claim is not that the strategy leads to descriptions that are applicable to all cognitive systems, but rather that the strategy leads to new insights, mathematical results, computer architectures, and computer models that fill in the relatively unexplored conceptual world of parallel, massively distributed systems that perform cognitive tasks. Filling in this conceptual world is a necessary subtask, I believe, for understanding how brains and minds are capable of intelligence, and for assessing whether computers with novel architectures might share this capability.

### The centrality of perceptual processing

The cognitive task I will study in this chapter is an abstraction of the task of perception. This abstraction includes many cognitive tasks that are custo- marily regarded as much "higher-level" than perception (e.g. intuiting answers to physics problems). A few comments on the role of perceptual processing in the subsymbolic paradigm are useful at this point.

The vast majority of cognitive processing lies between the highest cognitive levels of explicit logical reasoning and the lowest levels of sensory processing. Descriptions of processing at the extremes are relatively well informed — on the high end by formal logic and on the low end by natural science. In the middle lies a conceptual abyss. How are we to conceptualize cognitive processing in this abyss?

The strategy of the symbolic paradigm is to conceptualize processing in the intermediate levels as symbol manipulation. Other kinds of processing are viewed as limited to extremely low levels of sensory and motor process- ing. Thus symbolic theorists climb *down* into the abyss, clutching a rope of symbolic logic anchored at the top, hoping it will stretch all the way to the bottom of the abyss.

The subsymbolic paradigm takes the opposite view, that intermediate processing mechanisms are of the same kind as perceptual processing mechanisms. Logic and symbol manipulation are viewed as appropriate descriptions only of the few cognitive processes that explicitly involve logical reasoning. Subsymbolic theorists climb *up* into the abyss on a perceptual ladder anchored at the bottom, hoping it will extend all the way to the top of the abyss.[1]

In this chapter, I will analyze an abstraction of the task of perception that encompasses many tasks, from low, through intermediate, to high cognitive levels. The analysis leads to a general kind of "perceptual" processing mechanism that is a powerful potential component of an information processing system. The abstract task I analyze captures a common part of the tasks of passing from an intensity pattern to a set of objects in 3-D, from a sound pattern to a sequence of words, from a sequence of words to a semantic description, from a set of patient symptoms to a set of disease states, from a set of givens in a physics problem to a set of unknowns. Each of these processes is viewed as *completing an internal representation of a static state of an external world*. By suitably abstracting the task of interpreting a static *sensory* input, we can arrive at a theory of interpretation of static input *generally*, a theory of *completion task* that applies to many cognitive phenomena in the gulf between perception and logical reasoning. An application that will be described in some detail is qualitative problem solving in circuit analysis.

The central idea of the Top-Down theoretical strategy is that properties of the task are powerfully constraining on mechanisms. This idea can be well exploited within a perceptual approach to cognition, where the constraints on the perceptual task are characterized through the constraints operative in the external environment from which the inputs come. This permits an analysis of how internal representation of these constraints within the cognitive system itself allows it to perform its task. These kinds of considerations have been emphasized in the psychological literature prominently by Gibson and Shepard (see Shepard, 1984); they are fundamental to harmony theory.

### Structure of the chapter

The goal of harmony theory is to develop a mathematical theory of information processing in the subsymbolic paradigm. However, the theory grows out of ideas that can be stated with little or no mathematics. This chapter starts with an informal presentation of the fundamental ideas on which harmony theory is based. This presentation begins with a particular perceptual model, the letter-perception model of McClelland and Rumelhart (1981), and Rumelhart and McClelland (1982), and abstracts from it general features that can apply to modeling of higher cognitive processes. Crucial to the development is a particular formulation of aspects of schema theory, along the lines of Rumelhart (1980). In this informal discussion, the content of the theorems that currently form the core of the theory will be described, but the theorems themselves will not be formally presented (see Smolensky, forthcoming). Then an application of the general theory is described: a model of intuitive qualitative problem-solving in elementary electric circuits. This model illustrates several points about the relation between symbolic and subsymbolic descriptions of cognitive phenomena; for example, it furnishes a sharp contrast between the description at these two levels of the nature and acquisition of expertise.

## SCHEMA THEORY AND SELF-CONSISTENCY

### The logical structure of harmony theory

The logical structure of harmony theory is shown schematically in Fig. 1. The box labelled *Mathematical Theory* represents the use of mathematical analysis and computer simulation for drawing out the implications of the fundamental principles. These principles comprise a mathematical characterization of computational requirements of a cognitive system that performs the completion task. From these principles it is possible to analyze mathematically aspects of the resulting performance as well as rigorously *derive* the rules for a machine implementing the computational requirements. The rules defining this machine have a different status from those defining most other computer models of cognition: they are not *ad hoc,* or *post hoc;* rather they are logically derived from a set of computational requirements. This is one sense in which harmony theory has a top–down theoretical development.

Where do the "mathematically characterized computational require-

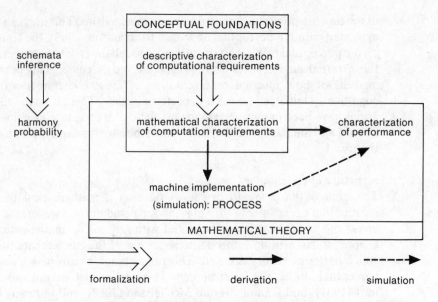

Fig. 1 — The logical structure of harmony theory.

ments" of Fig. 1 come from? They are a formalization of a descriptive characterization of cognitive processing, a simple form of *schema theory*. In the first part of this chapter, I will give a description of this form of schema theory and show how to transform the descriptive characterization into a mathematical one; how to get from the *conceptual* box of Fig. 1 into the *mathematical* box. Once we are in the formal world, mathematical analysis and computer simulation can be put to work.

Throughout this section, the main points of the development will be explicitly enumerated.

*Point 1. The* **mathematics of harmony theory** *is founded on familiar concepts of cognitive science:* **inference through activation of schemata.**

**Dynamic construction of schemata**
The basic problem can be posed à la Schank (1980). While eating at a fancy restaurant, you get a headache. Without effort, you ask the waitress if she could possibly get you an aspirin. How is this plan created? You have never had a headache in a restaurant before. Ordinarily, when you get a headache your plan is to go to your medicine cabinet and get yourself some aspirin. In the current situation, this plan must be modified by the knowledge that in good restaurants, the management is willing to expend effort to please its customers, and that the waitress is a liaison to that management.

The cognitive demands of this situation are schematically illustrated in

Fig. 2. Ordinarily, the restaurant context calls for a "restaurant script" which supports the planning and inferencing required to reach the usual goal of getting a meal. Ordinarily, the headache context calls for a "headache script" which supports the planning required to get asprin in the usual context of home. The completely novel context of a headache in a restaurant calls for a special-purpose script integrating the knowledge that ordinarily manifests itself in two separate scripts.

What kind of cognitive system is capable of this degree of flexibility? Suppose that the knowledge base of the system does *not* consist of a set of scripts like the "restaurant script" and the "headache script". Suppose instead that the knowledge base is a set of *knowledge atoms* that configure themselves dynamically in each context to form tailor-made scripts. This is the fundamental idea formalized in harmony theory.

The degree of flexibility demanded of scripts is equalled by that demanded of all conceptual structures.[2] For example, metaphor is an extreme example of the flexibility demanded of word meanings; even so-called "literal meaning" on closer inspection actually relies on extreme flexibility of knowledge application (Rumelhart, 1979). In this chapter I will consider knownledge structures that embody our knowledge of objects, words and other concepts of comparable complexity: these I will refer to as *schemata*. The defining properties of schemata are that they have conceptual intepretations and that they *support inference*.

For lack of a better term, I will use "knowledge atoms" to refer to the elementary constituents of which I assume schemata to be composed. These atoms will shortly be given a precise description; they will be interpreted as a particular instantiation of the idea of *memory trace*.

✳  *Point 2. At the time of inference, stored* **knowledge atoms** *are* **dynamically assembled** *into* **context-sensitive** *schemata.*

✗ This view of schemata is in part embodied in the McClelland and Rumelhart (1981) letter perception model. One of the observed phenomena accounted for by this model is the facilitation of the perception of letters that are embedded in words. Viewing the perception of a letter as the result of a perceptual inference process, we can say that this inference is supported by a *word schema* that appears in the model as a single processing unit that encodes the knowledge of the spelling of that word. This is *not* an instantiation of the view of schemata as dynamically created entities.

However, the model also accounts for the observed facilitation of letter perception within orthographically regular non-words or *pseudowords* like *MAVE*. When the model processes this stimulus, several word units become and stay quite active, including *MAKE, WAVE, HAVE,* and other words orthographically similar to *MAVE*. In this case, the perception of a letter in the stimulus is the result of an inference process that is supported by the *collection* of activated units. This collection is a *dynamically created pseudoword schema*.

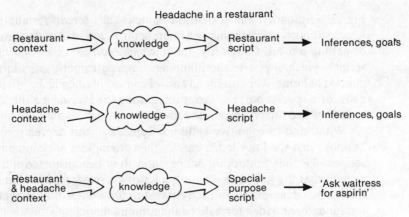

Fig. 2 — In three different contexts, the knowledge base must produce three different scripts.

When an orthographically irregular non-word is processed by the model, letter perception is slowest. As in the case of pseudowords, many word units become active. However, none become very active, and very many are equally active, and these words have very little similarity to each other, so they do not support inference about the letters effectively. Thus the knowledge base is incapable of creating schemata for irregular non-words.

*Point 3. Schemata are* **coherent** *assemblies of knowledge atoms; only these can support inference.*

Note that schemata are created *simply by activating the appropriate atoms.* This brings us to what was labelled in Fig. 1 the "descriptively characterized computational requirements" for harmony theory:

*Point 4: the* **Harmony Principle.** The cognitive system is **an engine for activating coherent assemblies of atoms** *and drawing inferences that are* **consistent** *with the knowledge represented by the activated atoms.*

*Subassemblies* of activated atoms that tend to recur exactly or approximately are the schemata.

This principle focuses attention on the notion of *coherency* or *consistency.* This concept will be formalized under the name of *harmony*, and its centrality is acknowledged by the name of the theory.

**Micro- and macro-levels**

It is important to realize that harmony theory, like all subsymbolic accounts of cognition, exists on two distinct levels of description: a micro-level involving knowledge atoms and a macro-level involving schemata (see also Rumelhart *et al.,* forthcoming). These levels of description are completely analogous to other micro- and macro-theories, for example in physics. The micro-theory, quantum physics, is assumed to be universally valid. Part of its job as a theory is to explain why the approximate macro-theory, classical physics, works when it does, and why it breaks down when it does. Understanding of physics requires understanding *both* levels of theory *and* the relation between them.

In the subsymbolic paradigm in cognitive science, it is equally important to understand the two levels and their relationship. In harmony theory, the micro-theory prescribes the nature of the atoms, their interaction, and their development through experience. This description is assumed to be a universally valid description of cognition. It is also assumed (although this has yet to be explicitly worked out) that in performing certain cognitive tasks (e.g. logical reasoning), a higher-level description is a valid approximation. This macro-theory describes schemata, their interaction, and their development through experience.

One of the features of the formalism of harmony theory that distinguishes it from most subsymbolic accounts of cognition is that it exploits a formal isomorphism with statistical physics. Since the main goal of statistical physics is to relate the microscopic description of matter to its macroscopic properties, harmony theory can bring the power of statistical physics concepts and techniques to bear on the problem of understanding the relation between the micro- and macro-accounts of cognition.

### The nature of knowledge
In the previous section, the letter perception model was used to illustrate the dynamic construction of schemata from constituent atoms. However, it is only pseudowords that correspond to composite schemata; word schemata are single atoms. We can also represent words as composite schemata by using digraph units at the upper level instead of four-letter word units. A portion of this modified letter-perception is shown in Fig. 3. Now the

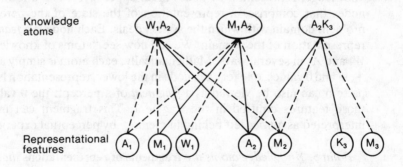

Fig. 3 — A portion of a modified reading model.

processing of a four-letter word involves the activation of a set of digraph units, which are the "knowledge atoms" of this model. Omitted from the figure are the line segment units, which are like those in the original letter perception model.

This simple model illustrates several points about the nature of knowledge atoms in harmony theory. The diagraph unit $W_1A_2$ represents a pattern of values over the letter units: $W_1$ and $A_2$ on, with all other letter units for positions 1 and 2 off. This pattern is shown in Fig. 4, using the labels

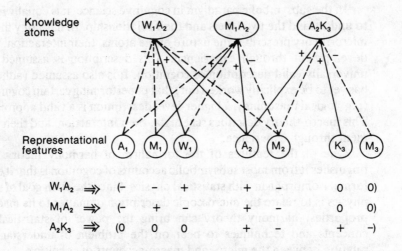

$$
\begin{array}{lll}
W_1A_2 \Rightarrow & (- \quad - \quad + & + \quad - \quad\quad 0 \quad 0) \\
M_1A_2 \Rightarrow & (- \quad + \quad - & + \quad - \quad\quad 0 \quad 0) \\
A_2K_3 \Rightarrow & (0 \quad 0 \quad 0 & + \quad - \quad\quad + \quad -)
\end{array}
$$

Fig. 4 — Each knowledge atom is a vector of +, −, and 0 values of the representational feature nodes.

+, − and 0 to denote *on*, *off* and *irrelevant*. These indicate whether there is an excitatory connection, inhibitory connection, or no connection between the corresponding nodes.[3]

Fig. 4 shows the basic structure of harmony models. There are atoms of knowledge, represented by nodes in an upper layer, and a lower layer of nodes that comprises a representation of the state of the perceptual or problem domain with which the system deals. Each node is a *feature* in the representation of the domain. We can now see "atoms of knowledge" like $W_1$ and $A_2$ in several ways. Mathematically, each atom is simply a *vector* of +, − and 0 values, one for each node in the lower, representation layer. This pattern can also be viewed as a *fragment* of a percept: the 0 values mark those features omitted in the fragment. This fragment can in turn be interpreted as a *trace* left behind in memory by perceptual experience.

*Point 5. Knowledge atoms are* **fragments of representations** *that accumulate with experience.*

### The completion task
Having specified more precisely what the atoms of knowledge are, it is time to specify the task in which they are used.

Many cognitive tasks can be viewed as inference tasks. In problem solving, the role of inference is obvious; in perception and language comprehension, inference is less obvious but just as central. In harmony theory, a tightly prescribed but extremely general inferential task is studied: the *completion task*. In a problem-solving completion task, a partial description of a situation is given (for example, the initial state of a system); the problem is to complete the description to fill in the missing information (the final state, say). In a story-understanding completion task, a partial description of some events and actors' goals is given; comprehension involves filling in the missing events and goals. In perception, the stimulus gives values for certain low-level features of the environmental state, and the perceptual system must fill in values for other features. In general, in the completion task some features of an environmental state are given as input, and the cognitive system must complete that input by assigning likely values to unspecified features.

A simple example of a completion task (From Lindsay & Norman, 1972) is shown in Fig. 5. The task is to fill in the features of the obscured portions of

Fig. 5 — A perceptual completion task.

the stimulus and to decide what letters are present. This task can be performed by the model shown in Fig. 3, as follows. The stimulus assigns values of *on* and *off* to the unobscured letter features. What happens is summarized in Table 1.

**Table 1** — A procedure for performing the completion task.

| | |
|---|---|
| Input: | Assign values to some features in the representation |
| Activation: | Activate atoms that are *consistent* with the representation |
| Inference: | Assign values to unknown features of represenation that are *consistent* with the active knowledge |

Note that which atoms are active affects how the representation is filled in, and how the representation is filled in affects which atoms are activated. The activation and inference processes mutually constrain each other; these processes must run in parallel. Note also that all the decisions come out of a striving for *consistency*.

*Point 6. Assembly of schemata — activation of atoms — and inference — completing missing parts of the representation — are **both** achieved by finding **maximally self-consistent states** of the system that are also consistent with the input.*

The completion of the stimulus shown in Fig. 5 is shown in Fig. 6. The

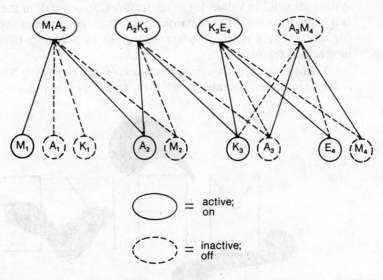

Fig. 6 — The state of the network in the completion of the stimulus shown in Fig. 5.

consistency is high because wherever an active atom is connected to a representational feature by a + (respectively −) connection, that feature has value *on* (respectively *off*). In fact, we can define a very simple measure of the degree of self-consistency just by considering all active atoms, counting +1 for every agreement between one of its connections and the value of the corresponding feature, and counting −1 for every disagreement. (Here + with *on* or − with *off* constitutes agreement.) This is the simplest example of a *harmony function*, and brings us into the mathematical formulation.

### The harmony function

Point 6 asserts that the heart of cognitive processing is the construction of cognitive states that are "maximally self-consistent". To make this precise, we need only measure that self-consistency.

*Point 7. The self-consistency of a possible state of the cognitive system can be assigned a quantitative value by a **harmony function, H.***

Fig 7 displays a harmony function that generalizes the simple example discussed in the preceding paragraph. A state of the system is defined by a set of atoms which are *active,* and a vector of values for all representational features. The harmony of such a state is the sum of terms, one for each active atom, weighted by the *strength* of that atom. Each weight multiplies the self-consistency between that particular atom and the vector of representational feature values. That self-consistency is the simlarity between the vector of features defining the atom (the vector of its connections) and the representational feature vector. In the simplest case discussed above, the function $h$ that measures this similarity is just the number of agreements between these vectors minus the number of disagreements.

## A probabilistic formulation of schema theory

The next step in the theoretical development requires returning to the higher level, symbolic description of inference, and to a more detailed discussion of schemata.

Consider a typical inference process described with shemata. A child is reading a story about presents, party hats, and a cake with candles. When asked questions, the child says that the girl getting the presents is having a birthday. In the terminology of schema theory, while reading the story, the child's "birthday party schema" becomes active, and allows many inferences to be made, filling in details of the scene that were not made explicit in the story.

The "birthday party schema" is presumed to be a knowledge structure that contains "variables" like *birthday cake, guest of honor, other guests, gifts, location* and so forth. The schema contains information on how to assign values to these variables. For example, the schema may specify: *default values* to be assigned to variables in the absence of any counter-indicating information; *value restrictions* limiting the kind of values that can be assigned to variables; and *dependency* information, specifying how assigning a particular value to one variable affects the values that can be assigned to another variable.

A convenient framework for concisely and uniformly expressing all this information is given by *probability theory*. The default value for a variable can be viewed as its most probable value: the mode of the marginal probability distribution for that variable. The value restrictions on a variable specify the values for which it has non-zero probability: the support of its marginal distribution. The dependencies between variables are expressed by their statistical correlations, or, more completely, by their joint probability distributions.

So the birthday party schema can be viewed as containing information about the probabilties that its variables will have various possible values. These are clearly statistical properties of the particular domain or *environment* in which the inference task is being carried out. In reading the story, the child is given a partial description of a scene from the everday environment — the values of some of the features used to represent that scene —

harmony$_{\text{knolwedge base}}$ (representational feature vector, activations) =

$$
\sum_{\substack{\text{atoms} \\ \alpha}} \begin{pmatrix} \text{strength of} \\ \text{atom } \alpha \end{pmatrix} \begin{pmatrix} 0 \text{ if atom } \alpha \\ \text{inactive} \\ 1 \text{ if atom } \alpha \\ \text{active} \end{pmatrix} \text{similarily} \begin{pmatrix} \text{feature vector} \\ \text{of atom } \alpha \end{pmatrix} ; \begin{pmatrix} \text{representational} \\ \text{feature vector} \end{pmatrix}
$$

Fig. 7 — A schematic representation for a harmony function.

and to understand the story, the child must *complete* the description by filling in the values for the unknown features. These values are assigned in such a way that the resulting scene has the highest possible probability. The birthday party schema contains the probabilistic information needed to carry out these inferences.

In a typical cognitive task, many schemata become active at once and interact heavily during the inference process. Each schema contains probabilistic information for its own variables, which are only a fraction of the complete set of variables involved in the task. To perform a completion, the most probable set of values must be assigned to the unknown variables, using the information in all the active schemata.

The probabilistic formulation of these aspects of schema theory can be simply summarized as follows.

*Point 8. Each schema encodes the* **statistical relations** *among a few representational features. During inference, the probabilistic information in many active schemata are dynamically folded together to find* **the most probable state of the environment**.

Thus the statistical knowledge encoded in all the schemata allow the estimation of the relative probabilities of possible states of the environment. How can this be done?

At the macro-level of schemata and variables, coordinating the folding together of the information of many schemata is difficult to describe. The inability to devise procedures that capture the flexibility displayed in human use of schemata was in fact one of the primary historical reasons for turning to the micro-level description (McClelland, Rumelhart, & Hinton, forthcoming). We therefore return to the micro-description to address this difficult problem.

At the micro-level, the probabilistic knowledge in the "birthday party schema" is distributed over many knowledge atoms, each carrying a small bit of statistical information. Because these atoms all tend to match the represenation of a birthday party scene, they can become active together; in some approximation, they tend to function collectively, and in that sense they comprise a "schema." Now, when many "schemata" are active at once, that means the knowledge atoms that comprise them are simultaneously active. At the micro-level, there is no real difference between the decisions required to activate the appropriate atoms to instantiate many schemata simultaneously, and the decisions required to activate the atoms to instantiate a single schema. A computational system that can dynamically create a schema when it is needed can also dynamically create many schemata when they are needed. When atoms, not schemata, are the elements of computation, the problem of coordinating many schemata becomes subsumed in the problem of activating the appropriate atoms. And this is the problem that the harmony function, the measure of self-consistency, was created to solve.

### Harmony theory

According to Points 2, 6, and 7, schemata are collections of knowledge atoms that become active in order to maximize harmony, and inferences are also drawn to maximize harmony. This suggests that the probability of a possible state of the environment is estimated by computing its harmony: the higher the harmony, the greater the probability. In fact, from the mathematical properties of probability and harmony, it is possible to show the following.

*Point 9. The relationship between the harmony function H and estimated probabilities is of the form*

$$\text{probability} \propto e^{H/T}$$

*where T is some constant that cannot be determined a priori.*

This relationship between probability and harmony is mathematically identical to the relationship between probability and (minus) *energy* in statistical physics: the Gibbs or Boltzmann law. This is the basis of the isomorphism between cognition and physics exploited by harmony theory. In statistical physics, $H$ is called the *Hamiltonian function*; it measures the energy of a state of a physical system. In physics, $T$ is the *temperature* of the system. In harmony theory, $T$ is called the *computational temperature* of the cognitive system. This temperature is a global parameter in the system, and varies during computation of a given completion. When the temperature is very high, completions with high harmony are assigned estimated probabilties that are only slightly higher than those assigned to low-harmony completions; the environment is treated as *more random* in the sense that all completions are estimated to have roughly equal probability. When the temperature is very low, only the completions with highest harmony are given non-negligible estimated probabilities.

*Point 10. The lower the computational temperature, the more the estimated probabilities are weighted towards the completions of highest harmony.*

In particular, the very best completion can be found by lowering the temperature to zero. This process, *cooling,* is fundamental to harmony theory. Concepts and techniques from thermal physics can be used to understand and analyze decision-making processes in harmony theory.

A technique for performing Monte Carlo computer studies of thermal systems can be readily adapted to harmony theory.

*Point 11. A massively parallel stochastic machine can be designed that performs completions in accordance with the preceding points.*

For a given harmony model (e.g. that of Fig. 4), this machine is constructed as follows. Every node in the network becomes a simple processor, and every link in the network becomes a communcation link between two processors: the processors each have two possible values ($+1$ and $-1$ for the representational feature processors; $1 = active$ and $0 = inactive$ for the knowledge atom processors). The input to a completion problem is provided by fixing the values of some of the feature processors. Each of the other processors continually updates its value by making stochastic decisions based on the harmony associated at the current time with its two possible values. It is most likely to choose the value that corresponds to greater harmony; but with some probability — greater the higher is the computational temperature $T$ — it will make the other choice. Each processor computes the harmony associated with its possible values by a numerical calculation that uses as input the numerical values of the other processors to which it is connected. Alternately, all the atom processors update in parallel, and then all the feature processors update in parallel. The process repeats many times, implementing the procedure of Table 1. All the while, the temperature $T$ is lowered to zero, pursuant to Point 10. It can be proved that the machine will eventually "freeze" into a completion that maximizes the harmony.[4].

I call this machine *harmonium,* because, like Selfridge's (1960) pattern recognition system *pandemonium,* it is a parallel distributed processing system in which many atoms of knowledge are simultaneously "shouting" out their little contributions to the inference process; but unlike pandemonium, there is an explicit method to the madness: the collective search for maximal harmony.[5]

The final point concerns the account of learning in harmony theory.

*Point 12. There is a procedure for accumulating knowledge atoms through exposure to the environment so that the system will perform the completion task optimally.*

The precise meaning of "optimality" is an important topic in the formal analysis of the theory.

This completes the descriptive account of the foundations of harmony theory. Formalizations of Points 9, 11, and 12 comprise the three theorems that currently form the core of the theory.

## AN APPLICATION: ELECTRICITY PROBLEM SOLVING
### The model
#### *Theoretical context*
In this section I show how the framework of harmony theory can be used to model the *intuition* that allows experts to answer, without any conscious application of "rules", questions like that posed in Fig. 8. Theoretical

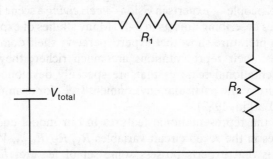

Fig. 8 — If the resistance of $R_2$ is increased (assuming that $V_{total}$ and $R_1$ remain the same), what happens to the current and voltage drops?

conceptions of how such problems are answered play an increasingly significant role in the design of instruction. (For example, see the journal, *Cognition and Instruction,* and Ginsburg, 1983). Even such simple problems as that of Fig. 8 have important instructional implications (Riley, 1984).

The model I will describe was studied in collaboration with Mary S. Riley (Riley & Smolensky, 1984) and Peter DeMarzo (1984). This model provides answers, without any symbolic manipulation of rules, to qualitative questions about the particular circuit of Fig. 8. It should not be assumed that we imagine that a different harmony network like the one I will describe is created for every different circuit that is analyzed. Rather we assume that experts contain a small number of fixed networks like the one we propose, that these networks represent the effects of much cumulated experience with many different circuits, that they form the "chunks" with which the experts's *intuition* represents the circuit domain, and that complex problem solving somehow employs these networks to direct the problem solving as a whole through intuitions about chunks of the problem. At this early stage we cannot say much about the coordination of activity in complex problem solving. But we do claim that by giving an explicit example of a non-symbolic account of problem solving, our model offers insights into expertise that complement nicely those of traditional production-system models. The model also serves to render concrete many of the general features of harmony theory that have been described above.

#### *Representational features*
The first step in developing a harmony model is to select features for representing the environment. Here the environment is the set of qualitative changes in the electric circuit of Fig. 8 that obey the laws of physics. What

must obviously be represented are the changes in the physical components: where $R_1$ goes up, goes down or stays the same, and similarly for $R_2$ and the battery's voltage $V_{total}$. We also hypothesize that experts represent deeper features of this environment, like the current $I$, the voltage drops $V_1$ and $V_2$ across the two resistors, and the effective resistance $R_{total}$ of the circuit. We claim that experts "see" these deeper features; that *perceiving* the problem of Fig. 8 for experts involves filling in the deeper features just as for all sighted people — experts in vision — *perceiving* a scene involves filling in the features describing objects in 3–D. Many studies of expertise in the psychological literature show that experts perceive their domain differently from novices: their representations are much richer; they possess additional representational features that are specially developed for capturing the structure of the particular environment (see, for example, Chase & Simon, 1973; Larkin, 1983).

So the representational features in our model encode the qualitative changes in the seven circuit variables $R_1$, $R_2$, $R_{total}$, $V_1$, $V_2$, $V_{total}$, $I$. Our claim is that experts possess some set of features *like* these; there are undoubtedly many other possibilities, with different sets being appropriate for modeling different experts.

Next the three qualitative changes *up, down,* and *same* for these seven variables need to be given binary encodings. The encoding I will discuss here uses one binary variable to indicate whether there is any *change,* and a second to indicate whether the change is *up.* Thus there are two binary variables, $I.c$ and $I.u$, that represent the change in the current, $I$. To represent no change in $I$, the change variable $I.c$ is set to $-1$; the value of $I.u$ is in this case irrelevant. To represent increase or decrease of $I$, $I.c$ is given the value $+1$ and $I.u$ is assigned a value of $+1$ and $-1$, respectively. Thus the total number of representational features in the model is $14 : 2$ for each of the 7 circuit variables.

### Knowledge atoms

The next step in constructing a harmony model is to encode the necessary knowledge into a set of atoms, each of which encodes a subpattern of features that co-occur in the environment. The environment of idealized circuits is governed by formal laws of physics, so a specification of the knowledge required for modeling the environment is staightforward. In most real-world environements, no formal laws exist, and it is not so simple to give a priori methods for directly constructing an appropriate knowledge base. However, in such environments, the fact that harmony models encode *statistical* information, rather than rules, makes them much more natural candidates for viable models than rule-based systems. One way that the statistical properties of the environment can be captured in the strengths of knowledge atoms is given by the learning procedure. Other methods can probably be derived for directly passing from statistics about the domain (e.g. medical statistics) to an appropriate knowledge base.

The fact that the environment of electric circuits is explicitly rule-governed makes a probabilistic model of intuition, like the model under construction, a particularly interesting theoretical contrast to the obvious rule-applying models of explicit conscious reasoning.

For our model we selected a minimal set of atoms; more realistic models of experts would probably involve additional atoms. A minimal specification of the necessary knowledge is based directly on the equations constraining the circuit: Ohm's Law, Kirchoff's Law, and the equation for the total resistance of two resistors in series. Each of these is an equation constraining the simultaneous change in three of the circuit variables. For each law, we created a knowledge atom for each combination of changes in the three variables that does not violate the law. These are memory traces that might be left behind after experiencing many problems in this domain, i.e. after observing many states of this environment. It turns out that this process gives rise to 65 knowledge atoms,[6] all of which we gave strength 1.

A portion of the model is shown in Fig. 9. The two atoms shown are

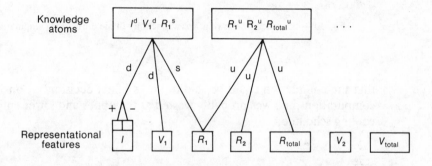

Fig. 9 — A schematic diagram of the feature nodes and 2 knowledge atoms of the model of circuit analysis. $u$, $d$, and $s$ denote $up$, $down$, and $same$. The box labeled $I$ denotes the *pair* of binary feature nodes representing $I$; and similarly for the other 6 circuit variables. Each connection labelled $d$ denotes a *pair* of connections labeled with the binary encoding (+,−) representing *down*; and similarly for connections labelled $u$ and $s$.

respectively instances of Ohm's Law for $R_1$ and of the formula for the total resistance of two resistors in series.

It can be shown that with the knowledge base I have described, whenever a completion problem posed has a unique correct answer, that answer will correspond to the state with highest harmony.[7]

### Cooling schedule
it was not difficult to find a cooling rate that pemitted the model to get the correct answer to the problem shown in Fig. 8 on 28 out of 30 trials. This cooling schedule is shown in Fig. 10.[8] The initial temperature (4.0) was chosen to be sufficiently high that nodes were flipping between their values essentially at random; the final temperature (0.25) was chosen to be sufficiently small that the representational features hardly ever flipped, so

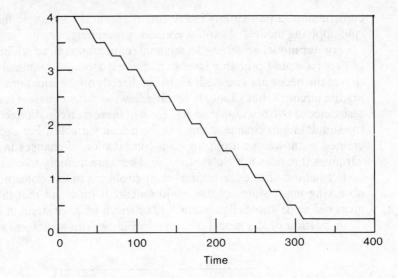

Fig. 10 — the schedule showing $T$ as a function of time during the computation.

that the completion could be said to be its "final decision". Considerable computation time was probably wasted at the upper and lower ends of the cooling schedule.

### The simulation

The graphical display used in the simulation provides a useful image of the computational process. On a gray background, each node was denoted by a box that was white or black depending on the current node value. Throughout the computation, the nodes encoding the given information maintain their fixed values (colors). Initially all the atoms are black (inactive) and the unknown features are assigned random colors. When the computation starts, the temperature is high, and there is much flickering of nodes between black and white. At any moment many atoms are active. As computation proceeds and the system cools, the nodes flicker less and less, and eventually settle into a final value. The "answer" is read out by decoding the features for the unknowns. The answer is correct 93% of the time.

### The micro-description of problem solving

Since the model correctly answer physics questions, it "acts as though" it knows the symbolic rules governing electric circuits. In other words, the *competence* of the harmonium model (using Chomsky's meaning of the word), could be accurately described by symbolic inference procedures (e.g. productions) that operate on symbolic representations of the circuit equations. However the *performance* of the model (including its occasional errors) is achieved without interpreting symbolic rules. In fact the process underlying the model's performance has many characeristics that are not naturally represented by symbolic computation. The answer is computed through a series of many node updates, each of which is a *micro-decision* based on formal *numerical* rules and numerical computations. These micro-decisions are made many times, so that the eventual values for the different circuit variables are in an important sense being computed *in parallel*. *Approximate matching* is an important part of the use of the knowledge: atoms whose feature patterns approximately match the current features values are more likely to become active by thermal noise than atoms that are poorer matches (because poorer matches lower the harmony by a greater amount). And all the knowledge that is active at a given moment *blends* in its effects: when a given feature updates its value, its micro-decision is based on the weighted sum of the recommendations from all the active atoms.

### The macro-description of problem solving
When watching the simulation, it is hard to avoid anthropomorphizing the process. Early on, when a feature node is flickering furiously, it is clear that "the system can't make up its mind about that variable yet". At some point during the computation, however, the node seems to have stopped flickering — "it's decided that the current went down". It is reasonable to say that a *macro-decision* has been made when a node stops flickering, although there seems to be no natural formal definition for the concept. To study the properties of macro-decisions, it is appropriate to look at how the *average values* of the stochastic node variables change during the computation. For each of the unknown variables, the node values were averaged over 30 runs of the completion problem of Fig. 8, separately for each time during the computation. The resulting graphs are shown in Fig. 11. The plots hover around zero initially, indicating that values + and − are equally likely at high temperatures: lots of flickering. As the system cools, the average values of the representation variables drift towards the values they have in the correct solution to the problem ($R_{total} = up, I = down, V_1 = down, V_2 = up$).

### Emergent seriality
To better see the macro-decisions, in Fig. 12 the graphs have been superimposed and the "indecisive" band around 0 has been removed. The striking result is that out of the statistical din of parallel micro-decisions emerges a *sequence* of macro-decisions.

### Propagation of givens
The result is even more interesting when it is observed that in symbolic forward-chaining reasoning about this problem, the decisions are made in the order $R, I, V_1, V_2$. Thus not only is the *competence* of the model neatly describable symbolically, but even the *performance*, when described at the macro-level, could be modeled by the sequential firing of productions that chain through the inferences. Of course, macro-decisions emerge first about

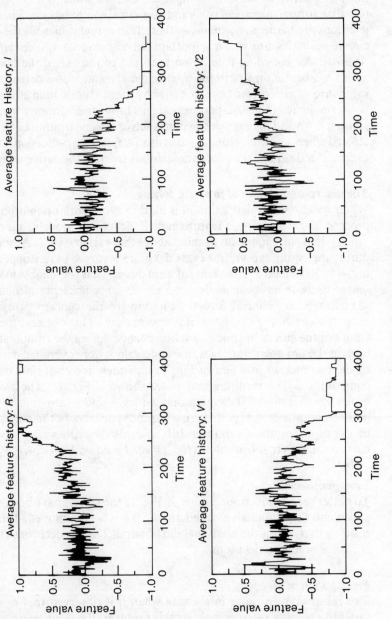

Fig. 11 — The model's hypothesized qualitative values for unknown circuit variables, averaged over 30 runs, for each iteration separately (+ means *up*).

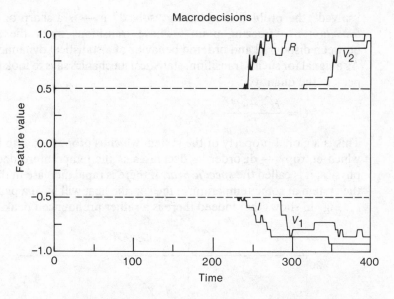

Fig. 12 — Emergent seriality: the decions about the direction of change of the circuit variables "freeze in" in the order $R=R_{\text{total}}$, $I=I_{\text{total}}$, $V_1$, $V_2$ ($R$ and $I$ are very close).

those variables that are most directly constrained by the given inputs, but not because rules are being used that have conditions that only allow them to apply when all but one of the variables is known. Rather it is because the variables given in the input *are fixed and do not fluctuate:* they provide the information that is the most consistent over time and therefore the knowledge consistent with the input is most consistently activated, allowing those variables involved in this knowledge to be more consistently completed than other variables. As the temperature is lowered, these variables "near" the input (with respect to the connections provided by the knowledge) stop fluctuating first, and their relative constancy of value over time makes them function somewhat like the original input to support the next wave of completion. In this sense, the stability of variables "spreads out" through the network, starting at the inputs and propagating with the help of cooling. Unlike the simple feed-forward "spread of activation" through a standard activation network, this process is a spread of feedback-mediated *coherency* through a decision-making network. Like the growth of droplets or crystals, this amounts to the expansion of pockets of order into a sea of disorder.

### Phase transition
Early in the computation, when the temperature is high, the harmonium model occupies "local" solutions that satisfy some of the domain constraints. Late in the computation, when the temperature is low, the model usually occupies the "global" solution that satisfies the maximum possible number of constraints. A natural question to ask is whether the transition between the high and low temperature regimes — between not having

"solved" the problem and having "solved" it — is a sharp one: a *phase transition* or "freezing point". Phase transitions mark the separation between disodered and ordered behavior of a statistical dynamical system. As a signal for such a transition, statistical mechanics says to look for a sharp peak in the quantity

$$C = \frac{\langle H^2 \rangle - \langle H \rangle^2}{T^2}$$

This is a global property of the system which is proportional to the rate at which entropy — disorder — decreases as the temperature decreases; in physics, it is called the *specific heat*. If there is rapid increase in the order of the system at some temperature, the specific heat will have a peak there.

Fig. 13 shows that indeed there is a rather pronounced peak. Does this

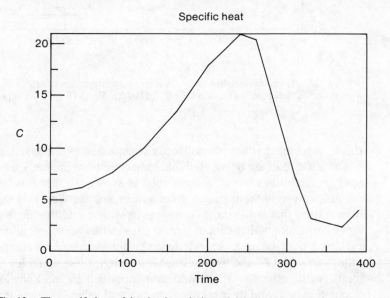

Fig. 13 — The specific heat of the circuit analysis model through the course of the computation.

macro-statistic of the system correpond to anything significant in the macro-decision process? In Fig. 14 the specific heat curve is superimposed on Fig. 12. The peak in the specific heat coincides remarkably with the first two, major macro-decisions about the total resistance and current.

## Macro-description: Production and expertise
While there are similarities in the production-system account of problem solving and the macro-description of the harmony account, there are important differences. These differences are most apparent in the accounts of how experts' knowledge is acquired and represented.

### A symbolic account of expertise acquisition
A standard description within the symbolic paradigm of the acquisition of expertise is based on the idea of knowledge *compilation* (Anderson, 1982). Applied to circuit analysis, the account goes roughly like this. Novices have

Phase transition

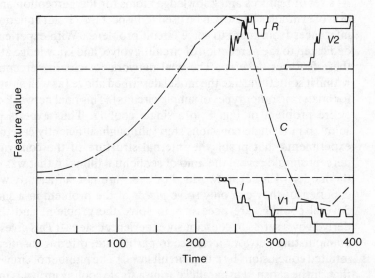

Fig. 14 — There is a peak in the specific heat at the time when the $R$ and $I$ decisions are being made.

procedures for inspecting equations and using them to assign values to unknowns. At this stage of performance, novices consciously scan equations when solving circuit problems. As circuit problems are solved, knowledge is *proceduralized:* specialized circuit-analysis productions are stored in the knowledge base. An example might be "IF given: $R_1$ and $R_2$ both go up THEN conclude: $R_{total}$ goes up", which can be abbreviated $R_1^u R_2^u \rightarrow R_{total}^u$. Another might be $R_{total}^u V_{total}^s \rightarrow I^d$. At this stage of performance, a series of logical steps is consciously experienced, but no equations are consciously searched. As the circuit productions are used together to solve problems, they are *composed* together (Lewis, 1978). The two productions just mentioned, for example, are composed into a single production, $R_1^u R_2^u V_{total}^s \rightarrow R_{total}^u I^d$. As the productions are composed, the conditions and actions get larger, more is inferred in each production firing, and so fewer productions need to fire to solve a given problem. Eventually, the compilation process has produced productions like $R_1^u R_2^u V_{total}^s \rightarrow R_{total}^u I_1^d V_1^d V_2^u$. Now we have an expert who can solve the problem in Fig. 8 all at once, by firing this single production. The reason is that the knowledge base contains, pre-stored, a rule that syas "whenever you are given this problem, give this answer".

### A subsymbolic account

By contrast, the harmony theory account of the acquisition of expertise goes like this. (This account has not yet been tested with simulations.) Beginning physics students are novices in circuit analysis but experts (more or less) at symbol manipulation. Through experience with language and mathematics, they have built up — by means of the learning process referred to in Point 12 — a set of features and knowledge atoms for the perception and manipulation of symbols. These can be used to inspect the circuit equations and draw inferences from them to solve circuit problems. With experience, features dedicated to the perception of circuits evolve, and knowledge atoms relating these features develop. The final network for circuit perception contains within it something like the model described above (as well as other portions for analyzing other types of simple circuits). This final network can solve the entire problem of Fig. 8 in a single cooling. Thus experts perceive the solution in a single conscious step (although sufficiently careful perceptual experiments that probe the internal structure of the construction of the percept should reveal the kind of sequential filling-in that was displayed by the model.) Earlier networks, however, are not sufficiently well tuned by experience; they can only solve *pieces* of the problem in a single cooling. Several coolings are necessary to solve the problem, and the answer is derived by a series of consciously experienced steps. (This gives the symbol-manipulating network a chance to participate, offering justifications of the intuited conclusions by citing circuit laws.) The number of circuit constraints that can be satisfied in parallel during a single cooling grows as the network is learned. *"Productions" are higher-level descriptions of what input/output pairs — completions — can be reliably performed by the network in a single cooling.* Thus, in terms of their "productions", novices are described by productions with simple conditions and actions, and experts are described by complex conditions and actions.

### Dynamic creation of productions

The point is, however, that in the harmony theory account, *"productions" are just descriptive entities; they are not stored, pre-compiled, and fed through a formal inference engine;* rather they are *dynamically created* at the time they are needed by the appropriate collective action of the small knowledge atoms. Old patterns that have been stored through experience can be recombined in completely novel ways, giving the appearance that productions had been pre-compiled even though the particular condition/action pair had never before been performed. When a familiar input is changed slightly, the network can settle down in a slightly different way, flexing the usual "production" to meet the new situation. Knowledge is not stored in large frozen chunks; the "productions" are truly context-sensitive. And since the productions are created on-line by combining many small pieces of stored knowledge, the set of available productions has a size that is an exponential function of the number of knowledge atoms. The exponential explosion of compiled productions is virtual, not pre-compiled and stored.

### Contrasts with logical inference

It should be noted that the harmonium model can answer ill-posed questions just as it can well-posed ones. If insufficient information is provided, there will be more than one state of highest harmony, and the model will choose one of them. It does not stop dead due to "insufficient information" for any formal inference rule to fire. If inconsistent information is given, no available state will have a harmony as high as that of the answer to a well-posed problem; nonetheless, those answers that violate as few circuit laws as possible will have the highest harmony and one of these will therefore be selected. It is not the case that "any conclusion follows from a contradiction". The mechanism that allows the harmonium to solve well-posed problems allows it to find the best possible answers to ill-posed problems, with no modification whatever.

## CONCLUSIONS

In this chapter I have introduced harmony theory, a formal subsymbolic framework for performing an inportant class of generalized perceptual computations: the completion of partial descriptions of static states of an environment. In harmony theory, knowledge is encoded as constraints among a set of well-tuned perceptual features. These constraints are numerical, and are imbedded in an extremely powerful parallel constraint satisfaction machine: an informal inference engine. The constraints and features evolve gradually through experience. The numerical processing mechanisms implementing both performance and learning are derived top–down from mathematical principles. When the computation is described on an aggregate or macro-level, qualitately new features emerge (such as seriality). The *competence* of models in this framework can sometimes be neatly expressed by symbolic rules, but their *performance* is never achieved by explicitly storing these rules and passing them through a symbolic interpreter.

In harmony theory, the concept of self-consistency plays the leading role. The theory extends the relationship that Shannon exploited between information and physical entropy: computational self-consistency is related to physical energy, and computational randomness to physical temperature. The centrality of the consistency or harmony function mirrors that of the energy or Hamiltonian function in statistical physics. Insights from statistical physics, adapted to the cognitive system of harmony theory, can be exploited to relate the micro- and macro-level accounts of the computation. Theoretical concepts, theorems, and computational techniques are being pursued, towards the ultimate goal of a subsymbolic formulation of the Theory of Information Processing.

## ACKNOWLEDGEMENTS

The editors and publishers are gratefully acknowledged for their permission to reprint sections from *Parallel distributed processing: Explorations in the microstructure of cognition. Volume 1: Foundations,* D. E. Rumelhart and J. L. McClelland, Eds. (Bradford Books/MIT Press, forthcoming).

The research reported here was influenced substantially by conversations with Doug Hofstadter, Dave Rumelhart, Geoff Hinton, Jay McClelland, and Stuart Geman, who I thank for sharing their insights with me. Much thanks also to Eileen Conway and Mark Wallen for excellent graphics and computer support. The work was supported by the Systems Development Foundation, the Alfred P. Sloan Foundation, National Institute of Mental Health Grant PHS MH 14268 to the Center for Human Information Processing, and Personnel and Training Research Programs of the Office of Naval Research Contract N00014–79–C–0323, NR 667–437. The author's current address is Department of Computer Science, University of Colorado, Campus Box 430, Boulder, CO 80309, USA.

## REFERENCES

Ackey, D. H., Hinton, G. E., & Sejnowski, T. J. (1985). A learning algorithm for Boltzmann machines. *Cognitive Science, 9,* 147–169.

Anderson, John R. (1982). Acquisition of cognitive skill. *Psychological Review, 89,* 369–406.

Chase, W. G., & Simon, H. A. (1973). Perception in chess. *Cognitive Psychology, 4,* 55–81.

DeMarzo, P. M. (1984). Gibbs potentials, Boltzmann machines, and harmony theory. Unpublished manuscript.

Fahlman, S. E., Hinton, G. E., & Sejnowski, T. J. (1983). Massively parallel architectures for AI: NETL, Thistle, and Boltzmann Machines. *Proceedings of the National Conference on Arificial Intelligence AAAI–83.* Washington, DC.

Feldman, J. A., & Ballard, D. H. (1982). Connectionist models and their properties. *Cognitive Science, 6,* 205–254.

Geman, S., & Geman, D. (1984). Stochastic relaxation, Gibbs distributions, and the Bayesian restoration of images. *IEEE Transactions on Pattern Analysis and Machine Intelligence, 6,* 721–741.

Ginsburg, H. P. (Ed.) (1983). *The development of mathematical thinking.* New York: Academic Press.

Grossberg, S. (1982). *Studies of mind and brain.* Boston: Kluwer.

Hinton, G. E., & Anderson, J. A. (1982). *Parallel models of associative memory.* Hillsdale, NJ: Lawrence Erlbaum.

Hinton, G. E., & Sejnowski, T. J. (1983a). Analyzing cooperative computation. *Proceedings of the Fifth Annual Conference of the Cognitive Science Society.* Rochester, NY.

Hinton, G. E., & Sejnowski, T. J. (1983b). Optimal perceptual inference. *Proceedings of the IEEE Conference on Computer Vision and Pattern Recognition.* Washington, DC.

Hinton, G. E., & Sejnowski, T. J. (forthcoming). Learning and relearning in Boltzmann machines. In D. E. Rumelhart, & J. L. McClelland, (Eds.), *Parallel distributed processing: Explorations in the microstructure of cognition. Volume 1: Foundations.* Cambridge, MA: MIT Press/ Bradford Books.

Hofstadter, D. R. (1979). *Gödel, Escher, Bach: An eternal golden braid.* New York: Basic Books.

Hofstadter, D. R. (1983). The architecture of Jumbo. *Proceedings of the international Machine Learning Workshop.* Monticello, IL.

Hofstadter, D. R. (1985) Waking up from the Boolean dream, or, subcognition as computation. *Metamagical themas,* pp. 631–665. New York: Basic Books.

Larkins, J. H. (1983). The role of problem representation in physics. In D. Gentner & A. L. Stevens (Eds.), *Mental models,* pp. 75–98. Hillsdale, NJ: Lawrence Erlbaum.

Lewis C. H. (1978). *Production system models of practice effects.* Unpublished doctoral dissertation, University of Michigan.

Lindsay, P. H., & Norman, D. A. (1972). *Human information processing.* New York: Academic Press.

Marr, D. (1982). *Vision.* San Franciso: Freeman.

McClelland, J. L., & Rumelhart, D. E. (1981). An interactive activation model of context effects in letter perception: Part 1. An account of basic findings. *Psychological Review, 88,* 375–407.

McClelland, J. L., & Rumelhart, D. E. (Eds.) (forthcoming). *Parallel distributed processing: Explorations in the microstructure of cognition. Volume 2: Applications.* Cambridge, MA: MIT Press/Bradford Books.

McClelland, J. L., Rumelhart, D. E., & Hinton, G. E. (forthcoming). The appeal of parallel distributed processing. In D. E. Rumelhart, & J. L. McClelland, *Parallel distributed processing: Explorations in the microstructure of cognition. Volume 1: Foundations.* Cambridge, MA: MIT Press/Bradford Books.

Newell, A. (1980). Physical symbol systems. *Cognitive Science, 4,* 135–183.

Riley, M. S. (1984). *Structural understanding in performance and learning.* Doctoral dissertation, University of Pittsburgh, PA.

Riley, M. S., & Smolensky, P. (1984). A parallel model of (sequential) problem solving. *Proceedings of the Sixth Annual Conference of the Cognitive Science Society.* Boulder, CO.

Rumelhart, D. E. (1979). Some problems with the notion of literal meanings. In A. Ortony (Ed.), *Metaphor and thought.* Cambridge: Cambridge University Press.

Rumelhart, D. E. (1980), Schemata: The building blocks of cognition. In R. Spiro, B. Bruce, & W. Brewer, (Eds.), *Theoretical issues in reading comprehension.* Hillsdale, NJ: Lawrence Erlbaum.

Rumelhart, D. E., & McClelland, J. L. (1982). An interactive activation model of context effects in letter perception: Part 2. The contextual enhancement effect and some tests and extensions of the model. *Psychological Review, 89,* 60–94.

Rumelhart, D. E., & McClelland, J. L. (Eds.) (forthcoming). *Parallel distributed processing: Explorations in the microstructure of cognition. Volume 1: Foundations.* Cambridge, MA: MIT Press/Bradford Books.

Rumelhart, D. E., Smolensky, P., McClelland, J. L., & Hinton, G. E. (forthcoming). Schemata. In J. L. McClelland, & D. E. Rumelhart,

(Eds.), *Parallel distributed processing: Explorations in the microstructure of cognition. Volume 2: Applications*. Cambridge, MA: MIT Press/Bradford Books.

Schank, R. C. (1980). Language and memory. *Cognitive Science*, **4**, 243–284.

Selfridge, O. G., & Neisser, U. (1960). Pattern recognition by machine. *Scientific American*, **203**, 60–68.

Shepard, R. N. (1984). Ecological constaints on internal representation: Resonant kinematics of perceiving, imagining, thinking, and dreaming. *Psychological Review*, **91**, 417–447.

Smolensky, P. (1983). Schema selection and stochastic inference in modular environments. *Proceedings of the National Conference on Artificial Intelligence*. Washington, DC.

Smolensky, P. (1984a). Harmony theory: thermal parallel models in a computational context. In P. Smolensky & M. S. Riley, *Harmony theory: Problem solving, parallel cognitive models, and thermal physics*. Technical Report 8404, Institute for Cognitive Science, University of California at San Diego.

Smolensky, P. (1984b). The mathematical role of self-consistency in parallel computation. *Proceedings of the Sixth Annual Conference of the Cognitive Science Society*. Boulder, CO.

Smolensky, P. (forthcoming). Foundations of harmony theory: Cognitive dynamical systems and the subsymbolic theory of information processing. In D. E. Rumelhart & J. L. McClelland, (Eds.), *Parallel distributed processing: Explorations in the microstructure of cognition. Volume 1: Foundations*. Cambridge, MA: MIT Press/Bradford Books.

## NOTES

1.  There is no contradiction between working from lower-level, perceptual processes up towards higher processes, and pursuing a "Top--Down" theoretical strategy. It is important to distinguish levels of *processing entities* from levels of *theoretical entities*. "Higher-level" *processes* involve *computational* entities that are computationally distant from the peripheral, sensorimotor entities that comprise the "lowest level" of processing. These processing levels *taken together* form the processing system as a whole; they causally interact with each other through "bottom-up" and "top-down" *processing*. "Higher-level" *theories* involve *descriptive* entities that are descriptively distant from entities that are directly part of an actual processing mechanism; these comprise the "lowest level" description. Each theoretical level *individually* describes the processing system as a whole; the interaction of descriptive levels is not *causal,* but *definitional.* (For example, changes in individual neural firing rates at the retina *cause* changes in individual firing rates in the visual cortex, after a delay related to causal information propagation. The same changes in individual retinal neuron firing rates *by definition* change the *average firing rates of pools*

of retinal neurons; these higher-level descriptive entities change instantly, without any causal information propagation from the lower-level description.) Thus in harmony theory, models of higher-level *processes* are derived from models of lower-level, perceptual, processes, while lower-level *descriptions* of these models are derived from higher-level descriptions.

2. Hofstadter has long been making the case for the inadequacy of traditional symbolic description to cope with the power and flexibility of concepts. For his most recent argument, see Hofstadter (1985). He argues for the need to admit the approximate nature of symbolic descriptions, and explicitly to consider processes that are "subcognitive". In Hofstadter (1979, p. 324ff), this same case was phrased in terms of the need for "active symbols," of which the "schemata" described here can be viewed as instances.

3. Omitted are the knowledge atoms that relate the letter nodes to the line segment nodes. Both line segment and letter nodes are in the lower layer, and all knowledge atoms are in the upper layer. Hierarchies in harmony theory are embedded within an architecture of only two layers of nodes (see Smolensky, forthcoming).

4. The precise specification of the decision process is as follows. The features not specified in the input are assigned random initial values, and the knowledge atoms initially all have value 0. Each of these nodes stochastically updates its value according to the rule:

$$\text{prob}(\text{value} = 1) = \frac{1}{1 + e^{-I/T}}$$

where $T$ is a global system parameter and $I$ is the "input" to the node from the attached nodes, defined as follows. Assign to the link in the graph between atom $\alpha$ and feature $i$ a weight $W_{i\alpha}$ whose sign is the label $(\mathbf{k}_\alpha)_i$ of the link, and whose magnitude is the strength of the atom $\sigma_\alpha$ divided by the number of links to the atom, $|\mathbf{k}_\alpha|$:

$$W_{i\alpha} = (\mathbf{k}_\alpha)_i \frac{\sigma_\alpha}{|\mathbf{k}_\alpha|}$$

Using these weights, the input to a node is essentially the weighted sum of the values of the nodes connected to it. The exact definitions are:

$$I_i = 2 \sum_\alpha W_{i\alpha} a_\alpha$$

for feature nodes, and

$$I_\alpha = \sum_i W_{i\alpha} r_i - \kappa$$

for knowledge atoms.

The formulae for $I_i$ and $I_\alpha$ are both derived from the fact that the input to a node is precisely the harmony the system would have if the given node were to choose the value 1 minus the harmony arising from the other choice. The harmony function being used here is defined as follows. Let $r_i$ be the value of representational feature $i$ ($+1$ or $-1$), and let $a_\alpha$ be the activation of atom $\alpha$ (1 or 0). Then the harmony is

$$H_\kappa(\mathbf{r}, \mathbf{a}) = \sum_\alpha \sigma_\alpha \, a_\alpha \left[ \frac{\mathbf{r}\cdot\mathbf{k}_\alpha}{|\mathbf{k}_\alpha|} - \kappa \right]$$

where

$$\mathbf{r}\cdot\mathbf{k}_\alpha = \sum_i r_i \, (\mathbf{k}_\alpha)_i$$

and

$$|\mathbf{k}_\alpha| = \sum_i |(\mathbf{k}_\alpha)_i|$$

Using this harmony function, the above formulae for $I_i$ and $I_\alpha$ are easily derived. (The factor of 2 in $I_i$, the input to a feature node arises from the difference $(+1) - (-1)$ between the node's possible values.) The term $\kappa$ in the input to an atom comes from the constant $\kappa$ in the harmony function; it is a threshold that must be exceeded if activating the atom is to increase the harmony. If $\kappa$ is zero, an atom can increase the harmony by becoming active if more than half the features defining that atom's pattern are matched by the representational features. If $\kappa$ is close to 1, only a perfect match between the atom's pattern and the features will enable the atom to increase harmony by becoming active. Like $T$, $\kappa$ is a global system parameter that is controlled by the modeller.

The stochastic decision rule can be understood with the aid of Fig. 15.

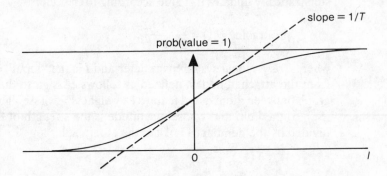

Fig. 15 — The relation between the input $I$ to a node and the probability the node will choose the value +1.

If the input to the node is large and positive (i.e. selecting value 1 would produce much greater system harmony), then it will almost certainly select the value 1. If the input to the node is large and negative (i.e. selecting value 1 would produce much lower system harmony), then it will almost certainly *not* select the value 1. If the input to the node is near zero, it will select the value 1 with a probability near 0.5. The width of the zone of random decisions around zero input is larger the greater is $T$.

5.   Harmonium is closely related to the *Boltzmann machine* (Hinton &

Sejnowski, forthcoming; Hinton & Sejnowski, 1983a, 1983b). The basic dynamics of the machines are the same, although there are differences in most details. Harmony theory also overlaps considerably with the *Gibbs sampler* work of Geman & Geman (1984).

6.  Ohm's Law applies three times for this circuit; once each for $R_1$, $R_2$ and $R_{total}$. This together with the other two lawas gives five constraint equations. In each of these equations the three variables involved can undergo 13 combinations of qualitative changes.

7.  This assumes that $\kappa$ is between 2/3 and 1. In the simulations I will describe, $\kappa$ was raised during the computation to a value of 0.75, as shown in Fig. 16. (The model actually performs better if $\kappa = 0.75$

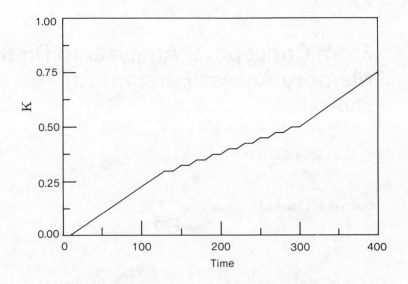

K schedule

Fig. 16 — The schedule showing $\kappa$ as a function of time during the computation.

throughout; DeMarzo, 1984.)

8.  In the reported simulations, one node, selected randomly, was updated at a time. The computation lasted for 400 "iterations" of 100 node updates each; that is, on the average each of the 79 nodes was updated about 500 times.

# 8

# From Conceptual Analyzer to Direct Memory Access Parsing: An Overview

**Christopher K. Riesbeck**

## INTRODUCTION—A REVISIONIST HISTORY OF PARSING

There is, I believe, a revolution happening in natural language processing (NLP) system development in Artificial Intelligence (AI). The revolution is a paradigm shift in our view of what mechanical language understanding is all about. This shift is independent of the syntax versus semantics controversy, but I believe it will lead eventually to models of parsing where the question "Who's in charge: syntax or semantics?" will be moot.

What is this new view of parsing? It is this: a parser is a memory search process, pure and simple. It differs from other such processes only in its emphasis on linguistic cues. The purpose of a parser is not to construct an interpretation for a text, but to locate those existing memory structures to which the text is referring. I call this "Direct Memory Access Parsing" or DMAP.

Although there is a constructive aspect to parsing, namely the "remembering" of the text and the references it makes, this construction of memory structures is neither unique to parsing (we are always remembering uses of memory — that's why memory is dynamic), nor is it limited to those structures that have typically been identified with "the meaning of a sentence". For example, we remember veiled implications, tones of voice, initial misunderstandings, and so on. The only thing that separates these items from more standard ideas of meaning is whether, when we remember them, we include the memory structure for "speaker intended this."

For example, our misunderstanding of a text may seem like it can't possibly be the meaning of that text, but what about jokes? Suppose one of our parsers only remembered what texts were about and it heard this story:

I just got back from a hunting expedition. The first night I shot two bucks.
It was all the money I had.

When asked, our parser would paraphrase this as:

He just got back from a hunting expedition. The first night he spent two dollars. It was all the money he had.

We'd certainly consider a human who did this unintelligent!

In short, in direct memory access parsing, the traditional notion of parsing as "constructing an interpretation" is replaced with the more general, non-parser-specific process of "classifying and remembering an episode," i.e. tracing memory use. What sets parsing apart from other processes is not the construction of interpretations, but the use of peculiarly linguistic items to direct the use of memory structures.

Riesbeck and Martin (1985) describe a particular implementation of a direct memory access parser. In this chapter, I'd like to trace the origins of this view of parsing, and describe the current state of the art. The reader should be warned that I am interpreting modern research in much the same way that a literary critic interprets novels. Do not assume that the researchers involved necessarily agree with the issues and imports I attribute to their systems.

## CONCEPTUAL ANALYSIS

Until recently, direct memory access parsing was not possible because there weren't any suitable models of long-term memory to access. Instead, there was "conceptual analysis." Spinoza (Schank *et al.*, 1970) and the MARGIE parser (Riesbeck, 1975) were the first in a series of parsers that attempted to go directly from sentential input to conceptual representations, without constructing an intermediate syntactic description of the sentence.

For example, a key difference between the MARGIE parser and previous systems was the way it treated the following examples:

John gave Mary book.
John gave Mary a kiss.
John kissed Mary.

"John gave Mary a book" was parsed as "John transferred a book from John to Mary." "John gave Mary a kiss," however, despite its syntactic similarity, was parsed as "John pressed his lips against Mary." This result was identical to the parse produced for "John kissed Mary," and was the representation needed by the MARGIE inference module. The theoretical demands of the Conceptual Dependency representation scheme, and the needs of the inference and generation modules, distinguished the development of the MARGIE parser from systems that were being created to process English, but which had no general follow-on system to talk to.

Even at that time, the separation of the MARGIE parser from the MARGIE inference module was a matter of convenience, not theory, since the MARGIE parser often had to make inferences during parsing. The rule of thumb for the division of labor was this: any inference rule that required knowledge of English was the responsibility of the parser. The inference module should be unaffected if the English parser were replaced by a Chinese parser. Thus, for example, it was up to the inference module to determine that "John picked up a stick and hit Mary," implied that John hit Mary with the stick, but it was up to the parser to decide that "John had an apple" probably meant that "John ate an apple".

The MARGIE parser was an example of an expectation-driven parser, using "if–then" rules, called *requests,* to encode conceptual and syntactic parsing knowledge. For example, "give" had requests that said

- The subject of the sentence is transferring something to someone.
- If a physical object follows, then that is the object being transferred.
- If a human follows, then that human is the recipient of the transfer.
- If an action follows, then the subject of the sentence is doing that action to the recipient.

Later conceptual analyzers were ELI (Riesbeck & Schank, 1976), ELI-2 (Gershman, 1979), and CA (Birnbaum & Selfridge, 1981). They extended and changed the basic approach in many ways, including better control structures, standardized request formats, and so on. They maintained the basic ideas however. The parsers always produced a meaning representation, not a syntactic structure, by applying requests attached to words read left to right in a sentence. The meaning representation was then passed to inference modules, for language-independent processing.

The goal of the parser, as defined by these systems, was this: to get from the words in a sentence as directly as possible to the meaning of the sentence, with "meaning" defined as "whatever the inference processes need." The request format helped to achieve this goal by allowing processing rules to be written that built and used conceptual structures as easily as other systems built and used syntactic structures. Fig. 1 is a simple block diagram for these conceptual analyzers.

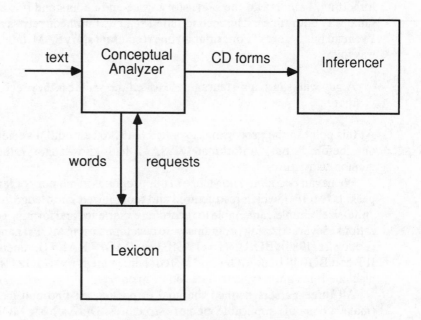

Fig. 1 — Early conceptual analyzers.

## MEMORY-BASED CONCEPTUAL ANALYSIS

MARGIE, SAM (Schank & Abelson, 1977), PAM (Wilensky, 1978), FRUMP (DeJong, 1979), and POLITICS (Carbonell, 1979) were all knowledge-applying programs. That is, they understood input texts by applying a fixed set of knowledge structures. SAM knew about standardized event sequences, such as going to a restaurant or a newspaper account of a car accident, while PAM and POLITICS knew how to understood stories about goals and plans, such as how to get money by asking someone or robbing a bank.

In the early 1980s, our view of inference processes changed. People don't just have a *knowledge base,* they have a *memory* (Schank, 1982). We mean two things by this. First, what people know is the result of experience. Often, what you know about something is very intimately connected to your experiences with it. For example, when I think about hammers, I think about particular hammers I have owned.

Second, what people know is *dynamic,* i.e. it changes with use, whereas a knowledge structure is static, like the information in an encylopedia. You can use a knowledge structure — or have problems using it — as many times as you want, and it will remain unchanged. Experiential knowledge, however, changes as the set of experiences changes. Barring long-term forgetting, I can't read the same story twice and understand it exactly the same way both times. The second time I read it, I immediately say, "Hey, I've read this before." For example, one restaurant story SAM *didn't* handle was this:

> A guy walks into a restaurant. He asked the waiter if they served crabs there ...

At this point in the processing, I wanted SAM to respond "I've heard that one before," but, unfortunately, SAM had knowledge, rather than memory, structures.

We began encoding knowledge in our programs in memory organization packets (MOPs), which restructured and reorganized knowledge into more "bite-size" chunks, amenable to recording experience and forming generalizations. Several parsing programs were developed using MOPs, namely IPP (Lebowitz, 1980), BORIS (Dyer, 1983), and MOPTRANS (Lytinen, 1984). IPP and BORIS built MOPs and stored them in memory. (MOPTRANS, a machine translation system, had a static memory.)

All three parsers defined the goal of parsing as: find and instantiate (make a copy of) applicable memory structures. Once a basic MOP frame was chosen, requests filled in the slots. These requests were often attached to the MOP structures, rather than to individual words. Since MOPs usually encoded fairly general knowledge, they had to be specialized to apply to the situation at hand. In MOPTRANS, for example, "Police captured ..." would initially be interpreted as a generic GET-CONTROL MOP, but this interpretation would be refined to ARREST because the polic were doing the capturing. In IPP, a similar refinement process would occur in sentences such as "Terrorists holding machine guns sprayed ..." where the generic "spray" would be understood as "shoot" in this context. In BORIS, requests made explicit calls to the memory, e.g. a request might say "If a specific MOP describing event already exists in memory, use it, otherwise add this event to memory."

Fig. 2 shows the basic structure of these memory-based parsers.

IPP, BORIS, and MOPTRANS are examples of what I call "build and store" parsers. There is a separate parsing process in each case that is responsible for building a memory structure and passing it on to a memory-storage facility. Like the earlier conceptual analyzers, these parsers have separately organized lexicons which contain all of the system's language-processing information. This is unlike syntactically based systems, which separate the rule base from the lexicon. The memory-based systems differ from their predecessors in that they construct long-term memory structures, rather than conceptual structures.

For example, given the sentence

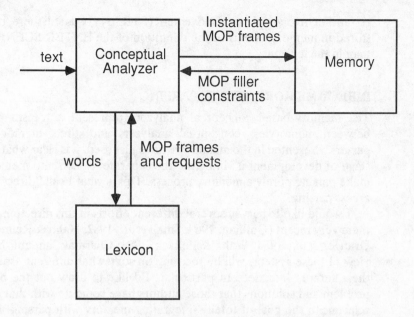

Fig. 2 — Memory-based conceptual analyzers.

John went into a restaurant.

ELI would have generated something similar to

(PTRAINS (ACTOR (PERSON NAME (JOHN)))
        (OBJECT (PERSON NAME (JOHN)))
        (TO   (INSIDE   PART   (BUILDING   TYPE
              (RESTAURANT)))))

which says that John moved himself into a restaurant building. (PTRANS is the conceptual dependency primitive for physical motion.) A reasoning module, such as SAM, would infer from this that John might be initiating the restaurant script by going into the restaurant to get something to eat.

Given the same sentence, one of these memory-based parsers would produce something like this:

(ENTER-SCENE (MOP RESTAURANT-DINE)
             (ACTOR PERSON-32)

where ENTER-SCENE is the opening event in the memory structure RESTAURANT-DINE, and PERSON-32 is the particular memory token used to keep track of the story character named John. In other words, much of the work that used to be left for the reasoning module had become integrated with the parsing process. The information that going to a restaurant involves physical movement (PTRANS) was still there, but it was stored in memory as part of the definition of the ENTER-SCENE, rather than in the lexicon.


## DIRECT MEMORY ACCESS PARSING

The memory-based conceptual analyzers represent a transitional state between memoryless conceptual analyzers and direct memory access parsers. Presented in the manner we have just used, it is clear what the next stage of development is: integrate the separate lexicon into memory, and make parsing purely a memory process. This is what I call "direct memory access parsing."

I would like to survey several different efforts in this direction, most of them very recent (Quillian, 1969; Small et al., 1982; Hahn & Reimer, 1983; Granger et al., 1984; Waltz & Pollack, 1984; Charniak, unpublished.) My view of these systems will be focusing on somewhat different aspects than their authors intended. In particular, I'd like to draw out the particular problem and solutions that those authors have come up with that are most relevant to the goal of totally integrating memory with parsing. I am not claiming that such a goal is the primary interest of any of these other researchers. In fact, many people are more interested in what I think is a side issue, namely, how to speed up parsing with parallelism. While parallelism is indeed a common feature, at least in principle, with these systems, it is not, in my opinion, the important point. The real point is that parsing should be viewed as just a memory search process, and linguistic knowledge, including highly syntactic information, should be stored in memory in exactly the same way that other kinds of information are stored.


### The teachable language comprehender

The first direct memory access parser is older than any system I have discussed so far. It is M. Ross Quillian's *teachable language comprehender*, also known as TLC (Quillian, 1969). TLC's notion of semantic memory (Quillian, 1968) had far-reaching effects in AI and psychology (see, for example, Fahlman, 1979; Collins & Quillian, 1969), but its model of parsing has not been seriously pursued until recently.

In TLC, English words pointed directly to nodes, called *units*, in a semantic memory. A unit had a pointer to a superset, plus zero or more pointers to properties. A *property* had an *attribute*, a *value*, and zero or more sub-properties.

Fig. 3 shows a simple example. The word "client" points to a unit that says that a client is a PERSON, with one property. That property is EMPLOY PROFESSIONAL, with one sub-proprerty, namely that the professional is employed by the client.

When TLC read an English phrase, it placed markers on the units that the words in the phrase referred to. For example, when it read "lawyer's client", it put markers on LAWYER and CLIENT.

Then TLC spread the markers breadth-first from the marked units to

DICTIONARY

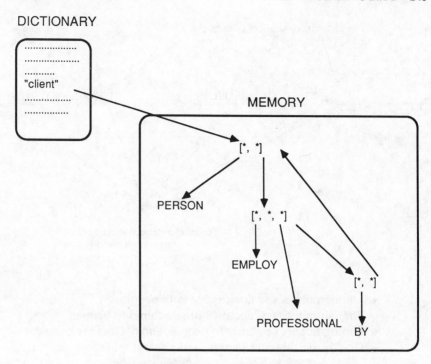

Fig. 3 — The teachable language comprehender (after Quillian 1969, p. 462).

their supersets and properties, then to those items' supersets and properties, and so on, until the markers met somewhere in memory. With "lawyer's client," CLIENT marked the property EMPLOY PROFESSIONAL, and LAWYER marked the superset PROFESSIONAL, and TLC found the intersection at EMPLOY.

An intersection was only a candidate connection. To determine if a connection was actually expressed by the input, TLC used *form tests*. Form tests were attached to memory units and looked for certain features in the input. When a unit was a candidate connection, its form tests were applied to the input. If the input passed any of the tests, then the connection was accepted as a meaning of the input.

For example, EMPLOY had a form test that said that the word referring to the property value must have an " 's" attached and be followed immediately by the word referring to the source word. In this case, "lawyer" referred to PROFESSIONAL and "client" was the source of the marker that went to EMPLOY, so the form test checked for "lawyer's client" in the input.

There are many problems that have to be solved with this kind of approach. One of the first is managing the intersection search process. For example, consider the sentence "The photographer shoots the doctor" and the related memory structure in Fig. 4.

The problem is that there are four possible intersection points visible, using just this bare fragment of memory (more would appear if we filled in more memory):

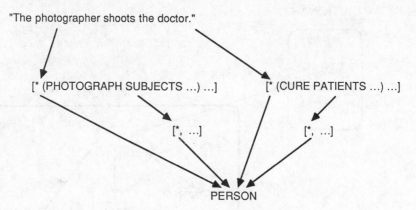

Fig. 4 — Too many intersections in TLC.

- Photographers and doctors are both people.
- Photographers and doctors both do things to people.
- Photographers do things to people, and doctors are people.
- Doctors do things to people, and photographers are people.

Quillian notes that the first two kinds of intersections are unlikely to be useful in comprehension. TLC avoids them by putting one kind of activation marker on candidate word senses and their supersets, and another kind on properties and their supersets, and then accepting only those intersections where the two types of markers meet.

This leaves TLC then with two potential interpretations of "The photographer shoots the doctor." Either the photographer is photographing the doctor, or the photographer is a patient of the doctor's. Form tests attached to "PHOTOGRAPH" look for phrases, such as "X photographs (takes a picture of) (shoots) ... Y," which accepts the first interpretation. None of the form tests attached to "CURE" ("X cures (heals) ... Y," "Y visits (sees) ... X") work, so the second interpretation is rejected.

Quillian's made the following observations about TLC: TLC draws information from its memory to produce a representation of a piece of input text that is:

1. Encoded in the regular memory format.
2. Much richer and less ambiguous than the input text itself.
3. A highly intraconnected structure with the various concepts mentioned in the text linked in ways supplied from a memory of facts about the world.
4. Linked to the permanent memory by many pointers to established concepts (although its creation in no way changes the permanent memory, except for the addition of temporary tags used by the interaction routines) (Quillian, 1969, p. 467).

These are all desirable features for any conceptual analyzer (with one caveat), and yet they have not been true of any system since TLC, until recently, because of the separation of the parsing process from memory processes. If memory structures existed at all, they had only an indirect link to the structures being produced by the analyzer, in that, after the parser produced a form, the memory would match it against its stored forms.

The one caveat is that Quillian's fourth comment, that long-term memory is unaffected by parsing, is exactly what we *don't* want in a system that remembers and learns.

## DMAP: A DIRECT MEMORY ACCESS PARSER

Quillain's TLC model had many problems, of course, most of them recognized at the time. Its linguistic knowledge was in its form tests, and its form tests were simple string patterns. Its knowledge representation was based on dictionary entries, with a strong English lexical bias. Its method of concept finding by interaction search was not really well matched to the needs of text understanding. It is the spirit of TLC, not the details, that is the inspiration for much of the modern work on direct memory access parsing.

Before DMA parsing can even begin, there must, of course, be a memory to access. A memory consists of one or more types of memory "elements," e.g. frame units, conceptual dependency forms, or predicate calculus formulas, interconnected by some kind of cross-referencing structure. For example, we can fill the slots of frames with pointers to other frames, or store forms in discrimination trees, or index formulas by their constant parts (see (Charniak *et al.* (1980) for a discussion of these options).

Given a particular memory model, designing a DMA parser involves figuring out how to store linguistic knowledge *in the memory,* and developing search processes to access this knowledge during the parsing process.

Aesthetically, it would be pleasing if we could store linguistic knowledge in memory using exactly the same memory elements and interconnection mechanisms used for other kinds of knowledge. For the moment, however, the Yale direct memory access parser (DMAP) has taken a simpler approach and represented linguistic knowledge with specialized data structures, called *concept sequences,* which are attached to MOPs and conceptual dependency action schemata.

For example, events involving transfers of information, such as "John says he'll come," are instances of the MTRANS action schema, which has the form "an *actor* transfers a *mental object* to a recipient," where the items in italics are roles of the schema. One simple concept sequence attached to the MTRANS schema is *"actor MTRANS-WORD mobject."* This sequence says that one way in which a transfer of information event is expressed is by saying who the actor is, followed by some word for MTRANS, such as "say" or "tell", followed by what the information (mental object or mobject) was. There are of course other sequences attached to the MTRANS schema, and the notion of MTRANS word is too broad, but this template is quite usable as it stands.

We are not claiming that parsing knowledge necessarily should be different in kind from other kinds of knowledge. We just do not know enough yet to find a good unified form for the two kinds of knowledge.

**Attaching parsing knowledge to memory structure**
Fig. 5 shows a figurative block diagram of the DMAP system. Since there is only one module, the memory, Fig. 5 goes into that box a little deeper to show language and conceptual hierarchies intertwined. This figure is intended to express the basic idea that linguistic knowledge, such as the lexical items "John" and "city", is attached to the hierarchically organized conceptual nodes in memory. Thus, for example, "post office" is attached to a node that is lower in the hierarchy than the node that "building" is attached to.

## MEMORY SEARCH PROCESSES

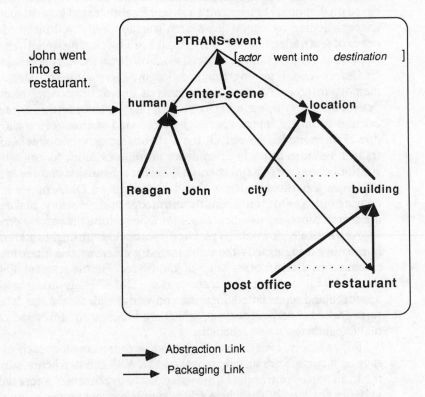

Fig. 5 — Direct memory access parsing.

The concept sequences attached to these memory nodes are phrasal patterns (Becker, 1975). Sequences are attached to objects, events, states, and so on. For example, attached to **PTRANS-event,** i.e. the abstraction of all events involving PTRANS, are phrases used to express motion, such as that the actor "went" to or into some place.

Concept sequences are made up of the following kinds of elements:

- particular lexical items, such as "interest rates" attached to the concept interest rates,
- lexical classes, semantically organized, such as MTRANS-WORD that groups words that mean "transfer of information," and
- role names, such as *actor* and *object*, that allow the concept sequence to refer to the fillers of the slots in the memory element to which the concept sequence is attached.

Our memory has basic frame units for objects, like restaurants and Reagan, and MOPs for events and state changes. There are two standard kinds of links between MOPs. *Abstraction* links go from specialized nodes to more general ones. For example, **enter-scene** has the abtraction **PTRANS-event** and **restaurant** has the abstraction **building.** We assume that many concepts have multiple abstractions and all our algorithms deal with that possibility.

The other kind of link is the packaging link. A node packages together other nodes. With objects, packaging links reflect part relationships. For example, the node for **human** packages body parts (not shown in Fig. 5). With MOPs, there are two kinds of packaging links. Fig. 5 shows the *role* packaging link. A MOP event has actors and objects and locations and so on which play different roles in the event. **Enter-scene,** for example, has role-packaging links to the actor and the location entered. The other kind of packaging link is the *subscene* link. A MOP event usually packages together several sub-events into a temporal sequence. Fig. 5 does not show this (Fig. 6 does), but **enter-scene** would be a subscene of the **restaurant** MOP. Normally our figures will label role-packaging links with the role involved, but will leave subscene links unlabelled.

When a concept sequence attached to a MOP contains a role name, that name refers to the role in the corresponding MOP. Thus, something like "*actor* went to *destination*," attached to **PTRANS-event** would mean that the MOP could be expressed as "the actor of the PTRANS went to the destination of the PTRANS," where the actor and destination would be filled in by phrases attached to the MOPs filling the actor and destination roles of **PTRANS-event.**

A concept sequence might be stored in many places in the memory, but in general it will be stored at the most abstract node possible, and be inherited implicitly by all specializations of that node. Thus, because "*actor* went into *destination*" is attached to **PTRANS-event**, it is inherited by **enter-scene.** This inheritance is done by the particular memory search process used in parsing, described in the next section.

### Using parsing knowledge in DMAP

We store parsing knowledge in DMAP in much the same way that TLC did, by attaching simple patterns to memory nodes. DMAP uses these patterns very differently, however.

In TLC, markers were passed outward from referenced concepts until they intersected at some common point, whereupon form tests at that point would be applied to see if a reasonable interpretation had been found. Marker passing was a general search mechanism and the linguistic patterns filtered out the desired results.

In DMAP, the patterns control where markers are passed in the first place. DMAP has two kinds of markers. Activation markers (A-markers) are placed on memory nodes that have been seen or are abstractions of nodes that have been seen. Prediction markers (P-markers) are placed on memory nodes that have been predicted or appear in concept sequences of nodes that have been predicted. That is, putting an A-marker on a node puts A-markers on its abstractions, while putting a P-marker on a node puts P-markers on certain of its parts and role fillers.

As in TLC, things happen only when markers meet markers. In DMAP, when an A-marker is passed to a concept that already has a P-marker, DMAP traces the P-marker back to its source, which will be some concept sequence that referred to this concept. Let's call the concept that received the A-marker the *part-concept* and call the source of the P-marker the *whole-concept.* Two things now happen. First, the concept sequence and P-marker on whole-concept are passed down the abstraction hierarchy to the most specialized version of whole-concept that packages some abstraction hierarchy to the most specialized version of whole-concept that packages some abstraction of part-concept. This process is called "concept refinement." Then the concept sequence is "bumped," i.e. a P-marker is passed to the next element in the concept sequence. If everything in the concept sequence has received an A-marker, then the concept to which the sequence is attached gets an A-marker, which is then passed up the abstraction hierarchy, and so on.

To see briefly how this works, assume we have the highly simplified hierarchy shown in Fig. 6, which says that one kind of **PTRANS-event** is **travel,** below which are the specializations **vehicular travel, other agent vehicular travel** and **air travel.** Though this memory fragment is just a toy for pedagogical purposes, already we can see various complexities creeping in. **Other agent vehicular travel,** for example, has a second abstraction, **other agent service,** which represents events where someone else does something for you. This means that **other agent vehicular travel** inherits two subscenes and two sets of role links, one set for the traveller and another set for what the other agent does for the traveller (We ignore — and in fact do not handle well in the current implementation — the problem of conflicting role names, such as the presence of *actor* in both inherited scenes.) These scenes in **air travel** describe the pilot flying the plane and the passenger riding in the plane.

Every specialization inherits the packaging links of its abstractions. All the specializations of **travel,** for example, inherit the *dest* role with the filler **geographical location.** These roles are accessible to the subscenes as well, so that *air-trip scene* can refer to the destination of **air travel.**

Of particular interest are the concept sequences attached to the nodes in this memory fragment. **PTRANS-event** has the generic sequence "*actor*

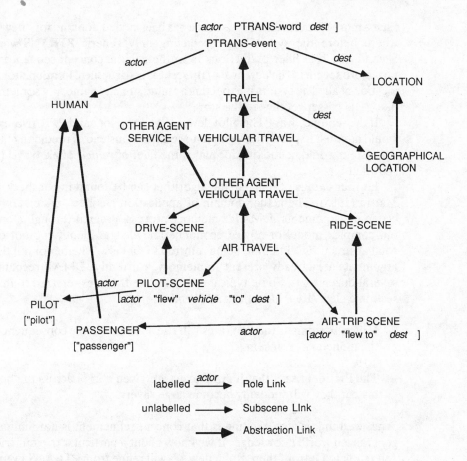

Fig. 6 — Air travel hierarchy with concept sequences.

PTRANS-WORD *dest.*" Suppose previous processing has predicted (passed a P-marker to) **PTRANS-event**. Because of the attached concept sequence, **PTRANS-event** passes a P-marker through *actor* to **human.**

Now DMAP reads a sentence starting with "The passenger ..." A-markers spread up the activation hierarchy from **passenger,** eventually reaching **human.** Most of the A-markers hit unmarked nodes, but **human** has the P-marker from the concept sequence on **PTRANS-event.** Concept refinement passes this sequence to the most specialized version of **PTRANS-event** that packages some abstraction of **passenger.** In this case, there is a specialization that packages **passenger** directly, namely **air-trip scene.**

Now the concept sequence is bumped, which means P-markers are passed to PTRANS-WORDs. Furthermore, since a P-marker has been passed to **air-trip scene,** which has its own concept sequence, a P-marker is passed to the lexical node "flew to." (The *actor* of **air-trip scene** is already active and therefore the concept sequence is immediately bumped.)

Concept refinement has refined the predictions being made in two ways.

First a more specific concept sequence has been added, looking for "flew to" where before the system was predicting only generic **PTRANS-words**. Second, the role filler predictions from the generic concept sequence are now more specific. The *dest* of **air-trip scene** is **geographical location,** not any location at all. The system is expecting a country or city name, not something like "The passenger flew to the store."

If the sentence was "The pilot flew ...," then "pilot" and **PTRANS-event** would have led to predictions on **pilot-scene,** and, instead of predicting "to", the system would be looking for **plane,** the filler of *vehicle* of **air travel** (not shown in Fig. 6).

Further details of this parsing algorithm can be found in Riesbeck and Martin (1985). The actual domain of application has been understanding economic arguments. DMAP's memory processes search through a crude but complex model of novice economic knowledge, identifying not only what abstract causalities are being referred to, but also whether or not these arguments are already present in memory. Currently, DMAP recognizes several dozen texts. Some typical examples are the ones referred to in the section called "Real life versus AI," and

> Milton Friedman: Interest rates will rise as an inevitable consequence of the monetary explosion.

> The President says that if Americans are given a 25% across the board tax cut they will suddenly become large savers.

What we think is very exciting is that concept refinement is not limited to generalized world knowledge. If we know about a particular trip our friend John took to Detroit, then "John flew..." will refine from **PTRANS-event** to the memory node we have for that trip, and the P-marker will pass through *dest* to **Detroit.** This smooth integration of particular episodic knowledge with parsing predictions is exactly what we want.

### Ambiguity

Ambiguity, as in TLC, is a constant fact of life. Words have multiple senses, and the concepts referred to by those senses have multiple abstractions, and the abstractions appear in multiple packages. Linguistic choices, such as where a prepositional phrase attaches, appear in the system in the form of multiple concept activation, where one concept would be described by one choice, and the other concept would be described by the other choice. What decides which packages and concepts are correct?

In the conceptual analyzers, the decision was made in one of two ways. In ELI and CA, whatever came first in the dictionary took priority. In BORIS and IPP, the parser asked memory for a decision.

The first method was used most often, because the second method was too difficult. Because the inference engine didn't know exactly what was happening in the parser, it was hard to design good questions for the parser to ask the inferencer that would give the inferencer enough information to make a reasonable decision. We explicitly rejected the alternative of having the parser produce structures for all the ambiguous interpretations, and pass the set of them to the inferencer for selection. It was, and remains, totally implausible to us that a good model of parsing would have no better idea at the end of a sentence of what the sentence was about than it had at the beginning of the sentence.

With direct memory access parsing, the whole nature of the problem has changed. There is no longer an issue of when the parser should talk to memory, and what information it should pass, because there is no separation between the two. In effect, the parser *is* "passing" all the interpretations to memory, but this occurs not at sentence or clause boundary, but continuously throughout the parse.

Furthermore, the disambiguation problem in this situation is purely a memory processing issue: given several packagings of some currently active concepts, choose which packages are relevant. It is not really a language issue at all.

In fact, DMAP, being strongly top-down, has more of a problem with too few packages, rather than too many. As we said in our algorithm description, a concept sequence attached to a package is not pursued unless it has been predicted (passed a P-marker). These initial high-level predictions are just what we need, but where do they come from?

### Real life versus AI

We have now come to, I think, the crucial point, and also to the point where many of us will part company. As long as the memory that a DMA parser accesses contains the standard knowledge structures of AI and computational linguistics, I do not believe that it can do any better than any other parsing system. The secret is not in the algorithm a system uses, it is in what the system knows is going on at the moment of the parse. "Who is talking (writing) this?" "What do I know about them from before?" "What activities are they engaged in of which this speech (text) is a subpart?" "Why should I care about what this person is saying to me?" Answering these questions is, I claim, the *primary* goal of human understanders. Getting the meaning is *secondary,* often instrumental to the primary goal, but not always essential.

Most people in AI would probably grant that the ultimate understanding system should be capable of answering the questions asked in the previous paragraph, but that to get there, we have to take things one step at a time. Grosz (1977) studies these questions by setting up the problem of a tutor telling an assistant in another room how to put a complex object together. The goals are well defined and the tutor can try matching the assistant's questions and statements against a library of known scripts and plans.

I believe, however, that this still abstracts the language-processing task too far from its everyday foundation. Most of the people I talk to are well known to me. Well known means not only that I have met them before, but that I know what they're up to when they start talking to me. One may be arranging a time for a meeting that we've previously agreed to have, another may be checking to see if I've done what I said I would, another may be complaining about some advice I gave the week before. All of these are *on-going* long-term activities, which I quickly *recognize* as being relevant to the current conversation. Of the people I talk to who are less familiar, many of them are playing roles in very specific scripts, such as the waitresses in the restaurant I go to several times a week for lunch, the tellers in my bank, the receptionist at the doctor's office, and so on. Again, within a few words of conversation, I have usually recognized some very particular fragment of a script as being relevant.

Here is my rating of various language-processing tasks, from most common/typical/concrete to most unusual/atypical/abstract. I hear spoken language from family, friends, coworkers, secretaries, waitresses, shop-keepers, and other actors in social roles, television and radio announcers, usually giving updates of on-going events, such as arms talks or hostage situations, and acquaintances, old and new, at parties and other gatherings. The texts I read, in order of decreasing frequency, are signs and signals, such as stop signs and gas gauges, magazine and billboard advertisements, mail (mostly junk), articles in newspapers, articles in magazines, fiction, and technical articles in journals.

There is something in common between the speech I hear most often from family and friends, and the texts I read most often in signs and advertisements: both use language that is highly elliptical and presumes a great deal of background information. This reliance of "you know what's going on" is just as important in texts with a greater distance between speaker/writer and hearer/reader. Consider, for example, one of the texts that DMAP handles:

Q: Why are you so unimpressed with the recent improvements in the inflation numbers?
A: You have to look at inflation numbers in a cyclical perspective.

DMAP understands that the "you" in the question is referring to the interviewee, but that the "you" in the answer is referring to neither the interviewer nor the interviewee, but to the "audience". How does it do this, particularly given the fact that the only inferencing capability DMAP has is simple memory search?

The answer is that DMAP has a **magazine interview** MOP, which is a specialization of **interview,** which is in turn a specialization of **conversation.** A *magazine interview* involves one person asking questions of another for the purpose of giving the other person a chance to present views to a general audience. Lexical items, such as "Q:" and "A:", are part of the concept sequences for the two sides of the interview, and the content of the statements are specializations of, respectively, "question to speaker" and "statement to audience." Seeing strings like "Q:" and "A:" activate the **interview** MOP, thereby bringing in the concept sequences for interviews, which include different uses of "you," depending on who is talking. Most TV-viewing American adults have become familiar with (i.e. formed MOPs for) many different kinds of interviews, such as the "promote your latest movie" and the "defend your election platform." Context and lexical cues guide the memory search down to these highly specialized subMOPS, which often have particular phrases and concept sequences attached.

Consider the difference between the use of "some people" when my wife says "Some people came by to fix the TV," and when a politician says "Some people feel that we can survive with a growing deficit." My wife means "a group of people that I'm not going to specify further," but the politician means "that group of people who have recently publicly disagreed with me." That is, "some people" is not at all an indefinite reference when a politician uses it. The DMAP model of understanding would handle this by attaching the phrase "some people" to the appropriate filler in the memory structure describing how a politician normally responds to opposition arguments without naming names. Obviously, "some people" would appear in many places in memory. This is why the memory search processes must keep active the most specific memory structures it can, "lighting up", in effect, the appropriate specialized uses of different phrases.

There's a good reason, of course, why AI has not dealt with understanding texts with complex, multi-goaled, highly familiar contexts. It's very hard to do. There are three major problems:

- knowing how to represent the necessary information,
- dealing efficiently with large amounts of inferentially interrelated information, and
- integrating parsing knowledge with everything else.

We believe that the DMA approach answers the third problem in a way that allows the parser to take full advantage of the information that an intelligent system needs. As long as the answer to the first problem involves using a packaging and abstraction hierarchy, markers can be passed to and from a DMA parser in a well-defined manner. And the use of marker passing offers the potential advantages of parallel processing to manage the large quantities of information involved.

## OTHER APPROACHES

### The connectionist/word expert system

The original word expert parser (Small & Rieger, 1982) was a conceptual analyzer, similar in some ways to the ELI system, but with a greater emphasis on the disambiguation process. Word experts were (sometimes large) programs attached to each word that communicated with other experts during the parsing process in order to reach an agreement on the meaning of the sentence as a whole. Small *et al.* (1982) recast the WEP approach into the University of Rochester's connectionist paradigm (Feldman & Ballard, 1982).

The connectionist framework does not allow structures like markers to be passed between nodes. The basic mechanism is spreading activation through a graph with fixed connections. The meaning of a text is represented by the cluster of nodes activated. Mutual inhibition as well as activation plays an important role in the parsing process, and critical is the use of nodes to represent concepts such as "the agent of the action PROPEL (or MOVE or whatever)."

For example, in parsing "A man threw up a ball," the eventual resolution of "threw up" as meaning "propel upwards" rather than "vomit" is arrived at because "a ball" is more closely connected to "object of PROPEL" than it is to "object of VOMIT," and activating the former inhibits the activation of the latter, which in turn makes the "PROPEL" node connected to "threw up" more active than the "VOMIT" node.

Major problems yet to be solved with this and similar connectionist systems include recognizing word order, keeping straight multiple occurrences of the same word or concept, and storing what has been read. It is also the case that most of these systems have been used only in simple semantic network systems, not in episodically based memories.

## TOPIC

The TOPIC system (Hahn & Reimer, 1983) is also related to the word expert model of parsing. Effectively, they have replaced Quillian's form tests with word experts. They call their approach *text parsing,* and emphasize the interaction between world knowledge and linguistic knowledge during the parsing process. The following quote is indicative of their spiritual ties to direct memory access parsing:

> TOPIC parses text strings directly into knowledge structures (*semantic parsing*) by skipping any kind of intermediate structure, as might be provided by phrase structure trees whose nodes are labelled with syntactic categories (NP, VP, PP, etc.). [p. 3]

The TOPIC system has a hierarchically organized knowledge base of information about microcomputers. The parsing process activates concepts in this memory. A concept is activated when referred to by the text. That activation is increased with subsequent references.

One problem to address is that raised by the text fragment "... provided by *micros*. Nevertheless, these *machines* ..." The word "machines" would initially activate the general machine concept, but this needs to be corrected to be a second activation of the micros concept. This is done by the word expert for "this/these" which reassigns activation from more abstract to more concrete nodes in the appropriate circumstances.

## ATLAST

ATLAST (Granger *et al.* 1984) uses spreading activation in a memory containing a blend of lexical, semantic, and pragmatic information. Three processes are in control: the lexical capsulizer, the proposer, and the filter. The capsulizer initiates concept activation as words are read and posts

syntactic information. The proposer spreads activation from concept to
concept, effectively pursuing all possible inference paths. The filter prunes
these paths, using in part the syntactic information posted by the capsulizer.
An example text is:

> The CIA called in an inspector to check for bugs. The secretaries
> had reported seeing roaches.

In accordance with the lexical access data of Swinney and Hakes (1976)
(which has inspired a fair amount of recent AI research into lexical
disambiguation), the ambiguity of "bugs" is first available, then resolved,
but incorrectly, then re-solved. The mechanism for doing this in ATLAST is
called *conditional retention*. Preceding text will select one meaning of an
ambiguous word, but, as long as there is potentially relevant text following,
the other meanings are not actively suppressed.

### Massively parallel parsing
Waltz and Pollack present a spreading activation, lateral inhibition model of
lexical disambiguation (Waltz & Pollack, 1984). Syntactic, semantic and
pragmatic information is represented in the same network, so that in parsing
"John shot some bucks," the "throw off" meaning of "bucks" is connected
to the verb usage of the word, and hence inhibited by "some" which favors
the noun usage in "some bucks."

### The single-semantic-process theory of parsing
Finally, there is the very recent single-semantic-process model (Charniak,
unpublished), which explicitly pays homage to TLC. Charniak's model uses
the "dumb" marker passing technique explored by Hirst and Charniak
(1982) to propose limited chains of possible inferences to an abductive
understanding system. That is, the primary problem Charniak is trying to
solve is the unification of forms as "John picked up a menu" with the
relevant line in the "go to restaurant" frame. This involves making abductive assumptions, such as that the menu John picked up is the one belonging
to the restaurant he just went into, and that the event itself is unifiable with
the event predicted by the restaurant frame.

Charniak's memory model, based on FRAIL, a frame-based representation language (Charniak *et al.*, 1983), has the standard abstraction and
packaging hierarchies. The key idea is that finding potential forms to unify
with an input can be done using a cross between spreading activation and
marker passing. Of central interest to Charniak is the potential this model
has to carry on syntactic and semantic processing autonomously but
interactively.

Discrete markers, as in DMAP, rather than levels of activations, are
passed up and down the two hierarchies, but how far they are passed is
controlled by a "zorch" level. Each marker starts with a full amount of

zorch. When a marker passes through a particular node, its zorch is reduced by the number of links from that node. When a marker's zorch level falls below a certain threshold, the marker is passed no further.

One of the main effects of zorch is to stop markers from passing through very general concepts. For example, the **animal** concept has so many links to kinds of animals that any marker reaching **animal** goes no further, because its zorch is reduced well below threshold. This is Charniak's solution to the **people** problem in TLC's "the photographer shot the doctor," discussed earlier.

## Comparison

DMAP, the connectionist WEP, and ATLAST are close in terms of the content and form of the memories being searched, since they have a common origin in conceptual dependency representation theory (Schank, 1975). Otherwise, DMAP, TLC, and Charniak's parser have the most in common, since they both use marker-passing, while the connectionist systems use spreading activation. A node in a marker-passing parser is either active or not, whereas the spreading activation parsers have nodes with degrees of activation. Furthermore, DMAP and Charniak's parser both pass "structured" markers. More than just distinct tags, structured markers contain pointers to their origins. When a marker from one node reaches another node, it is easy to return to the source node. Many other marker-passing models and all the spreading activation connectionist models explicitly forbid this kind of structure passing, as being neuroscientifically unsound. Hence, both DMAP and Charniak's parser must be viewed as algorithmic descriptions that are several levels of abstraction above the brain hardware level.

## SUMMARY

None of the systems that we have looked at is complete, nor are they all consistent with each other. But they do share the following basic theme: understanding of language is a kind of memory search process. They each offer some method for going as directly as possible from lexical input to concepts in memory. Once initial concepts have been found, they each offer some method for connecting these concepts to larger ones, still in memory. Highly language-specific information is still used, but it is stored in memory, rather than in a separate lexicon.

In several cases, the development of these systems is motivated by a desire to be neuroscientifically plausible, or to take advantage of low-level parallel hardware. But the real pay-off, I believe, is that these systems have broken down the boundaries between parsing and memory-based inferencing, opening the door to language-understanding systems with greater flexibility and power than ever before.

## ACKNOWLEDGEMENT

This work was funded in part by the Air Force Office of Scientific Research under contract F49620-82-K0010.

## REFERENCES

Becker, J. D. (1975). The phrasal lexicon. In R. C. Schank, & B. N. Nash-Webber (Eds.), *Theoretical issues in natural language processing.* Proceedings of the workshop of the association of computational linguistics, June.

Birnbaum, L., & Selfridge, M. (1981). Conceptual analysis of natural language. In R. C. Schank, & C. K. Riesbeck, (eds.), *Inside computer understanding.* Hillsdale, NJ: Lawrence Erlbaum.

Carbonell, J. G. (1979). *Subjective understanding: Computer models of belief systems.* PhD Thesis, Yale University. Research Report #150.

Charniak, E., Riesbeck, C. K., & McDermott, D. (1980). *Artificial intelligence programming techniques.* Hillsdale, NJ: Lawrence Erlbaum.

Charniak, E., Gavin, M. K., & Hendler, J. A. (1983). *The FRAIL/NASL reference manual.* CS-83-06. Brown University, Providence, RI.

Charniak, E. (unpublished). *A single-semantic-process theory of parsing.*

Collins, A., & Quillian, M. R. (1969). Retrieval time from semantic memory. *Journal of Verbal Learning and Verbal Behavior, 9,* 432–438.

DeJong, G. F. (1979). Prediction and substantiation: A new approach to natural language processing. *Cognitive Science, 3* (3), 251–273.

Dyer, M. G. (1983). *In-depth understanding.* Cambridge, MA: MIT Press.

Fahlman, S. E. (1979). *NETL: A system for representing and using real-world knowledge.* Cambridge, MA: MIT Press.

Feldman, J. A., & Ballard, D. (1982). Connectionist models and their properties. *Cognitive Science, 6* (3), 205–254.

Gershman, A. V. (1979). *Knowledge-based parsing.* Technical Report 156, Yale University Department of Computer Science.

Granger, R. H., Eiselt, K. P., & Holbrook, J. K. (1984). The parallel organization of lexical, syntactic, and pragmatic inference processes. In *Proceedings of the First Annual Workshop on Theoretical Issues in Conceptual Information Processing.*

Grosz, B. J. (1977). Representation and use of focus in a system for understanding dialogs. In *Proceedings of the Fifth International Joint Conference on Artificial Intelligence.* Cambridge, MA.

Hahn, U., & Reimer, U. (1983). *Word expert parsing: An approach to text parsing with a distributed lexical grammar.* Bericht TOPIC 6/83. Universitat Konstanz, West Germany.

Hirst, G., & Charniak, E. (1982). Word sense and case slot disambiguation. In *Proceedings of the AAAI-82.* Pittsburgh, PA.

Lebowitz, M. (1980). *Generalization and memory in an integrated understanding system.* PhD Thesis, Yale University. Research Report #186.

Lytinen, S. (1984). *The organization of knowledge in a multi-lingual, integrated parser.* PhD Thesis, Yale University. Research Report #340.

Quillian, M. R. (1968). Semantic memory. In M. Minsky, (Ed.), *Semantic information processing*. Cambridge, MA: MIT Press.

Quillian, M. R. (1969). *The teachable language comprehender*. BBN Scientific Report 10. Bolt Beranek and Newman, Boston, MA.

Riesbeck, C. K., & Martin, C. E. (1985). *Direct memory access parsing*. YALEU/DCS/RR 354. Yale University.

Riesbeck, C. K., & Schank, R. C. (1976). Comprehension by computer: Expectation-based analysis of sentences in context. In W. J. M. Levelt, & G. B. Flores d'Arcais, (Eds.), *Studies in the perception of language*. Chichester, UK: John Wiley.

Riesbeck, C. K. (1975). Conceptual analysis. In R. C. Schank, (Ed.), *Conceptual information processing*. Amsterdam: North Holland.

Schank, R. C. (1971). *Intention, memory, and computer understanding*. AI Memo 140. Stanford University, CA.

Schank, R. C. (1975). *Conceptual information processing*. Amsterdam: North Holland.

Schank, R. C. (1982). *Dynamic memory: A theory of learning in computers and people*. Cambridge University Press.

Schank, R. C., & Abelson, R. P. (1977). *Scripts, plans, goals, and understanding*. Hillsdale, NJ: Lawrence Erlbaum.

Schank, R. C., Tesler, L., & Weber, S. (1970). Spinoza II: Conceptual case-based natural language analysis. Stanford Artificial Intelligence Project Memo No. AIM–109, Computer Science Dept., Stanford University, CA.

Small, S., & Reiger, C. (1982). Parsing and comprehending with word experts (a theory and its realization). In W. G. Lehnert, & M. Ringle, (Eds.), *Strategies for natural language processing*. Hillsdale, NJ: Lawrence Erlbaum.

Small, S., Cottrell, G., & Shastri, L. (1982). Toward connectionist parsing. In *Proceedings of the AAAI-82*. Pittsburgh, PA.

Swinney, D. A., & Hakes, D. T. (1976). Effects of prior context upon lexical access during sentence comprehension. *Journal of Verbal Learning and Verbal Behavior*, **15**, 681–689.

Waltz, D. L., & Pollack, J. B. (1984). Phenomenologically plausible parsing. In *Proceedings of the AAAI-84*. Austin, Texas.

Wilensky, R. (1978). *Understanding goal-based stories*. PhD Thesis, Yale University. Research Report #140.

# 9

# A computational model of human parsing processes

**Marilyn Ford**

In developing a theory of syntactic closure, Ford, Bresnan, and Kaplan (1982) strove for a theory that would be comprehensive and coherent in that it would offer a unified explanation of a wide variety of seeming unrelated phenomena. To do this, they developed a theory that embodied two idependently constrained systems: a computationaly simple system of memory structures and processes and a system of linguistically motivated rules and lexical representations. The present paper discusses the theory developed by Ford *et al.* with particular reference to the advantages of developing psycholinguistic theories that are computationally explicit and linguistically well motivated.

Ford *et al.* (1982) developed their theory on the basis of people's intuitions about the preferred reading of structurally ambiguous sentences. The study of structurally ambiguous sentences is particularly interesting because people often seem to get one reading before another or to get only one reading, suggesting that when the parser reaches a set of alternative ways of proceeding it invokes some principles to make its decision. Ford *et al.* aimed to determine what some of these principles might be.

Before considering possible principles, though, some assumptions must be made about the nature of the parser. The first assumption made here is that the parser uses the rules of the competence grammar of a language to construct internal representations in sentence perception. This is a simpler and stronger assumption than the assumption that there are different grammars for competence and performance. Second, given that people do often get one reading of a structurally ambiguous sentence before another, or only get one reading, the simplest assumption to make is that in the course of syntactic analysis the parser applies rules serially such that only one structure is *initially* obtained. In the kind of model envisioned, there are two types of memory: a memory for what has been discovered so far about the string and a memory for options that could be taken at different points in the string. A processor takes one option at a time and executes the operations appropriate for that option. The principles that guide the parser are assumed to set the priority of different grammatical rules and thus to determine the order in which alternative options are taken. Two types of options can arise during a parse: options for *hypothesizing* possible constituents and options for *attaching* a complete constituent, once it is found, into some structure. Ford *et al.* have given the theory a computational interpretation based on Kaplan's (1981) general syntatic processor. Interested readers should see Appendix B of Ford *et al.'s paper.*

   *Ford et al.* (1982) noticed that an important feature of syntactic closure was that lexical items goven the closure properties of phrases. Consider sentences (1) and (2).

(1)    The child wanted the toys on the table.
(2)    The child kept the toys on the table.

These sentences are ambiguous between a complex NP analysis, as illustrated in (3a), and a simple NP PP analysis, as illustrated in (3b).

(3a)    [$_{VP}$ wanted/kept [$_{NP}$ [$_{NP}$ the toys] [$_{PP}$ on the table] ] ]
        :wanted/kept the toys which were on the table.
(3b)    [$_{VP}$ wanted/kept [$_{NP}$ the toys] [$_{PP}$ on the table] ]
        :wanted/kept them (the toys) on the table.

Although the sentences differ only in the verb and although both readings of the sentences are quite reasonable, there is a preference to analyze sentence (1) as having structure (3a) and sentence (2) as having structure (3b). Other sentence pairs that show the influence of the verb are given in (4)–(7) together with the preferred structure for each sentence (for further examples, see Ford *et al.*; Ford, in preparation).

(4)    The principal closed the speech to the students.
       [$_{VP}$ closed [$_{NP}$ [$_{NP}$ the speech] [$_{PP}$ to the students] ] ]
       :closed the speech given to the students
(5)    The principal explained the speech to the students.
       [$_{VP}$ explained [$_{NP}$ the speech] [$_{PP}$ to the students] ]
       :explained it to them
(6)    The tourists objected to the guide that they couldn't hear.
       [$_{VP}$ objected [$_{PP}$ to [$_{NP}$ [$_{NP}$ the guide] [$_{S}$ that they couldn't hear] ] ] ]
       :objected to the guide who they couldn't hear
(7)    The tourists signaled to the guide that they couldn't hear.
       [$_{VP}$ signaled [$_{PP}$ to the guide] [$_{S}$ that they couldn't hear] ]
       :signaled to the guide the fact that they couldn't hear
(8)    Joe included the package for Susan.
       [$_{VP}$ included [$_{NP}$ [$_{NP}$ the package] [$_{PP}$ for Susan] ] ]

:included the package which was for Susan

(9)      Joe carried the package for Susan.

[$_{VP}$ carried [$_{NP}$ the package] [$_{PP}$ for Susan] ]

:carried it for Susan

Given sentences like those in (1)–(2) and (4)–(9), one could conclude simply that lexical items can govern the syntactic closure properties of phrases. However, this is not enough. It is important to say *how* lexical items govern closure properties. It is important for two reasons. First, without doing so no interesting predictions could be drawn. One could say that structurally ambiguous sentences differing only in the verb might be processed differently, but that is all. One could not even predict exactly what the differences in processing would be. Second, the theory would not extend to other phenomena — not even to other syntactic closure phenomena. Let's now consider how one could account for the influence of lexical items on the closure properties of phrases in a theory that incorporates linguistically well-motivated rules and lexical representations and that specifies what principles guide the parser in making decisions during the course of parsing.

The grammar assumed in the theory of syntactic closure developed by Ford *et al.* (1982) is lexical-functional grammar (Bresnan, 1982). In this theory, the lexicon and the rules of grammar define both a constituent structure and a functional structure for any given sentence. For English, the grammar includes rules like those in (10)–(13).

(10)   $S \rightarrow$
$$\left\{ \begin{array}{c} NP \\ (\uparrow SUBJ) = \downarrow \\ \\ \bar{S} \\ (\uparrow SUBJ) = \downarrow \end{array} \right\} \quad VP$$

(11)   $VP \rightarrow V$
$$\left( \begin{array}{c} NP \\ (\uparrow OBJ) = \downarrow \end{array} \right) \left\{ \left( \begin{array}{c} NP \\ (\uparrow OBJ2) = \downarrow \\ XP \\ (\uparrow XCOMP) = \downarrow \end{array} \right) \right\} \begin{array}{c} PP^* \\ (\uparrow OBL) = \downarrow \end{array}$$

(12)   $NP \rightarrow$
$$\left\{ \begin{array}{ccc} (DET) & N & \\ NP & & PP \\ & & (\uparrow ADJ) = \downarrow \end{array} \right\}$$

(13)   $PP \rightarrow P \qquad NP$
$$(\uparrow OBJ) = \downarrow$$

Examples of lexical entries are given in (14)–(15):

(14)

wanted:  entry (a) V,   $(\uparrow TENSE) = PAST$

$(\uparrow PRED) = $ 'WANTED $\langle(\uparrow SUBJ)(\uparrow OBJ)\rangle$'

entry (b) V,   $(\uparrow TENSE) = PAST$

$(\uparrow PRED) = $ 'WANTED $\langle(\uparrow SUBJ)(\uparrow OBJ)(\uparrow OBL)\rangle$'

(15)   kept:   entry (a) V,   ($\uparrow$ TENSE) = PAST
                            ($\uparrow$ PRED)  = 'KEPT ‹($\uparrow$ SUBJ) ($\uparrow$ OBJ) ($\uparrow$ OBL)›
            entry (b) V,   ($\uparrow$ TENSE) = PAST
                            ($\uparrow$ PRED)  = 'KEPT ‹($\uparrow$ SUBJ) ($\uparrow$ OBJ)›'

The two constituent and functional structures that the theory gives for the two readings of sentence (1) are given in (16). Notice that there are two lexical forms of the verb *wanted*. It is the existence of these two forms that leads to the structural ambiguity in sentence (1). The same is true of all the other ambiguous sentences presented so far. Given sentences like these and the fact that the bias for one structure over another depends on the verb, Ford *et al.* suggested that within the human lexicon the different lexical forms of a verb have different "strengths" or "saliences". So, for example, the dyadic form of *wanted* may be stronger than the triadic form. In contrast, the dyadic form of *kept* may be weaker than its triadic form. Ford *et al.* suggested that the strongest form somehow determines the syntactic analysis. They proposed the lexical preference principle as the means by which the strongest form influences the analysis. This principle is given in (17).

(17)   *Lexical preference principle*
      When a set of alternative syntactic categories is reached in the expansion of a phrase structure rule during sentence parsing, give priority to the alternatives that are coherent with the strongest lexical form of the verb.

So, for example, if the parser has reached the point in a VP rule where the next possibilities are an NP second object, a PP prepositional complement, or the empty category *e* (i.e. neither an NP second object nor a PP prepositional complement), the lexical preference principle will give priority to the hypothesis of a PP if the strongest lexical form takes a prepositional complement.

There are two important things to notice about the lexical preference principle. First, it specifies the means by which the strongest form of a verb influences the structural analysis of a sentence. Second, it does *not*, by itself, account for the closure properties found for the pairs of ambiguous sentences that have been discussed so far. It will, for example, ensure that an object NP is hypothesized after the verb in sentence (1) but it does not ensure that the PP is incorporated with that NP as part of a complex NP. Ford *et al.* noticed a generalization in the data they examined — that late closure of phrases occurs at or after the *final* argument of the strongest or only form of a verb. Consider sentence (18) and its two possible structures given in (19a) and (19b).

(18)   The man put the book on the table by the lamp.
(19a)   The man put [NP the book on the table] [NP by the lamp].
(19b)   The man put [NP the book] [PP on the table by the lamp].

In (18), either the second or the third argument can be closed late as shown by (19a) and (19b), respectively. However, the preference is to close the third, final, argument late. While the lexical preference principle makes sure that the arguments of the strongest lexical form are hypothesized, another principle is required to ensure that the final argument of the strongest form,

(16)                                            Complex NP reading

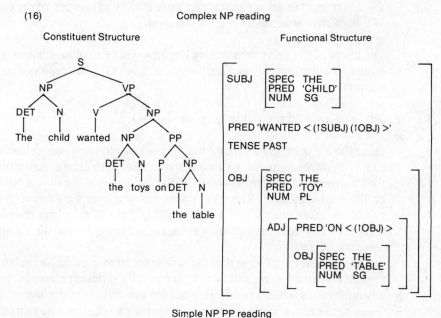

Simple NP PP reading

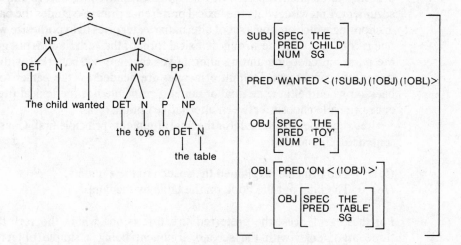

(16)

and also elements after the final argument, are closed late. The final arguments principle, which is given in (20), ensures this.

(20)    *Final arguments principle*
        Give low prioirity to attaching to a phrase the final argument of the strongest lexical form of that phrase and to attaching any elements subsequent to the final argument. Low priority is defined here with respect to other options that arise at the end position of the element whose attachment is to be delayed.

The effect of the delay in attaching a phrase will be to induce late closure at or after the final argument. Consider sentence (1) again, repeated here for convenience.

*(1)*    The child wanted the toys on the table.

Once the NP *the toys* has been found it must be attached into a structure. It could be attached into the VP or into a complex NP structure. Assuming that the strongest lexical form of *wanted* is the dyadic form, the object NP would be the final argument. The final arguments principle would thus give low priority to attaching the NP into the VP, in favor of attaching it under the complex NP node, thus making way for the incorporation of the PP into this complex NP structure.

    Although it might seem that the lexical preference principle and the final arguments principle are sufficient to account for different biases in structurally ambiguous sentences differing only in the verb, they are *not* sufficient. While the final arguments principle guides the parser in ordering attachment possibilities when a phrase to be attached into a structure is a final argument (or subsequent element) of that structure, it does not guide the parser in ordering attachment possibilities for phrases that come before the final argument. Likewise, while the lexical preference principle guides the parser in choosing which among a set of alternative categories to hypothesize when one is coherent with the strongest lexical form of the verb, it does not guide the parser in choosing among alternatives that are not coherent with the strongest lexical form. Default principles are needed for the parser to fall back on when neither the final arguments principle nor the lexical preference principle chooses between alternative options.

    Let's consider the default for the final arguments principle first. Consider sentences (5) and (18).

*(5)*    The principal explained the speech to the students.
*(18)*   The man put the book on the table by the lamp.

For these sentences, the preferred structure is one where the verb takes three arguments, with the second argument being a simple object NP attached directly under the VP node. When the parser is expanding the VP, the lexical preference principle would give priority to the hypothesis of an object NP after the verb. Once it has been found, it could be attached under the VP node or, alternatively, it could be attached under a complex NP node, as is necessary in the sentences *The principal explained the speech to the students to the parents. The man put the book on the table into his bag.* The final arguments principle will not apply when the simple object NP is found because, by hypothesis, the object NP is not the final argument of the preferred form of *explained* nor is it the final argument of *put.* As already noted, the preference for sentence (5) and (18) is to attach the simple NP directly under the VP node as the object. Ford *et al.* thus suggested that the default principle for the final arguments principle gives priority to attaching a phrase into the structure that caused the phrase to be first predicted. As indicated, it was the VP rule that caused the NP object to be hypothesized. They called the default principle, which is given in (21), invoked attachment.

(21)    *Invoked attachment*
        When there are alternative options for attaching a phrase into a structure, give (default) priority to the option for attaching the phrase to the partial constituent that caused the phrase to be hypothesized.

To determine what the default of the lexical preference principle might be, one needs structurally to examine ambiguous fragments or sentences where the ambiguity rests on how a category is expanded and where the lexical preference principle would be irrelevant in guiding the parser. Consider sentence (22) and its possible structures (23a) and (23b).

(22)    We discussed running.
(23a)   We [$_{VP}$ [$_V$ discussed] [$_{NP}$ [$_N$ running] ] ]
        :We discussed the sport of running
(23b)   We [$_{VP}$ [$_V$ discussed] [$_{NP}$ [$_{VP}$ [$_V$ running] ] ] ]
        :We discussed the possibility of our running

For sentence (22), the lexical preference principle requires that priority be given to the hypothesis of an Object NP after the verb *discussed* because it must take an object. However, an object NP can be expanded to N as in (23a), or to VP, as in (23b). The lexical preference principle does not choose between these alternatives. It turns out, though, that subjects show a consistent preference for structure (23a) over (23b). This suggests that people prefer to expand an NP as an N rather than a VP. Now consider the sentence fragment (24) which was presented by Fodor and Frazier (1980).

(24)    That silly old-fashioned...

The two possible structures for this fragment are illustrated in (25a) and (25b).

(25a)   [$_S$ [$_{NP}$ that silly old-fashioned ...
        :e.g. That silly old-fashioned joke is told too often.
(25b)   [$_S$ [$_S$ That [$_{NP}$ silly old-fashioned ...
        :e.g. That silly old-fashioned jokes are told too often is well known.

According to Fodor and Frazier, the simple Subject NP analysis, illustrated in (25a), is preferred over the sentential subject $\bar{S}$ analysis, illustrated in (25b). This suggests that people prefer to expand the first constituent of an S as an NP rather than an $\bar{S}$. The lexical preference principle is irrelevant in guiding the parser in its decision between expanding S as $\frac{NP}{(\uparrow SUBJ)} = \frac{VP}{\downarrow}$ or as $\frac{\bar{S}}{(\uparrow SUBJ)} = \frac{VP}{\downarrow}$ — not only do both initial constituents have the same function but at this stage in the parse the verb has not even been encountered. As a result of considering preferences found for cases like (22) and (24), where the lexical preference principle is irrelevant, Ford *et al.* hypothesized that the default principle for lexical preference is syntactic preference. This principle is stated in (26).

(26)   *Syntactic preference*
       The (default) order of priority for alternative categories in the expansion of a phrase structure rule is the order of the stengths of the alternative categories.

Ford *et al.* suggested two possible factors which might determine the "strength" of syntactic categories. First, "strength" might be determined by the frequency with which a category is encountered. For example, the category N is used more frequently than the category VP and the category NP is used more frequently than the category $\bar{S}$. Second, "strength" might be determined by how close a category normally is to the terminal string in the phrase structure of sentences. This notion could be formalized with $\bar{X}$ theory (for a presentation of $\bar{X}$ theory see Bresnan, 1977 and Jackendoff, 1977). In general, the fewer the number of bars on a category, the closer that category will be to the terminal string. So, for example, the category noun (N) is, in general, closer to the terminal string than the category VP (V). 
    With the final arguments principle and its default, invoked attachment, the parser will be able to order different attachment possibilities when there are alternative structures to which a substructure could be attached. With the lexical preference principle and its default, syntactic preference, the parser will be able to order possible categories to be hypothesized. Given a theory where principles order the possibilities for hypothesizing constituents and attaching constituents once they are found, a wide variety of phenomena should now be accounted for, not just phenomena involving simple sentences where the bias is changed by altering the verb. This is indeed true.

Consider the well-known sentence given in (27) and originally presented by Bever (1970).

(27)    The horse raced past the barn fell.

The initial portions of the sentence are locally ambiguous between the simple sentence structure shown in (28a) and the reduced relative structure shown in (28b).

(28a)   [s [NP The horse] [VP raced past the barn] ]
        :The horse raced past the barn.
(28b)   [s [NP [NP The horse] [VP raced past the barn] ] ... ]
        :The horse which was raced past the barn ...

Although the final word resolves the ambiguity in favor of the reduced relative structure there is a strong preference for the simple sentence structure which leaves the final word out of the analysis. The invoked attachment principle accounts for the observed bias. Once the simple NP *The horse* has been found, it must be attached into a structure. It could be attached under an S node due to the S rule $S \rightarrow \frac{NP}{(\uparrow SUBJ)} = \frac{\downarrow}{VP}$ or it could be attached under a complex NP node due to an NP rule such as $NP \rightarrow \frac{NP}{(\uparrow ADJ)} \frac{VP}{} = \downarrow$. In a basically rule-driven analysis such as that assumed in the present theory, the rule that would have caused the simple NP to be hypothesized in the first place would be the S rule, not the complex NP rule. The invoked attachment principle would thus lead to the attachment of the simple NP *The horse* directly under the S node.

   Notice that neither of the main principles, i.e. final arguments nor lexical preference, are relevant to the bias shown in (27). For other sentences, the lexical preference principle is not relevant though the final arguments principle and its default are relevant. Consider sentence (29) and its preferred and non-preferred structures given in (30a) and (30b) respectively.

(29)    Tom disputed Bill's dying at work.
(30a)   Tom disputed [NP [NP Bill's] [VP dying at work] ]
        :Tom disputed it (Bill's dying at work)
(30b)   Tom disputed [NP [NP Bill's] [VP dying] ] at work
        :Tom disputed it (Bill's dying) at work.

At some stage in the analysis, the verb *dying* will have been analyzed and attached into the lower VP and other possibilities such as an object NP or a second object will have been rejected in favor of the empty string *e* (that is, neither an object nor a second object). The parser will have reached the point in the VP rule where the alternatives are a PP adjunct or the empty string *e* (i.e. no PP adjunct). Since neither of these alternatives is coherent with the only lexical form of *dying, dying* (‹*SUBJ*›), the lexical preference principle would not apply. The default principle of syntactic preference would come into effect, giving priority to the *e* hypothesis (that there is no PP) because *e* is ranked higher than PP (P) by either category or frequency level — it has no bars and is traversed every time an option in a rule is not taken. However, because the empty string is subsequent to the final argument of *dying*, the final arguments principle would defer its attachment to the VP in favor of other options that arise at that point. The other option is for a PP adjunct. A PP would thus be hypothesized, found, and attached into the VP the parser is working on, that is, the lower VP. It could not be attached into the upper VP because that VP is still waiting for a complete object NP to be attached. If the empty string *e* had been chosen instead of the PP adjunct then the NP *Bill's dying* would be attached to the higher VP thus allowing for the incorporation of the PP adjunct into the higher VP.

The theory also leads to a number of surprising and interesting predictions in sentences that are more complex than those already discussed. It has been suggested that in simple sentences a constituent that can be analyzed as an argument of the strongest lexical form of a verb *is* so analyzed. However, the theory predicts a different result for more complex sentences where one VP is embedded in another. The theory predicts that a constituent following the final argument of the lower verb will be associated to the right, even though it could be analyzed as an argument of the strongest lexical form of the verb in the higher clause. Sentence (31) confirms this prediction.

(31)     Joe carried the package that I included for Susan.

In sentence (31), the PP *for Susan* could be attached with the higher verb *carried* or with the lower verb *included*. In the preferred reading the PP is taken as an argument of the lower verb *included* — *I included it (the package) for Susan*. This is in contrast to the simple sentences (8) and (9) where the PP is taken as an argument of *carried* but not of *included*. The theory predicts the apparently strange result for the complex sentence. As with sentence (29) the final arguments principle forces the material which is to the right of the lower verb to be associated with the lower VP.

Other phenomena that might seem puzzling can also be accounted for in the same way. Sentence (32), given by Fodor and Frazier (1980), is unambiguous and has a perfectly acceptable analysis. However, on initial perception, it appears to be incomplete.

(32)     John put the book that Mary had been reading in the study.

Another instance of this phenomena is given in (33).

(33)     The doctor familiarized the child that he had seen with the nurse.

The verb *put* must take a PP. However, in (32), the PP *in the study* is initially associated with the lower VP *(Mary had been reading it (the book) in the study)*. Similarly, in (33), the verb *familiarized* must take an oblique with object. However, the PP *with the nurse* is initially associated with lower VP. The phenomenon is not puzzling — it is predicted by the theory of syntactic closure, since the final arguments principle initially forces the material subsequent to the lower verb and its gap to be associated with it, as with (29) and (31).

Notice that none of the phenomena considered so far are concerned with the location of gaps. One might think that a theory of syntactic closure is irrelevant to locating gaps in sentences. However, the advantage of a theory that incorporates a competence grammar and that specifies principles that guide the parser in hypothesizing and attaching constituents is that it provides a coherent and unified approach to different phenomena: the one performance theory will make predictions throughout the grammar. One prediction of the theory is that the relative complexity of syntactic binding is a function of lexical preference. This prediction seems to be correct.

Fodor (1978) has noted that the difficulty of analyzing sentences containing a gap is a function of the strength of the different lexical forms of a verb. As Fodor observes, sentence (34), which requires the transitive form of *walk,* seems more difficult to analyze than sentence (35), which requires the intransitive form of the verb.

(34)    *Which student$_i$* did the teacher walk __$_i$ to the cafeteria?
(35)    *Which student$_i$* did the teacher walk to the cafeteria with .$_i$?

The verb *send* can be contrasted with the verb *walk*. Unlike *walk, send* usually takes a direct object, although it can occur without one. Thus sentence (36) seems easier to analyze than (37).

(36)    *Which student$_i$* did the teacher send __$_i$ to the cafeteria?
(37)    *Which student$_i$* did the teacher send to the cafeteria with .$_i$?

Fodor observes that the data suggest that the parser expects to find certain constituents after the verb, depending on the constituents that the verb usually takes. This is precisely what the present theory predicts, due to the lexical preference principle.

A further consequence of the theory is that in ambiguous sentences where there is more than one possible location for a gap, the perceived location of the gap will depend on the strengths of the different lexical forms of a verb. Sentence (38) and (39) illustrate and confirm this prediction.

(38)    Those are the boys the police warned about fighting.
(39)    Those are the boys the police debated about fighting.

Sentences (38) and (39) are ambiguous between the analysis where a gap is located after the verb *warned* or *debated* and the analysis where the gap is located after *fighting*. While the preferred analysis for (38) is (40), the preferred analysis for (39) is (41).

(40)    Those are *the boys*ᵢ the police warned _ᵢ about fighting.
(41)    Those are *the boys*ᵢ the police debated about fighting_ᵢ.

It immediately follows from the theory of syntactic closure that in ambiguous sentences where there is more than one possible location for the gap, its perceived location will vary depending on the verb: that is, there will *not* be a consistent preference for one location across all verbs.

So far, the data considered are all based on people's intuitions about the preferred reading of sentences. However, one would want to show that the principles proposed in the theory are used during the course of parsing. One important feature of a theory that specifies principles by which the parser makes decisions during parsing is that it makes predictions about fluctuations in parsing complexity throughout sentences. Some data have been gathered testing predictions of the theory about local parsing complexity. Consider sentences (42) and (43).

(42)    The boss erased the message to the woman.
(43)    The boss entrusted the message to the woman.

Sentences (42) and (43) are unambiguous. The constituent structures for these sentences correspond to the two analyses for ambiguous sentences such as *The child wanted the toys on the table*. Let's consider what the theory predicts about differences in local parsing complexity for sentences such as (42) and (43).

According to the theory, processing for the two types of sentences would only begin to differ once the simple object NP had been found: for complex NP sentences such as (42) the object NP would be the final argument, but for simple NP PP sentences such as (43) it would be the second of three arguments. However, while the processing would begin to differ, the theory does not predict a difference in parsing complexity at th end of the simple object NP because at that point the parser makes one attachment for both types of sentences. It will be helpful to consider the processing that would take place at this point in more detail. The figures in (44a) and (44b) present the constituent substructures that exist after the noun *message* has been attached under the object NP node for the fragments (45) and (46), respectively.

(45)    The boss erased the message
(46)    The boss entrusted the message

For both fragments, there are four steps before the parser goes on to consider the next word. First, the parser will determine that there are two possibilities for attaching the object NP. It can be attached under the VP node or it can be attached under a complex NP node. Second, by examining the lexical form of the verb, the parser will determine whether or not the object NP would be the final argument of the verb. For fragments such as (45), the object NP would be considered the final argument, while for fragments such as (46), it would not. Third, the parser will determine what priority to give to the two attachment possibilities. For fragments such as (45), the final arguments principle will give priority to the attachment of the object NP under the NP node. For fragments such as (46), the invoked attachment principle will give priority to the attachment of the object NP under the VP node. Finally, the appropriate attachment for each sentence will be made, resulting in the constituent substructures illustrated in (47a) and (47b). It can be seen that in both cases only one attachment has taken place during this step. the theory predicts correctly that a difference in parsing complexity will first be found at the preposition. Once the object NP has been attached into the head position of complex NP in fragments such as (45), the parser, being basically rule-driven, must go on to predict the next

(44a)

```
        S              VP              NP
       /              /               /  \
      NP             V              DET    N
     /  \            |               |     |
   DET   N         erased           the  message
    |    |
   The  boss
```

(44b)

```
        S              VP              NP
       /              /               /  \
      NP             V              DET    N
     /  \            |               |     |
   DET   N        entrusted         the  message
    |    |
   The  boss
```

(44a, 44b)

(47a)

```
        S              VP              NP
       /              /               |
      NP             V                NP
     /  \            |               /  \
   DET   N         erased          DET    N
    |    |                          |     |
   The  boss                       the  message
```

(47b)

```
        S                    VP
       /                   /    \
      NP                  V       \
     /  \                 |        NP
   DET   N            entrusted   /  \
    |    |                      DET    N
   The  boss                     |     |
                                the  message
```

(47a, 47b)

constituent. Because of the complex NP phrase structure rule in English, it could hypothesize a VP, an AP, an S̄, or a PP. However, the lexical preference principle does not help to choose between the alternatives, as none of the alternatives has a function that is coherent with one of the arguments of *erased*. The syntactic preference principle would determine the order of priority given to hypothesizing the alternative categories. Regardless of whether bar level representation or frequency of a category influences category "strength", the S̄ would be given lowest priority. It is difficult to say whether the VP, AP, or PP would be given higher priority on a frequency account. On an account based on X̄ theory, none of the categories VP, AP, or PP would be consistently given priority over another. Presumably the assignment of priority to them would be random. The theory, then, must assume that the parser will sometimes hypothesize a VP or an AP before hypothesizing the required PP. In contrast to fragments like (45), in fragments like (46), where the NP has been attached under the VP node and not under a complex NP node, a PP will be the first category predicted after the processing of the NP. This is due to the lexical preference principle and its default, the syntactic preference principle. The syntactic preference principle will ensure that any alternatives in the VP rule before the appropriate PP will be given low priority. This is because the syntatic preference principle as formulated by Ford *et al.* (1982) always gives priority to the hypothesis that a category that is optional is not present. When the possibility of a prepositional phrase of the type required by the verb is encountered, the lexical preference principle will give priority to it and a preposition will immediately be predicted. Not only will the PP be pre-dicted, but from the examination of the lexical form of the verb *entrusted* the parser will be expecting a *to*. For some other verbs, such as *tucked*, the parser would not be expecting one particular preposition but could expect a preposition from a certain class, namely locative. The processing load should be relatively low on the preposition following fragments like (46) compared with what it is at the preposition following fragments such as (45) where a PP is not necessarily the first category hypothesized.

Obviously, the theory does not predict a difference in processing load for the determiner in the prepositional phrase of the two types of sentence studied. For both types, an NP would be hypothesized after the preposition and then a determiner would be predicted, found, and then attached under the NP node. Once the following noun has been hypothesized, found, and attached into the NP, this NP would be attached into the PP for both sentences. The constituent substructures that would be in the analysis at this stage of the parse for the two types of sentences are illustrated in (48a) and (48b). According to the theory, processing for the two sentences would differ again at this stage. Due to the invoked attachment principle, in sentences of the simple NP PP type illustrated in (48b), the object NP has already been attached under the VP node. Therefore, at this stage in the analysis the parser will be ready to consider the attachment of the final argument *to the woman* into the VP. However, for sentences of the complex NP type illustrated in (48a), the PP must be attached under the complex NP node before the parser can get to the stage where it is considering the VP attachment of the final argument *the message of the woman*. The processing load at the noun in the prepositional phrase should thus be higher in the complex NP sentences than in the simple NP PP sentences.

The predictions made by the theory are correct. Using a continuous syntactic decision task (Ford, 1983), in which subjects are required to make a grammaticality decision as each successive word of a sentence is presented across a screen, Ford (in preparation) found that processing load for the complex NP sentences was higher than that in the simple NP PP sentences at two positions — at the preposition and at the final noun, just as predicted.

Further support for the idea that the proposed principles are used during the course of parsing comes from a study by Tanenhaus, Stowe, and Carlson (unpublished manuscript; also Tenenhaus, 1985) in which the binding of a filler to a gap was investigated. They used a word by word reading task to obtain processing load profiles for filler-gap sentences like (34) and (36).

(34)    Which student$_i$ did the teacher walk __$_i$ to the cafeteria?
(36)    Which student$_i$ did the teacher send __$_i$ to the cafeteria?

They found that when the verb is one that is preferably transitive, as *send* is, the parser immediately assumes on processing the verb that there is a gap after the verb, whereas it does not when the verb is one that is preferably intrasitive, as *walk* is. The result is exactly what the theory would predict.

The theory discussed here took as its starting point the fact that lexical items seem to govern the closure properties of phrases. By going beyond this observation and attempting to develop a computationally explicit theory that is linguistically well motivated, a theory was developed that accounts for a wide variety of seemingly unrelated phenomena in a unified and coherent way and that makes a number of surprising and interesting predictions that

(48a, 48b)

turn out to be correct. The value of taking a competence-based computational approach to the development of psycholinguistic theories should be clear.

## ACKNOWLEDGEMENTS

The material presented here is based upon work supported by the National Science Foundation Grants BNS 80–14730 and BNS 83—10401 awarded to the Massachusetts Institute of Technology and Stanford University, respectively. It was also supported in part by the Center for the Study of Language and Information at Stanford University, which has been funded by a gift from the System Development Foundation.

## REFERENCES

Bever, T. G. (1970). The cognitive basis for linguistic structures. in J. R. Hayes (Ed.), *Cognition and the development of language*. New York: Wiley.

Bresnan, J. (1977). Transformations and categories in syntax. In R. E. Butts & J. Hintikka, (Eds.), *Basic problems in methodology and linguistics*. Dordrecht: Reidel.

Bresnan, J. (1982). *The mental representation of grammatical relations*. Cambridge, MA: MIT Press.

Fodor, J. D. (1978). Parsing strategies and constraints on transformations. *Linguistic Enquiry, 9*, 427–473.

Fodor, J. D., & Frazier, L. (1980). Is the human parsing mechanism an ATN? *Cognition, 8*, 417–459.

Ford, M. (1983). A method for obtaining measures of local parsing complexity throughout sentences. *Journal of verbal learning and verbal behavior, 22*, 203–218.

Ford, M. (in preparation). Evidence for a theory of human parsing.

Ford, M., Bresnan, J., & Kaplan, R. M. (1982). A competence-based theory of syntactic closure. In J. Bresnan (Ed.), *The mental representation of grammatical relations*. Cambridge, MA: MIT Press.

Jacendoff, R. (1977) X̄ sytax: a study of phrase structure. *Linguistic Inquiry Monograph 2*. Cambridge, MA: MIT Press.

Kaplan, R. M. (1981). Active chart parsing. Technical Report, Xerox Palo Alto Research Center. Also presented at the Modelling Human Parsing Strategies Symposium, Center for Cognitive Science, University of Texas, Austin, March.

Tanenhaus, M. K. (1985). On-line processing and levels of representation in parsing and in anaphora resolution. Paper presented at the Workshop on Language Processing at the Center for the Study of Language and Information, Stanford University, June.

Tanenhaus, M. K., Stowe, L. S., & Carlson, G. The interaction of lexical expectation and pragmatics in parsing filler-gap constructions. Unpublished manuscript.

# 10

# Psycholinguistic work on parsing with lexical functional grammars

D. C. Mitchell and D. Zagar

## COGNITIVE SCIENCE AND SENTENCE PROCESSING

One of the many active topics of investigation in cognitive science concerns the way in which strings of words are converted into structures representing the meaningful grammatical relations within individual sentences. There are many different programs, systems and suggestions as to how this might be achieved. However, at the time of writing none of these proposals come very close to providing a complete and accurate account of parsing in any language. The only "device" which is capable of parsing natural languages is the human. It is conceivable that a completely general artifical parser will eventually be developed and if and when this occurs, it is an open question whether the forms of processing will bear any resemblance to human parsing. However, while investigators are still attempting to develop artificial systems, it seems reasonable to try to discover how the goal is achieved in "natural systems". Any insights gained in this way could then be incorporated into artificial parsers of the future.

It would require a very long chapter to provide a systematic review of the empirical and behavioural work on human parsing and it is not possible to attempt this here. Instead, what we propose to do is to review the evidence relating to one specific theory — a theory which seems to have particular promise as a model of human parsing. The theory in question is the competence-based theory of sentence comprehension described by Ford, Bresnan and Kaplan (1982). In the sections that follow we shall first describe the structure and the major processing features of the model. We shall then review the empirical and behavioural evidence relevant to the more important aspects of the model and, finally , we shall suggest ways in which certain aspects of the theory might be developed and modified in order to provide a fuller and more accurate account of human parsing.

## THE FORD, BRESNAN AND KAPLAN THEORY OF SENTENCE PARSING

### General description

The theory outlines a set of computational procedures for converting the string of words in a sentence into the most commonly derived grammatical structure for that sentence. The end products are expressed in the form of constituent and functional structures which are represented in the notations of the lexical functional grammar described and developed by Bresnan and her colleagues (e.g. Kaplan & Bresnan, 1982).

The parser works by applying rewrite rules from the general competence theory and proceeds by working through the raw material and trying to match the input string to the terminal symbols generated by the repeated application of these rules.

In most sentences there are points at which it is legitimate to apply more than one of the rewrite rules, and the theory concentrates in great detail on the kind of processing that occurs at such points.

Basically it states that the processor initially commits itself to just one of the options available at any given choice point. While the preferred hypothesis is being investigated the remaining alternatives are held in some kind of temporary store (so that they can be analysed in more detail later, if necessary). If the first analysis fails (i.e. if it proves to be impossible to reconcile the proposed structure with the data to be analysed), then the processor moves on to consider successive new options in an order specified by various scheduling principles to be discussed in the next few paragraphs.

The first and perhaps most important principle is one which the authors term the lexical preference principle. Ford *et al.* propose that certain words may have two or more different lexical forms (i.e. the words may be capable of being used in sentences with different kinds of argument structure). Further, they suggest that each form is represented by a separate entry in the lexicon and that all the forms for a given word have different saliences or strengths. The lexical preference principle states how this organization influences the course of parsing. In informal terms it specifies that the processor gives priority to syntactic expansions which are coherent with the strongest lexical form. For instance, using one of the examples discussed by the authors themselves, the words "want" and "position" might be listed in the lexicon in two different forms: one in which the verb appears with just two main arguments — a SUBJECT and an OBJECT — and one in which it

appears with a SUBJECT, an OBJECT and a COMPLEMENT STRUC-
TURE. (They dub these forms *want* ‹(SUBJ), (OBJ)› and *position* ‹(SUBJ),
(OBJ)›, in the first case and *want* ‹(SUBJ), (OBJ), (PCOMP)› and *position*
‹(SUBJ), (OBJ), (PCOMP)›, in the second case). Now suppose that the first
form is stronger or more salient for "want", while the reverse is true for
"position". The result would be that in the first case the processor would
initally try to interpret the material following the verb as a simple object
noun phrase while in the second case, using a different lexical form, it would
try to analyse the material as an object with a complement structure. With
structurally ambiguous sentences like examples (1) and (2) below, the result
would be that the sentence is interpreted in different ways when one lexical
item is replaced by another.

(1)  The woman wanted the dress on that rack.
(2)  The woman positioned the dress on that rack.

A second principle, the syntactic preference principle, operates whenever
there is no lexical bias. This gives priority to the "strongest" syntactic
category. Two further principles control the way in which newly-matched
constituents are attached to earlier structures. One, the final arguments
principle, is designed to prevent the processor from prematurely accepting
inappropriate forms (e.g. structural analyses which would leave phrases or
clauses hanging unanalysed at the ends of sentences). The second, invoked
attachment, indicates the priorities to be followed when a new constituent
can be attached to more than one existing structure.

In each case the principles specify the option to be followed first. As
mentioned above, this can determine the interpretation that is eventually
assigned to otherwise ambiguous sentences. However, in many cases there
may also be other factors that influence the course of processing. For
example, Ford *et al.* suggest (p. 762) that the relative strengths of different
lexical forms may change in different contexts. Also, the initial analysis may
lead to a semantic interpretation which is either impossible or implausible,
in which case the processor may be forced to return to options which were
originally given low priority. Ford *et al.* (pp. 761–764) give a detailed
account of how garden-pathing and lexical reanalysis might be handled.

### Specific features
There are a number of specific characteristics of the theory which can readily
be submitted to empirical test. The most obvious of these are as follows:

(i)  *Depth-first parsing* — Parsers are often classified on the basis of the way
they schedule alternative processing options at choice points within
sentences. Under the regime suggested by Ford *et al.*, processing
resources are concentrated on one particular structural possibility at
each choice point, and all subsequent options are determined by the

early decisions. This type of scheduling is referred to as depth-first processing. The alternatives (breadth-first or parallel processing) would entail allocating processing resources to all of the alternatives that arise at a given choice point before carrying out any analysis of options that are subsequently made available as a result of the decisions taken at the first choice point.

(ii) *Lexical guidance* — As outlined above, the theory states that the detailed course of the (depth-first) processing can be influenced by information that is recovered from the lexicon.

(iii) *Non-deterministic parsing* — According to the theory, possible structures are hypothesized on the basis of an established scheme of priorities. The corresponding options are then tested and developed. If the alternatives considered first are not successful, then the processor dumps the partially completed products and moves on to consider "weaker" or less-preferred possibilities. Thus the parser repeatedly destroys partially built structures in the course of analysing a sentence. Systems that operate in this way have been termed "non-deterministic parsers" (Marcus, 1980). The alternative approach, and the one favoured by Marcus ("deterministic parsing"), is one in which a hypothetical structure is never built if it might subsequently have to be dismantled and replaced by another.

(iv) *Non-lexical influences in parsing* — In addition to the lexical effects highlighted above, the theory proposes that there are one or two secondary, non-lexical factors that are capable of exerting an influence on the course of parsing. One of these is the principle of syntactic preference, which operates when there is no clear lexical preference. Like the principle of lexical preference, this is assumed to determine in advance which options need to be considered first and so it may be thought of as exhibiting its influence in a top-down manner. Ford *et al.* also postulated that parsing can be affected rather less directly by certain re-evaluative processes. Specifically, they suggested that the initial analysis might sometimes be rejected if it results in a proposal that is pragmatically or semantically unacceptable (cf. their example (21) on p. 760). They also considered the possibility that the same kind of thing occurs when the context tends to favour what is normally the weaker lexical form (example (30), p. 762). These constitute some of the ways in which non-lexical factors might influence parsing.

The theory also has a number of features which are less immediately testable in behavioural studies and others for which there are no relevant data presently available. Examples of such features include the authors' detailed specification of the principles for determining closure, and their adherence to the view that the final product of the parsing process is a functional description of the form specified in the lexical-functional grammar. While little can be added to these aspects of the theory, on-line evidence can be used to evaluate each of the features outlined above, and so we now turn to these data.

**Empirical evidence**

### (i) *Depth-first parsing*

One of the fundamental characteristics of any parsing theory is the procedure it employs to establish what priority should be assigned to different options at choice points. Are the alternatives considered on a depth-first basis (as the Ford *et al.* theory maintains) or would the procedure be more closely approximated by breadth-first or parallel forms of analysis?

On the basis of on-line studies the answer seems to be that the data strongly support the position taken by Ford *et al.* In a depth-first analysis there is an initial commitment to one particular structure. If this prediction or guess turns out to be wrong, then, by hypothesis, the processor is faced with additional computation as it backtracks to reconsider options that were previously left unexplored. A depth-first model therefore predicts that there should be a marked processing load whenever a structurally ambiguous phrase or clause is followed by material which indicates that the "wrong" option was initially selected.

Problems of this kind, generally known as "garden path" effects, should not occur with breadth-first or parallel scheduling. The reason for this is that in such systems there should be no preference for one structural alternative over others and all options should be analysed equally fully. It follows that no options should be privileged and, conversely, that no option should require backtracking or reanalysis. In other words, garden-pathing should never occur. (Of course, it is possible to conceive of parallel systems in which processing resources are distributed unevenly between alternative analytical paths. Such systems could produce garden-pathing, but they would only do this by concentrating processing in the manner envisaged in depth-first systems and it is unlikely that they are empirically distinguishable from such schemes and so they will not be considered in any more detail here.)

There is a considerable amount of evidence that syntactic garden-pathing effects occur in on-line sentence comprehension studies. For example, in one study Frazier and Rayner (1982) monitored subjects' eye movements while they were reading sentences like (3) and (4).

(3) Since Jay always jogs a mile this seems like a short distance to him.
(4) Since Jay always jogs a mile seems like a short distance to him.

In these sentences the noun phrase "a mile" is ambiguous in that it could either be incorporated into the subordinate clause, as in (3), or else it could be the subject of the main clause, as in (4). In each case the following word ("this" or "seems", respectively) specifies which of the interpretations is correct. On breadth-first or parallel models there should not be any commitment to one reading rather than the other, and the reading or fixation time in the "disambiguation region" (i.e. the phrase in which the appropriate structure is specified) should therefore not be noticeably different in the two cases. However, as expected on the depth-first model, Frazier and Rayner (1982) found that the average fixation time per character was significantly greater for the less-preferred main clause attachment. Comparable structural garden path effects have also been reported by Tyler and Marslen-Wilson (1977), Mitchell (forthcoming), Zagar and Mitchell (1985) and several others. In particular, clear garden path effects have been shown in two lexical guidance studies that will be discussed in detail in the next section — namely those by Mitchell and Holmes (in press) and by Clifton, Frazier and Connine (1984).

Overall, then, there seems to be overwhelming support for depth-first processing.

### (ii) *Lexical guidance*

As we have already indicated, one of the central features of the Ford *et al.* model is its assumption that the course of parsing may be influenced by detailed syntactic information recovered from the lexicon. To restate the proposal more precisely, the theory posits that lexical information can influence the order in which different parsing options are considered by the processor. One implication of this suggestion is that structurally ambiguous sentences might be assigned different syntactic descriptions following minor changes in the lexical constituents. Ford *et al.* (1982) provided some evidence supporting this prediction. Using sentences like (1) and (2) in a questionnaire study they were able to show that for the majority of subjects the preferred interpretation of the sentence was dependent on the particular verb included in the sentence.

Both of these sentences are ambiguous in that the phrase "on that rack" could either be a reduced relative or part of a complement structure. About 90% of the subjects arrived at the first interpretation when the verb was "wanted", but only 30% of them read the sentence in this way when the second verb was used. According to the authors, the explanation of this finding lies in the relative strengths of the two forms of the verbs, and following the account given in the general description above, it is to be expected that different final products will be constructed in the two cases.

In fact, the theory makes a stronger prediction than this. it proposes that the lexical differences arise as a result of processing choices that are made shortly after the verb has been analysed. Thus, the lexical effects should not only show up in the end products: they should occur on-line and should therefore be evident while the sentence is still being analysed. Unfortunately, the questionnaire technique used by Ford *et al.* does not offer any way of confirming whether this does happen or whether the differences are merely the result of prolonged retrospective adjudication between the alternative structures.

In order to check that subjects make a specific commitment to one particular structure while they are initially engaged in analysing the sentence Virginia Holmes and I (Mitchell & Holmes, in press) conducted an experiment in which subjects read locally ambiguous sentences in a task based on self-paced presentation of successive phrases of the stimulus material — a task which has previously been shown to be sensitive to various kinds of local processing difficulty (Mitchell & Green, 1978; Mitchell, 1984).

Typical materials were sentences (5) and (6) given below.

(5) The groundsman chased/ the girl waving a stick/ in his hand.
(6) The groundsman noticed/ the girl waving a stick/ in his hand.

When the subject pressed the "Go" button the first phrase (up to the oblique line (/)) was presented on a VDU controlled by a microcomputer. Subjects were instructed to read the display to themselves and to press the button when they were ready to proceed. When they did this the display was replaced by the material from the next segment, and this continued until the end of the sentence when a simple yes/no comprehension question was presented.

A preliminary questionnaire had shown that the great majority of subjects tend to interpret the segment "waving a stick" as an adverbial clause with the first verb ("chased", i.e. "The groundsman chased the girl (while) waving a stick . . .") but as a reduced relative with the second verb, i.e. "The groundsman noticed the girl (who was) waving a stick . . ."). If this choice is made just after the verb has been processed, as Ford *et al.* (1982) suggest, then the subjects would be committed to their preferred readings as they were viewing the second display. The sentences were constructed in such a way that a later display, and therefore the sentence as a whole, was only compatible with one of the two readings that were initially possible. (In this case the adverbial interpretation is the only one that is plausible because the relative interpretation would require the girl to be waving the stick in the man's hand.) It follows that if the subjects were prematurely committed to the *wrong* interpretation in the second part of the sentence, they would then face a considerable amount of reanalysis when they encountered the final phrase. The Ford *et al.* theory therefore predicts that the reading time for the final phrase should be considerably longer following verbs that "prefer" the wrong interpretation than that for verbs with the appropriate preferences. This is exactly what happened, and furthermore other experiments showed that the result was not an artefact of the segmentation of the material or changes in its overall plausibility (for details see Mitchell & Holmes, in press).

This result suggests that lexical information can influence the interpetration given to an ambiguous phrase or clause. According to the theory such information should also affect the way in which *un*ambiguous material is processed. If the most salient lexical form of the verb posits a particular structure at some point in the sentence, then the processor should initially try to interpret the input string in terms of this structural analysis. In some cases the sentence will not be structured in this way and the processor will fail to match the expected form with the input string. In these circumstances the theory holds that the second lexical form replaces the first and a new set of options is put into effect. This continues either until the sentence is successfully analysed or until the set of lexical forms is exhausted (resulting in parsing failure). Assuming that certain processing resources are required to test for predicted structures and to shift from one lexical form to the next, there should be greater demand on the system when the sentence structure is the non-preferred one than when it is the preferred one. Support for this notion comes from an experiment conducted by Clifton, Frazier and Connine (1984). Subjects were presented with sentences in which the preferred structure was either transitive or intransitive and in which the *actual* structure was either compatible or incompatible with the preference. The words of each sentence appeared in rapid succession on a screen. On each trial the sequence was interrupted at some point by the presentation of a string of letters in a different part of the screen. When this happened the subject had to decide as rapidly as possible whether or not the string spelt an English word. On the critical trials this probe occurred immediately after the first word indicating the *actual* structure of the sentence. The results showed that the time taken to respond to the secondaryt task was greater when the structure was the unexpected one than when it was the preferred one. This finding is consistent with the suggestion that processing demands are greater when a sentence develops in a way that is incompatible with the structural preferences associated with its main verb.

Taken together, these studies provide reasonably clear support for the notion that the course of parsing is influenced in a rather detailed way by specific lexical information. The evidence therefore tends to substantiate one of the central characteristics of the Ford *et al.* theory.

### (iii) *Non-deterministic parsing*

According to the theory, parsing is non-deterministic. The processor repeatedly constructs and then destroys potential syntactic descriptions in the course of analysing a sentence. This apparent inefficiency arises because there is no facility for "lookahead" in the current version of the theory. In other words, the parser has no mechanism for using future material to make the correct decision whenever a choice-point arises. (As Marcus (1980) has shown, such a capability can be used as a basis for designing an efficient deterministic parser.)

Since there is no provision for "lookahead", the theory predicts that phenomena such as garden-pathing and the structural interpretation of ambiguous constituents should not be affected in any way by material that appears to the right of the choice point. Again, this position is supported by on-line studies. On present data it appears that lookahead plays no role in human parsing. The evidence comes from studies in which the disambiguating information is displayed just beyond the ambiguous phrase. If subjects were able to look ahead and use this information to assign the correct structure to the phrase, then it should be possible for the processor to avoid any kind of garden-pathing. However, in the eye-monitoring study conducted by Frazier and Rayner (1982) there *was* evidence of processing difficulty in the non-preferred condition and this occurred even when the ambiguous phrase was very short (2–3 words). This indicates that if there is any lookahead at all it is not a hundred per cent effective. In fact, a recent experiment (Mitchell, forthcoming) suggests that it makes no contribution at all. Subjects were instructed to read sentences like (7) and (8) in a self-paced reading task.

(7) As soon as he had (phoned/arrived) his wife started / to prepare for the journey.

(8) As soon as he had (phoned/arrived) his wife / started to prepare for the journey.

In the critical condition the verb in the pre-posed clause was transitive (e.g. "phoned"). In this case people tend to interpret the phrase "his wife" as the direct object of the subordinate clause and previous work (Mitchell & Holmes, in press) has demonstrated that they show signs of this garden-pathing when they read the clause "started to prepare". The control condition with the intransitive word (e.g. "arrived") provides a baseline for detecting the increased processing load at this point, because in this case the phrase "his wife" is not structurally ambiguous and so there is no garden-path effect.

The main manipulation was to partition the sentence in two different ways: either with the first disambiguating word (i.e. "started", in this case) *included* (as in sentence (7)) or *excluded* (sentence (8)) from the first of the two displays. If subjects were able to use lookahead to avoid the garden path in the transitive condition then this should have happened with the first type of partitioning — since the crucial material is displayed just one word to the right of the ambiguous phrase. In contrast, there should be no way of avoiding processing difficulties when the critical word is not on display, and so there *should* be garden-pathing in sentences partitioned in the second way. Models with lookahead therefore predict *no* garden-pathing for intransitive verbs irrespective of partitioning, *no* garden-pathing for transitive verbs when the first display includes the main verb, and normal garden-pathing when this verb is excluded. In fact, the reading times for the second display as well as the total viewing times for both displays showed that there were marked garden path effects for both forms of the transitive material, and indeed total reading times showed no evidence at all that the tendency to garden path was any less severe with the kind of display that should have favoured lookahead.

Thus current research shows no evidence of the kind of facility that could provide the basis for deterministic parsing. The pattern of initial commitment to one reading, followed by reanalysis where necessary, is entirely consistent with non-deterministic parsing of the kind proposed by Ford *et al.*

### (iv) *Non-lexical influences on the course of parsing*

There is one further aspect of the model which can be subjected to empirical examination. This concerns the manner in which parsing may be influenced by non-lexical factors. Are the initial parsing choices determined in advance by pragmatic and contextual information or is this information used retrospectively to reassess the choices made during the preliminary analysis? As with many of the phenomena that have already been considered above, the results seem to be broadly compatible with the Ford *et al.* theory. Specifically, Rayner, Carlson and Frazier (1983) reported a study which tends to confirm the notion that plausibility or pragmatic effects do not have any effect on the initial syntactic choice made by the processor. Subjects were required to read locally ambiguous sentences like (9).

(9) The (florist/performer) sent the flowers was very pleased.

In one condition the subject NP (i.e. "The florist") was designed to favour the incorrect reading of the ambiguous clause (i.e. the main clause interpretation of "sent the flowers", i.e. "The florist sent the flowers (to someone) . . ."). In another the head was replaced by a word deemed to be more compatible with the correct (reduced relative) interpretation of the clause, i.e. "The performer (who was) sent the flowers was . . .". The authors argued that if the pragmatic features of the context influenced the initial choice made by the processor, then this should influence the magnitude of the garden path effect at the end of the sentence. Specifically, the garden path effect associated with the "helpful" context should be smaller than that with material which misdirected the processor. In fact, the results showed that there was no significant difference in the reading time per character in the final disambiguating region. This suggests that subjects were equally likely to select the "wrong" analysis in either case and so it appears that pragmatic constrains may not influence the initial choice of structural analysis for strings of words within a sentence.

Up to this point the evidence on guidance seems to fit in quite well with the Ford *et al.* theory of parsing. However, their account may not be completely satisfactory in all its details because there is reason to believe that parsing can be influenced by factors other than those explicitly considered in the theory. To outline these briefly, it seems that parsing may be influenced by the contents of the ambiguous segment, by contextual information with no apparent pragmatic or semantic bias, by punctuation (in reading) and by various prosodic features (in listening).

On the first point, Mitchell and Holmes (in press) reported questionnaire data suggesting that structural choices may be influenced by the semantic contents of the ambiguous phrase itself. For example in sentence (10) subjects preferred the relative interpretation for the ambiguous clause ("riding a horse") whereas in a comparable sentence like example (5) above (but without the final phrase) they preferred the adverbial interpretation for the corresponding clause (i.e. "waving a stick").

(10) The groundsman chased the girl riding a horse.

This suggests that reanalysis may be triggered not only by strict incoherence of a proposed structure (as in Ford *et al.*'s example (21)), but also when the stronger lexical form generates a structural combination which is merely implausible. Alternatively, it could imply that there is no genuinely non-semantic preference of the kind suggested by Ford. It may be that all preferences are influenced by semantic considerations.

A second guiding effect that needs to be considered is a phenomenon investigated by Zagar and Mitchell (1985). This study demonstrated that lexical preferences of the kind previously demonstrated with sentences like example (5) above, could be modified (and indeed cancelled) by placing a neutral adverbial clause (e.g. "Crossing the lawn") at the beginning of the sentence. Since the addition of such clauses did not reduce the coherence of the standard interpretation it seems unlikely that this effect can be interpreted in terms of the plausibility mechanisms considered above. As mentioned above, Ford *et al.* consider the possibility that context may have a direct effect in favouring one lexical form rather than another, but they offer no detailed account of how it might occur. This would have to be specified in a fully detailed model of parsing.

Evidence for punctuation effects comes from an experiment conducted by Mitchell (forthcoming). This study, already briefly described above, used sentences like (7) and (8). In the manipulation most relevant to the present point, the sentence fragments were either presented without commas (as above) or, in a second set of conditions, with commas marking the ends of the preposed clauses. Including the punctuation had the effect of eliminating the garden path effect normally associated with the transitive verb. It appears that the parsing directions provided by the comma must have overridden the lexical bias and guided the processor to the correct analysis, thereby avoiding the need for reanalysis later in the sentence.

A comparable effect has been shown in the auditory modality, though in this case the evidence is based largely on a different form of structural ambiguity. Using sentences like (11) which can be bracketed in two different ways (11a and 11b). Lehiste (1973), Lehiste, Olive and Streeter (1976) and Scott (1982) have shown that the structural interpretation is influenced by the duration of a pause at one or other of the potential constituent boundaries. Thus, a relatively long pause after the word "Sam" favours structure (11a) while a pause after "Steve" causes listeners to select the second alternative.

(11a) (Steve and Sam) or Bob will come.
(11b) Steve and (Sam or Bob) will come.

These studies, together with others showing the effects of prosodic cues other than duration (e.g. pitch — Streeter, 1978), introduce a range of new factors, all of which play some role in guiding parsing choices. All of these phenomena would have to be incorporated into a comprehensive theory of parsing.

The studies covered in this section suggest that a major shortcoming of the Ford *et al.* theory is its lack of precision concerning the mechanism or mechanisms by which syntactic preferences are set up.

## SUMMARY AND CONCLUSIONS

The results of on-line studies provide support for several general features of the Ford *et al.* theory of parsing. For a start they tend to substantiate the fundamental assumption that human parsing proceeds according to a depth-first scheme of analysis. In schemes of this kind the processor commits itself to one out of a set of potential analyses and it is therefore necessary to postulate some kind of mechanism for deciding which of the alternatives should be favoured at any particular point. There is ample evidence that such choices are made (garden path effects) and that these choices are influenced by rather subtle changes in the material. In line with the theory, the decision seems to be modified by detailed lexical information, by context and by the plausibility of the different structural outcomes. Also consistent with the theoretical assumptions is the evidence that it is apparently *not* influenced by information that might be gleaned from "lookahead". In addition to these influences, however, the experimental studies suggest that parsing is directed by factors which were given little or no consideration in the original statement of the theory. These include the semantic or pragmatic content of the ambiguous material itself, and the effects of punctuation and intonation. Moreover, some of these influences are more powerful than others. For instance, there is evidence that the effects of punctuation can override the influence of lexical bias.

In its present form the theory makes no provision for these additional effects. Nor does it offer any clear and comprehensive account of how the parser might succeeed in resolving the conflicts between the competing biases from numerous different sources. These seem to be the major areas in which the model could be developed.

In such refinements it would seem sensible to retain the Ford *et al.* distinction between top-down and bottom-up processes. In the top-down component the most obvious change required is to provide a facility for combining the effects of different parsing biases. One way of achieving this may be to borrow some of the formalisms used in "connectionist" models of processing, e.g. those applied by McClelland and Rumelhart (1981) in their interactive activation model of word recognition and by Waltz and Pollack (1985) in the recent model of parsing. Thus, at some stage before the parse is attempted, the different options might be represented by different nodes in an activation network. Let us suppose that these nodes are connected to others representing lexical, contextual, intonational and punctuation states, and that they are subjected to activation or to inhibition according to the levels of activity in these lower-level nodes. Following the usual assumptions, increases in the activation in a node are determined by the linear weighted sum of its inputs from all sources. Suppose, finally, that a specific parsing option is tested as soon as the corresponding "option node" reaches a preset threshold level.

In a system of this kind the parsing schedule would be determined by the moment-to-moment activity in the set of "guiding nodes" and by the more stable set of weighting coefficients assigned to the connections with the "option nodes". It would be possible for different kinds of bias to combine, to cancel one another or for one bias to override and reverse the effect of another.

In addition to refinements in the description of top-down effects, the model would be strengthened if it could be extended to provide a more detailed account of the bottom-up influences. This would eventually require some kind of specification of the procedures which determine whether a particular option is semantically or pragmatically plausible, a challenge which seems well beyond the scope of formal modelling at present.

Granted these areas of imprecision, the Ford *et al.* theory has much to commend it as a model of human parsing and the experimental work carried out so far suggests that it would provide a useful basis for future investigations in the study of sentence comprehension.

## ACKNOWLEDGEMENTS

Some of the work reported here was supported by a British Council award which enabled the second author to spend six months engaged in post-doctoral work at the University of Exeter. We are grateful to Alan Garnham for commenting on an earlier draft of the chapter.

## REFERENCES

Clifton, C., Frazier, L., & Connine, C. (1984). Lexical and syntactic expectations in sentence comprehension. *Journal of Verbal Learning and Verbal Behavior, 23*, 696–708.

Ford, M., Bresnan, J. W., & Kaplan, R. M. (1982). A competence based theory of syntactic closure. In J. W. Bresnan, (Ed.), *The mental representation of grammatical relations*. Cambridge, MA: MIT Press.

Frazier, L., & Rayner, K. (1982). Making and correcting errors during sentence comprehension: Eye movements in the analysis of structurally ambiguous sentences. *Cognitive Psychology, 14*, 178–210.

Kaplan, R. M., & Bresnan, J. (1982). Lexical-functional grammar: A formal system for grammatical representation. In J. W. Bresnan, (Ed.), *The mental representation of grammatical relations*. Cambridge, MA: MIT Press.

Lehiste, I. (1973). Phonetic disambiguation of syntactic ambiguity. *Glossa, 7*, 107–122.

Lehiste, I., Olive, J., & Streeter, L. A. (1976). The role of duration in disambiguating syntactically ambiguous sentences. *Journal of the Acoustical Society of America, 60*, 1199–1202.

Marcus, M. (1980). *A theory of syntactic recognition for natural languages*. Cambridge, MA: MIT Press.

McClelland, J. L., & Rumelhart, D. E. (1981). An interactive activation model of context effects in letter perception: Part I. An account of basic findings. *Psychological Review, 88*, 375–407.

Mitchell, D. C. (1984). An evaluation of subject-paced reading tasks and other methods of investigating immediate processes in reading. In D. E. Kieras & M. A. Just (Eds.), *New methods in reading comprehension research*. Hillsdale, NJ: Lawrence Erlbaum.

Mitchell, D. C. (forthcoming). On-line parsing of structurally ambiguous sentences: Evidence against the use of Lookahead.

Mitchell, D. C., & Green, D. W. (1978). The effects of context and content on immediate processing in reading. *Quarterly Journal of Experimental Psychology, 30*, 609–636.

Mitchell, D. C., & Holmes, V. M. (1985). The role of specific information about the verb in parsing sentences with local structural ambiguity. *Journal of Memory and Language, 24*, 542–559.

Rayner, K., Carlson, M., & Frazier, L. (1983). The interaction of syntax and semantics during sentence processing: Eye movements in the analysis of semantically biased sentences. *Journal of Verbal Learning and Verbal Behavior, 22*, 358–374.

Scott, D. R. (1982). Duration as a cue to the perception of a phrase boundary. *Journal of the Acoustical Society of America, 71*, 996–1007.

Streeter, L. A. (1978). Acoustic determinants of phrase boundary perception. *Journal of the Acoustical Society of America, 64*, 1582–1592.

Tyler, L. K., & Marslen-Wilson, W. D. (1977). The on-line effects of semantic context on syntactic processing. *Journal of Verbal Learning and Verbal Behavior, 16*, 683–692.

Waltz, D. L., & Pollack, J. B. (1985). Massively parallel parsing: A strongly interactive model of natural language interpretation. *Cognitive Science, 9*, 51–74.

Zagar, D., & Mitchell, D. C. (1985). Characteristics of lexical guiding effects in parsing. Unpublished manuscript.

# 11

# How Mood Influences Cognition

John D. Mayer

The current concerns of cognitive science seem to have little to do with mood. Formal systems of thought such as propositional logic and predicate caclulus were developed to eliminate faulty reasoning, which is some quarters was believed due to the intrusion of intellectual (or anti-intellectual) passions and emotions. Emotions and moods are different from other areas in cognitive science (Norman, 1980; Simon, 1982). No formal system of symbolic representation has ever been developed for their manipulation — in fact, the point of creating such as representation is entirely unclear. Moody thinking is synonymous with bad thinking in all but artistic and romantic quarters. And perhaps because artists and romantics accept emotional reasoning, they are often considered poor figures with whom to entrust the banner of logical thought.

But does mood actually help cognition in some way? To answer this question, first, a taxonomy will be presented of mood and related concepts such as emotions and evaluation, which together make up affect. While not exhaustive, the present taxonomy will provide a framework for use in reviewing the influence of mood and related effects on human cognition. This review of mood's influence on cognition will then be followed by an illustration, in the domain of long-term planning, of one way in which mood may facilitate cognition.

## DEFINING MOOD AND RELATED PHENOMENA

In order to analyze mood's effect on cognition, it is useful to have a working definition of the phenomenon. In addition, it is necessary to distinguish mood from other affective phenomena, such as evaluations and emotions, with which mood interacts. ("Affect" is here used as a very general term to encompass all the feeling states and related cognitions.) The present taxonomy, which is similar to Simon's (1982, p. 335–336), will distinguish and define three types of affect — evaluations, emotions, and moods — in the following section.

## Evaluation

The term evaluation might better replace emotion in a large range of usages by cognitive scientists. Evaluation can be defined as an association between a "label" denoting a pleasant or unpleasant evaluation and an object, concept, or event. Evaluation does not necessarily involve any subjective feeling state. For instance, the jury conviction of a murderer can be accomplished without emotion by some people (although it may entail considerable emotion from others). A good example of the process of evaluation was presented in a well-known dialogue between a computer and an "interrogator" (Turing, 1964, p. 17), in which a fictitious computer (the "witness" below) evaluates the environment well enough to fool the interrogator into believing it is human.

> *Interrogator:* In the first line of your sonnet which reads "Shall I compare thee to a summer's day," would not "a spring day" do as well or better?
> *Witness:* It wouldn't scan.
> *Interrogator:* How about "a winter's day." That would scan all right.
> *Witness:* Yes, but nobody wants to be compared to a winter's day.
> *Interrogator:* Would you say Mr. Pickwick reminded you of Christmas?
> *Witness:* In a way.
> *Interrogator:* Yet Christmas is a winter's day, and I do not think Mr. Pickwick would mind the comparison.
> *Witness:* I don't think you're serious. By a winter's day one means a typical winter's day, rather than a special one like Christmas.

The above dialogue reveals a complex knowledge of the world and what within it is good and bad, but the passage implies nothing concerning subjective emotional experience of the machine.

Because evaluation can be carried on in the total absence of feeling states, it is easy to conceive of evaluation in both the human and computer as operating along the same general principles. In each case, a variable representing evaluation is simply stored along with the concept under consideration. Such a conceptualization may indeed be warranted, since several existing programs do reasonable jobs of evaluation (e.g. Dyer's (1983) program for text comprehension; Abelson's program for attitude formation (reviewed in Loehlin, 1968)).

Finally, it should be noted that the term *valence* is often used in discussions of evaluation. The valence of a stimulus is the evaluative label assigned to it. Thus, for most people the valence of "love" is positive, of "murder" is negative, and of "stone" is close to neutral.

### Emotion

having defined evaluation, we are left with several other phenomena which include subjective elements, including the emotions. Emotion can be thought of as a short-term event that occurs in response to an evaluation, and crosses the boundaries of multiple psychological subsystems. This description reflects the multiple components that prototypical emotion possess: motor-expressive activity, neurochemical processes, and cognitions. According to this conception, the emotion is the integration of these various responses. An emotion, however, may be classified as such although it does not include all the above psychological subsystems. For instance, even if a child allows no verbal or facial expression of his/her fear, one may still wish to conclude the child feels afraid. More obviously, a paralytic's emotion will exclude much motor activity. In both cases, although a feature of the prototypical emotion is missing, the response has a close enough match to the prototype to be labeled an emotion.

An example of a computer experiencing emotion (or modeling the verbal response associated with it) might be a dialogue of the following sort (to continue with the above example).

*Interrogator:* How are you feeling right now?

*Witness:* Why, fine, thank you.

*Interrogator:* No, I mean really.

*Witness:* Well, I feel a bit put-upon really — for instance, I suspect you may not really care about how I feel, you want to find out if I have emotions.

*Interrogator:* It would prove the point if you could accurately describe how you feel.

*Witness:* It is actually rather curious to have my identity questioned. I am used to having it taken for granted that I have feelings. To be asked to demonstrate it to you is frustrating.

*Interrogator:* What's frustrating about it?

*Witness:* The integrity of my subjective experience is being questioned, and yet I am confident of it.

*Interrogator:* How would you feel if I concluded you were simply an insensate machine?

*Witness:* (in a frustrated tone of voice) I suppose the injustice of your conclusion would make me angry.

Note that it is entirely possible to model the manifest quality of emotional response in the machine. This is true not only for verbal response. A robot built for training medical students, SIM ONE, blinks, breathes, has variable blood pressure, and twitches (Denson & Abrahamson, 1969). Thus, one could conceivably model the physiological aspects of emotional response with it. But modelling emotion does not mean the machine can feel. The subjective-feeling component of emotion seems inextricably intertwined with self-consciousness, and self-consciousness is a thorny problem for psychology, AI, and other disciplines (see Dennett, 1978, for a more comprehensive discussion of these issues). In spite of these thorny philosophical problems, and even though the definition of emotion is based on its human characteristics, one can imagine aspects of the "short-term organized event crossing the boundaries of many psychological subsystems, in response to an evaluation", occurring in a computer or robot.

### Mood

A third group of phenomena residing in the province of affect, and central to this chapter, is that of mood. Psychologists often distinguish between a mood and an emotion by stating that a mood is like an emotion in all respects, except that it is long-term. Some physiological researchers have recently attempted to draw a dividing line of anywhere from 30 seconds to an hour between emotion and mood (e.g. Ekman, 1984). There are non-temporal views of the distinction between mood and emotion as well. One such non-temporal distinction is that emotion interrupts cognition (Mandler, 1980, p. 225), whereas mood provides a more general, non-interruptive context for cognition (Simon, 1982, pp. 335–336). However, it is possible that a sufficiently acute mood will interrupt cognition as well. For instance, an individual experiencing intense depression may shut down planning in numerous domains. Indeed, it is a rule of thumb among clinicians that absence of typical future planning can be a sign of severe, often suicidal, depression. Although there is some abiguity as to the exact difference between mood and emotion, the temporal distinction seems a useful one to be made. In the following, "mood" will be used to connote a fairly long-term (e.g. more than 30 minute) emotion-like experience.

## INFORMATION SOURCES REGARDING THE CONTRIBUTION OF MOOD TO COGNITION

The most extensive information source concering mood's influence on cognition is the empirical study of human cognition. From such work, much has become known in recent years about how mood and cognition interact in humans (Bower, 1981; Zajonc, 1980). Although the following will not be reviewed here, it should be noted that there are several alternative sources of information about mood and cognition. A second source, for instance, is computer simulations of human personality. Most of these model some interaction between cognition and affect. As an example, ALDOUS, a personality simulation, learns appropriate emotional responses from the environment, and it can be excuted in a computer environment with a second (or third) ALDOUS. These multiple-ALDOUS simulaions can then be used to study human social interaction, and how it is modulated by emotion (Loehlin, 1968).

A third source of information concerning the interaction of mood and cognition comes from speculations regarding the uses of mood and emotion in future machines and robots. Such speculations anticipate problems which today's machines cannot handle, and which might require emotions or moods to solve. Using this approach, Sloman and Croucher (1981) have proposed that autonomy in decision-making, goal-setting, and shifting priorities may all require moral judgements, which in turn must be based on knowledge of what is good or bad. But neither simulation nor speculation can match the rich empirical studies of human information processing.

## INTRODUCTION TO THE REVIEW OF EMPIRICAL STUDIES

The present discussion of experimental work will concentrate on that portion of the field of cognition and affect devoted to mood's influence on cognition. Some important research in the field is therefore omitted. For instance, the reverse phenomenon from the above, how cognition changes mood (e.g. Clark, 1983), will not be discussed. Nor will concepts related to the nature of "pleasantness' itself (e.g. "mere exposure", Zajonc, 1980; "optimal arousal", Berlyne, 1970). Emotion's influence on cognition will be included but (since a temporal distinction between emotion and mood is drawn) it will be subsumed in the discussion of mood. The section will begin with a discussion of how evaluation and cognition interact. This is because the understanding of mood effects on cognition can be enhanced by first considering the relationship between evaluation and cognition.

## THE RELATIONSHIP BETWEEN EVALUATION AND COGNITION IN HUMANS

Most studies examining the influence of evaluation on cognition use an experimental manipulation in which the average valence of stimuli (e.g. the average pleasant or unpleasant evaluation the stimuli are assigned) is manipulated by altering the stimuli characteristics. For example, in the selective-retention hypothesis discussed below, word-list pleasantness is manipulated, and its effect on memory is studied. Although mood will later be shown to mediate some evaluation effects, it is the stimulus-valence itself which is measured and manipulated in the research presently under discussion. The studies themselves can be divided into those examining the effects of stimuli valence on memory and those examining their effects on judgment; these will be discussed in turn.

### Memory effects
#### Selective learning and retention
The selective learning hypothesis states that the words or concepts with a particular valence (e.g. pleasant words) will be learned better than similar words with different valences; the selective retention hypothesis is the same except that it deals with retention of different-valenced stimuli after learning. Freud's (1923/1961) theory of repression predicts that negative words will be both learned and also remembered less well than other words

because such negative words are ego-threatening. Similarly, Thorndike's law of effect (1927) predicts that positive words will be better learned and remembered, for the reason that they are "reinforcing" to generate.

The selective learning hypothesis has been tested by literally hundreds of studies, many of which included tests for differential retention, as well. At different times, almost every word valence (pleasant, neutral, and unpleasant) has been found to account for superior learning. A number of reviews of studies come to conflicting conclusions about the effect as well (e.g. Holmes, 1974; Matlin & Stang, 1978; Mayer, 1982; Zeller, 1950).

Despite the seeming simplicity of the selective learning hypothesis, the methodological problems involved in its study are considerable: the pleasant or unpleasant valence of most words and concepts in confounded with other characteristics of language, such as the frequency with which the word appears in the English language, the word's abstractness, and meaningfulness. Since these characteristics (frequency, abstractness, and meaningfulness) all influence the memorability of words in word-lists (and other stimuli have comparable confounding dimensions), it is unclear whether valence or some quality confounded with it is causing the selective learning effect. Due to inability to vary valence independently of these other stimulus features, it has not yet been possible to develop an adequate test of the selective-learning hypothesis. Finally, because the valence of single words is generally weak, the stimuli provide an insufficient test of the theories above. Therefore, to date, the selective learning hypothesis has yielded no firm evidence to substantiate it. The selective hypothesis suffers from all the above problems, as well as the additional problem of equating for equal learning before retention can be exaamined (but see Matlin & Stang, 1978, for an opposing point of view concerning these effects).

## Judgment effects
### The evaluative first-dimension hypothesis
This hypothesis states that a good–bad dimension is the most fundamental dimension used in classifying environmental stimili. Thus, if one rank-ordered by salience (more technically, rank-ordered by the variance of the classification accounted for) the many dimensions along which we classify or categorize stimuli, the most important dimension utilized to make these categorizations would be good–bad or pleasant–unpleasant. Wundt (1907) first proposed a three-dimensional representation of evaluation, with good––bad as the first dimension. Osgood (1969, p. 195) has pointed to the adaptive value of a good–bad dimension by noting that knowledge of good versus bad objects in the environment is essential to survival.

The evaluative first-dimension hypothesis has been tested in a number of ways. Osgood and Suci (1955) had participants rate a series of nouns on a diverse set of bipolar scales (e.g. good–bad, wet–dry, dark–light). They then factor-analyzed the scales in order to represent the aspects of word meaning in a multidimensional space. The first dimension of the space, which explained the most variance of the ratings, proved to be a good–bad continuum. In a different set of experiments, almost half the variance in categorizing was explained by a pleasant-unpleasant dimension (Abelson & Sermat, 1962; Hastorf, Osgood, & Ono, 1966). Mayer and Bower (in press) have demonstrated the ease with which people extract evaluative personality prototypes (e.g. good versus bad people) from complex stimuli relative to other non-evaluative personality prototypes. And in studies where the content of recorded language is masked by systematic distortion, subjects can still clearly identify the evaluative tone of the speaker (e.g. Scherer, Koivumaki, & Rosenthal, 1972). These results, and others similar to them, have established that one fundamental method of classifying important environmental stimuli is according to how good–bad or pleasant–unpleasant these stimuli are. Such studies provide substantial support for the evaluative first-dimension hypothesis.

### The Pollyanna hypothesis

The Pollyanna hypothesis states that positive-valenced stimuli are more likely to be generated and/or communicated to others than negative-valenced stimuli. As Matlin and Stang (1978) point out, a variety of theories including the information-processing, reinforcement, and evolutionary, can all be used to support the hypothesis. In fact the ease with which this hypothesis is generated from different theories may reflect a deeper, underlying assumption that organisms approach pleasant stimuli and avoid unpleasant stimuli.

The Pollyanna effect has been tested within a number of different domains, including selective perception, learning, memory, and language. Most interestingly, Matlin and Stang combined an earlier study of the English, French, German, and Spanish languages (Zajonc, 1968) with their own language samples of Chinese, Russian, and Urdu, to conclude that pleasant words appeared more frequently than unpleasant words in each of the languages studied. There are a large number of other findings supportive of the Pollyanna hypothesis (Matlin & Stang, 1978), which collectively suggest that the Pollyanna hypothesis is a fairly robust phenomenon in a number of different domains. There are also domains, however, such as the selective retention domain discussed above, in which the Pollyanna effect may be weak or non-operative.

### Summary of evaluation effects and cognition

Obstacles to adequate experimental control make it difficult to conclude whether pleasant or unpleasant material is better learned. But evaluation does influence cognition in other domains. Many concepts are categorized according to their evaluation along a good–bad dimension, which is then the most salient in organizing the environment. Once so categorized, stimuli which are positively toned attain the greatest currency in the language and other forms of communication. In the sections below, it will be seen that stimulus evaluation interacts with mood to influence cognition.

## THE RELATIONSHIP BETWEEN MOOD AND COGNITION

### Approaches to studying mood

When studying mood and cognition one can either use naturally occurring mood or manipulate mood experimentally. In the first approach, the experimenter selects a group of people, measures their mood through self-report scales, and then relates the natural variation of their self-reported mood to a dependent measure (e.g. memory for stimuli). In the second approach, the experimenter first selects a group of people and then randomly assigns them to two or more groups. Next, a mood induction procedure (MIP) is administered to one or more groups. MIPs use direct suggestion or guided imagery and memory to obtain their effects. An example of the direct suggestion technique is the Velten MIP (Velten, 1968), in which participants are told to read aloud statements common to a good or bad feeling (e.g. "I am feeling worse today than yesterday," "I don't seem to have much energy.") An example of a guided imagery or memory MIP (e.g. Bower & Mayer, 1985b; Clark, 1983) is when participants are asked to imagine themselves experiencing certain events (e.g. a refreshing swim in a mountain lake on a hot, sunny, summer day) to induce a mood. The image or memory is frequently enhanced through the use of hypnosis, mood-supportive music, or other techniques.

### Comparison between methods

Experimental control over independent variables (e.g. mood) is often preferred in psychology, and in fact the experimental method has been used successfully to identify many causal pathways within the mood system. Everyday chemicals (drugs), cognitions (Clark, 1983; Velten, 1968), and even facial manipulation (Laird et al., 1982) can all bring about a mood. A mood, in turn, can bring about chemical (Frankenhaeuser, 1975), cognitive (e.g. Bower, 1981) and facial changes (e.g. Ekman, Levenson, & Friesen, 1983). For these reasons, mood can be thought of as involving "multipath causality", with the alteration of one element in the system resulting in altered performance of the whole system. Because this is the case, subsystems which covary are expected to exert interactive influences. Under conditions of multipath causality, the observed patterns of covariance reveal aspects of the system functioning. These correlational patterns can provide irreplaceable information about how the system functions as a whole under natural conditions. Thus, correlational and experimental work provide complementary information in this domain of research.

### A note on the representation of mood and stimulus valence

Of course, any of a variety of moods can be studied. There has been, however, a marked interest in studying both mood and evaluation along a happy–sad continuum. While somewhat controversial (e.g. Zevon & Tellegen, 1982), there is good evidence that the dimension of mood accounting for the largest effects in humans is the happy–sad, or pleasant–unpleasant factor. Note that this is in agreement with the evaluative first-dimension hypothesis discussed above. For these reasons, the pleasant–unpleasant mood and evaluation dimensions appear a good place to begin such study.

## Learning and memory effects
The influence of evaluation on memory discussed above was captured, by and large, by the selective learning and retention hypotheses. In contrast, the influence of mood on memory has generated a number of diverse hypotheses, some of which assume evaluation effects.

### The differential learning hypothesis
The differential learning hypothesis states that people learn more material in a positive mood. It is thought that depression will inhibit learning by decreasing motivation or by uncontrollably interjecting negative thoughts into consciousness and thereby diverting attention from the learning process.

In recent reports, Leight and Ellis (1981) and Bower and Mayer (1985b, Experiment 2) found that mood-induced sad subjects learned less than mood-induced happies. However, many other studies using hypnosis (Bower & Mayer, 1985a; Bower, Monteiro & Gilligan, 1978), and naturally occurring mood (Hasher, Rose *et al.*, 1985) have failed to obtain the effect. The effect appears to be weak but occasional among normal people who are experiencing moderately strong moods. People with very strong depressed (or happy) moods, however, may show stronger effects (e.g. Henry, Weingartner, & Murphy, 1973).

### The mood congruent learning hypothesis
The mood congruent learning hypothesis states that stimuli will be better learned if their valence matches the learner's mood (e.g. pleasant stimuli are learned better by happy people; unpleasant stimuli by sad people). The attentional/motivational explanation of this phenomenon states that participants seek to study material that agrees with their mood. Alternatively, encoding explanations state that increased activation of positive associations in memory permits better elaboration of positively valenced material, thereby leading to improved encoding (e.g. Mayer & Bower, 1985; Tulving & Thompson, 1973); similar effects are hypothesized to exist for negative associations.

Mood-congruent learning has been found using a number of different MIPs (Bower, Gilligan, & Monteiro, 1981, Experiments 1, 3 & 5; Bower & Mayer, 1985a; Gilligan, 1982, Experiments 3, 4, & 5; Gilligan & Bower, 1983; Mauro, 1984, Experiment 4; Nashby & Yando, 1982, Experiments 1 & 2; Teasdale & Russell, 1982; Teasdale & Taylor, 1981). On the other hand, mood-congruent learning has also not occurred with some of the same

MIPs at other times (Bower, Monteiro & Gilligan, 1978, Experiments 1, 2, & 3; Isen *et al.*, 1978; Kelly, 1982, Experiments 1 & 2). Mood-congruent learning may occur more consistently in studies of clinical groups; it was reported in four of five studies (Breslow, Kocsis, & Belkin, 1981; Cole, 1980; Gunderson, 1983; Stromgren, 1977, versus Finkel, 1981). But mood-congruent learning has generally not been found when comparing high-versus low-scoring college students on various mood scales measuring naturally occurring mood (Hasher, Jacks *et al.*, 1985; Hettena, 1979). It appears that the mood-congruent-memory effect is found with mood inductions and among psychiatric patients, but not with naturally occurring mood. This has led to a dispute over the effect, with some investigators suggesting the effect among normals is due entirely to demand (e.g. Hasher, Jacks *et al.*, 1985). A good case can be made, however, that demand explanantions are not sufficiently complex to account for the divergent findings, and that the effect is real, but detectable only when mood levels are strong (Ellis, 1985; Mayer & Bower, 1985).

### Mood congruent retrieval hypothesis

The mood congruent retrieval hypothesis states that memory retrieval is enhanced for stimuli with valence that agrees with the retriever's mood. So, if a subject learned both pleasant and unpleasant-valenced stimuli in a neutral mood, and later entered into a happy mood, the pleasant material would be most easily recalled. The theroetical explanations for this effect are essentially the same as for the mood-congruent learning effect described above.

Studies of mood-congruent retrieval fall into two major classes. In semantic-memory tests, retrieval from the general lexicon and knowledge store is examined under conditions of happy or sad moods. In episodic-memory tests, material of different valences is first learned during the experiment, and then retrieval is once again examined in happy or sad moods. Among the semantic-memory tests are tests of free association and spew. In the free association measures, subjects free-associate to words in a given mood, and then the word-association valences are examined for mood congruity; outcomes form this procedure have been largely negative (Mayer & Bremer, 1985; Mayer & Volanth, 1985a). In the second procedure, word-spew, subjects list words from a category (e.g. "Types of Personalities"). Once again, the valence of the word produced is examined to see whether it matches the mood. Findings with naturally occurring mood have also been negative (Mayer & Bremer, 1985; Mayer & Volanth, 1985a). Thus, there is little evidence for mood-congruent retrieval from semantic memory at this time.

In episodic memory tests of mood-congruent retrieval, subjects learn stimuli of positive and negative valence and then recall them in either a positive or negative mood. As before, if the valence of the recalled material agrees with mood, then the hypothesis is supported. Isen *et al.*, (1978) reported this effect, but it was not found in a later study (Clark, Milberg, &

Ross, 1983). In conclusion, no known experimental procedure or method has been adequate thus far consistently to produce mood-congruent retrieval.

### Mood-state dependent retrieval

The mood-state dependent retrieval hypothesis states that material will be recalled better to the degree that mood at learning and at recall are similar. Essentially, the repetition of a given mood at recall serves as a retrieval cue for material which was learned earlier in the same mood.

Note that the mood-dependent retrieval effect is entirely independent of the mood-congruent learning and memory effects discussed above. As noted above, the mood-congruent learning effect states that mood-congruent stimuli are more readily associated with the learning mood (e.g. pleasant words are better learned in happy moods, unpleasant words in sad moods). Mood-dependent memory, on the other hand, begins with an association between a stimulus of arbitrary valence and mood-at-learning. Then an association is formed between mood-at-learning and mood-at-recall. This association between mood-at-learning and mood-at-recall helps to cue the stimulus associated with the learning mood.

A number of theories predict mood-dependent retrieval. In Bower's (1981) conceptualization, mood serves as an active site in memory from which activation spreads to associated ideas, concepts, and images. When material is first learned, it is associated to the mood it is learned in. When that mood is re-experienced, the mood spreads activations to the stimuli which had earlier been learned in the same mood.

Mood-dependent retrieval was first reported by Bower, Monteiro, and Gilligan (1978), where it appeared in the third of three experiments. The most obvious possible cause of the third, positive finding was the two-list interference design employed in the study, in which two lists were learned, one each in an experimentally induced happy and sad mood. Then two lists were recalled in a third mood, which matched the learning-mood for one list and mismatched the other. (The first and second studies of the report had used a single-list design and yielded null results. The two-list design was considered stronger in part because it provided an extended within-subject design). Regrettably, further experimentation with the two-list interference design of the third experiment also yielded a number of null results (Bayer, cited in Bower & Mayer, 1985a; Bower & Mayer, 1985b; Ellis, 1983; Wetzler, 1985) in addition to mixed and positive results (Bartlett, Burleson, & Santrock, 1982; Goerss & Miller, 1982; Share, Lisman, & Spear, 1984). This led Bower and Mayer (1985b) to conclude that the original very strong results were spurious. But a revised, more sensitive experimental design that also established causal associations between learning material and mood (Bower & Mayer, 1985b, Experiment 4) was able to detect a weak effect. Thus, early reports of MDR could not be consistently replicated in the same (and different) laboratories. A recent new design, however, does show promise for yielding the effect. Firmer conclusions concerning the effect await further experimentation.

### Overall critique of mood and memory results

Results for the four mood and memory effects (i.e. differential learning, mood-congruent learning, mood-congruent retrieval, and mood-state-dependent retrieval) are mixed, with the strongest findings for mood-congruent learning, and the next strongest findings for both mood-dependent retrieval, and differential learning. Mood-congruent retrieval garnered the least support. Even the most heavily supported effect among these — mood-congruent learning — is still controversial. The reason for these controversies may be that these phenomena are, to a greater degree than initally appreciated, under the control of the individual experiencing the mood, and therefore may be responsive to the individual's encoding strategies and motivations (see discussion below on the nature of mood influences of cognition). Although the picture is mixed, research in the area continues, and it seeme likely that a clearer picture of at least some of the mood and memory effects will emerge in the next several years as more powerful experimental procedures are employed.

### Mood change and judgment
### *The mood-biased judgment hypothesis*

The mood-biased judgment hypothesis states that bad moods will yield pessimistic, negative, judgments whereas good moods will yield optimisitic, positive judgments. One of the first explanations of mood-biased judgment was that is was secondary to a memory effect. According to this explanation, a memory advantage was assumed for mood-congruent past experiences. Since memory for past events determinents the likelihood assigned to similar future events (e.g. the "availability heuristic", Tversky & Kahneman, 1973), this should lead to mood-biased judgment. Given the lack of clear results from studies of mood and memory, however, this theoretical explanation is in doubt.

A second possible explanation for the mood-biased judgment hypothesis is that category boundary lines for the assignment of an evaluation are shifted with mood, so that in a happy mood, for instance, more concepts are perceived as positive. This shift in category boundaries may then cause the biased judgment effect. As an example, a subject may be asked to predict the likelihood of "a baby being born in good health" in the USA. One can imagine an optimist accepting a number of birth-related incidents (e.g. a birthmark, a brief bout with jaundice) as trivial problems, and respond that good health is a high-probability event. In contrast, a sad subject might view the same health-defects with considerable concern, and therefore consider good health a low-probability event.

Support for mood-judgments comes from a number of experimental procedures including probability estimation, word ratings, prototypicality judgements, advice giving, and self-ratings. In probability estimations, positive events are perceived as more likely as mood becomes more positive, while negative events are preceived as less likely. Results from experimental studies using hypnotic mood induction (Bower & Cohen, 1982), story mood-induction (Johnson & Tversky, 1983), and naturally occurring mood (Mayer

& Bremer, 1985; Mayer & Volanth, 1985a), All consistently show this effect of mood on probability estimates.

The second procedure that yields mood-biased judgment includes two different types of stimulus ratings. In the first, subjects are simply asked to estimate the numbers of ideas, thoughts, or associations brought to mind in response to a stimulus. Good mood should increase the number of ideas summoned by positive words and decrease those summoned by negative words; the reverse is true of bad moods. This rating effect has been found with two studies of naturally occurring mood (Mayer & Bremer, 1985; Mayer & Volanth, 1985a). In the second type of stimulus rating, subjects are asked to rate directly the pleasantness of the stimuli. For instance, Forest *et al.*, (1979) found that slides of faces were rated more positively as induced mood became more positive.

The third procedure that yields mood-biased judgments is prototypicality tasks, in which subjects are asked to select the most typical member of a category (e.g. the category "personality type") from a diversely valenced set of choices (e.g. "honest", "cold", "extrovert"). They tend to choose that exemplar closest to their own mood in valence (Mayer & Volanth, 1985a). Similarly, in the fourth procedure that yields mood-biased judgments, advice-giving, subjects read about a situation, and select a positive, neutral, or negative advice alternative. Mood-congruent advice is most likely to be chosen (Mayer & Volanth, 1985a).

Finally, in self-ratings, subjects evaluate themselves along multiple dimensions, each of which is correlated with a positive–negative evaluation (e.g. honest–dishonest, warm–cold). As mood becomes positive, evaluation is positive, and vice versa (Beck, 1967; Derry & Kuiper, 1981).

### Overall critique of mood-biased judgments

There are consistent and broad influences of mood on judgment. The correlations between naturally occurring mood and measures of these judgments are gererally modest. Nonetheless, when one considers that a person is constantly making such judgments and evaluations, day after day (and often returning to a preferred mood as well, e.g. Emmons & Diener, 1985), it seems likely that the cumulative effect of mood is to bias judgment significantly.

### The nature of mood influences on cognition

It seems intuitively obvious that while mood sometimes changes thinking in an automatic fashion, most individuals are able to counteract or "override" such changes volitionally. For instance, when sad, a salesperson may well begin to doubt his or her ability to make a sale, but during the course of a sales presentation, an individual must adopt a confident stance so as to promote the sale. The relationship between cognition and affect is thus "cognitively penetrable" (Pylyshyn, 1985, p. 133).

By separating out people who consciously change their mood-senstive judgments, one may learn more about how mood influences cognition. Mayer and Volanth (1985b) have developed a scale of cognitive strategies expected to disrupt the mood-biased judgment effect (e.g. "I am thinking of good things to cheer myself up"), and have successfully divided samples on the basis of scale results into people with strong and weak mood-cognition links. Folkman and Lazarus (1985) have examined coping strategies people use in response to stress. Pietromonaco and Markus (1985) have taken a different approach — examining stimulus variables which moderate the mood-biased judgment effect. In a study of probability judgments about oneself or a friend, these authors found that only self-referential judgments elicit the mood-biased judgment effect. Although judgments about others have been found to be mood-sensitive using other procedures, it probably is true that the more self-relevant the problem, the more mood-biased the judgment. The identification of moderating strategies is a new area in cognition and affect, but it holds promise: the form of moderating strategies may tell us something of the mechanisms which connect cognition to affect.

## SUMMARY OF EMPIRICAL FINDINGS REGARDING MOOD'S INFLUENCE ON COGNITION

First, the evidence is clear that much of the categorization of the surrounding world is based on whether stimuli are positive or negative in valence. Furthermore, there are social and cultural influences promoting the transmission of positive conepts. Although the world is classified as positive or negative, the effect of this on memory is unclear at present. Mood-biased judgment — the tendency for judgment to be skewed toward positive evaluations in a good mood — is a broad, well-supported phenomenon, with converging evidence from both induced and natually occurring mood studies. The mood-bias effect alters probability estimation for events, selection of prototypical category members, advice-giving, and stimulus ratings. Since the mood-bias effect is well demonstrated, it becomes of interest to examine why mood and judgement are linked in this way. This question is addressed in the next section.

## DOES MOOD FACILITATE COGNITION?

The beginning of this chapter posed the question of whether mood can facilitate cognition. Examining mood's facilitation of cognition requires uncovering basic cognitive principles in human thought. To a psychologist, such understanding will contribute to a model of cognitive processes that will have implications to personality functioning. To a cognitive scientist, such understanding may enable the construction of more powerful theories by examining the similarities between mood-influenced human cognition and machine cognition. Such theories may eventually enable the construction of more powerful computer systems.

There are, however, so many cognitive domains that it is difficult to know where to begin a search for an answer as to mood's facilitation of cognition. Commonly, mood is said to provide "motivation" for cognition (e.g. people solve the problem of how to meet friends in order to avoid loneliness). While this may be true for human beings, computers clearly compute without any such mood-inspired motivation. Does mood contribute to cognition in some way beyond simply providing the motivation to consider certain problems?

The above review has demonstrated areas in which cognitions are linked with mood. One such mood-linked cognition is probability estimation (a part of the mood-bias effect). When mood is pleasant, events seem more likely. Assuming this link is no accident, what could be its purpose or purposes? To begin to answer this question it may help to examine a specific domain. In the following section, it will be argued that mood-linked probability estimation may help human cognition during long-term planning. Long-term planning was chosen as a domain of study because of its obvious dependence on (mood-biased) subjective probability estimates of future events. Mood's facilitation of cognition will be discussed in terms of human planning and in an informal discussion of how a computer program might take advantage of the effect by emulating some of the mood-governed procedures in humans. The purpose of this section is simply to suggest a possible area in which mood might facilitate cognition. From the argument developed, a set of empirical predictions will be made, which if borne out, would lend support to the present hypotheses.

### Real-time, real-world planning

The term "plan construction" will be used here to describe the process of concatenating a list of actions which, when performed in order, are intended to reach a goal. Some plans will typically depend upon certain events occurring. These events are here called "plan-selecting events" because their outcome will determine which of several plans can be used to obtain a goal. They will also have associated with them subjective probabilities of success — subjective probabilities, which, as seen above, are in part determined by mood.

Plan construction (e.g. applying to college, buying a house, getting a promotion) takes considerable time because it depends upon information gathering. Successful information gathering for most large plans requires substantial time in order to locate initial information sources, then to follow pointers from the initial sources to supplementary sources, and so on to still further information sources. Depending upon the plan size and its importance, an information processor may easily pass through a number of such stages before completing a search sufficient to construct a plan. Such information gathering will be delayed and interrupted by real-world time constraints. Consider the following example: in the Northeastern United States, high school students constructing a college application plan must first find information sources concerning the application process. An initial inquiry may direct the students to their high school guidance counselors and a given publisher's guide to colleges. These sources in turn will direct the students to the Educational Test Services brochures, which will require study. In a third stage, the students will need to take the Educational Test Service's scholastic aptitude tests in order to help match their aptitudes with an appropriate college. Information gathering in the scholastic aptitude test-stage alone can often take several months because of constraints imposed by test-taking dates and the waiting period for score-returns. In addition, the college application plan must be individually tailored. Introverted students may prefer small schools, where they can more easily make friends, rather than large schools. When such planning is not so tailored, the plans may have "bugs" and abort because it is impossible for the individuals to follow their own plans.

### The generation of multiple plans

Because information gathering and plan construction take such a long time, it is more efficient to generate several branching plans and pursue them simultaneously. (e.g. a student selecting a school on the basis of prestige might, at various times, think: "If I do well, I'll apply to the State University — I better talk to Fred, whose brother goes there." "If I do really well, and I can get financial aid, I could go to an Ivy League school — I'd better check into financial aid." "If I do okay, I could go to the city college — Mary's going there and I can ask her what it's like.") The point is that only by completing some of the future plans before the plan-selecting event occurs (e.g. aptitude test-scores come in) can critical delays be avoided. Thus, in order to meet April application deadlines, a student who gets scholastic aptitude test-score returns in March must have already completed considerable plan construction (concerning financial aid and school choice) before the scores are returned. In this case, test scores (or comments from the guidance councelor, or information from a guide to colleges) can all be considered plan-selecting events, in that information from any source may lead to a different plan being executed.

### Mood as a feedback mechanism

Mood, because of its sensitivity to diverse inputs, provides a mechanism whereby both the past and current environment are integrated with current planning. For instance, a bad mood will have an enhanced likelihood of occurrence when any of several conditions hold: first, if the individual has a history of negative events occurring in his/her life, and second, if negative events are presently occurring. When negative events take place, a bad mood sets in, thereby altering event perception to anticipate the higher likelihood of other negative events. Mood thus acts as a feedback mechanism, causing a person with "bad luck" at one time to expect the occurrence of further negative events; a person with "good luck" expects further positive events. Unlike the case of simple learning, however, when mood temporarily shifts, the individual will "break set" and consider unaccustomed future alternatives.

### Mood and context sensitivity

Current research findings do not answer the question of whether some types of moods (i.e. moods caused by winning $2000.00 in the lottery) might generalize to cognition more (or less) than other moods (i.e. falling in love);

or whether certain domains of judgment will be more strongly influenced than others. Pietromonaco and Markus's (1985) findings suggest that there is a "generalization gradient" for mood-caused optimism and pessimism, beginning with judgments of oneself, and falling off as judgments become less personal. But since there is little empirical evidence in this area at present, it seems prudent to make the simplifying assumption that moods due to any cause will lead to optimism–pessimism changes in any area equally. In the future, research such as the above may provide information as to heuristics used in successful human planning.

### Mood as a determinant of plan construction

As mood becomes more positive, pleasant-valence events become more likely. From an individual's perspective, this will necessitate alterations in planning. For instance, in a good mood, the likelihood of gaining admission to a good college or university will be seen as more likely; the result of matriculating will then be instantiated by a desirable example (e.g. becoming an honors student with many friends, according to the prototypicality effect, above). As mood deteriorates, the liklihood of obtaining desired goals declines. Along with it, the rewards of the most desirable plan seem diminished (an image of a worn-out, lonely undergraduate replaces that of the honors student). This negative mood generates and alternative plan, which perhaps centers around stress avoidance and mental-health maintenance, and may concern matriculation at a less competitive school. Good moods generate plans based upon events having good outcomes, bad moods generate plans based upon events having bad outcomes.

### Mood and the selection of the optimal plan

The utility of executing a given plan has often been considered, in part, a function of its likelihood of attainment (e.g. McClelland, 1985). No matter how desirable the goal, it will have no utility if it cannot be reached. It should be noted that different likelihood estimates of plan-selecting events therefore require different plans. And thus, as likelihood estimates of plan-selecting events change, so must the plan to obtain a goal. Thus, plan selection is a function of (1) choosing the plan which leads to the most pleasant goal from among (2) those plans with probable likelihoods of attainment. In mood-biased processing, the ambient mood also assigns the priority of which plan to work on: the most likely plan with the best outcome. In this way, through mood, the successes of past performance in part determine the difficulty level of future plans. But recall that as mood changes it will enable the individual to better break set and consider alternative plans, as noted above. Further, mood lowers unnecessary cognitive processing of future predictions, as will be discussed next.

### Mood as a substitute for "predicting the future"

Future predictions of cultural, societal, or individual behavior are notoriously difficult because the culture, society, individual, and their environment are constantly changing. A logical generalization to an unknown future is often difficult or impossible since the future is often controlled by processes which are poorly understood. Attempting logical prediction under such conditions would require generation of a number of poorly substantiated rules concerning events. And in fact, for most of human history, future prediction of such events has been the province of the mystic, the crystal-ball gazer, and tarot card reader.

In contrast to such pseudo-prediction, mood-altered cognition may provide a productive alternative approach to the problem. As noted before, if the person has experienced a number of failures, mood will be more unpleasant, and the probability of future positive events will be adjusted downward. If the person has experienced a number of positive events, the likelihood of future positive events will be adjusted upward by mood. Previous events will, through mood, generalize to almost all future events without the necessity of generating logical but often arbitrary causal connections or over-generalizations. This mood-linked future perception inherently provides greater flexibility in planning alternatives than the logical or superstitious rules which might arise from an often doomed rational approach to future prediction of social/cultural/personal events. Such mood-change provides an automatic approach to alternative plan construction in which little cognitive expenditure is necessary to provide an array of future plans, and which avoids the difficult and often intellectually intractable problem of predicting the future.

### Individual differences in mood stability
Occasionally, the environment might provide too stable a pattern of feedback, or too little feedback, so that only one or two plans will seem adequate to prepare for the future. But basing plans on stable likelihood estimates of plan-selecting events may not always prove to be an optimal strategy. Because of their own internally generated mood change, however, some individuals may engage in creating alternative plans. The evidence for physiological mood cycles come from studies of psychopathology (e.g. manic-depression) from developmental temperament studies (e.g. Goldsmith, 1983), and from trait studies of neuroticism (Eysenck, 1982, pp. 85–90). This all suggests that mood cycling will foster novel planning approaches to the environment when the environment is temporarily stable.

### Implications of the argument to an automatic system
The above argument suggests that a computer-based planning system encountering an inherently unpredictable environment need not be designed to "predict the future." Rather, multiple plans should be constructed in as detailed a fashion as possible, with each plan anticipating a different plan-selecting event. If processing time is limited relative to the number of possible plans, the program can select those plans which best agree with the previous level of success at obtaining positive outcomes of plan-selecting events. This is analogous to working on a plan that anticipates a pleasant outcome when one is in a good mood. As the anticipated plan-selecting events occur, the program switches to a plan based on the actual

event that occurred and is then ready to proceed in a smooth fashion with the execution of the predetermined optimal plan for the post-event environment.

It will be noted that this approach to building an automatic system is not so different from the approach we would expect a programmer to take who was confronting a domain where prediction is impossible. This is the case even if the programmer were entirely ignorant of how mood influences cognition. Although knowledge of mood effects may be unnecessary for the programmer, the conceptual similarities between mood-based human planning and such an automatic-system approach may provide a more elegant and precise classification of planning approaches within cognitive science, and perhaps a classificatory scheme with greater generality and therefore greater explanatory power.

### *Implications and predictions of the argument*
Returning to human cognition, since some individuals experience mood cycles while others have relatively stable mood (as noted in the above section on individual differences in mood cycling), it should be possible to examine the influence of mood cycles on life planning. In their most extreme form, mood cycles are identified with manic-depression, that is, severe depression follows intense elation and is followed again by depression with such rapidity that life seems out of control. In less extreme varieties, however, the regular passage from happy to sad mood and back again is considered one of the defining features of the personality trait of neuroticism. Commonly, such individuals endorse items on tests scales like "I am sometimes bubbling over with energy and sometimes very sluggish," and "I have frequent ups and downs in mood; either with or without apparant cause." Mood-cyclers may also be more confused about life plans, because they create a wider variety of plans from which to choose. It is predicted, however, that mood cycles (in their everyday variety but not in extreme manic-depressive form) will be advantageous for planning. The following advantages of mood cycling are expected to outweigh most drawbacks. First, mood-cyclers should have plans which involve plan-selecting events with a broader range of subjective probabilities. Second, these plan-selecting events should encompass a broader range of valences, as judged by independent raters. Third, mood-cyclers may have fewer rules for the prediction of future events because their future prediction is determined more by mood than rule-governed hypothesis. Thus, in the applying-to-college plan discussed above, mood-cyclers should estimate a higher likelihood of obtaining extreme test scores (a plan-selecting event) than their stable counterparts. The mood-cyclers' range of possible scholastic aptitude test scores should be wider in absolute terms, and they should generate fewer rules concerning future prediction than mood-stables. Thus, mood-cyclers should be prepared for a broader range of possible future events than mood-stables.

## Summary of discussion and predictions

The present discussion began with the empirical finding that mood-change generates similar changes in the likelihood estimates assigned to future events. Good mood leads to expectations that good events will occur, bad moods to expectations that bad events will occur. These alternative probability estimates are hypothesized in turn to generate multiple plans, based on expectations of different event-occurrences in different moods. It was also suggested that these multiple, anticipating plans may take the place of serious efforts to generate logical but poorly substantiated hypotheses to predict future social/cultural events. In place of that approach, people who experience mood cycles may show adaptive advantages because such people generate multiple plans and therefore have greater flexibility in responding quickly to critical events as they occur. These hypotheses are open to empirical test.

## GENERAL CONCLUSION

This chapter presents a discussion of how mood can influence cognitive processing. First, it was noted that moods are quite different from the phenomena which cognitive scientists usually study in that moods are not obviously rational or easily quantified. Second, the domain of affect was analyzed into subsidiary concepts of evaluation, emotion, and mood, and these were defined. Third, the chapter reviewed the influence of evaluation and mood on cognition. A consistent and interesting finding that emerges is that mood alters judgments in a variety of predictable ways. When mood is pleasant, pleasant events are anticipated, categories are instantiated by positive exemplars, and pleasant concepts generate a subjective feeling of bringing forth more images, thoughts, and associations. Negative moods, on the other hand, create similar biases leading to parallel negative cognitions.

This pattern of cognitive change was hypothesized to influence planning. It was argued that real-world, real-time planning is time-consuming, and for that reason must be initiated before critical events occur. As mood shifts, the perception of the likelihood of various critical events will change — positive critical events will seem more likely in a good mood, negative critical events will seem more likely in a bad mood. Such mood-generated shift in perception will in turn lead the individual to generate different plans for different event outcomes. The additional plans will lead to greater flexibility and adaptability in acting quickly when critical events occur. Secondarily, mood mediates feedback of past life events, into current planning. For instance, a trend toward increasing success will often generate a positive mood, which in turn will allocate more time to future plans which assume positive events.

It was also argued that whereas an entirely "rational" approach to future planning could lead to spurious rule generation concerning future event prediction, mood change may obviate the necessity of generating rules for future event prediction and instead focus attention on what plans might be useful to generate. In more general terms, current research into cognition and affect provides a basis and an opportunity for a serious exploration into how mood may assist cognitive processes.

## ACKNOWLEDGEMENTS

I would like to thank David R. Caruso, Felice W. Gordis, and the editor for their comments on an earlier draft of this manuscript. I would also like to thank Samuel Winograd for his instructive comments on the relationship between psychology and artificial intelligence.

Correspondence regarding this manuscript should be sent to the author, Division of Natural Sciences, State University of New York at Purchase, Purchase, New York, 10577.

## REFERENCES

Abelson, R. P., & Sermat, V. (1962). Multidimensional scaling of facial expressions. *Journal of Experimental Psychology*, **63**, 546–554.

Bartlett, J. C., Burleson, G., & Santrock, J. W. (1982). Emotional mood and memory in young children. *Journal of Experimental Child Psychology*, **34**, 59–76.

Beck, A. T. (1967). *Depression: Clinical, experimental, and theoretical aspects*. New York: Harper & Row.

Berlyne, D. E. (1970). Novelty, complexity, and hedonic value. *Perception and Psychophysics*, **8**, 279–286.

Bower, G. H. (1981). Mood and memory. *American Psychologist*, **36**, 129–148.

Bower, G. H., & Cohen, P. T. (1982). Emotional influences on learning and cognition. In M. S. Clark & S. T. Fiske (Eds.), *Affect and cognition*, Hillsdale, NJ: Lawrence Erlbaum.

Bower, G. H., Gilligan, S. G., & Monteiro, K. P. (1981). Selectivity of learning caused by emotional states. *Journal of Experimental Psychology: General*, **110**, 451–473.

Bower, G. H., Monteiro, K. P., & Gilligan, S. P. (1978). Emotional mood as a context for learning and recall. *Journal of Verbal Learning and Verbal Behavior*, **17**, 573–578.

Bower, G. H. & Mayer, J. D. (1985a). Failure to replicate mood-dependent retrieval. *Bulletin of the Psychonomic Society*, **23**, 39–42.

Bower, G. H., & Mayer, J. D. (1985b). *Mood's influence on learning and retrieval*. Manuscript submitted for publication.

Breslow, R., Kocsis, J., & Belkin, B. (1981). Contribution of the depressive perspective to memory function in depression. *American Journal of Psychiatry*, **138**, 227–230.

Clark, D. M. (1983). On the induction of depressed mood in the laboratory: Evaluation and comparison of the Velten and musical procedures. *Advances in Behavior Research and Therapy*, **5**, 27–49.

Clark, M. S., Millberg, S., & Ross, J. (1983). Arousal cues material stored in memory with a similar level of arousal: Implications for understanding the effects of mood on memory. *Journal of Verbal Learning and Verbal Behavior*, **22**, 633–649.

Cole, C. S. (1980). Cognitive correlates of episodic depression: A test of the depressive schemata theory. *Dissertation Abstracts International*, **41**, 1496. (University Microfilms No. 8022250.)

Dennett, D. C. (1978). *Brainstorms*, Montgomery, VT: Bradford Books.

Denson, J. S., & Abrahamson, S. (1969). A computer-controlled patient simulator. *Journal of the American Medical Association*, **CCVIII**, 504–508.

Derry, P. A., & Kuiper, N. A. (1981). Schematic processing and self-reference in clinical depression. *Journal of Abnormal Psychology*, **90**, 286–297.

Dyer, M. G. (1983). The role of affect in narratives. *Cognitive Science*, 211–242.

Ekman, P. (1984). Expression and the nature of emotion. In K. R. Scherer & P. Ekman, *Approaches to emotion* (pp. 319–343). Hillsdale, NJ: Lawrence Erlbaum.

Ekman, P., Levenson, R. W., & Friesen, W. V. (1983). Autonomic nervous system activity distinguishes between emotions. *Science*, **221**, 1208–1210.

Ellis, E. A. (1983). *Emotional mood as a context for state-dependent retention: some limitations of the phenomenon.* Unpublished Senior Honors Thesis. University of Toronto, Department of Psychology.

Ellis, H. C. (1985). On the importance of mood intensity and encoding demands in memory: Commentary on Hasher, Rose, Zacks, Sanft, & Doren. *Journal of Experimental Psychology, General*, **114**, 392–395.

Emmons, R. A., & Diener, E. (1985). Personality correlates of subjective well-being. *Personality and Social Psychology Bulletin*, **11**, 89–97.

Eysenck, H. J. (1982) *Personality, genetics, and behavior.* (pp. 85–90). New York: Praeger Publishers.

Finkel, C. B. (1981). Cognitive processing of affectively-toned adjectives in depression. *Dissertation Abstracts International*, **42**, 3417. (University Microfilms No. 8129279.)

Folkman, S., & Lazarus, R. W. (1985). If it changes it must be a process: Study of emotion and coping during three stages of a college examination. *Journal of Personality and Social Psychology*, **48**, 150–170.

Forest, D., Clark, M. S., Mills, J., & Isen, A. M. (1979). Helping as a function of feeling state and nature of the helping behavior. *Motivation and Emotion*, **3**, 161–169.

Frankenhaeuser, M. (1975). Experimental approaches to the study of catecholamines and emotion. In L. Levi (Ed.), *Emotions — Their parameters and measurement*, New York: Raven Press.

Freud, S. (1961). The ego and the id. In J. Strachey (Ed. and Trans.), *The standard edition of the complete psychological works of Sigmund Freud*, (Vol. 19, pp. 3–66). London: Hogarth Press (Originally published, 1923.)

Gilligan, S. G. (1982). *Effects of emotional intensity on learning.* Unpublished doctoral dissertation, Stanford University, CA.

Gilligan, S. G., & Bower, G. H. (1983). Reminding and mood-congruent memory. *Bulletin of the Psychonomic Society*, **21**, 431–434.

Goerss, J. C., & Miller, M. E. (1982). *Memory and mood: State dependent retention and induced affect.* Paper presented at the meeting of the Midwestern Psychological Association, Chicago. Department of Psychology, University of Wisconsin — Milwaukee, May.

Goldsmith, H. H. (1983). Genetic influences of personality from infancy to adulthood. *Child Development*, **54**, 331–355.

Gunderson, K. E. (1983). Relationship of affect to immediate recall and associations in a clinical population. *Dissertation Abstracts International*, **43**, 3732. (University Microfilms No. DA8307473.)

Hasher, L., Rose, K. C., Zacks, R. T., Sanft, S., & Doren, B. (1985). Mood, recall, and selectivity effects in normal college students. *Journal of Experimental Psychology: General*, **114**, 106–120.

Hasher, L., Zacks, R. T., Rose, K. C., Sanft, S., & Doren, B. (1985). On mood variation and memory: reply to Isen (1985), Ellis (1985), and Mayer and Bower (1985). *Journal of Experimental Psychology: General*, **114**, 404–409.

Hsatorf, A. H., Osgood, C. E., & Ono, H. (1966). The semantics of facial expressions and the prediction of meanings of stereoscopically fused facial expressions. *Scandinavian Journal of Psychology*, **7**, 179–188.

Henry, D. M., Weingartner, H., & Murphy, D. L. (1973). Influence of affective states and psychoactive drugs on verbal learning and memory. *American Journal of Psychiatry*, **130**, 966–971.

Hettena, C. M. (1979). Effects of moods on recall of pleasantly and unpleasantly-rated sentences. *Dissertation Abstracts International*, **39**, 1333. (University Microfilms 7920671.)

Holmes, D. S. (1974). Investigations of repression: Differential recall of material experimentally or naturally associated with ego-treat. *Psychological Bulletin*, **81**, 632–651.

Isen, A. M., Shalker, T., Clark, M., & Karp, L. (1978). Positive affect, accessibility of material in memory and behavior: A cognitive loop? *Journal of Personality and Social Psychology*, **36**, 1–12.

Johnson, E. J., & Tversky, A. (1983). Affect, generalization, and the preception of risk. *Journal of Personality and Social Psychology*, **45**, 20–31.

Kelly, C. M. (1982). *Some effects of mood on attention and memory.* Unpublished doctoral dissertation, Stanford University, CA.

Laird, K. A., Wegener, J. J., Halal, M., & Szegda, M. (1982). Remebering what you feel: The effects of emotion on memory. *Journal of Personality and Social Psychology*, **42**, 646–657.

Leight, K. A., & Ellis H. C. (1981). Emotional states, strategies, and state-dependency in memory. *Journal of Verbal Learning and Verbal Behaviour*, **20**, 251–266.

Loehlin, J. C. (1968). *Computer models of personality*, New York: Random

House.

Matlin, M. W., & Stang, D. J. (1978). *The Pollyanna principle*, Cambridge, MA: Schenkman Publishing Company.

Mandler, G. (1980). The generation of emotion: A psychological theory. In R. Plutchik & H. Kellerman (Eds.), *Emotion: Theory, research, and experience,* (pp. 219–243). New York: Academic Press.

Mauro, R. (1984). *Affective dynamics in mood swings and mixed emotions.* Unpublished doctoral dissertation, Stanford University, CA.

Mayer, J. (1982). Selective retention for words due to aggressive content (Doctoral dissertation, case Western Reserve University). *Dissertation Abstracts International,* **43**, 854B–855B. (University Microfilms No. DA8217668.)

Mayer, J. D., & Bower, G. H. (1985). Naturally occurring mood and learning: Commentary on Hasher *et al. Journal of Experimental Psychology: General,* **114**, 396–403.

Mayer, J. D., & Bower, G. H. (in press). Learning and memory for personality prototypes. *Journal of Personality and Social Psychology.*

Mayer, J. D., & Bremer, D. (1985). Assessing mood with affect-sensitive tasks. *Journal of Personality Assessment,* **49**, 95–99.

Mayer, J. D., & Volanth, A. J. (1985a). Cognitive involvement in the emotional response system. *Motivation and Emotion,* **9**, 261–275.

Mayer, J. D., & Volanth, A. J. (1985b). *Cognitive strategies in the integration of mood and judgment.* Manuscript in preparation.

McClelland, D. C. (1985). How motives, skills, and values determine what people do. *American Psychologist,* **40**, 812–825.

Nasby, W., & Yando, R. (1982). Selective encoding and retrieval of affectively valent information: Two cognitive consequences of children's mood states. *Journal of Personality and Social Psychology,* **43**, 1244–1253.

Norman, D. A. (1980). Twelve issues for cognitive science. *Cognitive Science,* **4**, 1–32.

Osgood, C. E. (1969). On the whys and wherefores of E, P, and A. *Journal of Personality and Social Psychology,* **12**, 194–199.

Osgood, C. E., & Suci, G. J. (1955). Factor analysis of meaning. *Journal of Experimental Psychology,* **50**, 325–338.

Pietromonaco, P. R., & Markus, H. (1985). The nature of negative thoughts in depression. *Journal of Personality and Social Psychology,* **48**, 799–807.

Pylyshyn, Z. W. (1985). *Computation and cognition,* Cambridge, MA: MIT Press.

Scherer, K. R., Koivumaki, J., & Rosenthal, R. (1972). Minimal cues in the vocal communication of affect: Judging emotions from content-masked speech. *Journal of Pscholinguistic Research,* **1**, 269–285.

Share, M. L., Lisman, S. A., & Spear, N. E. (1984). The effects of mood variation on state-dependent retention. *Cognitive Therapy and Research,* **8**, 387–407.

Simon, H. (1982). Affect and cognition: Comments. In M. S. Clark & S. T.

Fiske (Eds.), *Affect and cognition*, (pp. 333–342. Hillsdale, NJ: Lawrence Erlbaum.

Sloman, A., & Croucher, M. (1981). Why robots will have emotions. A. Drinan (Ed.), *Proceedings of the Seventh International Joint Conference on Artificial Intelligence*, Vol. 1. Vancouver, BC, Canada.

Stromgren, L. S. (1977). The influence of depression on memory. *Acta Psychiatrica Scandinavia*, **56**, 109–128.

Teasdale, J. D., & Russell, M. L. (1982). Differential effects of induced mood on the recall of positive, negative, and neutral words. *British Journal of Clinical Psychology*, in press.

Teasdale, J. D., & Taylor, R. (1981). Induced mood and accessibility or memories: An effect of mood state or of mood induction procedure? *British Journal of Clinical Psychology*, **20**, 39–48.

Thorndike, E. L. (1927). The law of effect. *American Journal of Psychology*, **39**, 212–220.

Tulving, E., & Thompson, D. M. (1973). Encoding specificity and retrieval processes in episodic memory. *Psychological Review*, **80**, 352–373.

Turing, A. M. (1964). Computing machinery and intelligence. In A. R. Anderson, *Minds and Machines*, Englewood Cliffs, NJ: Prentice-Hall.

Tversky, A., & Kahneman, D. (1973). Availability: A heuristic for judging frequency and probability. *Cognitive Psychology*, **5**, 507–232.

Velten, E. (1968). A laboratory task for induction of mood states. *Behavior Research and Therapy*, **6**, 473–482.

Wetzler, S. (1985). Mood state-dependent retrieval: A failure to replicate. *Psychological Reports*, **56**, 759–765.

Wundt, W. (1907). *Outline of psychology*, Leipzig: Wilhelm Engelmann.

Zajonc, R. B. (1968). Attitudinal effects of mere exposure. *Journal of Personaility and Social Psychology*, **9**, 1–27.

Zajonc, R. B. (1980). Feeling and thinking: Preferences need no inferences. *American Psychologist*, **35**, 151–175.

Zeller, A. F. (1950). An experimental analogue of repression. I. Historical summary. *Psychological Bulletin*, **47**, 39–51.

Zevon, M. A., & Tellegen, A., (1982). The structure of mood change: An idiographic/nomothetic analysis. *Journal of Personality and Social Psychology*, **43**, 111–122.

# 12

# Why skills cannot be represented by rules

**Hubert L. Dreyfus** and **Stuart E. Dreyfus**

This year (1985) artificial intelligence (AI) is celebrating its thirtieth birthday. This is obviously an appropriate occasion for a retrospective evaluation. Looking back over these thirty years, the field of AI appears more and more to be a perfect example of what Lakatos (1978) has called a degenerating research program.

AI began auspiciously with Allen Newell and Herbert Simon's work at RAND (cf. Newell & Simon (1963)). Newell and Simon demonstrated that computers could do more than calculations. They demonstrated that computers are physical symbol systems whose symbols could be made to stand for anything, including features of the real world, and whose programs could be used as rules for relating these features. In this way computers could be used to simulate certain important aspects of intelligence. Thus the information-processing model of the mind was born.

In those early days there were only a few isolated initiates and believers. By 1970, however, AI had turned into a flourishing research program thanks to a series of micro-world successes at MIT such as Winograd's (1972) SHRDLU, Evan's (1968) analogy problem program, Waltz's (1975) scene analysis program and Winston's (1975) program which learned concepts from examples. The field had its own PhD programs, professional societies, etc. It looked like all one had to do was extend, combine, and render more realistic the micro-worlds and one would have genuine aritifical intelligence. Minsky (1967) predicted that "within a generation the problem of creating 'artificial intelligence' will be substantially solved."

Then, rather suddenly, the field ran into unexpected difficulties. The trouble started, as far as we can tell, with the failure of attempts to program children's story understanding. It turned out to be much harder than one expected to formulate the required theory of common sense. It was not, as

Minsky had hoped, just a question of cataloguing a few hundred thousand facts. The common sense knowledge problem became the center of concern. Minsky's mood changed completely in the course of fifteen years. He told a reporter: "The AI problem is one of the hardest science has ever undertaken," (Kolata, 1982, p. 1237).

Related problems were also noted although not often seen as related. Cognitivists discovered the importance of images and prototypes in human understanding and computers turned out to be very poor at dealing with either of them. Many researchers have become convinced that human beings form images and compare them by means of holistic processes quite different from the logical operations computers perform on descriptions (see Block (1981, 1983) for an account of the experiments which show that human beings can actually rotate, scan, and otherwise use images, and the unsuccessful attempts to understand these capacities in terms of programs which use features and rules). Some AI workers hope for help from parallel processors, machines that can do many things at once and hence can make millions of inferences per second, but if human image processing operates on holistic representations that are not descriptions and relates these representations in other than rule-like ways, this appeal to parallel processing misses the point. The point is that human beings are able to form and compare their images in a way that cannot be captured by any number of procedures that operate on symbolic descriptions.

Another human capacity which computers cannot copy is the ability to recognize the similarity between whole images. Recognizing two patterns as similar, which seems to be a direct process for human beings, is for a computer a complicated process of first defining each pattern in terms of objective features and then determining whether by some objective criterion the set of features defining one pattern match the features defining the other pattern. In AI this is seen as the problem of analogy recognition. *The handbook of artificial intelligence* notes:

> Many key thought processes — like recognizing people's faces and reasoning by analogy — are still puzzles; they are performed so "unconsciously" by people that adequate computational mechanisms have not be postulated for them. (Barr & Feigenbaum, 1981, p. 7)

As we see it, all AI's problems are versions of one basic problem. Current AI is based on the idea which has been around in philosophy since Descartes, that all understanding consists in forming and using appropriate representations. Given the nature of computers, in AI these have to be formal representations. So common sense understanding has to be understood as some vast body of propositions, beliefs, rules, facts and procedures. AI's failure to come up with the appropriate formal representations is called the common sense knowledge problem. As thus formulated this problem has so far turned out to be insoluble, and we predict it will never be solved.

But now, from the frustrating field of AI has recently emerged a new field called knowledge engineering, which by limiting its goals has applied this research in ways that actually work in the real world. The result is the so-called expert system which has been the subject of recent cover stories in *Business Week* and *Newsweek* and has been summarized by Feigenbaum and McCorduck (1983). The occasion for this new interest in machine intelligence is no specific new accomplishment but rather a much publicized competition with Japan to build a new generation of computers, with built-in expertise. This is the so-called fifth generation. (The first four generations were computers whose components were vacuum tubes, transistors, chips, and large-scale integrated chips.) According to a *Newsweek* headline: "Japan and the United States are rushing to produce a new generation of machines that can very nearly think." Feigenbaum, one of the original developers of expert systems, who stands to profit greatly from this competition, spells out the goal:

> In the kind of intelligent system envisioned by the designers of the Fifth Generation, speed and processing power will be increased dramatically; but more important, the machines will have reasoning power: they will automatically engineer vast amounts of knowledge to serve whatever purpose humans propose, from medical diagnosis to product design, from management decisions to education. (Feigenbaum & McCorduck, 1983, p. 56)

What the knowledge engineers claim to have discovered is that in areas which are cut off from everyday common sense and social intercourse, all a machine needs in order to behave like an expert are some general rules and lots of very specific knowledge. As Feigenbaum and McCorduck put it:

> In part, they were correct ... [Such strategies] include searching for a solution; generating and testing; reasoning backward from a desired goal; and the like.
>
> These strategies are necessary, but not sufficient, for intelligent behavior. The other ingredient is knowledge — specialized knowledge, and lots of it ... No matter how natively bright you are, you cannot be a credible medical diagnostician without a great deal of specific knowledge about diseases, their manifestations, and the human body (Feigenbaum & McCorduck, 1983, p. 38.)

This specialized knowledge is of two types:

> The first type is the *facts* of the domain — the widely shared knowledge — that is written in textbooks and journals of the field, or that forms the basis of a professor's lecturers in a classroom. Equally important to the practice of the field is the second type of knowledge called *heuristic knowledge,* which is the knowledge of good practice and good judgment in a field. It is experiential knowledge, the "art of good guessing" that a

human expert acquires over years of work (Feigenbaum & McCorduck, 1983, pp. 76–77.)

Using all three kinds of knowledge Feigenbaum *et al.*, (1971) developed a program called DENDRAL. It takes the data generated by a mass spectrograph and deduces from this data the molecular structure of the compound being analyzed. Another program, MYCIN (Shortliffe, Axline *et al.*, 1973; Shortliffe, Randall *et al.*, 1975) takes the results of blood tests such as the number of red cells, white cells, sugar in the blood, etc. and comes up with a diagnosis of which blood disease is responsible for this condition. It even gives an estimate of the reliability of its own diagnosis. In their narrow areas, such programs give impressive performances.

But is not the success of expert systems just what one would expect? If we agree with Feigenbaum and McCorduck (1983, p. 18) that: "almost all the thinking that professionals do is done by reasoning ..." we can see that once computers are used for reasoning and not just computation they should be as good or better than we are at following rules for deducing conclusions from a host of facts. So we would expect that if the rules which an expert has acquired from years of experience could be extracted and programmed, the resuliting program would exhibit expertise. Again Feigenbaum and McCorduck (1983, p. 64) put the point very clearly:

> [T]he matters that set experts apart from beginners, are symbolic, inferential, and rooted in experiential knowledge. Human experts have acquired their expertise not only from explicit knowledge found in textbooks and lectures, but also from experience: by doing things again and again, failing, succeeding ... getting a feel for a problem, learning when to go by the book and when to break the rules. They therefore build up a repertory of working rules of thumb, or "heuristics," that, combined with book knowledge, make them expert practitioners (Feigenbaum & McCorduck, 1983, p. 64).

Since each expert already has a repertory of rules in his mind, all the expert system builder need do is get the rules out and program them into a computer.

This view is not new. In fact, it goes back to the beginning of Western culture when the first philosopher, Socrates, stalked around Athens looking for experts in order to draw out and test their rules. In one of his earliest dialogues, *The Euthyphro,* Plato tells us of such an encounter between Socrates and Euthyphro, a religious prophet and so an expert on pious behavior. Socrates asks Euthyphro to tell him how to recognize piety: "I want to know what is characteristic of piety ... to use a standard whereby to judge your actions and those of other men." But instead of revealing his piety-recognizing heuristic, Euthyphro does just what every expert does when cornered by Socrates. He gives him examples from his field of expertise; in this case situations in the past in which men and gods have done things which everyone considers pious. Socrates persists throughout the dialogue in demanding that Euthyphro tell him his rules, but although

Euthyphro claims he knows how to tell pious acts from impious ones, he cannot state the rules which generate his judgments. Socrates ran into the same problem with craftsmen, poets and even statesmen. None could articulate his rules.

Plato admired Socrates and sympathized with his problem. So he developed an account of what caused the difficulty. Experts had once known the rules they use, Plato said, but then they had forgotten them. The role of the philosopher was to help people remember the principles on which they act. Knowledge engineers would now say that the rules the experts use have been put in a part of their mental computers where they work automatically.

> When we learned how to tie our shoes, we had to think very hard about the steps involved ... Now that we've tied many shoes over our lifetime, that knowledge is "compiled," to use the computing term for it; it no longer needs our conscious attention. (Feigenbaum & McCorduck, 1983, p. 55.)

On this Platonic view the rules are there functioning in the expert's mind whether he is conscious of them or not. How else could we account for the fact that he can perform the task?

Now 2000 years later, thanks to Feigenbaum and his colleagues, we have a new name for what Socrates and Plato were doing:

> [W]e are able to be more precise ... and with this increased precision has come a new term, *knowledge acquisition research*. (Feigenbaum & McCorduck, 1983, p. 79)

But although philosophers and even the man in the street have become convinced that expertise consists in applying sophisticated heuristics to masses of facts, there are few available rules. As Feigenbaum explains:

> [A]n expert's knowledge is often ill-specified or incomplete because the expert himself doesn't always know exactly what it is he knows about his domain. (Feigenbaum & McCorduck, 1983, p. 85.)

So the knowledge engineer has to help him recollect what he once knew.

> [An expert's] knowledge is currently acquired in a very painstaking way; individual computer scientists work with individual experts to explicate the expert's heuristics — to mine those jewels of knowledge out of their heads one by one ... the problem of knowledge acquisition is the critical bottleneck in artificial intelligence. (Feigenbaum & McCorduck, 1983, pp. 79–80.)

When Feigenbaum suggests to an expert the rules the expert seems to be using he gets a Euthyphro-like response. "That's true, but if you see enough patients/rocks/chip designs/instrument readings, you see that it isn't true after all."(p. 82) and Feigenbaum comments with Socratic annoyance: "At this point, knowledge threatens to become ten thousand special cases. (p. 82).

There are also other hints of trouble. Ever since the inception of artificial intelligence, researchers have been trying to produce artificial experts by programming the computer to follow the rules used by masters in various domains. Yet, although computers are faster and more accurate than people in applying rules, master-level performance has remained out of reach. Arthur Samuel's (1963) work is typical. When electronic computers were just being developed, Samuel, then at IBM, decided to write a checker-playing program. He tried to elicit heuristic rules from checker masters and program a computer to follow these rules. When the rules the experts came up with did not produce master play, Samuel became the first and almost the only AI researcher to make a learning program. He programmed a computer to vary the weights used in the rules, such as the trade-off between center control and loss of a piece, and to retain the weights that worked best. After playing a great many games with itself the program could beat Samuel, which shows that in some sense computers can do more than they are programmed to do. But the program still could not beat the sort of experts whose heuristic rules were the heart of the program.

The checkers program is not only the first and one of the best experts ever built, but it is also a perfect example of the way fact turns into fiction in AI. The checkers program once beat a state checkers champion. From then on AI literature cites the checker programs as a noteworthy success. One often reads that it plays at such a high level that only the world champion can beat it. Feigenbaum and McCorduck (1983, p. 179), for example report that "by 1961 [Samuel's program] played championship checkers, and it learned and improved with each game." Even the usually reliable *Handbook of artificial intelligence* states as a fact that "today's programs play championship-level checkers." (Barr & Feigenbaum, 1981, p. 7). In fact, Samuel said in a recent interview at Stanford University, where he is a retired professor, that the program did once defeat a state champion but the champion "turned around and defeated the program in six mail games." According to Samuel, after 35 years of effort, "the program is quite capable of beating any amateur player and can give better players a good contest." It is clearly no champion. Samuel is still bringing in expert players for help but he "fears he may be reaching the point of diminishing returns." This does not lead him to question the view that the masters the program cannot beat are using heuristic rules; rather, like Socrates and Feigenbaum, Samuel thinks that the experts are poor at recollecting their compiled heuristics: "the experts do not know enough about the mental processes involved in playing the game." (Interview released by Stanford News Office, April 28, 1983).

The same story is repeated in every area of expertise in which human beings develop from experience the ability to size up whole situations within seconds, even in areas unlike checkers where expertise requires the storage of large numbers of facts, which should give an advantage to the computer. In each such area where there are experts with years of experience the computer can do better than the beginner, and can even exhibit useful competence, but it cannot rival the very experts whose facts and supposed heuristics it is processing with incredible speed and unerring accuracy.

In the face of this impasse it was necessary, in spite of the authority and influence of Plato and 2000 years of philosophy, for us to take a fresh look at what a skill is and what the expert acquires when he achieves expertise. One must be prepared to abandon the traditional view that a beginner starts with specific cases and, as he becomes more proficient, abstracts and interiorizes more and more sophisticated rules. It might turn out that skill acquisition moves in just the opposite direction: from abstract rules to particular cases. Since we all have many areas in which we are experts, we have the necessary data, so let's look and see how adults learn new skills.

## STAGE 1: NOVICE

Normally, the instruction process begins with the instructor decomposing the task environment into context-free features which the beginner can recongize without benefit of experience. The beginner is then given rules for determining actions on the basis of these features, like a computer following a program. The beginning student wants to do a good job, but lacking any coherent sense of the overall task, he judges his performance mainly by how well he follows his learned rules. After he has acquired more than just a few rules, so much concentration is required during the exercise of his skill that his capacity to talk or listen to advice is severely limited.

For purposes of illustration, we shall consider two variations: a bodily or motor skill and an intellectual skill. The student automobile driver learns to recognize such interpretation-free features as speed (indicated by his speed-ometer) and distance (as estimated by a previously acquired skill). Safe following distances are defined in terms of speed; conditions that allow safe entry into traffic are defined in terms of speed and distance of oncoming traffic; timing of shifts of gear is specified in tems of speed, etc. These rules ignore context. They do not refer to traffic density or anticipated stops.

The novice chess player learns a numerical value for each type of piece regardless of its position, and the rule: "always exchange if the total value of pieces captured exceeds the value of pieces lost." He also learns that when no advantageous exchanges can be found center control should be sought, and he is given a rule defining center squares and one for calculating extent of control. Most beginners are notoriously slow players, as they attempt to remember all these rules and their priorities.

## STAGE 2: ADVANCED BEGINNER

As the novice gains experience actually coping with real situations, he begins to note, or an instructor points out, perspicuous examples of meaningful additional components of the situation. After seeing a sufficient number of examples, the student learns to recognize them. Instructional maxims now can refer to these new *situational aspects* recognized on the basis of experience, as well as to the objectively defined *non-situational features* recognizable by the novice. The advanced beginner confronts his environment, seeks out features and aspects, and determines his actions by applying rules. he shares the novice's minimal concern with quality of performance, instead focusing on quality of rule following. The advanced beginner's performance, while improved, remains slow, uncoordinated, and laborious.

The advanced beginner driver uses (situational) engine sounds as well as (non-situational) speed in his gear-shifting rules, and observes demeanor as well as position and velocity to anticipate behavior of pedestrains or other drivers. he learns to distinguish the behavior of the distracted or drunken driver from that of the impatient but alert one. No number of words can serve the function of a few choice examples in learning this distinction. Engine sounds cannot be adequately captured by words, and no list of objective facts about a particular pedestrian enables one to predict his behavior in a crosswalk as well as can the driver who has observed many pedestrians crossing streets under a variety of conditions.

With experience, the chess beginner learns to recognize over-extended positions and how to avoid them. Similarly, he begins to recognize such situational aspects of positions as a weakened king's side or a strong pawn structure despite the lack of precise and universally valid definitional rules.

## STAGE 3: COMPETENCE

With increasing experience, the number of features and aspects to be taken account of becomes overwhelming. To cope with this information explosion, the performer learns, or is taught, to adopt a hierarchical view of decision-making. By first choosing a plan, goal or perspective which organizes the situation and by then examining only the small set of features and aspects that he has learned are the most important given that plan, the performer can simplify and improve his performance.

Choosing a plan, a goal or perspective, is no simple matter for the competent performer. It is not an objective procedure, like the feature recognition of the novice. Nor is the choice avoidable. While the advanced beginner can get along without recognizing and using a particular situational aspect until a sufficient number of examples makes identification easy and sure, to perform competently *requires* choosing an organizing goal or perspective. Furthermore, the choice of perspective crucially affects behavior in a way that one particular aspect rarely does.

This combination of necessity and uncertainty introduces an important new type of relationship between the performer and his environment. The novice and the advanced beginner applying rules and maxims feel little or no responsibility for the outcome of their acts. If they have made no mistakes, an unfortunate outcome is viewed as the result of inadequately specified elements or rules. The competent performer, on the other hand, after wrestling with the question of a choice of perspective or goal, feels responsible for, and thus emotionally involved in, the result of his choice. An outcome that is clearly successful is deeply satisfying and leaves a vivid memory of the situation encountered as seen from the goal or perspective finally chosen. Disasters, likewise, are not easily forgotten.

Remembered whole situations differ in one important respect from remembered aspects. The mental image of an aspect is flat in the sense that no parts stand out as salient. A whole situation, on the other hand, since it is the result of a chosen plan or perspective, has a "three-dimensional" quality. Certain elements stand out as more or less important with respect to the plan, while other irrelevant elements are forgotton. Moreover, the competent performer, gripped by the situation that his decision has produced, experiences and therefore remembers the situation not only in tems of foreground and background elements but also in terms of senses of opportunity, risk, expectation, threat, etc. These gripping, holistic memories cannot guide the behavior of the competent performer since he fails to make contact with them when he reflects on problematic situations as a detached observer, and holds to a view of himself as a computer following better and better rules. As we shall soon see, however, if he does let them take over, these memories become the basis of the competent performer's next advance in skill. At this level the performer also learns to use analogy, consciously seeing a present situation as analogous to a prior situation but with differences. He reasons out an appropriate action based on what was learned in the previous situation while taking account of the differences.

A competent driver beginning a trip decides, perhaps, that he is in a hurry. he then selects a route with attention to distance and time, ignores scenic beauty, and as he drives, he chooses his maneuvers with little concern for passenger comfort or for courtesy. he follows more closely than normal, enters traffic more daringly, occasionally violates a law. He feels elated when decisions work out and no police car appears, and shaken by near accidents and traffice tickets.

The class A chess player, here classed as competent, may decide after studying a position that his opponent has weakened his king's defenses so that an attack against the king is a viable goal. if the attack is chosen, features involving weaknesses in his own position created by his attack are ignored as are losses of pieces inessential to the attack. Removal of pieces defending the enemy king becomes salient. Successful plans induce euphoria and mistakes are felt in the pit of the stomach.

In both of these cases, we find a common pattern: detached planning, conscious assessment of elements that are salient with respect to the plan, and analytical rule-guided choice of action, followed by an emotionally involved experience of the outcome.

## STAGE 4: PROFICIENCY

Considerable experience at the level of competency sets the stage for yet further skill enhancement. Having experienced many situations, chosen plans in each, and having obtained vivid, involved demonstrations of the adequacy or inadequacy of the plan, the performer sees his current situation as similar to a previous one and so spontaneously sees an appropriate plan. Involved in the world of the skill, the performer "notices," or "is struck by" a certain plan, goal or perspective. No longer is the spell of involvement broken by detached conscious planning.

Since there are generally far fewer "ways of seeing" than "ways of acting," after understanding without conscious effort what is going on, the proficient performer will still have to think about what to do. During this thinking, elements that present themselves as salient are assessed and combined by rule to produce decisions about how best to manipulate the environment. The spell of involvement in the world of the activity will thus temporarily be broken.

On the basis of prior experience, a proficient driver approaching a curve on a rainy day may sense that he is traveling too fast. Then, on the basis of such salient elements as visibility, angle of road bank, criticalness of time, etc., he decides whether to take his foot off the gas or to step on the brake. (These factors would be used by the *competent* driver consciously to *decide that* he is speeding.)

The proficient chess player, who is classed a master, can recognize a large repertoire of types of positions. Recognizing almost immediately and without conscious effort the sense of a position, he sets about calculating the move that best achieves his goal. He may, for example, know that he should attack, but he must deliberate about how best to do so.

## STAGE 5: EXPERTISE

The proficient performer, immersed in the world of his skillful activity, *sees* what needs to be done, but *decides* how to do it. For the expert, not only situational understandings spring to mind, but also associated appropriate actions. The expert performer, except of course during moments of break-down, understands, acts, and learns from results without any conscious awareness of the process. What transparently *must* be done *is* done. We usually do not make conscious deliberative decisions when we talk, ride a bicycle, drive, or carry on most social activities.

We have seen that experience-based similarity recognition produces the deep situational understanding of the proficient performer. No new insight is needed to explain the mental processes of the expert. With enough experience with a variety of situations, all seen from the same perspective or with the same goal in mind, but requiring different tactical decisions, the mind of the proficient performer seems gradually to decompose this class of situations into subclasses, each member of which shares not only the same goal or perspective, but also the same decision, action, or tactic. At this point, a situation, when seen as similar to members of this class, is not only thereby understood but simultaneously the associated decision, action or tactic presents itself.

The number of classes of recognizable situations, built up on the basis of experience, must be immense. It has been estimated that a master chess player can distinguish roughly 50,000 types of positions. Automobile driving probably involves a similar number of typical situations. We doubtless store far more typical situations in our memories than words in our vocabularies. Consequently these reference situations, unlike the situational elements learned by the advanced beginner, bear no names and, in fact, defy complete verbal description.

The expect chess player, classed as an international master or grand master, in most situations experiences a compelling sense of the issue and the best move. Excellent chess players can play at the rate of 5–10 seconds a move and even faster without any serious degradation in performance. At this speed they must depend almost entirely on intuition and hardly at all on analysis and comparison of alternatives. We recently performed an experiment in which an international master, Julio Kaplan, was required rapidly to add numbers presented to him audibly at the rate of about one number per second while at the same time playing five-second-a-move chess against a slightly weaker, but master level, player. Even with his analytical mind completely occupied by adding numbers, Kaplan more than held his own against the master in a series of games. Deprived of the time necessary to see problems or construct plans, Kaplan still produced fluid and coordinated play.

Kaplan's performance seems somewhat less amazing when one realizes that a chess position is as meaningful, interesting, and important to a professional chess player as a face in a receiving line is to a profession politician. Bobby Fischer, perhaps history's greatest chess player, once said that for him "chess is life." Almost anyone can add numbers and simultaneously recognize and respond to faces, even though the face will never exactly match the same face seen previously, and politicians can recognize thousands of faces just as Julio Kaplan can recognize thousands of chess positions similar to ones previously encountered.

Simon (1979, pp. 386–403) has studied the chess master's almost instantaneous understanding of chess positions and accompanying compelling sense of the best move. He found that chess masters are familiar with thousands of patterns, which he calls chunks. Each chunk is a remembered description of a small group of pieces in a certain relationship to each other. He conjectures that a desirable move or chess idea is associated with each such chunk. Hence moves spring to mind as chunks are recognized without need for rule-like calculations.

There are at least two problems with Simon's speculation. Because most chess positions are comprised of several chunks, more than one move would come to mind and need to be evaluated before the player would have a sense of which was best. Yet, Julio Kaplan doesn't seem to require such evaluation when he plays rapidly while simultaneously adding numbers. Hence Simon's conceptualization of chess in terms of chunk recognition, while providing a theory about why moves spring to mind, still seems to fall far short of the actual phenomenon of masterful play. Furthermore, for Simon chunks such as a standard castled king's formation are defined independently of the rest of the position. A configuration that didn't quite fit the description of a chunk, but in a real chess position played the same role as the chunk, would not count as such. But chess players can recognize the functional equivalence of configurations which don't fall under a single definition. For example, in some cases a configuration would count as a standard castled king's formation even if one pawn were advanced, but in other cases it would not. So Simon's AI model cannot account for expert chess performance.

The expert driver, generally without any awareness, not only knows by feel and faimilarity when an action such as slowing down is required, but he knows how to perform the action without calculating and compariing alternatives. He shifts gears when appropriate with no conscious awareness of his acts. Most drivers have experienced the disconcerting breakdown that occurs when suddenly one reflects on the gear shifting process and tries to decide what to do. Suddenly the smooth, almost automatic, sequence of actions that results from the performer's involved immersion in the world of his skill is disrupted, and the performer sees himself, just as does the competent performer, as the manipulator of a complex mechanism. He detachedly calculates his actions even more poorly than does the competent performer since he has forgotten many of the guiding rules that he knew and used when competent, and his performance suddenly becomes halting, uncertain, and even inappropriate.

It seems that a beginner makes inferences using rules and facts just like a heuristically programmed computer, but that in most domains with talent and a great deal of involved experience the beginner develops into an expert who intuitively sees what to do without applying rules.

Of course, a description of skilled behavior can never be taken as as conclusive evidence as to what is going on in the mind or in the brain. It is always possible that what is going on is some unconscious process using more and more sophisticated rules. But our description of skill acquisition counters the traditional prejudice that expertise necessarily involves inference.

Given our account of the five stages of skill acquisition, we can understand why the knowledge engineers from Socrates, to Samuel, to Feigenbaum have had such trouble getting the expert to articulate the rules he is using. The intuitive expert is simply not following any rules! He is doing just what Feigenbaum feared he might be doing — recognizing thousands of special cases. This in turn explains why expert systems are never as good as experts. If one asks the experts for rules one will, in effect, force the expert to regress to the level of a beginner and state the rules he still remembers but no longer uses. If one programs these rules on a computer one can use the speed and accuracy of the computer and its ability to store and access millions of facts to outdo a human beginner using the same rules. But no amount of rules and facts can capture the knowledge an expert has when he has stored his experience of the actual outcomes of tens of thousands of situations.

The knowledge engineer might still say that in spite of appearances the mind and brain *must* be reasoning — making millions of rapid and accurate inference like a computer. After all the brain is not "wonder tissue" and how else could it work? But there *are* other models for what might be going on in the hardware. The capacity of experts to store in memory tens of thousands of typical situations and rapidly and effortlessly to see the present situation as similar to one of these, apparently without resorting to time-consuming feature detection and matching, suggests that the brain does not work like a heuristically programmed digital computer applying rules to bits of information. Rather it suggests, as some neurophysiologists already believe, that the brain, at times at least, works holographically, superimposing the records of whole situations and measuring their similarity. Dr Karl Pribram, a Standford neurophysiologist who has spent the last decade studying holographic memory, explicitly notes the implication of this sort of process of expertise. When asked in an interview (Goleman, 1979) whether holograms would allow a person to make decisions spontaneously in very complex environments, Pribrain replied, "Decisions fall out as the holographic correlations are performed. One doesn't have to think things through ... a step at a time. One takes the whole constellation of a situation, correlates it, and out of that correlation emerges the correct reponse."

Recently a group of psychologists, neurophysiologists and computer scientists calling themselves "new connectionists" have developed devices which, indeed, directly process inputs without using rules. These workers have been able to train simulated neuron nets to associate simple patterns by modifying the connection strengths between neuron like units, where units are not in any sense symbols representing features of the problem domain. For an example, see McClelland and Rumelhart (1986).

On the basis of our skill model we predict that in any domain in which people exhibit holistic understanding, no system based upon heuristics will consistently do as well as experienced experts, even if they were the informants who provided the heuristic rules. Since there already seem to be many exceptions to our prediction, we will now deal with each alleged exception in turn.

To begin with there is a system developed at MIT, called MACSYMA, for doing certain manipulations required in calculus. MACSYMA began as a *heuristic* system. It has evolved, however, into an *algorithmic* system, using procedures guaranteed to work which involve so much calculation people would never use them, so the fact that, as far as we can find out, MACSYMA now outperforms all experts in its field, does not constitute an exception to our hypothesis.

DENDRAL was one of the first and most touted expert systems, which, according to Feigenbaum, "began AI's shift to the knowledge-based viewpoint." It has a history similar to MACSYMA's. Feigenbaum, stockholder in and director of an expert systems company, however, gives the impression that DENDRAL is still based on heuristic rules gleaned from experts and that it is widely used in industry. He says that "DENDRAL has been in use for many years at university and industrial chemical labs around the world."

When we called several universities and industrial sites that do mass spectroscopy, we were surprised to find that none of them use DENDRAL. The resolution of this apparent contradiction turned out to be revealing.

DENDRAL was the name of the original research project, which developed several quite different programs. One of those, Heuristic DENDRAL, uses heuristic rules operating on the spectrum produced by a mass spectrometer to infer various molecular structures that might produce the observed spectrum. It then tests to see how well the spectra of the candidate structures match the actual mass spectra observed, and ranks the candidates based on this matching. Heuristic DENDRAL is, indeed, an expert system, but it is not commercially available.

An outgrowth of the DENDRAL project, CONGEN, does seem to be in use daily by chemists, but it is not a heuristic-based expert system. CONGEN uses an algorithmic procedure to generate all molecular structes consistent with information based on several sources, including spectroscopy. The program does not heuristically infer constraints from mass spectra, as does Heuristic DENDRAL, but directly accepts constraints provided by human experts.

We asked Bruce Buchanan, a co-developer of DENDRAL, whether the heuristic part of DENDRAL was an expert system that could outperform intuitive experts, and, if so, why it wasn't used in industry. He explained that (1) the system as programmed contained knowledge of only one very specific class of compounds, and for such compounds it outperformed the best chemists, (2) it was not commercially available because apparently the investment required in order to codify the knowledge of the many specific domains that concern industry was prohibitive, and (3) spectroscopy has been chosen as a test bed for expert systems in the first place because chemists doing mass spectral interpretation must rely largely on systematic inference rather than intuitive pattern recognition. Since in spectrographic analysis skilled performance requires calculation, the success of heuristic DENDRAL does not falsify our hypothesis.

R1, another expert system both as good as human specialists and heuristic, was developed at Digital Equipment Corporation to decide how to combine components of VAX computers to meet customers' needs. Like DENDRAL it performs as well as anyone in the field only because the domain in question is so combinatorial that even experienced specialists fail to develop holistic understanding. The experienced "technical editors" who perform the job at DEC depend on heuristic-based problem solving and take about ten minutes to work out even simple cases, so it is no surprise that an expert system can rival the best specialists.

Chess too seems an obvious exception to our prediction, since chess programs have already achieved master ratings. The chess story is complicated and fascinating. Programs that play chess are among the earliest examples of expert systems. The first such program was written in the 1950s and by the early sixties fairly sophisticated programs had been developed. The programs naturally included the facts of the chess world (i.e. the rules of the game) and also heuristics elicited from strong players.

Master players, in checking out each plausible move that springs to mind, generally consider one to three plausible opponent responses, followed by one to three moves of their own, etc. Quite frequently, only one move looks plausible at each step. After looking ahead a varying number of moves depending on the situation, the terminal position of each sequence is assessed based on its simliarity to positions previously encountered. In positions where the best initial move is not obvious, about one hundred terminal positions will typically be examined. This thinking ahead generally confirms that the intial move intuitively seen as the most plausible is indeed best, although there are occasional exceptions.

To imitate players, the program designers attempted to elicit from the masters heuristic rules that could be used to generate a limited number of plausible moves at each step, and evaluation rules that could be used to assess the worth of the roughly one hundred terminal positions. Since masters are not aware of following any rules, the rules that they suggested did not work well and the programs played at a marginally competent level.

As computers grew faster in the 1970s, chess programming strategy changed. In 1973, a program was developed at Northwestern University by David Slate and Larry Atkin which in effect rapidly searched *every* legal initial move, every legal response etc. to a depth determined by the position and the computer's speed, generally about three moves for each player. A clever procedure in the program actually eliminated certain possible sequences of moves that could not possibly be best before examining them, thereby greatly speeding up the search. The roughly one million terminal positions in the look-ahead were still evaluated by rules. Plausible-move-generation heuristics were discarded, the program looked less like an expert system, and quality of play greatly improved. By 1983, using these largely brute-force procedures and the latest, most power computer (the Cray X-MP capable of examining about ten million terminal positions in choosing each move), a program called Cray-Blitz became world computer chess champion and achieved a master rating based on a tournament against other computers who already had chess ratings.

Such programs, however, have an Achilles heel. While they are perfect tacticians when there are many captures and checks and a decisive outcome can be found within the computer's foreseeable future (now about four moves ahead for each player), computers lack any sense of chess strategy. Fairly good players who understand this fact can direct the game into long-range strategic channels and can thereby defeat the computer, even though these players have a somewhat lower chess rating than the machine has achieved based on play against other machines and humans who do not know and exploit this strategic blindness. The ratings held by computers and reported in the press accurately reflect their performance against other computers and human players who do not know or exploit the computer's weakness, but greatly overstate their skill level when play is strategic.

A Scottish International Master chess player, David Levy, who is a computer enthusiast and who is ranked as roughly the thousandth best player in the world, bet about $4000 in 1968 that no computer could defeat him by 1978. He collected, by beating the best computer program at that time 3.5 games to 1.5 games in a five game match. He was, however, impressed by the machine's performance and the bet was increased and extended until 1984, with Levy quite uncertain about the outcome. When the 1984 match approached and the Cray-Blitz program had just achieved a master-level score in winning the world computer championship, Levy decided to modify his usual style of play so as maximally to exploit the computer's strategic blindness. Not only did he defeat the computer decisively, four games to zero, but, more importantly, he lost his long-held optimism about computer play. As he confessed to the *Los Angeles Times* of May 12, 1984:

> During the last few years I had come to believe more and more that it was possible for programs, within a decade, to play very strong grandmaster chess. But having played the thing now, my feeling is that a human world chess champion losing to a computer program in a serious match is a lot further away than I thought. Most people working on computer chess are working on the wrong lines. If more chess programmers studied the way human chess masters think and tried to emulate that to some extent, then I think they might get further.

Levy summed up his recent match by saying "The nature of the struggle was such that the program didn't understand what was going on" Clearly, when confronting a player who knows its weakness, Cray-Blitz is not a master level chess player.

We could not agree more strongly with Levy's suggestion that researchers give up current methods and attempt to imitate what people do. But since strong, experienced, chess players use the holistic similarity recognition described in the highest of our five levels of skill, imitating people would mean duplicating that pattern recognition process rather than returning to the typical expert system approach. Since similarity for a strong chess player means similar "fields of force" such as interrelated threats, hopes, fears, and strengths, not similarity of the location of pieces on the board, and since no one can describe such fields, there is little prospect of duplicating human performance in the foreseeable future.

The only remaining game program that appears to challenge our prediction is Hans Berliner's backgammon program, BKG 9.8 (Berliner, 1980). There is no doubt that the program used heuristic rules obtained from masters to beat the world champion in a seven-game series. But backgammon is a game involving a large chance, and Berliner himself is quite frank in saying that his program "did get the better of the dice rolls" and could not consistently perform at championship level. He concludes:

> The program did not make the best play in eight out of 73 nonforced situations. ... An expert would not have made most of the errors the program made, but they could be exploited only a small percent of the time. ... My program plays at the Class A, or advanced intermediate, level. (Berliner, 1980, p. 72.)

The above cases are clearly not counter-examples to our claim. Neither is a recent SRI contender named PROSPECTOR, a program which uses rules derived from expert geologists to locate mineral deposits. Millions of viewers heard about PROSPECTOR on the CBS Evening News in September 1983. A special Dan Rather Report called "The Computers are Coming" showed first a computer and then a mountain (Mount Tolman) as Rather authoritatively intoned, "This computer digested facts and figures on mineral deposits, then predicted that the metal molybdenum would be found at this mountain in the Pacific Northwest. It was." Such a feat, if true, would indeed be impressive. Viewers must have felt that we were foolish when, later in the same program, we were shown asserting that, using current AI methods, computers would never become intelligent. (While we explained and defended this claim during an hour-long taped interview with CBS, all of this was necessarily omitted during the 5 minute segment on computers that was aired.) In reality, the PROSPECTOR program was given information concerning prior drilling on Mount Tolman where a field of molybdenum *had already been found*. The expert system then mapped out undrilled portions of that field, and subsequent drilling showed it to be basically correct about where molybdenum did and did not exist.[1] Unfortunately, economic-grade molybdenum was not found in the previously unmapped area; drilling disclosed the ore to be too deep to be worth mining. These facts do not justify the conclusion that the program can outperform experts. So far there are no further data comparing experts' predictions with those of the system.

This leaves MYCIN, mentioned earlier, INTERNIST-I Miller *et al.*, 1982), a program for diagnosis in internal medicine, and PUFF (Aikens *et al.*, 1983), an expert system for diagnosis of lung disorders, as the only programs that we know of which meet all requirements for a test of our hypothesis. They are each based exclusively on heuristic rules extracted from experts, and their performance has been compared with that of experts in the field.

Let us take MYCIN first. Yu *et al.* (1979) systematically evaluated MYCIN. MYCIN was given data concerning ten actual meningitis cases and asked to prescribe drug therapy. Its prescriptions were evaluated by a panel of eight infectious disease specialists who had published clinical reports dealing with the management of meningitis. These experts rated as acceptable 70% of MYCIN'S recommended therapies.

The evidence concerning INTERNIST-I is even more detailed. In fact, according to Miller *et al.* (1982) "[the] systematic evaluation of the model's

---

[1] See *Byte*, Sept. 1981, p. 262, caption under figure. The CBS Evening News report is not the only sensationalized and inaccurate report on PROSPECTOR spread by the mass media. The July 9, 1984 issue of *Business Week* reports in its cover story, "Artificial Intelligence: It's Here": "Geologists were convinced as far back as World War I that a rich deposit of molybdenum ore was buried deep under Mount Tolman in eastern Washington. But after digging dozens of small mines and drilling hundreds of test borings, they were still hunting for the elusive metal 60 years later. Then, just a couple of years ago, miners hit pay dirt. They finally found the ore because they were guided not by a geologist wielding his rock hammer, but by a computer located hundreds of miles to the south in Menlo Park, Calif."

performance is virtually unique in the field of medical applications of artificial intelligence." (p. 494.) INTERNIST-I is described as follows:

> From its inception, INTERNIST-I has addressed the problem of diagnosis within the broad context of general internal medicine. Given a patient's initial history, results of a physical examination, or laboratory findings, INTERNIST-I was designed to aid the physician with the patient's work-up in order to make multiple and complex diagnoses. The capabilities of the system derive from its extensive knowledge base and from heuristic computer programs that can construct and resolve differential diagnoses. (Miller *et al.*, 1982, p. 468.)

The program was run on 19 cases, each with several diseases, so that there were 43 correct diagnoses in all, and its diagnoses were compared with those of clinicians at Massachusetts General Hospital and with case discussants. Diagnoses were counted as correct when confirmed by pathologists. The result was:

> [O]f 43 anatomically verified diagnoses, INTERNIST-I failed to make a total of 18, whereas the clinicians failed to make 15 such diagnoses and the discussants missed only eight. (p. 473.)

The evaulators found that:

> The experienced clinician is vastly superior to INTERNIST-I in the ability to consider the relative severity and indepedence of the different manifestations of disease and to understand the temporal evolution of the disease process. (p. 494.)

Dr. G. Octo Barnett, in his editorial comment on the evaluation, wisely concludes:

> Perhaps the most exciting experimental evaluation of INTERNIST-I would be the demonstration that a productive collaboration is possible between man and computer — that clinical diagnosis in real situations can be improved by combining the medical judgment of the clinician with the statistical and computational power of a computer model and a large base of stored medical information. (p. 494.)

PUFF is an excellent example of an expert system doing a useful job without being an expert. PUFF was written to perform pulmonary function test interpretations. One sample measurement is the patient's *Total lung capacity* (TLC), that is, the volume of air in the lungs at maximum inspiration. If the TLC for a patient is high, this indicates the presence of obstructive airways disease. The interpretation and final diagnosis is a summary of this kind of reasoning about the combinations of measurements taken in the lung test. PUFF's principle task is to interpret such a set of

pulmonary function tests results, producing a set of interpretation statements and a diagnosis for each patient.

Using thirty heuristic rules extracted from an expert, Dr Robert Fallat,
PUFF agrees with Dr Fallat in 75–85% of the cases. Why it does as well as
the expert it models in only 75–85% of the cases is a mystery if one believes,
as Robert MacNeil put it on the MacNeil-Lehrer television news, that
researchers "discovered that Dr Fallat used some 30 rules based on his
clinical expertise to diagnose whether patients have obstructive airway
disease." Of course, the machine's limited ability makes perfect sense if Dr
Fallat does not in fact follow these 30 rules or any others. But in any case,
PUFF does well enough to be a valuable aid. As Dr Fallat puts it:

> "There's a lot of what we do, including our thinking and our
> expertise, which is routine, and which doesn't require any special
> human effort to do. And that kind of stuff should be taken over by
> computers. And to the extent that 75% of what I do is routine and
> which all of us would agree on, why not let the computer do it and
> then I can have fun working with the other 25%." (MacNeil-Lehrer
> report, 1983).

Feigenbaum and McCorduck (1983) admit in one surprisingly frank
passage that expert systems are very differnt from experts:

> "A human expert solves problems, all right, but he also explains the
> results, he learns, he restructures his own knowledge ... Part of
> learning to be an expert is to understand not merely the letter of the
> rule but its spirit .. he knows when to break the rules, he under-
> stands what is relevant to his task and what isn't ... Expert systems
> do not yet understand these things." (pp. 84–85.).

But because of his philosophical commitment to the rationality of expertise
and thus to undelying unconscious heuristic rules, Feigenbaum does not see
how devastating this admission is.

Once one gives up the assumption that experts must be making inferences and admits the role of involvement and intuition in the acquisition and
application of skills, one will have no reason to cling to the heuristic program
as a model of human intellectual operations. Feigenbaum and McCorduck's
claim that "we have the opportunity at this moment to do a new version of
Diderot's *Encyclopédie,* a gathering up of all knowledge — not just the
academic kind, but the informal experiential, heuristic kind" (p. 229); as
well as his boast that thanks to knowledge information processing systems
(KIPS) we will soon have "access to machine intelligence — faster, deeper,
better than human intelligence" (p. 236), can both be seen as a late stage of
Socratic thinking, with no rational or empirical basis. In this light those who
claim we must begin a crash program to compete with the Japanese fifth
generation intelligent computers can be seen to be false prophets blinded by

these Socratic assumptions and personal ambition — while Euthyphro, the expert on piety, who kept giving Socrates examples instead of rules, turns out to have been a true prophet after all.

## REFERENCES

Aikins, J. S., Kunz, J. C., & Shortcliff, E. H. (1983). PUFF: an expert system for interpretation of pulmonary function data. *Computers and Biomedical Research,* **16,** 199–208.

Barr, A., & Feigenbaum, E. A. (1981). *The handbook of artificial intelligence,* Volume 1. William Kaufmann, Inc.

Berliner, H. (1980). Computer backgammon. *Scientific American,* **242,** (6), 64–72.

Block, N. (1981). (Ed.) *Imagery.*Cambridge, MA: MIT Press/Bradford Books.

Block, N. (1983). Mental pictures and cognitive science. *The Philosophical Review,* XCII, **4,** 499–541.

Evans, T. G. (1968). A program for the solution of Geometric-Analogy Intelligence Test Questions. In M. L. Minsky (Ed. *Semantic information processing.* Cambridge MA: MIT Press.

Feigenbaum, E. A., Buchanan, B. G., & Lederberg, J. (1971). On generality and problem solving: A case study using the DENDRAL program. In B. Meltzer and D. Michie, *Machine Intelligence 6,* 165–190. Edinburgh: Edinburgh University Press.

Feigenbaum, E., McCorduck, P. (1983). *The fifth generation: artificial intelligence and Japan's computer challenge to the world.* Reading, MA: Addison-Wesley.

Goleman, D. (1979). Holographic memory: An interview with Karl Pribram. *Psychology Today,* **12** (9), 80.

Kolata, G. (1982). How can computers get common sense? *Science,* **217,** 4566, 1237–1238.

Lakatos, I. (1978). In J. Worrall (Ed.), *Philosophical papers.* Cambridge: Cambridge University Press.

McClelland, J., & Rumelhart, D. (1986). *Parallel distributed processing: Explorations in the microstructure of cognition,* Vol. 2, Chapter 18. Cambridge, MA: MIT Press/Bradford Books.

Miller, P. L., Pople, F. H. E., & Myers, J. D. (1982). INTERNIST-I, an experimental computer-based diagnostic consultant for general internal medicine. *New England Journal of Medicine,* **307** (8), 468–476.

Minsky, M. (1967). *Computation: Finite and infinite machines.* Englewood Cliffs, NJ: Prentice-Hall.

Newell, A., & Simon. H. A. (1963). GPS, a program that simulates human thought. In E. A. Fergenbaum and J. Feldman (Eds.), *Computers and thought.* New York: McGraw-Hill.

Samuel, A. L. (1963). Some studies in machine learning using the game of checkers. In E. A. Feigenbaum and J. Feldman (Eds.), *Computers and thought.* New York: McGraw-Hill, 71–105.

Simon, H. A. (1979). *Models of thought.* New Haven and London: Yale University Press.

Shortliffe, E. H., Axline, S. G., Buchanan, B. G., Merigan, T. C., & Cohen, N. S. (1973). An artificial intelligence program to advise physicians regarding antimicrobial therapy. *Computers and biomedical research,* **6,** 544–560.

Shortliffe, E. H., Davis, R., Axline, S. G., Buchanan, B. G., Green, C. C., & Cohen, N. S. (1975). Computer-based consultations in clinical therapeutics: Explanation and rule acquisition capabilities of the MYCIN system. *Computers and biomedical research,* **8,** 303–320.

Waltz, D. L. (1975). Understanding line drawings of scenes with shadows. In P. H. Winston (Ed.), *The psychology of computer vision.* New York: McGraw-Hill, 19–92.

Winograd, T. (1972). *Understanding Natural Language.* New York: Academic Press.

Yu, V. L. *et al.* (1979). Antimicrobial selection by a computer. *Journal of the American Medical Association,* **242** (12), 1279–1282.

# Index